Opening the Black Box of Editorship

Opening the Black Box of Editorship

Edited by

Yehuda Baruch

Alison M. Konrad

Herman Aguinis

and

William H. Starbuck

Selection and editorial matter © Yehuda Baruch, Alison M. Konrad, Herman Aguinis and William H. Starbuck 2008
Individual chapters © contributors 2008

All rights reserved. No reproduction, copy or transmission of this publication may be made without written permission.

No paragraph of this publication may be reproduced, copied or transmitted save with written permission or in accordance with the provisions of the Copyright, Designs and Patents Act 1988, or under the terms of any licence permitting limited copying issued by the Copyright Licensing Agency, 90 Tottenham Court Road, London W1T 4LP.

Any person who does any unauthorised act in relation to this publication may be liable to criminal prosecution and civil claims for damages.

The authors have asserted their rights to be identified as the authors of this work in accordance with the Copyright, Designs and Patents Act 1988.

First published 2008 by
PALGRAVE MACMILLAN
Houndmills, Basingstoke, Hampshire RG21 6XS and
175 Fifth Avenue, New York, N.Y. 10010
Companies and representatives throughout the world

PALGRAVE MACMILLAN is the global academic imprint of the Palgrave Macmillan division of St. Martin's Press, LLC and of Palgrave Macmillan Ltd. Macmillan® is a registered trademark in the United States, United Kingdom and other countries. Palgrave is a registered trademark in the European Union and other countries.

ISBN-13: 978-0-230-01360-5   hardback
ISBN-10: 0-230-01360-0   hardback

This book is printed on paper suitable for recycling and made from fully managed and sustained forest sources. Logging, pulping and manufacturing processes are expected to conform to the environmental regulations of the country of origin.

A catalogue record for this book is available from the British Library.

Library of Congress Cataloging-in-Publication Data

Opening the black box of editorship / edited by Yehuda Baruch, Alison
   M. Konrad, Herman Aguinis and William H. Starbuck.
       p. cm.
   Includes index.
   ISBN 0-230-01360-0 (alk. paper)
   1. Manuscripts—Editing. 2. Journalism—Editing. 3. Academic writing.
   I. Baruch, Yehuda.
   PN162.O64 2008
   808'.027—dc22   2008016166

10 9 8 7 6 5 4 3 2 1
17 16 15 14 13 12 11 10 09 08

Printed and bound in Great Britain by
CPI Antony Rowe, Chippenham and Eastbourne

I am grateful for the support of my husband, Mark.
Alison M. Konrad

Thanks to my wife, Heidi, and daughters, Hannah and Naomi, for their infinite patience and love.
Herman Aguinis

Great many thanks to my wife, Avital, for her love and care, and to my children, Ben, Aya, Neta Bat-El, and Avinoam for their understanding.
Yehuda Baruch

Contents

List of Figures	x
List of Tables	xi
Notes on Contributors	xii
Preface	xxi
Acknowledgments	xxvi
List of Abbreviations	xxvii

Part I General/Introductory Chapters

1. Knowledge Creation and the Journal Editor's Role — 3
   Alison M. Konrad

2. The Role of Editing in Knowledge Development: Consensus Shifting and Consensus Creation — 16
   John R. Hollenbeck

3. How May I Help You? Editing as Service — 27
   Ann Marie Ryan

4. A Letter to Editors — 39
   Stephen R. Barley

Part II Effective Editorship

5. Setting up an Effective Manuscript-Review Process — 49
   K. Michele Kacmar

6. Communicating with Authors — 56
   Sara L. Rynes

7. Building and Maintaining a Strong Editorial Board and Cadre of Ad Hoc Reviewers — 68
   Daniel C. Feldman

8. Managing the Editorial Review Process: It's the People That Matter — 75
   Angelo S. DeNisi

9. Being an Ethical Editorial Board Member and Editor: The Integral Role of Earned Trust — 88
   Debra L. Shapiro and Jean Bartunek

10	Using Technology to Improve the Editorial Process *Martin Kilduff*	97
11	Moving a Journal up the Rankings *Gerard P. Hodgkinson*	104
12	The Developmental Editor: Assessing and Directing Manuscript Contribution *Donald D. Bergh*	114
13	The Case for an Activist Editorial Model *Jerry A. Jacobs*	124
14	Balancing Authorial Voice and Editorial Omniscience: The "It's My Paper and I'll Say What I Want To" versus "Ghostwriters in the Sky" Minuet *Arthur G. Bedeian*	134

Part III Editing Different Types of Journals

15	Editing a Top Academic Journal *Sheldon Zedeck*	145
16	Editing a Bridge Journal *Theresa M. Welbourne*	157
17	Developing a Global Journal: Embracing Otherness *Haridimos Tsoukas*	167
18	Sustaining Independent Journals *Timothy Clark and Mike Wright*	176
19	Reflections on Creating a New Scholarly Journal: Perspectives from a Founding Editor *Larry J. Williams*	188
20	Running an Electronic Journal: Considerations and Possibilities *Bernard Forgues and Jeanie M. Forray*	197

Part IV Editorship and Academic Career

21	Opening the Black Box of Editorship: Editors' Voice *Yehuda Baruch*	209
22	The Motivating Potential of an Associate Editor's Role *Carol T. Kulik*	223
23	How Editors are Selected *Wayne F. Cascio*	231

24	What Authors Need to Know to Navigate the Review Process Successfully: Understanding and Managing the Editor's Dilemma *Dov Eden*	239
25	Epilogue: Trade-Offs among Editorial Goals in Complex Publishing Environments *William H. Starbuck, Herman Aguinis, Alison M. Konrad, and Yehuda Baruch*	250
Author Index		271
Subject Index		276

Figures

Figure 25.1	Impact factors with four editors	251
Figure 25.2	Percentages of business journals with different impact factors in 2004	263
Figure 25.3	Percentages of articles that received different numbers of citations over 17 years	264

Tables

Table 1.1	Tywoniak's (2007) complexity definition of knowledge	4
Table 1.2	Relationships between the four types of knowledge	6
Table 12.1	Contribution typology	116
Table 21.1	Support from various sources	217
Table 21.2a	Positive outcomes	220
Table 21.2b	Negative outcomes	220

Notes on Contributors

Coeditors

Yehuda Baruch (DSc Technion, Israel) is professor of management at the University of East Anglia, Norwich, UK. He formerly held visiting positions at London Business School and the University of Texas at Arlington. His research interests are global and strategic human resource management (HRM), careers, and technology impact on management. He has published over 80 papers in refereed journals, including *Human Resource Management* (*HRM*), *Organizational Dynamics*, *Journal of Vocational Behavior*, *Human Relations*, and *Organization Studies* (*OSS*), and some 20 books and book chapters, including the coedited book *Winning Reviews: A Guide for Evaluating Scholarly Writing*. Professor Baruch is the editor of *Group & Organization Management* and former editor of *Career Development International*, serving on the editorial board of several journals, including the *Journal of Management* (*JOM*). He has edited special issues for leading journals such as the *Journal of Vocational Behavior* and *HRM*. Professor Baruch served as the chair for the careers division of the Academy of Management (AOM).

Alison M. Konrad was 2003–7 editor of *Group & Organization Management*. She joined the Richard Ivey School of Business, University of Western Ontario, in 2003 as a professor of organizational behavior and also holds the Corus Entertainment Chair in Women in Management. Previously, she was professor of HR administration at Temple University's Fox School of Business and Management, where she taught for 15 years. She was chair of the AOM's gender and diversity in organizations division in 1996–7 and received the division's Sage Scholarship Award for contributions to the field of gender and diversity in organizations in 1998. She has published two books and over 50 articles and chapters on topics relating to workplace diversity. Professor Konrad's current work focuses on organizational diversity initiatives and making workplaces more inclusive.

Herman Aguinis is professor of management and holds the Mehalchin Term Professorship of Management in the Business School at the University of Colorado Denver (UCD). He has been a visiting scholar at universities in the People's Republic of China (Beijing and Hong Kong), Malaysia, Singapore, Argentina, France, Spain, and Australia. He has written *Performance Management* (Prentice Hall, 2nd edition, 2009), *Applied Psychology in Human Resource Management* (with Wayne F. Cascio, Prentice Hall, 6th edition, 2005), and *Regression Analysis for Categorical Moderators* (Guilford, 2004) and has edited

Test-Score Banding in Human Resource Selection (Praeger, 2004). He has published about 60 journal articles in the *Academy of Management Journal* (*AMJ*), *Academy of Management Review* (*AMR*), *Journal of Applied Psychology* (*JAP*), *Personnel Psychology*, and elsewhere. He is a fellow of the American Psychological Association (APA), the Association for Psychological Science, and the Society for Industrial and Organizational Psychology (SIOP), and past editor of *Organizational Research Methods*. His work on this book was completed, in part, while he was on sabbatical leave from UCD and held a visiting appointment at the University of Salamanca (Spain) and University of Puerto Rico.

William H. Starbuck is professor-in-residence at the University of Oregon and professor emeritus at New York University (NYU). He has held faculty positions in economics, sociology, or management at Purdue University, Johns Hopkins University, Cornell University, University of Wisconsin-Milwaukee, and NYU, as well as visiting positions in England, France, New Zealand, Norway, Sweden, and the United States. He was also senior research fellow at the International Institute of Management in Berlin. He edited the *Administrative Science Quarterly* (*ASQ*), chaired the screening committee for Fulbright awards in business management, directed the doctoral program in business administration at NYU, and was president of the AOM. He has published over 140 articles on accounting, bargaining, business strategy, computer programming, computer simulation, forecasting, decision making, human-computer interaction, learning, organizational design, organizational growth and development, perception, scientific methods, and social revolutions. He has also authored two books and edited 16 books.

Contributors

Stephen R. Barley is the Charles M. Pigott Professor of Management Science and Engineering and the codirector of the Center for Work, Technology and Organization at Stanford's School of Engineering. He holds a PhD in organization studies from the Massachusetts Institute of Technology. Prior to coming to Stanford in 1994, Barley served for ten years on the faculty of the School of Industrial and Labor Relations at Cornell University. He was editor of the *ASQ* from 1993 to 1997 and the founding editor of the *Stanford Social Innovation Review* from 2002 to 2004. In collaboration with Gideon Kunda of Tel Aviv University, Barley has recently published a book on contingent work among engineers and software developers, entitled *Gurus, Hired Guns and Warm Bodies: Itinerant Experts in the Knowledge Economy*, with Princeton University Press.

Jean M. Bartunek is the Robert A. and Evelyn J. Ferris Chair and Professor of Organization Studies at Boston College, as well as a fellow (since 1999) and a past president (2001–2) of the AOM. Her PhD in social and organizational psychology is from the University of Illinois at Chicago. Her substantive research interests focus on organizational change, conflict associated with it, and organizational cognition, and her methodological interests center around ways in which external researchers can collaborate with inside members of a setting, to study the setting. She is an associate editor of the *Journal of Applied Behavioral Science* and serves on the editorial boards of many other journals. She has published more than 90 journal articles and book chapters and five ([co]authored or coedited) books.

Arthur G. Bedeian is a Boyd Professor at Louisiana State University. He is a past president of the AOM, a former dean of the Academy's Fellows Group, and a recipient of the Academy's Distinguished Service Award, the Ronald G. Greenwood Lifetime Achievement Award, and the Richard M. Hodgetts Service Award. A former editor of the *JOM*, he has served on the editorial boards of 16 journals, including *AMR*, *JAP*, and *Organizational Research Methods*. A former chair of the J. William Fulbright Foreign Scholar Board, he has been an external reviewer for the National Science Foundation, the National Academy of Science, and the Research Council of Canada.

Donald D. Bergh is an associate professor at the University of Denver. He received a PhD from the University of Colorado at Boulder and an MBA and BS from Utah State University. He is a former associate editor of the *AMJ* and is a coeditor (with David Ketchen, Jr.) of the book series *Research Methodology in Strategy and Management* (Elsevier), now in its fourth volume. He also serves on the review boards of the *Strategic Management Journal*, *Organization Science*, and *Organizational Research Methods*. Beginning in 2008, Dr. Bergh will serve as an associate editor for *Organizational Research Methods* and will rejoin the review board of the *AMJ*.

Wayne F. Cascio is US Bank Term Professor of Management at the UCD. He is past chair of the HR division of the AOM and past president of the SIOP. He has consulted with more than 150 organizations on six continents, and has published more than 80 journal articles, 35 book chapters, and 20 books, most recently, *Investing in People: Financial Impact of HR Initiatives* (with John Boudreau, FT Press, February 2008). An elected fellow of the AOM, he also has received the Distinguished Career Award from the Academy's HR division. In 2004 he was the first HR leader ever to receive an honorary doctorate from the University of Geneva, Switzerland. Chair of the Society for Human Resource Management (SHRM) Foundation, he wrote and hosted the five DVDs that the foundation has produced: *HR Role Models*, *HR in Alignment*, *Fueling the Talent Engine*, *Ethics – The Fabric of Business*, and *Trust Travels*.

Timothy Clark is professor of organizational behaviour at Durham Business School. He has been involved in editing journals since 1997, when he was an associate editor of *Human Relations*, before he joined the *Journal of*

Management Studies (*JMS*), where he became a general editor in 2002. He conducts research into different aspects of consultancy, including the role of management gurus. These have resulted in a series of publications, including *Managing Consultants* (Open University Press, 1995) and *Critical Consulting: New Perspectives on the Management Advice Industry* (with R. Fincham, Blackwell, 2002). His latest book focuses on the nature of speaker-audience interaction within management guru lectures (*Management Speak*, with David Greatbatch, 2005). He also serves on the editorial boards of *Journal of Management Inquiry* and *Management Communication Quarterly*.

Angelo DeNisi is dean of the A. B. Freeman School of Business and Albert Cohen Chair in Business Administration at Tulane University. He received his PhD in industrial/organizational psychology from Purdue University and taught at Kent State University, University of South Carolina, Rutgers, and Texas A&M University, before moving to Tulane. He is a fellow of the SIOP (division 14 of the APA) and the APA, and he also served as president of SIOP. He is also a fellow of the Southern Management Association and of the AOM and the president-elect for the AOM. Angelo has been an active researcher, whose work has been funded by the Army Research Institute and the National Science Foundation, among others, and has appeared in the top journals in management. In addition, he has written, coauthored, or coedited several books and served as the editor of the *AMJ*.

Dov Eden (PhD, University of Michigan) is the Saltiel Professor of Corporate Leadership at Tel Aviv University's Faculty of Management, where he has chaired the organizational behavior program and directed the Israel Institute of Business Research. He is a past associate editor of *AMJ* and has served on the editorial boards of *JAP*, *Organizational Behavior and Human Decision Processes* (*OBHDP*), and *Leadership Quarterly*. Lexington Books published his book *Pygmalion in Management: Productivity as a Self-Fulfilling Prophecy*. His article "Leadership and expectations: Pygmalion effects and other self-fulfilling prophecies in organizations" won the Leadership Quarterly Best Article Award. He is a fellow of the AOM, APA, and SIOP. He has held visiting appointments at NYU, the University of Maryland, and Baruch College and has consulted for leading Israeli public and private corporations, the Israel Defense Forces, and kibbutz enterprises.

Daniel C. Feldman (PhD, Yale University) is Associate Dean for Research, Synovus Chair of Servant Leadership, and director of the Leadership Research Consortium at the University of Georgia's Terry College of Business. Professor Feldman has served as editor-in-chief of the *JOM*, associate editor for *HRM*, and consulting editor for the *Journal of Organizational Behavior*. He has also served as Chair of the Careers Division of the AOM and on the executive committee of its Organizational Behavior Division. He has written six books and over 125 articles on career development and on topics such as socialization, early career indecision, job choice, career mobility and embeddedness, contingent employees, career plateaus, international assignments, layoffs, downsizing, and early retirement.

Bernard Forgues (PhD, Paris-Dauphine University) is currently professor of organization theory at the University of Lille's Business School, in Lille, France. Starting September 2008, he will join EM-Lyon Business School. In 1998, he founded *M@n@gement*, which is probably the oldest scholarly electronic journal in management with continuous operations. He served as the founding editor of *M@n@gement*, then as one of its coeditors, and in 2005, when *M@n@gement* became the official journal of AIMS (Association Internationale de Management Stratégique), he joined the publications advisory committee of the association. He also serves on the editorial boards of *Strategic Organization*, *European Management Review*, and *Service Business*. He has published in *Organization Science*, *Organization Studies*, *International Studies of Management and Organization*, *Service Business*, as well as several French outlets. His current research interests are twofold: he studies organizations over the long run, with an evolutionary perspective, and looks at location strategies of multiunit businesses.

Jeanie M. Forray (PhD, University of Massachusetts Amherst) is associate professor of management at Western New England College in Springfield, MA. She served as founding editor-in-chief of *Organization Management Journal (OMJ)* from 2001–6, and currently serves as a member of the journal's advisory committee. She is on the editorial review board of *Gender, Work & Organization*, *Management Learning* and *Journal of Management Education*. Her work has been published in *Organization*, *OSS*, *Group & Organization Management*, *Time and Society*, *Journal of Organizational Change Management*, *Management Learning*, and *Journal of Management Education*, among others. Her research interests are eclectic, with principal attention given to organizational justice and management education, and she tends to look at the world through feminist, ethnomethodological, and critical discursive lenses.

Gerard P. Hodgkinson is Professor of Organizational Behavior and Strategic Management and Director of the Centre for Organizational Strategy, Learning and Change at the University of Leeds, UK. His principal research interests center on the cognitive processes underpinning the strategic management of organizations. The author of two books and over 50 scholarly articles and chapters in edited volumes, his work has appeared in a number of major outlets including the *Annual Review of Psychology*, *Organizational Research Methods*, *OSS*, *Personnel Psychology*, *Risk Analysis*, and *Strategic Management Journal*. He was the Editor-in-Chief of the *British Journal of Management (BJM*: 1999–2006) and currently serves on the editorial boards of the *AMR*, *Journal of Organizational Behavior*, *Journal of Occupational and Organizational Psychology*, and *Organization Science*.

John R. Hollenbeck received his PhD in management from NYU in 1984 and is currently the Eli Broad Professor of Management at the Eli Broad Graduate School of Business Administration at Michigan State University. Dr. Hollenbeck served as the acting editor at *OBHDP* in 1995, the associate editor of *Decision Sciences* from 1999 to 2004, and the editor of *Personnel Psychology* from 1996 to 2002. Prior to serving as editor, he served on the editorial board of these journals, as well as the boards of the *AMJ*, *AMR*, *JAP*, and the *JOM*. Dr. Hollenbeck has published over 60 articles and book chapters on the topics of team decision making and work motivation, much of which was funded by the Office of Naval Research and the Air Force Office of Scientific Research. According to the Institute for Scientific Research this body of work has been cited over 1,300 times.

Jerry A. Jacobs is Merriam Term Professor of Sociology at the University of Pennsylvania. He has served as the editor of the *American Sociological Review* (*ASR*) and the president of the Eastern Sociological Society. His research has addressed a number of aspects of women's employment, including authority, earnings, working conditions, part-time work, and entry into male-dominated occupations. His research has been funded by the National Science Foundation, the Spencer Foundation, the Sloan Foundation, Atlantic Philanthropies, and the Macy Foundation. His research projects include a study of women's entry into the medical profession, funded by the Macy Foundation, and a study of working time and work-family conflict among university faculty.

K. Michele (Micki) Kacmar is the Durr-Fillauer Chair of Business Ethics at the University of Alabama. She received her PhD in HRM from Texas A&M University. Her general research interests fall in the area of impression management, organizational politics, ethics, and work-family conflict. She has published over 75 articles in journals such as *AMJ*, *JAP*, *OBHDP*, and *Human Relations*. Dr. Kacmar served as editor of the *JOM* from 2000 to 2003, as an associate editor of the *HRM Journal* from 1996 to 1999, and on the board of directors of the SHRM Foundation from 1993 to 2000. She is an associate editor of the *AMJ* for the term 2007–10.

Martin Kilduff (PhD, Cornell) is a professor of management and the editor of *AMR*. His work focuses on social networks including the two coauthored books *Social Networks and Organizations* (Sage, 2003) and *Bringing the Individual Back In: Organizational Behavior and Interpersonal Networks* (Cambridge University Press, forthcoming). He has also published articles on social networks, in the major research journals including *ASQ*, *Organization Science*, *Journal of Personality and Social Psychology*, and *AMJ*.

Carol T. Kulik is a research professor of HRM at the University of South Australia. Her interests encompass cognitive processes, demographic diversity, and procedural fairness in organizations, and her research focuses on explaining how HRM interventions influence the fair treatment of people in organizations. Carol is particularly interested in bridging the academic-practice divide and ensuring that academic research addresses problems of interest to the business community. She authored a book titled *Human Resources for the Non-HR Manager* (published by Erlbaum in 2004), which makes the cutting-edge research on HR issues accessible to managers with no formal training in human resources. She has served as the senior associate editor at the *JOM* and is currently the division chair for the organizational behavior division of the AOM.

Ann Marie Ryan is a professor of organizational psychology at Michigan State University. Her major research interests involve improving the quality and fairness of employee-selection methods, and topics related to diversity and justice in the workplace. In addition to publishing extensively in these areas, she regularly consults with organizations on improving assessment processes, including work with Procter & Gamble, Ford Motor Company, Dow Chemical, Kelly Services, and many other private sector organizations. She also has worked extensively on the design of hiring processes for public sector organizations, particularly for police and fire departments. She currently serves on the Defense Advisory Committee on Military Personnel Testing. She is a past president of the SIOP and past editor of the journal *Personnel Psychology*. She received her BS with a double major in psychology and management from Xavier University and her MA and PhD in psychology from the University of Illinois at Chicago. Further information about her research and consultation work can be found at http://psychology.msu.edu/People/faculty/ryanVITA.pdf.

Sara Rynes (PhD, University of Wisconsin) is the John F. Murray Professor of Management and Organizations at the University of Iowa. Her research interests are compensation, selection and recruitment, management education, and knowledge transfer between academics and practitioners. She is currently editor of the *AMJ* and has served on the editorial review boards of the *JAP*, *Personnel Psychology*, *Quality Management Journal*, *Academy of Management Learning and Education*, and *Frontiers in Industrial and Organizational Psychology*. She is a fellow of the AOM, the APA, the SIOP, and the Management Education Research Institute and a recipient of the Herbert G. Heneman Career Achievement Award in Human Resource Management. She was formerly on the faculties of Cornell University and the University of Minnesota.

Debra L. Shapiro (PhD, Northwestern University) is the Clarice Smith Professor of Management at the University of Maryland's Robert H. Smith School of Business. Before joining the Smith School in 2003, Shapiro was the Willard J. Graham Distinguished Professor at the University of North

Carolina's Kenan-Flagler Business School (where she was on the faculty [1986–2003] and also served as associate dean [1998–2001]). Shapiro's research regards antecedents and consequences of workplace-related conflicts such as perceived mistreatment and/or injustice, including how to effectively resolve these (e.g., via third-party procedures, negotiation strategies, explanations, and other communication tactics), especially when disputing parties are from different cultures. Shapiro's publications include a book *Managing Multinational Teams: Global Perspectives* (published by Elsevier/JAI Press, 2005) and over 60 journal articles and book chapters in outlets including premier management journals such as *ASQ, AMJ, AMR, JAP, JPSP, OBHDP, Handbook of Organizational Justice*, and *Handbook of Negotiation and Culture*. Shapiro is a past member of the AOM's board of governors (2002–5) and currently an associate editor of the *AMJ*.

Haridimos Tsoukas is the George D. Mavros Research Professor of Organization Theory at ALBA, Greece; professor of organization studies at Warwick University, UK; and the editor-in-chief of *OSS*. He has coedited the *Oxford Handbook of Organization Theory: Meta-theoretical Perspectives* (Oxford University Press, 2003) and is the author of *Complex Knowledge: Studies in Organizational Epistemology* (Oxford University Press, 2005). He has published articles on organizational knowledge, organizational change and the management of social reforms, and meta-theoretical issues in organization and management studies in leading journals, including the *AMR, Strategic Management Journal, Organization Science, OSS*, and the *JMS*.

Theresa M. Welbourne (PhD, University of Colorado, Boulder) is president and CEO of eePulse, Inc., a technology- and management-research company. Prior to founding the company, she worked full time in academics with Cornell University and the University of Michigan. She also has affiliated roles with executive education at the Ross School of Business, University of Michigan, and the Center for Effective Organizations, University of Southern California. Her research has been featured in popular publications such as *Inc.* magazine, *Wall Street Journal*, and *The Financial Times* and has been published in books and journals such as the *AMJ, JOM, Journal of Organization Behavior*, and *JAP*. She is the editor-in-chief of *HRM*.

Larry J. Williams received his PhD in organizational behavior from Indiana University's School of Business, and he is University Professor of Management at Virginia Commonwealth University. His main interests involve structural equation methods. He is the founding editor of *Organizational Research Methods* and previously served as consulting editor for the *JOM*. Dr. Williams has served as chairperson for the research methods division of the AOM and also established the Center for the Advancement of Research Methods and Analysis at Virginia Commonwealth University. Dr. Williams received the

2005 Distinguished Career Contributions Award by the AOM's research methods division. In 2004, he was recognized by the Southern Management Association as an author of two of the six most highly cited articles in the 30-year history of the *JOM*. He was also elected in 2004 to be a member of the Society for Organizational Behavior.

Mike Wright is professor of financial studies at Nottingham University Business School, director of the Center for Management Buy-out Research, and visiting professor at INSEAD, Erasmus University, and University of Siena. He received an honorary doctorate from the University of Ghent in 2006. He was an editor of *Entrepreneurship Theory and Practice* from 1994 to 1999. He has been an editor of *JMS* since 2003. He is a consulting editor for the *International Journal of Management Reviews*. He has edited special issues of the *AMJ*, *Journal of Business Venturing*, *JMS*, *JOM*, *Research Policy*, *Journal of Business Finance and Accounting*, *Accounting and Business Research*, *Journal of Corporate Finance*, *Industrial and Corporate Change*, *Managerial and Decision Economics*, etc. He serves on six editorial review boards, including that of *Strategic Entrepreneurship Journal* and *Journal of Business Finance and Accounting*. His recent books include *Academic Entrepreneurship in Europe* (Edward Elgar, 2007; with B. Clarysse, P. Mustar & A. Lockett) and *Private Equity and Management Buy-outs* (Edward Elgar, 2008; ed. with H. Bruining).

Sheldon Zedeck, University of California at Berkeley, is editor of the *JAP*; former editor and associate editor of *Human Performance*, a journal that he and Frank Landy founded; as well as former associate editor of *Applied Psychology: An International Review*. He has written numerous journal articles and has served on the editorial boards of *Contemporary Psychology* and *Industrial Relations*. Dr. Zedeck has been active in the SIOP, in addition to consulting with private and public sector organizations and serving as an expert witness in employment discrimination cases.

Preface

Goals and audiences for this volume

Scientific publications are at the heart of science as a system (Luhmann, 1984; Stichweh, 1998), and publishing is perhaps the most desired outcome of academics' work (Cummings & Frost, 1995). The cliché "publish or perish" is reflected in academic careers (Baruch & Hall, 2004; Rynes et al., 2005). Individual and departmental scholarly reputations grow through publication in refereed journals (Daft, 1995; Huff, 1999), and peer pressure maintains and reinforces this trend (Bedeian, 2004). Editors have significant power over the selection of manuscripts to publish. They occupy a key position in the publishing process and thus influence the shape of future knowledge. As a result, editorship carries with it strong scholarly position and prestige, and becoming an editor is a major event in anyone's academic career. Serving as an editor requires the community's trust and shows career success. Serving as an editor is a significant honor and responsibility, accompanied by substantial hard work.

In spite of the centrality of the editorship role, there is much mystery surrounding the nature and notion of editorship. Sometimes, more myth than reality prevails. Many scholars, not merely the novices, are unaware of editorial practices, processes, and strategies. Misinformation and lack of awareness might obstruct judgment in navigating the publication process. It might even lead to poor handling of the process, which would hamper the chances of eventually publishing good manuscripts. It can cause people to become editors for the wrong reasons, to perform poorly as editors once they are in the role, and to miss opportunities to learn from the experience of others.

This book contributes towards a more transparent system. It brings to light the "behind the scene" processes. Further, we relate to issues concerned with editorial work, its perils and benefits, and explicate a normative system of knowledge creation.

In a nutshell, this book aims to be

(1) an academic scholarly work on the roles of editors and processes of editorship in knowledge creation and dissemination,
(2) a guide for editors and professional associations in charge of setting editorial policies for developing and maintaining high-quality editing processes,
(3) a guide and realistic job preview for scholars who wish to become editors, and
(4) an important socialization tool for all doctoral students and scholars who wish to learn the intricacies of the publishing process.

Brief description

Understanding editorial work and how to become an effective editor is highly relevant for most scholarly academics working in the social, behavioral, and organizational sciences (e.g., members of the AOM, SIOP, APA, American Sociological Association, Strategic Management Association, and other professional organizations). This book offers essential scholarly reading for gaining knowledge and insights that can enhance scholarly achievements and explicate the relevance of editorship to the academic career.

The need for this book is clear: with much at stake in the "publish or perish" environment, understanding editorial work and processes is crucial for academic scholars. Further, from an individual career perspective, becoming an effective editor is an important goal for scholars at the peaks of their academic careers – a goal that contributes to the development and dissemination of knowledge. This book not only contributes to the growing field of academic careers but also provides tips on how to succeed in them (Baruch & Hall, 2004; Frost & Taylor, 1996; Miller, Glick, & Cardinal, 2005).

Despite the importance of editorship, there is no formal preparation or specific advice to prepare people for this role. To date, most scholars have learned how to edit by trial and error or via mentoring. The book offers a vital additional resource to success in the role. This is the first book dedicated entirely to the topic of editorship. It enables scholars around the world to learn from shared experiences and knowledge. The scholars who wrote the chapters for this book come from a variety of perspectives and backgrounds, but all have had major editorial experience. These represent a highly acclaimed set of prestigious, truly international journals.

Structure for the book

This book comprises four parts: (I) General, Introductory Chapters; (II) Effective Editorship; (III) Editing Different Types of Journals, and (IV) Editorship and Academic Careers.

In the opening chapter, Alison Konrad, former editor of *Group & Organization Management*, links the editorial process with perspectives on knowledge creation. She concludes that the goal of editing is "to *adjudicate the intersubjective knowledge-conversion process* whereby a manuscript representing the personal knowledge of the author(s) becomes part of the common body of knowledge in the field" and, from this definition, draws several conclusions about the editorial process. In chapter 2, John Hollenbeck, former acting editor of *OBHDP*, former associate editor of *Decision Sciences*, and former editor of *Personnel Psychology*, elaborates on what types of articles have the greatest unique contribution and value-adding potential and, consequently, are most likely to be accepted for publication. Ann Marie Ryan, former editor of *Personnel Psychology*, regards editing as a vital professional service that the editors conduct for the community, and takes us to the servant-leadership view. Closing the first part in reflection on editorship experience, Steve Barley, former editor of *ASQ*, addresses present and prospective editors with the enlightening and revealing article "A Letter to Editors."

The second part moves to the debate about how to be an effective editor. Micki Kacmar, former editor of the *JOM*, offers her wise advice about how to set up an effective manuscript review process, whereas Sara Rynes, former editor of the *AMJ*, explains emerging issues in communicating with authors and discusses how to guide and support authors in their journey to publication (or otherwise). Daniel Feldman, another former editor of the *JOM*, tells us about the important role of team building. The editor is a leader of several teams – the small one, that of associate editors, who share editorial decision making; the editorial board, as a wider team closely associated with the journal; and the cadre of ad-hoc reviewers – without whom editors will not be able to make a learned, validated decision on manuscripts. Feldman discusses how to develop and maintain strong bonds with these constituencies of the journal. Angelo Denisi, former editor of the *AMJ*, has significant experience in dealing with authors who are not so happy with either the decision or the process, or both. Another group that needs careful handling are reluctant reviewers. Debra Shapiro, former associate editor of the *AMJ*, and Jean Bartunek, associate editor of the *Journal of Applied Behavioral Science*, take us to the ethical minefield of issues needing consideration, during the review, revision, and decision-making processes. Martin Kilduff, editor of the *AMR*, focuses on the increasingly important element that is essential in dealing with the increasing number of submissions – the use (and sometimes misuse) of technology in the editorial process – how to improve editorial work and yet keep the human touch in dealing with multiple constituencies in the process. Gerard Hodgkinson, former editor of the *BJM*, maps out the critical factors that ultimately determine the standing of academic journals in the global marketplace of scholarly excellence and addresses the question regarding what steps might be taken in order to improve a journal's performance in that regard. Donald Bergh, former associate editor of the *AMJ*, explains how editors can help authors in creating added value in the review process. Jerry Jacobs, editor of the *ASR*, provides a slightly different view and advocates an "activist" role for editors, whereas Arthur Bedeian, former editor of the *JOM*, takes a strong stance in support of letting authors express their own view (instead of being influenced by "ghostwriters in the sky").

The third part of the book explores a diversity of issues associated with the editorship of different types of journals. Sheldon Zedeck, former editor of the *JAP*, reflects on his experiences as the editor of a top academic journal, including both challenges and gratifications. He provides a realistic job preview for those interested in becoming an editor and those who wish to understand some of the realities faced by editors on a daily basis. Theresa Welbourne, editor of *HRM*, expresses her own views, as well as those of her editorial board, in describing a bridge journal and opens the reader's eyes to the need to reach for both the academic and the practitioner communities, a demanding task which she leads successfully. Haridimos Tsoukas, editor of *OSS*, describes how his journal transformed from being European into a truly international journal, which keeps a distinct identity but embraces the global rather than only the European community. Timothy Clark and Mike Wright, coeditors of the *JMS*, describe how to push a journal up the ranking order, making it truly international, and doing so as an independent journal rather than being under the "cover" of a major publisher or association. Larry J. Williams, founding editor of *Organizational Research Methods*, an extremely successful journal, delineates his experience of creating a new journal and making it known and respected by the scholarly community. The last chapter in this part, by Bernard Forgues, coeditor of *M@n@gement*, and Jeanie Forray, founding editor of *OMJ*, examines new horizons that emerged only in the last decade – that of online publications and how to manage a purely electronic journal.

The fourth and last part includes considerations of the association between editorship and the academic career. Yehuda Baruch, editor of *Group & Organization Management* and former editor of *Career Development International*, describes the results of an empirical study on the impact of editorship on the academic career of editors. Carol Kulik, former associate editor of the *JOM*, analyzes her experience as an associate editor and offers diagnostic tips to academics who are considering an associate editorship, looking at the possibilities of this position as either a dead-end or springboard for future progress. Wayne Cascio, who served as chair of the journals committee of the AOM, writes about how editors are selected by AOM, though acknowledging that editors at other journals are selected using a variety of processes. The final chapter in this part, by Dov Eden, former associate editor of the *AMJ*, explains what authors need to know to navigate the review process successfully. His advice should be instrumental for authors ready and willing to understand the editor's dilemma. He reveals the most well-kept secret in journal publishing – editors want and need to publish papers – and suggests how authors can help editors to help themselves.

In the book's concluding chapter, we (Starbuck, Aguinis, Konrad, & Baruch) discuss several editorial choices that editors can make at both the practical and strategic levels of editorship and how these choices have implications for both editors and authors.

We close by thanking each of the contributors of this volume for offering such candid and open information that we hope will be useful for many generations of scholars.

References

Baruch, Y. & Hall D. T. (2004). The academic career: A model for future careers in other sectors? *Journal of Vocational Behavior*, 64, 241–62.

Baruch, Y., Sullivan, S. E., & Schepmyer, H. N. (Eds.) (2006). *Winning reviews: A guide for evaluating scholarly writing*. Basingstoke: Palgrave Macmillan.

Bedeian, A. G. (2004). Peer review and the social construction of knowledge in the management discipline. *Academy of Management Learning and Education*, 3, 198–216.

Cummings, L. L., & Frost, P. J. (1995). *Publishing in the organizational sciences* (2nd edition). Thousand Oaks, CA: Sage.

Daft, R. L. (1995). Why I recommended that your manuscript be rejected and what you can do about it. In L. L. Cummings & P. J. Frost (Eds.), *Publishing in the organizational sciences* (2nd edition, pp. 164–82). Thousand Oaks, CA: Sage.

Frost, P. J., & Taylor, M. S. (Eds.) (1996). *Rhythms of academic life: Personal accounts of careers in academia*. Thousand Oaks, CA: Sage.

Huff, A. S. (1999). *Writing for scholarly publication*. Thousand Oaks, CA: Sage.

Luhmann, N. (1984). *Soziales systeme: Grundriss einer allgemeine theorie*. Frankfurt, Germany: Suhrkamp.

Miller, C. C., Glick, W. H., & Cardinal L. B. (2005). The allocation of prestigious positions in organizational science: Accumulative advantage, sponsored mobility, and contest mobility. *Journal of Organizational Behavior*, 26, 489–516.

Rynes, S. L., Hillman, A., Ireland, R. D., Kirkman, B., Law, K., Miller, C. C., Rajagopalan, N., & Shapiro, D. (2005). From the editors. *Academy of Management Journal*, 48, 732–7.

Stichweh, R. (1998). Systems theory and the evolution of science. In G. Altman & W. A. Koch (Eds.), *Systems: New paradigms for the human sciences* (pp. 303–17). Berlin, Germany: Walter de Gruyter.

Tywoniak, S. A. (2007). Knowledge in four deformation dimensions. *Organization*, 14, 53–76.

Acknowledgments

This book would not be possible without the guidance and support of our editorial, production and marketing teams at Palgrave. We want to thank Jacky Kippenberger for commissioning the book, Virginia Thorp and Emily Bown for the editorial work, the production manager Ian Evans, the marketing manager Beverley Millar, and the staff of Macmillan India Ltd.

In addition, Alison M. Konrad thanks the support of the Corus Entertainment Chair in Women in Management from the Richard Ivey School of Business, and Herman Aguinis thanks the support of the University of Salamanca and University of Puerto Rico, where he spent his 2007–8 sabbatical year.

Lastly, our thanks to our many wonderful authors, who enthusiastically devoted much time, thoughts, and effort to writing their respective chapters. Our sincere appreciation to our many colleagues in the AOM, SIOP, and other associations, who encouraged and supported our efforts to produce this book.

Baruch, Konrad, Aguinis, and Starbuck

Abbreviations

AE	action editor
AIM	Advanced Institute of Management Research
AMJ	*Academy of Management Journal*
AMLE	*Academy of Management Learning and Education*
AMP	*Academy of Management Perspectives*
AMR	*Academy of Management Review*
AOM	Academy of Management
APA	American Psychological Association
ASQ	*Administrative Science Quarterly*
ASR	*American Sociological Review*
BAM	British Academy of Management
BJM	*British Journal of Management*
DOAJ	Directory of Open Access Journals
EAM	Eastern Academy of Management
EJROT	*Electronic Journal of Radical Organization Theory*
EMT	Emergency Medical Technicians
HRM	Human resource management
HRM	*Human Resource Management*
I/O	psychology industrial/organizational psychology
ISI	Institute of Scientific Information
JAP	*Journal of Applied Psychology*
JCCP	*Journal of Consulting and Clinical Psychology*
JCT	Job Characteristics Theory
JFE	*Journal of Financial Economics*
JMS	*Journal of Management Studies*
JOM	Journal of Management
JPSP	*Journal of Personality and Social Psychology*
KSAOs	knowledge, skills, abilities, and other characteristics
MPS	Motivating Potential Score
NFL	National Football League
NYU	New York University
OB	Organizational Behavior
OBHDP	*Organizational Behavior and Human Decision Processes*
OCB	Organizational citizenship behavior
OED	Oxford English Dictionary
OMJ	*Organization Management Journal*
ORM	*Organizational Research Methods*
OSS	*Organization Studies*
PDA	Personal digital assistant

PNAS	*Proceedings of the National Academy of Sciences*
R&R	Revise and resubmit
RMD	Research Methods Division
SCI	Social Science Index
sd	Standard Deviation
SHRM	Society for Human Resource Management
SIOP	Society for Industrial and Organizational Psychology
SSCI	Social Sciences Citation Index
UCD	University of Colorado Denver

Part I General/Introductory Chapters

1
Knowledge Creation and the Journal Editor's Role

Alison M. Konrad

Much has been written on the role of reviewers in the academic publishing process, yet little guidance is available to new editors of academic journals. When I took over as a new editor, what I received in the form of guidance was a set of cardboard boxes in the mail (filled with manuscripts) with all the best wishes of the previous editor. Upon asking senior people in the field for suggestions, I was told that I can do "anything I want."

Autonomy is a wonderful thing, and something that many academics value; however, I do not believe that editors should be able to do "anything they want." Given that the editorial role is so crucial to the development of the field as well as to the lives and careers of academics, it is important to start developing a set of process standards for assessing the quality of editorship. Outcome standards such as journal rankings by the ISI and other evaluation lists (e.g. Starbuck, 2005) already exist, but due to long lead times and the distal nature of outcomes, process standards are needed to help editors spend their time in ways that are most likely to result in the publication of high-quality manuscripts.

Given that the editor's work is to create, maintain, and extend the body of knowledge in the field, I thought that reading about knowledge creation might provide some useful implications for editorial action. By no means did I conduct a thorough reading of all of the knowledge-management literature, and I do not claim to provide a comprehensive synthesis of it here. I did find some very useful ideas, however, that helped to clarify and justify some of my own thoughts on what constitutes a high-quality editorial process.

First, the knowledge-creation literature suggests that the work of an editor is to *adjudicate the intersubjective knowledge-conversion process* whereby a manuscript representing the personal knowledge of the author(s) becomes part of the common body of knowledge in the field. As such, the work of an editor requires judgment, and the process is wrought with subjectivity. Subjectivity brings with it a set of knowledge-related exchange hazards, which others have considered in detail (Aguinis & Henle, 2002; Shapiro & Bartunek, this volume). The major point of this chapter will be that *the subjectivity and complexity of the content which editors work with means that the use of editorial judgment and extensive communication with authors and reviewers is essential.*

What is knowledge?

Defining knowledge is a nontrivial task, and the extant literature provides several definitions and debates about what knowledge is (see Calhoun & Starbuck, 2003). I found Tywoniak's (2007) "complexity" definition to be particularly interesting and useful for the discussion of the role of editors. Tywoniak begins by defining knowledge as "rules that reduce environmental uncertainty through connections between ideas and facts," which serve as guides for behavior (p. 53). He then suggests that this definition considers knowledge only as a structure, whereas a complexity perspective considers knowledge as a structure, a process, and a system (see Table 1.1).

As a structure, knowledge is stable, and as such can only be useful under stable conditions. Under conditions of instability, individuals must be able to generate new rules linking new sets of facts and ideas in order to adapt their behaviors to complicated and changing environments (Tywoniak, 2007, p. 57). Hence, knowledge must be more than a structure; it is also a process incorporating feedback loops to enable the generation of new heuristics. As individuals face new features in their environments, old behaviors may no longer result in desired outcomes, motivating a search for new solutions. Individuals continually modify and update their personal stores of knowledge by adjusting their behaviors to fit the new conditions they encounter, testing the new behaviors, and storing representations of the new behavioral contingencies in memory. This knowledge-development process, which is similar to Argyris and Schon's (1978) concept of single-loop learning, benefits individual survival in a complex and changing environment.

Tywoniak (2007) considers knowledge to have yet another level of complexity, arising due to the use of language. Human language facilitates the development of knowledge purely through the manipulation of symbols.

Table 1.1 Tywoniak's (2007) complexity definition of knowledge

Knowledge is ...	Description
a structure	A set of rules that reduce environmental uncertainty through connections between ideas and facts which serve as guides for behavior
a process	A process incorporating feedback loops that enable the generation of new links between ideas and facts or heuristics
a system	The common language and the rules used to generate and validate new links between facts and ideas within a given community

This human capacity to increase understanding of the environment in the absence of immediate experience allows for the development of "ever greater quantities of knowledge, going beyond the cognitive ability of a single individual" (Tywoniak, 2007, p. 57). In other words, humans are able to learn from the experiences of others, through the process of communication. At this level, knowledge is a system or "network of rule generating processes inter-linked through social interaction" (Tywoniak, 2007, p. 58).

As the research of Nonaka and colleagues shows (Nonaka, von Krogh, & Voelpel, 2006), knowledge is not transmitted between individuals in a simple linear manner wherein one person speaks and the other absorbs. Rather, knowledge transmission is based on an intersubjective process whereby individuals compare similar experiences in order to develop a more refined set of links between facts and ideas. The challenge faced by individuals engaged in the knowledge-sharing process is to persuade others that they have interpreted their personal experiences accurately and in a way that is useful for others to know. When individuals, each of whom has a subjective experience of the world, reach agreement about a particular piece of knowledge, it is "converted" from the personal to the common realm (Nonaka et al., 2006).

Hence, the body of common knowledge is basically a judgment among a community that a particular set of links between ideas and facts is valid. It is continually evolving as the environment changes and as community members have new experiences from which they draw conclusions that they then discuss and debate with others. Using the rules of language, community members reach agreements to add new links to the extant knowledge structure. The common language and the rules used to generate and validate new links between facts and ideas constitute the *system* of knowledge of a given community (Tywoniak, 2007).

Types of knowledge

Tywoniak (2007) suggests that there are (at least) four different types of knowledge. Personal knowledge is distinguished from common knowledge, and tacit knowledge is distinguished from explicit knowledge as follows (Tywoniak, 2007):

- Personal knowledge consists of the set of behavioral rules developed by a particular individual to reduce environmental uncertainty.
- Common knowledge is embedded in an interactive environment and consists of that evolving set of truth claims that has been validated through the intersubjective process discussed earlier.
- Tacit knowledge is processual in nature or "knowledge in action" that reflects the limitations of cognition.
- Explicit knowledge is the set of links between ideas and facts that has been formally codified.

Table 1.2 Relationships between the four types of knowledge

	Personal	**Common**	**Tacit**	**Explicit**
Personal				
Common	Interrelated			
Tacit	Capacity to act	Routines		
Explicit	Analogy	Formalized	Application	

Note: Summary of Tywoniak (2007).

Tywoniak relates all four knowledge types to each other, not in a two-by-two typology, but rather, in more of an association matrix (summarized briefly in Table 1.2).

For instance, according to Tywoniak (2007), personal and common knowledge are *interrelated*. Personal knowledge is based on common knowledge because individuals use language to organize their personal understanding of the world. Common knowledge depends upon personal knowledge for its existence also, because the body of common knowledge requires individuals to share their personal knowledge with others. When personal knowledge is validated through the intersubjective knowledge-conversion process (Nonaka et al., 2006), the body of common knowledge is honed, refined, modified, and extended. This process is absolutely essential if common knowledge is to remain useful as a guide to behavior in a complex and changing environment.

To fully appreciate all six of the associations, the reader is referred to Tywoniak's (2007) original article. Here, I mention those associations that I believe are most closely linked to the process of knowledge generation and validation in the social-science fields.

One such link is the association between tacit knowledge and personal knowledge. Tywoniak (2007) argues that tacit knowledge is related to personal knowledge through the capacity to act. Individuals may know many things explicitly, but they are only able to act effectively on those ideas for which they have sufficient tacit knowledge. This tacit knowledge on *how to use* the explicit knowledge is not codified, and hence, cannot be transmitted through language, but must be developed from experience.

Common knowledge is related to tacit knowledge through the development of organizational routines (Tywoniak, 2007). An example of this association occurs when a set of organizational positions and/or processes results in a particularly synergistic outcome that no one individual understands explicitly. Yet, if the organization can reliably produce this outcome without an explicit understanding of how it occurs, then the organization can be said to have a piece of common tacit knowledge.

Journal editors work with *explicit knowledge*. Manuscripts represent authors' *personal explicit knowledge* that they hope will be raised to the level of *common explicit knowledge* through publication. The editor's goal is to identify those submissions that critique, modify, and extend the body of *common explicit knowledge* to do a better job of reducing environmental uncertainty for action.

The interrelatedness of common explicit knowledge with other types of knowledge has interesting implications for the development of research. *It implies that researchers can and perhaps should do more than just work with the extant body of common explicit knowledge.* The work of an author likely can be enriched by engaging in action to create personal tacit knowledge, which authors then make explicit and fit into the common body of knowledge (Vermeulen, 2005). Authors can also examine organizational routines in which common tacit knowledge is embedded, and then explicate and extend that knowledge. By linking the extant literature (our body of common explicit knowledge) with sources of personal tacit knowledge and common tacit knowledge, authors may be more likely to identify research questions constituting revolutionary advances to the field, rather than incremental adjustments to current thinking.

Although the sources of tacit knowledge have important implications for the research process, journal editors are not working with the personal tacit knowledge or common tacit knowledge that might have inspired any given manuscript submission. Editors receive only the text presenting the author(s)' views and has no access to the direct personal experience or organizational arrangements that inspired the author(s)' work. Hence, the editor works with the personal explicit knowledge of the author(s). The editor's job is to *guide the knowledge-conversion process* (Nonaka et al., 2006) to determine which of the many submissions containing statements of author(s)' explicit personal knowledge will become part of the body of common explicit knowledge in the field.

Implications for journal editors

At least five implications for journal editors can be derived from the knowledge-creation literature:

- Editorial gatekeeping is necessary
- Judgment is critical to the editor's role
- Subjectivity enters into the editorial process
- Interests and the potential for moral hazard enter into the process
- Communication is essential

I discuss each of these implications briefly.

Editorial gatekeeping is necessary

One of the implications of the knowledge-creation field is that editorial gatekeeping is a necessary activity. This conclusion is less than obvious, given the ongoing debate in the fields of management and organization studies regarding the development of a paradigm (De Cock & Jeanes, 2006). Pfeffer (1993) argued that the openness of these fields to a wide variety of research questions, epistemologies, and methodologies has resulted in the failure to develop a strong paradigm, which he believes reduces the ability to make scientific progress. Pfeffer's ideas were quickly rebutted by Van Maanen (1995), who argued that a diversity of voices and approaches is essential for improving what he views as an overly consistent, unimaginative and mind-numbingly banal field. Van de Ven (1999) characterized the former of these two views as a "Pfefferdigm" aiming to weed the unruly garden of organization and management theory to support only the oaks; "They can be red oaks, American oaks, dwarf oaks, or Mexican oaks – as long as they're oak trees" (p. 119). Of the latter view, Van de Ven states that Van Maanen wants "a thousand flowers to bloom" (p. 120), so that the field will become "A quilt of a thousand rhetorical patches sewn together with the voices of many people … singing their rounds of a chorus that has become disentrained" (p. 120).

Should we engage in editorial gatekeeping, or should we let a thousand flowers bloom? In the field of knowledge creation, Nonaka et al. (2006) provide a clear and unambiguous answer. These authors argue that gatekeeping through the knowledge-conversion process is absolutely necessary. One reason we must limit the amount of information added to the common body of knowledge is to prevent information overload among members of our community. Another reason is to safeguard against poor-quality papers, misleading papers, or even worse, fraud and plagiarism. By gatekeeping, we help our community identify the more important links between ideas and facts, without having to go through all possible manuscripts that any academic has ever thought to write. Given the fact that more and more academics are pressured to produce refereed journal publications around the world, the sheer volume of manuscripts being produced is increasing geometrically, and any respected journal has seen its submissions increase dramatically in the last five years.

Although I advocate the need for gatekeeping, *I do not mean that certain types of methods, epistemologies, or conceptual frames should be banned.* Rather, each piece of research should be judged for quality, such that our knowledge base reflects the best of what our various scholarly traditions have to offer. Furthermore, different research questions are best addressed with different epistemologies and methodologies, and the best work demonstrates a strong fit between the research question and the data. Achieving inclusion of a variety of research approaches requires a variety of journals reflecting different perspectives, as well as diverse editorial boards capable of properly assessing the quality of scholarship from the various traditions.

Judgment is critical to the editor's role

Judgment is critical to the editor's role because the ideas scholars are working with are so complex. Especially in the field of organization studies, where the number of theories and paradigms is large and growing, judgments are very complex because there is much disagreement about many factors, including epistemology, conceptual frameworks, research methods, and appropriate conclusions to be drawn from any given piece of research (Pfeffer, 1993; Van Maanen, 1995, Van de Ven, 1999).

The importance of judgment has some very clear implications for editorial practice. Some editors seem to use a "vote-counting" method, which entails "averaging" the judgments of the reviewers to come to a conclusion (e.g., one revise-and-resubmit [R&R] plus two rejects = reject). Such editors return manuscripts to authors with a form letter, and authors receiving the coveted "R&R" decision obtain little or no guidance as to how they can best craft their revision. In my view, vote counting is not appropriate, given the complexity of the content editors are working with and the complexity of the intersubjective knowledge-conversion process that they are adjudicating. Editors must assess the quality of the reviews before determining the weight they'll place on any reviewer's comments, and that means they must read both the manuscript and the reviews carefully before making a decision. Because the editor must synthesize the information from multiple sources to make a judgment, the editorial job is a step more complex than that of any individual reviewer.

The task of the editor also differs substantially from that of the reviewers. Reviewers only need to judge the quality of submissions, while the editor, on top of recruiting reviewers, overseeing the review process, and making judgments on final publication decisions, in the end, for the benefit of the readership (and the publisher), *must fill the pages of the journal*. In my experience, reviewers are better at rejecting manuscripts than they are at selecting them, and for my first several months as an editor, my review teams rejected absolutely everything that was submitted. At that point, I had to send them all a message explaining that we needed to publish *something*, so please do not hold these manuscripts to an impossible standard of perfection.

Perhaps it is the "validity threat" paradigm in which we social scientists are raised that makes it so easy for us to perceive the flaws in our work and so difficult for us to see its strengths. As authors, we are advised to list the limitations of our work, which is important to ensure that it is interpreted properly. Unfortunately, these sections can often leave the reader feeling as if the study accomplished pretty much nothing of value. It is important to remember that we usually make our methodological decisions for sound reasons. It is very valuable for authors to include the reasons for their methodological choices in the limitations section. No individual piece of research is perfect, and the best we can ask of authors is to choose the best methodological tradeoffs possible, given the research question, the state of the extant literature, and the realistic availability of data.

Subjectivity enters into the editorial process

Although editorial judgment is necessary to the knowledge-creation process, neither the editorial process nor our judgments as editors are perfect. All of these judgments are affected by the limitations of the human cognitive structure. Editors are plagued with all of the perceptual biases that human beings are subject to, including personal biases (Is work in our own area of expertise really more worthy of publication than work in other subfields?), stereotyping (Is the work of an established scholar really higher in quality than that of an unknown author?), recency effects (Is a topic recently published in *Academy of Management Journal*, *Administrative Science Quarterly*, or *Academy of Management Review* really more worthy than others?), sunk costs (Does the fact that the author has gone through two R&Rs mean that I have to accept the article at this point?), and more. These biases mean that editors are subject to both Type I and Type II errors, such that articles that should be published are rejected and vice versa.

Furthermore, the editorial process is inherently subjective because editors work only with texts and do not have access to the original data, that is, the material reality against which to validate or invalidate those texts. The only resources we have at our disposal to assess the quality of manuscripts are (1) our judgment as experienced professionals, (2) the judgments of the reviewers, and (3) the system of rules for generating, communicating, and validating knowledge within our field. Hence, our editorial work is very much like Nonaka et al.'s (2006) knowledge-conversion process. It is *intersubjective*, meaning that one person's knowledge can be validated or invalidated by another's knowledge, depending upon whether the authors and the editorial team can reach an agreement regarding the validity of the knowledge claim.

The editorial process is also *reflexive*, by which I mean that process of converting each piece of knowledge affects the character of the knowledge itself. The fact that scholarly papers are changed through the review process is a well-known frustration in the field, and recently, some have called for "as is" publication decisions allowing no requests for revision (Tsang & Frey, 2007). Although the reflexivity of the editorial process may seem ominous to authors, the nature of these changes is generally quite positive. In my experiences as an editor, the manuscripts submitted to my journal improved substantially over the course of the review and revision process. Given that manuscripts generally improve with revision, authors probably serve themselves and the field best when they are highly responsive to input from the editor and reviewers (not necessarily agreeing with the editorial team, but responding to all of their concerns thoroughly to maximize the strength of the methods used and to minimize needless confusion generated by the writing).

Interests and the potential for moral hazard enter into the process

Beyond cognitive and process limitations, the subjectivity of the editorial process also invites what Foss (2007) terms "knowledge-related exchange hazards" (p. 40). Foss identified two types of such hazards: knowledge appropriation and strategic knowledge accumulation. Knowledge appropriation is what we might call plagiarism. Strategic knowledge accumulation is what we might call lack of collegiality or unwillingness to help other scholars. The field of organization and management studies has seen the development of mechanisms to minimize both of these issues. The Academy of Management (December 2005) recently developed formal mechanisms for enforcing rules about plagiarism and other ethical violations in the field. We are also doing better with knowledge sharing, due to the statistical and measurement tools that are now available on the Internet, as well as information sharing on list serves. Many subtle ethical issues remain, however, and editors must grapple with these on occasion (see Shapiro & Bartunek, this volume).

One of the issues is whether editors should publish their own work in their journal. Although the editor may be capable of contributing a fine piece to a journal, as human decision makers, editors cannot be free from bias in assessing their own work. Hence, publishing one's own research is a questionable practice, at best.

Editors can and often do publish work by associate editors and members of their editorial boards, however. This practice is acceptable for multiple reasons. First, editors can provide such manuscripts with the same blind review process experienced by other authors, ensuring an equitable process. Second, given the substantial increase in the number of submissions to refereed academic journals in recent years, editorial boards have grown larger. Often, many of the finest contributors in the field are members of prestigious editorial boards. Not only would disallowing their contributions greatly reduce participation on these boards, it would also reduce the ability of the journal to publish the highest quality work with the best chance of subsequent citation and impact.

Communication is essential

As adjudicators of a complex and evolving intersubjective knowledge-conversion process, communication is core to what editors do. First, a manuscript's quality of writing can often obscure the quality of a contribution. For authors, this means that the more effort you put into your writing, the better your chances of publication.

Perhaps less obviously, the quality of reviewer communication is also critical. Sometimes, reviewers do not communicate well by failing to provide citations or failing to clearly explain what they want authors to do. Such communication failures obviously create difficulties not only for the authors, who have a hard time satisfying the reviewer, but also for the editor, who is trying to evaluate the review and provide guidance to the authors. If, as a reviewer, you are not invited to join an editorial board or if you stop receiving manuscripts to review from your favorite journal, you might consider how well your communication has served the editor in the past.

Most importantly, communication from the editor is critically important to the process (Feldman, 2006). I learned this lesson from my experience as an author working with Nancy Eisenberg, who was the editor of *Psychological Bulletin* at the time. The first round of the review process resulted in three of the most challenging reviews ever written (at least, it seemed so to me). Fortunately, these reviews were accompanied by a detailed cover letter from Nancy Eisenberg, who made many suggestions for dealing with the concerns raised by the reviewers. She provided conceptual advice, methodological suggestions, and citations. She also helped me deal with two contradictory reviews by adjudicating them. She decided which reviewer's advice was more appropriate, and indicated so in the letter, as in, "on point 19, do what Reviewer X said and do not do what Reviewer Y suggested." This detailed advice was absolutely essential to the publication of the article, and I sent her a thank-you note for her contribution as editor. Since then, Nancy Eisenberg has been my role model for how I conduct myself as an editor.

Conclusions for editors

As adjudicators of the knowledge-conversion system in our fields, editors are very powerful in many ways. Editors have substantial decision-making power, especially in the typical case where multiple reviewers disagree with one another (Calhoun & Starbuck, 2003). If the reviewers are in agreement, the editor must have a very strong rationale for contradicting them. If the reviewers disagree, however, the editor has almost absolute power to decide whether or not to invite a revision.

Beyond the power to affect the lives and careers of our fellow academics, one of the greatest powers editors have is to influence the content of the common body of knowledge. Given that common knowledge is the foundation upon which personal knowledge is built (Tywoniak, 2007), by influencing the common body of knowledge, we hope to influence personal knowledge and action in the material world. A small portion of the articles we select become incorporated into academic texts and classrooms, and eventually influence the thinking of practitioners. Although most articles are never cited, the ones that are cited influence subsequent research, a small portion of which eventually influences practical thought and action. Increasing the value of academic research for improving practice by helping to develop and select high-quality articles is an editor's primary power and primary goal.

With power comes substantial responsibility. I strongly disagree that editors should be able to do anything they want. On the other hand, I do not believe that editors should be completely beholden to reviewers. Following reviewers blindly means abdicating our responsibility to judge the quality of the reviews as well as the quality of manuscripts ourselves. Because the editor has more information available, s/he is the only person who can provide authors with a higher level of judgment that synthesizes the content of the manuscript with the content of multiple reviews. Exercising that higher-level judgment is essential to the editorial process because of the complexity of the decisions we must make about complicated and abstract ideas (Tywoniak, 2007; Nonaka et al., 2006).

Conclusions for authors

The complexity definition of knowledge suggests some avenues through which authors can enhance the impact of their research to advance the field in a more revolutionary and less incremental fashion. Research questions derived solely through deduction from even a thorough knowledge of the extant literature are likely to generate only incremental contributions to the field. Adding information from other sources, such as personal tacit knowledge and common tacit knowledge, and working to articulate and integrate those sources of knowledge with the extant academic literature holds considerably greater promise for enhancing understanding in a revolutionary way. Given that editors wish to enhance the impact of their journals by increasing citations, doing research that advances the field in revolutionary ways, or at least larger than average increments, is probably the best method for achieving publication.

Beyond doing high-quality research that advances the field, authors can also increase their probability of publication by attending to the communication process (Feldman, 2006). The manuscript should be viewed as a means of persuasion to readers who are well-versed in the area. The fact that the readers are very knowledgeable means that they will not be persuaded by an argument unless the author has demonstrated an understanding of the extant state of knowledge and debate on the topic. Leaving out a critical concept or debate in the field leaves an opening for reviewers to question whether the work is really adding anything new or is simply a replication of previously published work. Hence, it is very helpful for authors to begin their papers with a persuasive introduction that

- States the research question
- Summarizes existing knowledge on the topic
- Identifies the contribution of the current study
- Explains why that contribution is important for advancing the field (see chapters by Bergh and Hollenbeck in this volume for guidance on how to effectively craft a statement of a paper's contribution)

A two- to four-page introduction that accomplishes these four goals makes considerable progress in the author's quest for publication. The reason a statement of contribution is valuable up front is because most of the time, the editor and the ultimate readers of the journal are not experts in every subfield covered by every submission. Hence, without a clear statement of contribution up front, my experience as an editor has been that I'll read through the whole paper and wonder, what is new about this? Haven't I read something like this before? As an editor, I find those reactions very frustrating because it makes me feel like I have to do a comprehensive literature search in order to be able to judge whether this new submission makes a contribution. And reviewing the extant literature is not the editor's job, it is the author's job. Specifically, it is the author's job to put the reader in a position where s/he can judge the value of the contribution to the literature based on the paper alone. If the author can accomplish that goal convincingly, the probability of publication is greatly enhanced.

Throughout the paper, authors should work to make their writing as clear and accessible as possible. Because readers do not have access to the data (i.e., the social and material reality the author is writing about), authors need to provide a clear chain of evidence from the data to their conclusions. That means providing full information on data collection, measurement, and analysis. For example, if survey items are new or have been modified from their original published versions in any way, providing the reader with full information on all items is essential to validate the authors' interpretations of their findings. If qualitative methods are used, authors need to provide a thorough description of how the data were systematically analyzed, to allow the reader to judge the validity of the conclusions drawn. Importantly, making explicit the reasons for the methodological tradeoffs made between the study's strengths and weaknesses can help to persuade the editorial team that the study merits publication despite its (inevitable) flaws.

Finally, if authors don't agree with the reviewers or the editor, often the source of the confusion is the quality of the original writing. If reviewers are asking authors to add something that the authors believe is already in the paper, it is likely that the point needs to be elaborated or emphasized, and simply telling the reviewer that the idea is already in the paper is probably insufficient. If the editor or reviewers make a methodological suggestion that is incorrect or unnecessary, the authors probably have to do a better job explaining the chosen method *in the paper* as well as in a rebuttal directed to the reviewers. Editors are likely to believe that issues raised by the reviewers are going to be raised in the mind of other readers as well, so authors serve themselves best by responding very fully to every issue and concern raised by the reviewers and the editor. Going beyond what is requested explicitly to *fulfill the spirit as well as the letter of all comments* helps authors to win the debate with the reviewers and move their work from the personal to the common realm of knowledge.

References

Academy of Management. (December 2005). *Academy of Management Code of Ethics: Policies and Procedures for Handling Charges of Ethical Standards Violations*. Available online at http://www.aomonline.org/aom.asp?id=271 (last accessed May 7, 2007).

Aguinis, H., & Henle, C. A. (2002). Ethics in research. In S. G. Rogelberg (Ed.), *Handbook of Research Methods in Industrial and Organizational Psychology* (pp. 34–56). Malden,

MA: Blackwell Publishers [available online at http://carbon.cudenver.edu/~haguinis/ AguinisHenle2002.pdf].

Argyris, C., & Schon, D. (1978). *Organizational Learning: A theory of action perspective*, Addison-Wesley, Reading MA, 1978.

Calhoun, M. A., & Starbuck, W. H. (2003). Barriers to creating knowledge. In M. Easterby-Smith & M. A. Lyles (Eds.), *Handbook of Organizational Learning and Knowledge* (pp. 471–90). London: Blackwell.

De Cock, C., & Jeanes, E. L. (2006). Questioning consensus, cultivating conflict. *Journal of Management Inquiry*, 15, 18–30.

Feldman, D. C. (2006). Communicating more effectively with editors: Strategies for authors and reviewers. In Y. Baruch, S. E. Sullivan, & H. N. Schepmyer (Eds.), *Winning Reviews: A guide for evaluating scholarly writing* (pp. 236–50). Basingstoke: Palgrave Macmillan.

Foss, N. J. (2007). The emerging knowledge governance approach: Challenges and characteristics. *Organization*, 14, 29–52.

Nonaka, I., von Krogh, G., & Voelpel, S. (2006). Organizational knowledge creation theory: Evolutionary paths and future advances. *Organization Studies*, 27, 1179–208.

Pfeffer, J. (1993). Barriers to the advance of organizational science: Paradigm development as a dependent variable. *Academy of Management Review*, 18, 599–620.

Starbuck, W. H. (2005). How much better are the most-prestigious journals? The statistics of academic publication. *Organization Science*, 16, 180–200.

Tsang, E. W. K., & Frey, B. S. (2007). The as-is journal review process: Let authors own their ideas. *Academy of Management Learning & Education*, 6, 128–36.

Tywoniak, S. A. (2007). Knowledge in four deformation dimensions. *Organization*, 14, 53–76.

Van de Ven, A. H. (1999). The buzzing, blooming, confusing world of organization and management theory: A view from Lake Wobegon University. *Journal of Management Inquiry*, 8, 118–25.

Van Maanen, J. (1995). Style as theory. *Organization Science*, 6, 133–43.

Vermeulen, F. (2005). On rigor and relevance: Fostering dialectic progress in management research. *Academy of Management Journal*, 48, 978–82.

2
The Role of Editing in Knowledge Development: Consensus Shifting and Consensus Creation

John R. Hollenbeck

> "You know, the Sheriff's got his problems too;
> he will surely take them out on you."
> —Warren Zevon ("Mohammed's Radio," 1976)

When I was first approached about writing this specific chapter, I must admit to being a little intimidated by the title I was asked to speak to – particularly because of its assumption that those who occupy editorial roles "develop knowledge." Even if some do, the thought that I may have ever done this in any of my editor or associate-editor roles is a claim or idea that I might have a hard time defending if pressed.

However, when I considered the formal definition of "knowledge" as provided by Webster's dictionary as "acquaintance with and understanding of a body of facts" and the definition of "fact" in Webster's as "an idea that is universally considered to be true" (Guralnik, 1972), then I got a little less defensive. If one divorces the words "knowledge" and "fact" from any kind of ultimately stable and unchanging truth with a capital "T," and instead views these terms as reflecting a valuable, but momentary universal consensus on ideas, then the role of the editor as knowledge developer becomes a little more visible – even as enacted by me.

Indeed, even a cursory review of much of the literature on the philosophy of science reveals the emphasis that science places on a consensus as a criterion, rather than the discovery of some form of ultimate truth. In defending the need for the scientific process, Charles Peirce wrote that "To satisfy all doubts, it is necessary that a method should be found by which our beliefs may be determined by nothing human, but some external permanency – by something upon which our thinking has no effect. The method must be such that *the ultimate conclusion of every person should be the same*. Such is the method of science" (Buchler, 1955). The history of science is often discussed in terms of revolutions that shift fields from one consensus to another (Kuhn, 1963), and the lack of consensus on basic ideas within a scholarly area has been cited as a sign of disciplinary weakness and immaturity (Platt, 1964).

With this as a background, it is clear to me that an editor has an important role in the development of knowledge if one accepts a definition of knowledge that, at its core, relies on "consensus creation" and "consensus shifting". The editor's role is to make sure that each published article contributes to either increasing consensus about the validity and utility of some idea or changing the consensus away from one idea toward some other idea that everyone agrees is better. Consensus has to occur on many levels. At the most abstract level, it has to be clear how the manuscript being considered contributes to a higher level of consensus in the literature.

At a more practical level, it is also useful to form a consensus among reviewers, as well as between the reviewers and the authors. Obviously, achieving perfect consensus among these different parties is unlikely to be achieved. Still, all else equal, if the editor can provide value added in at least moving all the parties toward agreement, it is directly beneficial to everyone directly involved, as well as for the general health of the discipline. In the face of total lack of consensus among reviewers, and between reviewers and authors, it is impossible for decision making by an editor not to look arbitrary, political, or imperial. Thus, whereas it is clear that, in the end, the editor can and must sometimes make a unilateral decision without ever achieving any consensus, the more he or she can do to create consensus at this level the better. Since other chapters in the book are devoted to managing this aspect of the editor's job, this chapter will focus on the abstract side of consensus and what an editor might be able to contribute to knowledge development at the discipline level, operationalized in consensus terms.

On the practical side, reaction data to the editorial team by authors, whether it is directly solicited or just distributed through the "grapevine," will be immediate and affect the number and quality of submissions that the team will receive. On the abstract side, the contribution that the editorial team has made to their discipline will take longer to assess. If the editor is successful, the evidence for his or her having contributed to consensus will be provided by history in the form of citations for the articles he or she published. If an article is cited over 2,000 times (see Sternberg, 1992 for several examples of these), then there seems to be pretty good consensus that what was written in this article was important to a large number of people. If no one ever cites an article (not even a gratuitous self-citation by the original author), then what was written there has been judged by history – as has the person who decided to publish that work.

With this last statement in mind, it is critical to remember that, like the sheriff in Warren Zevon's "Mohammed's Radio," the editor "has his problems too." He or she is going to be judged by history in terms of how well his or her decisions contributed to the knowledge base, in terms of creating or shifting consensus on ideas, and his or her journal is going to be ranked in terms of its prestige by how well it performs by this outcome, as operationalized in terms of citation counts. People who take on such time consuming, difficult, and uncompensated roles typically care deeply about their discipline and are achievement oriented. No one wants to see the impact of the journal he or she is stewarding on his or her discipline sink during his or her reign.

Hence, the imperial view of editors as being accountable to no one other than themselves is as inaccurate as it is unhelpful. Authors or reviewers would be better armed for success if they approach the editor as someone with a big problem on his or her hands; that is, how am I going to create or shift consensus with this manuscript so that I can raise or maintain the prestige of this journal and contribute to the discipline? As in any domain in life, if you understand people's problem and help them deal with it, you will be successful, and this also applies to people who wish to be accomplished authors or reviewers.

Thus, with these ideas in mind, the rest of this article will focus on what editors can do, at the abstract level, to be effective "consensus shifters" or "consensus creators". Although the focus that I was asked to take is on the leadership role of the editor in this process, obviously leadership can emerge from reviewers and authors as well, and in an ideal world, all parties involved should be striving to create consensus at the abstract level. Indeed, the more the focus of the review process can be kept on the level of abstract ideas, and away from the personalities involved, the more likely is it to obtain consensus at the practical level as well.

Although there are an infinite number of frames that can be used for manuscripts, in my experience, there are six very discernable and widely applied frames that are used for manuscripts in the applied organizational sciences. The relative strength of each of these frames is directly related to the motivation behind the manuscript and how the justification for the work is tied to an existing consensus. In the first section of this chapter, I will focus on two frames that focus on the current consensus and are very powerful. In the second section, I will focus on four less powerful frames that do not explicitly invoke a specific consensus as part of their justification. If authors present their work using either of the two frames mentioned in the first section, I believe they will have better long-term success in terms of publication outcomes and citations. If authors fail to use these frames, and instead invoke one of the four frames mentioned in the second section, editors or reviewers who can help reframe those works in consensus terms will have provided a value-added service in terms of increasing the impact that work has on the current stock of knowledge.

Framing the manuscript in consensus terms

Consensus shifting

The strongest frame for a paper is a frame that "shifts consensus." The frame for this type of paper was described most lucidly by Davis (1971). Davis (1971, p. 312) describes the frame for such a paper in these generic terms:

(1) The author articulates the taken for granted assumptions of the imagined audience by reviewing the literature ("It has long been thought that ...").
(2) The author adduces one or more propositions that deny what has been traditionally assumed ("But this is false ...").
(3) The author spends the body of the work "proving" by various devices that the old, routinely assumed propositions are wrong, while the new ones being asserted are right ("We have seen instead that ...").
(4) The author suggests the practical consequences of these new propositions for his imagined audience's ongoing research, specifically how they ought to deflect it unto new paths ("Future investigation is necessary to ...").

This frame is powerful because of it creates a sense of urgency. It is one thing to "not know something" and in a very real sense, in the applied organizational sciences, there is almost no limit to what we do not know. However, it is quite another to think one knows something, and then find out one is wrong. As Kuhn (1963) notes, "the prelude to much discovery and to all novel theory is not ignorance, but the recognition that something has gone wrong with the existing knowledge and beliefs" (p. 49). This conclusion is reiterated by Platt (1964), who notes more simply that the prelude to discovery is "error rather than confusion" (p. 350).

Space limitations preclude me from going into more detail, but for evidence of the strength of this frame, go to volume 112 of the 1992 edition of *Psychological Bulletin*, or more gratuitously, volume 51 of the 1998 edition of *Personnel Psychology* (the journal I was stewarding at that time), where authors of the most highly rated papers published in those outlets over the last several decades discuss their paper's historical contribution. In almost every case, even if the articles they wrote were not explicitly introduced with the frame described above, it is easy to see how their contribution could be expressed in these terms. If authors presented their papers in similar terms, their contribution would be easier for editors to detect. However, if the authors fail to do this, and if an editor can spin the frame in this direction, the contribution would have more impact, even if the manuscript is really only placing important boundary conditions on a well-accepted consensus (in terms of who, where, or when it holds).

Consensus creation

Another very powerful frame is one where the author uses the literature to show that there is currently a clear lack of consensus in the discipline regarding some important phenomenon. In this case, rather than demonstrating a consensus and then challenging it (or placing boundaries on it), the authors shows that there are two (or more) clear lines of discrepant thought simultaneously existing in the literature. As noted earlier, it is dangerous to think something is true when it is not, and hence, this grants urgency to studies that invoke the consensus shifting frame. The consensus creation frame generates urgency because lack of consensus is embarrassing. Lack of consensus within a discipline is a public advertisement, to external constituencies, that the discipline is immature, and it would be much better for those within the discipline to remain silent than to engage in a contentious, public, external debate regarding topics where well-intentioned and informed parties generally disagree.

In this context, what is needed is a vigorous internal debate in the professional literature, with the aim of shedding light (and not just heat) on the issue. Clearly, if an author can come along and shed such light with a manuscript that contributes meaningfully to ending the debate or restricting its boundaries, this would be highly valuable in terms of generating knowledge as defined here. If the author's paper is not framed this way, but could be, an editor who reframed it would make a value-added contribution.

A "close but not quite" variant of this frame is one where the author suggests something along the lines that "several papers have examined this relationship; half have found effects and half have not, so we are going to do it again." This is a much weaker frame for several reasons. First, in many cases, the inference that half have found it and half have not is based on an inappropriate overreliance on the "Statistical Hypothesis Inference Testing" paradigm, where effects not significant (n.s.) at the $p < 0.05$ level are treated as if the effects are zero (Cohen, 1994). With a sample of 80, the critical value for a correlation coefficient is 0.22. If three studies with this sample size obtained correlations of 0.21 (n.s.) and three obtained correlations of 0.22 ($p < 0.05$), it is not really legitimate to conclude that half the studies got it and half did not.

Even if one can show via a direct test (e.g., meta-analysis) that the obtained findings are actually different from each other, simply "piling on" another correlation, in and of itself, does little to create consensus. This paper can be converted into a genuine consensus creation paper only if the authors (either on their own or strongly encouraged by the editorial team) can explain exactly why there are two different sets of results and how these can all be reconciled if one takes "X" into consideration. If the three authors that failed to find the effect and the three authors that did find the effect were all in agreement about the effect after reading the manuscript under consideration (and by the way, two of them are probably reviewers), then this paper has real value as an exercise in consensus creation, and hence knowledge generation. This is especially the case if there were strongly held, long standing, and publicly declared positions on both sides, because this new manuscript will be instrumental in "putting this embarrassing incident behind us" (or at least placing boundaries on it). Internal debates within a discipline have real value in terms of highlighting where the knowledge base is weak, but their value is inversely related to how long they last.

Whereas "consensus creation" and "consensus shifting" frames are two of the most powerful, the next four frames to be discussed are less powerful. I believe this partially because of my editorial experience, but also because I have employed them myself as an author on one or more occasions to less than satisfactory effect. I think most active researchers have, at one point or another, invoked one or more of these frames because they are ubiquitous in the literature, and hence serve as legitimate models. Being a legitimate model, however, does not mean these are the best models, and I have come to the conclusion that the following four frames are less powerful relative to the two identified above. Hence, if an author or reviewer or editor could reframe these papers into more explicit consensus shifting or consensus creation, he or she would be helping to solve the editors' problem.

Reframing manuscripts in consensus terms

This has never been done before

One very common, but very weak, frame justifies the research by stating something of the form "this has never been done before." Few would accept the idea that "such and such has never been done before" as a legitimate reason for letting their teenage son or daughter do something, and this reluctance should generalize to one's responsibilities as editor. There are probably many good reasons why what the author is doing has never been done before, but even if there are not, it may be very difficult to link this outlier manuscript to any existing consensus in the literature. Thus, the paper is unlikely to either promote greater consensus or shift the consensus because it never comes directly in contact with any consensus.

The reviewers or the editor may be able to help the author if some case could be made that the reason that "this was never been done before" is because it flies in the face of some consensus that clearly states it cannot or should not be done. This could potentially convert the paper into a "consensus shifting" paper, which as noted below can be a powerful frame. It would take a great deal more effort on the part of someone (author, reviewers, or editors) to establish exactly why what is being proposed flies in the face of the existing consensus (and that may not even be possible), and this is unlikely to be accomplished with a single round of revision.

This frame becomes particularly weak, and harder to save, when it is invoked with a very narrow interpretation of what "this" is. In my experience, most of the time, the "this has never been done before" frame was invoked; one or more of the reviewers were able to directly contradict the authors by showing that "this" had indeed been done before. That is, previous studies had linked the same independent variable, dependent variable, mediator and/or moderators. The author would often come back and say, "yes but not with a sample like this (workers from Eastern Europe!) or a task context like this (Emergency Medical Technicians [EMTs]!) or at a time like this (after 9/11!)."

Generally, if there was a compelling theoretical reason why the nature of the sample, task or time made it highly plausible that "what everyone believes is true is actually false with some people, some tasks or at some times," then this might again be converted into a meaningful "consensus shifting" frame by the editorial team. However, the conceptual reason would have to be compelling and it might also require data collected from both this "new" context (sample, task or time), with data from more "traditional" contexts (samples, tasks, and times) to refute alternative conceptual or methodological reasons for differences between this new context and all the existing contexts.

And yes, there need to be differences in results between this context and traditional contexts or else this is straight replication, which is valuable, but not urgent in the eyes of most editors. No two contexts are exactly alike, and hence there is no end to this for an editor that accepts a narrow definition of "this" along with a "this has never been done before" frame as sufficient justification to publish a paper. It will not be viewed as generating new knowledge nor will it generate a large number of future citations – which of course, is a problem for the editor.

Filling a gap

A slight variation on the "This has never been done before" frame is the "Filling a gap" frame. This is a variant in the sense that the author recognizes that someone has done "this," and someone has done "that," but no one has done both "this and that" at the same time. This frame shares many of the same limitations of the frame that preceded it, in terms of (a) there may be good reasons why "this and that" have never been done at the same time and (b) defining "this and that" too narrowly may not be possible. However, if these limitations can be overcome, this frame is slightly stronger. The key to this frame is the relationship between "this and that."

If the consensus is "this and that" have well-known effects, and that they are largely independent (and hence no reason to expect anything other than additive effects), then this reverts to an act or pure replication. This is consensus-confirming research, and as noted earlier, this is valuable, but less urgent relative to consensus-shifting or consensus-creation research in terms of generating new knowledge and impact. Moreover, the number of "gaps" in the literature, if defined this way, is very large, and an editor would quickly run out of space if he or she treated this type of spackle work as equivalent in terms of knowledge generation relative to consensus-creation or consensus-shifting research.

Fortunately, under certain conditions, it is often possible to convert this frame into one of these two other frames. First, if "this and that" are potentially negatively related or in some way inconsistent in conceptualization or in implications for practice, then this frame can be potentially converted in a consensus-creation frame. That is, if one can make a compelling case that "this and that" cannot both be true, and yet this has not been recognized in the literature, then the stage is set for consensus creation. Second, if "this and that" have interactive, rather than additive effects, then the stage is set for consensus-shifting research. That is, if one can argue that "it is generally believed that 'this' has certain effects, but this is not true when 'that' is high or low," then the current consensus has effectively been refined and bounded more definitively (although not necessarily shifted a great deal).

Why ask why why?

Bacharach (1989) has noted that at the core of all strong theories is an explanation of "why" two variables are related or "why" a particular cause leads to a specific effect. Given this, it should not be surprising that someone might frame a paper in generic terms such as "Although everyone knows that this and that are related, no one has ever been establish *why* this is the case," and this is a common frame. Although expressed in consensus terms, authors that invoke this frame are directly claiming right from the start that consensus creation has already been accomplished, and they have no intention of shifting it. Instead, their goal is to more fully elucidate it.

This frame is particularly weak if (a) there is one single mediator that has been implied but never directly tested, or (b) if no mediator has ever been proposed, but the one tested here is the most obvious. In both of these cases, the paper is likely to confirm that what everyone thinks is true, is in fact true. There is some value in this as an extended replication, but what is learned from this does not really create a sense of urgency for a would-be publisher.

This frame is also weak when one moves beyond the first level of mediation and asks, "why, why?" That is, when the frame becomes "everyone knows A leads to C because of B, but *why* does A lead to B?" Now, the authors are suggesting that not only is there consensus, but that this consensus is already pretty well elucidated. Cook and Campbell (1979) refer to this type of second, third, or higher order mediation question as "micromediation," and they show that this can go on forever. In the end, what is learned from it never really changes the basic reality that if you need to control C, all you really need to worry about is A. Particularly in applied contexts, when research goes beyond the first level of mediation, one starts to hear complaints from practice-oriented reviewers that the paper is too academic.

This frame becomes more powerful, on the other hand, if the authors can make the case (or the editors or reviewers can induce the authors to make the case) that the literature has proposed alterative reasons "why" A leads to C, and that these may not be compatible. Thus, although there is consensus about the A-C relationship, there is a clear lack of consensus about why this is the case, and thus, this has now been framed in "consensus creation" terms at a different level. This frame also becomes more powerful if the mediators being tested have strong implications for helping uncover future moderators. That is, if one knows the exact and precise reason why A leads to C (i.e., B), it may be easier to imagine contexts where A may not lead to C because in these contexts, B is not possible, or B is not caused by A, or B may not cause C. This at least sets the stage for "consensus shifting" research where the well-known relationship between A and C turns out not to hold after all because of contingencies associated with B.

Linear problem solving

In many applied areas of science, research questions are driven by the need to solve real-world problems. When that is the case, solving the problem becomes the justification for conducting the research. The frame that is set for such research follows a form where (1) some important problem is introduced, (2) the lack of solution to the problem is established, (3) the existing literature base or knowledge base is reviewed for potential solutions, (4) those solutions that seem most relevant or applicable are invoked, and (5) the results of that are reported, more often than not – resulting in a happy ending.

Both knowledge generation and problem solving are good things, but unfortunately, they are not necessarily the same thing. When the problem is used to justify the research, the theory and the hypotheses become "problem driven," and not necessarily "knowledge driven." Indeed, Weick (1989) has noted that "most descriptions of theory construction sound very much like conventional linear descriptions of problem solving which is unfortunate ... when theory building is modeled after linear problem solving, the outcomes are unremarkable" (p. 519).

The reason for this is that good problem solving, for obvious reasons, more often than not tries to *leverage* the existing knowledge base, not *extend* it. That is, the most logical steps to take when solving the problem are those steps for which there is a strong consensus that the steps will work, and it would seem odd (if not unethical) to try something controversial or unproven in any context where there was some consensually approved alternative. Authors will sometimes try to suggest that the existing knowledge base says absolutely nothing about the problem that they are trying to solve, but that is usually only true in a very narrow sense (i.e., "no one has tried to improve personnel selection outcomes with Eastern European EMTs after 9/11). When people speak of the need for close ties between researchers and practitioners, the most important thing that researchers bring to that relationship, in my opinion, would be a recommendation about what should be done in this specific context given the current consensus. This maximizes the practitioner's likelihood of success, as well as the defensibility of what the practitioner did if it turns out the problem was not solved.

Paradoxically, the potential contribution of the linear problem-solving frame to knowledge generation is inversely related to the success of the problem-solving effort. When all works out well, then the research is totally knowledge confirming, and more likely than not, replicates past studies (although perhaps in a different context). The potential for knowledge generation is highest when all hell breaks loose. When nothing that was promised by the existing knowledge base actually works when invoked in this specific context, then this sets the stage for consensus shifting, because some aspect of the sample, task, or time is serving as boundary condition on what is known.

Again, the prelude to new discovery is not ignorance, but rather something that we all truly believe in has gone terribly, terribly wrong. Even when things do not go terribly wrong, unforeseen problems in implementing consensus-based practices often call for more refined levels of consensus. What might be serendipitously learned in the aftermath of these events could have critical implications for extending the knowledge base. When people speak of the need for close ties between researchers and practitioners, this is the most important thing that practitioners bring to the relationship, in my opinion.

Finally, for the record (i.e., so that I am not quoted out of context), let me directly reiterate that problem solving is a good thing, and I am not saying that knowledge generation should be given a higher priority than problem solving. If my doctor follows all of the textbook protocols and cures me of some malady, this is a good thing for me. However, he or she may not have generated any new knowledge in the process, and although my problem has been solved, my doctor has *not solved the problem* of the editor of some prestigious medical journal. If my doctor wants to ignore the textbook protocols and try out some new and unproven procedure on me, in the hope of generating new knowledge, this may or may not be good for me. On the other hand, the editor of a prestigious journal might be curious about how this new and unusual treatment works out for me, and not because we are close friends. Alternatively, if my doctor goes through all the textbook protocols and all hell breaks loose – this is definitely bad for me – but the editor of a prestigious medical journal may want to "stop the presses" and rush off and publish my case. The editor of a prestigious medical journal, like the sheriff, has his problems too.

Implications for authors, reviewers, and editors

If, like many philosophers of science, one accepts a definition of "knowledge" that is expressed in terms of a momentary, but valuable universal consensus about ideas, then manuscripts that are cleanly framed in consensus terms have the clearest potential for impact and knowledge development. In particular, manuscripts that explicitly induce a "consensus shifting" or "consensus creation" frame can be powerful in terms of generating a sense of urgency with respect to their publication and eventual citation.

There are many other potential frames an author could employ, and four specific frames that are widely seen in the applied organizational sciences that are less powerful in the sense of creating a sense of urgency, were identified here. The implication that this has for authors, reviewers, and editors is basically the same, in the sense that if any one of these parties can convert a manuscript that starts out with a less powerful frame into a more powerful consensus-shifting or consensus-creation frame, the better it would be for all parties. Many specific ways of making this conversion were presented in this paper, and anyone who can take the lead in reframing such papers is consensus terms helps promote a win-win-win situation for the authors, the editor, and the journal in terms of maximizing the potential impact that the article has on the knowledge base.

References

Bacharach, S. (1989). Organizational theories: Some criteria for evaluation. *Academy of Management Review*, 14, 516–31.
Buchler, J. (1955). *Philosophical writings of Peirce*. New York: Dover.
Cohen, J. (1994). The earth is round (p < .05). *American Psychologist*, 49, 997–1003.
Cook, T. D., & Campbell, D. T. (1979). *Quasi-experimentation: Design and analysis issues for field settings*. Rand McNally: Chicago.
Davis, M. (1971). That's interesting! Towards a phenomenology of sociology and a sociology of phenomenology. *Philosophy of the Social Sciences*, 1, 309–344.
Guralnik, D. B. (1972). *Webster's new world dictionary of the American language*. Southwestern: Nashville, TN.
Kuhn, T. S. (1963). The essential tension: Tradition and innovation in scientific research. In C. W. Taylor and F. Barron (Eds.) *Scientific creativity: Its recognition and development*. New York: Wiley and Sons.
Platt, J. R. (1964). Strong inference. *Science*, 146, 347–53.
Sternberg, R. J. (1992). Psychological Bulletins top ten "hit parade." *Psychological Bulletin*, 112, 387–8.
Weick, K. E. (1989). Theory construction as disciplined imagination. *Academy of Management Review*, 14, 516–31.
Zevon, W. (1976). *Mohammed's Radio*. Elektra Records, New York.

3
How May I Help You? Editing as Service

Ann Marie Ryan

A reductionist view of the role of an editor would be that it is but a series of service transactions – receive a manuscript, assign reviewers, read the manuscript, read the reviews, write a decision letter, pick up the next one and repeat the process. Lest the reader be horrified that as an editor I have viewed my decision letters as no more than hamburgers at a fast food drive-through (and you are probably grumbling about applying the word "fast" to editorial decisions), let me elaborate on why applying a service lens to the editor's role is appropriate and useful.

Service on the part of editors is integral to the continued vitality of the peer review process. Priem and Rasheed (2006) noted that reviewing is an "invisible service"; in contrast, the role of an editor is quite a visible one as the name authors associate with an acceptance or rejection is the editor's. The "service provider" that is directly identifiable to those seeking to publish is the editor. Further, editing is a professional service that is quite involving in terms of time and effort commitment relative to many other forms of voluntary professional activities.

In this chapter, I discuss different ways of considering editing as a service role, drawing upon literature on volunteerism to highlight why individuals might choose to serve the profession in this way, and the literatures on organizational citizenship, customer service, and servant leadership to discuss the nature of service provided by editors. Throughout, ways in which editors should and should not adopt a service orientation to the task of editing are highlighted. Finally, I end with brief advice to both the person and the profession on how to better cultivate editors and to cultivate better editors.

Editing as sustained volunteerism

The literature on sustained volunteerism addresses why individuals choose to take on and remain in roles that require "long-term, planned, prosocial behaviors that benefit strangers and occur within an organizational setting" (p. 448; Penner, 2002). The editor's role can be characterized as one of sustained volunteerism, and hence Penner's model of why individuals take on such roles has relevance as to why individuals might choose to serve a profession through editing.

Penner (2002) suggests that volunteer-related motives affect decisions to volunteer. Clary, Snyder, & Ridge (1992) developed the most oft-cited framework of volunteer motives, noting that individuals will volunteer if they perceive volunteering as fulfilling one or more of six functions: (values) expression of altruistic values, (esteem) for ego-growth and development, (career) to gain career-related benefits, (social) in response to the normative influence of friends, family, or a social group, (understanding) to better understand the population being helped, and (protective) to facilitate guilt reduction associated with being more fortunate than others. Any combination of these motives can lead to editorial service.

First, editing can serve as an expression of professional values. Mael and Ashforth (1992) defined professional identification as the extent to which an individual defines him/herself in terms of the work he/she does. When individuals have a greater professional identification, it leads to a greater congruence between their personal work values and the values of the profession. Editors generally have high professional identification or they would not take on such a large professional service burden, and the process of editing itself will lead to an increase in professional identification and a reinforcement of values. Piliavin and colleagues discuss the concept of volunteer role identity, the extent to which a volunteer role is part of a person's self-concept (Piliavin, Callero, & Grube, 2002; also see Grube & Piliavin, 2000). Being an editor is a service with which an individual must have a strong role identity to be successful, lest the service be seen as a chore.

Second, editorships are considered highly influential roles, and so the esteem function likely often plays a part. Similarly, the career function of editing is apparent – one does gain broader name recognition and one develops one's own skills as an author and reviewer. While the motives to take on the service of editing probably have some basis in the desire for career enhancement, status, and recognition, I would argue that the esteem and career functions simply aren't enough to induce one to become an editor. There are many paths to achieving high status as a scholar, and editing has costs that may affect those other paths (e.g., time spent editing may mean less time on conducting and publishing one's own research). Editors must possess some of those other motives as well.

Penner (2002) notes that a major determinant of the decision to volunteer is social pressure. There is likely explicit and implicit social pressure to be an editor – one obviously is asked to do it directly (although some journals solicit self-nominations), and it is considered a prestigious honor. Hence, in most cases we could say that there is social pressure to volunteer one's services as editor. If one were to ask why I became an editor, it is in no small measure because many individuals I admire and respect (my advisor, his advisor, and a number of current and former colleagues) had been editors. Admiring their contributions to my field led me to internalize the belief that being an editor is important (the value function), but it also created social pressures to serve.

There also may be some creeping social pressures working in an opposing direction (e.g., if one's department is not supportive through offering released time, relaxing expectations, or rewarding editorial duties). While these social pressures against taking on editing roles are not as strong as those toward accepting the position, their existence is a concern as it lessens the likelihood of individuals accepting editorial positions.

The understanding and protective functions of volunteering may be less apparent motives for an editor, or at least they weren't apparent to me when I took on the role. However, I do think these relate to outcomes gained from service as an editor. One understands a great deal more about initially unfamiliar research topics from editing and gains understanding of how individual authors and reviewers approach the task of crafting manuscripts. In terms of a protective function, I have come to realize how fortunate I was in my early academic career to collaborate with colleagues that facilitated my growth as a researcher and as a writer. Editing reinforces what many graduate educators have long observed – there are many intelligent individuals with creative ideas who put a lot of energy into their research but produce papers that "need lots of revision." Individuals such as myself, who have been fortunate to interact with so many talented scholars in their career, can contribute through the service of editing to assist others in learning how to take that unpolished manuscript to a highly influential article.

In addition to motives, Penner (2002) suggests personality influences decisions to volunteer. The literature supports two dispositional predictors of volunteering, Other-oriented Empathy and Helpfulness (Penner, 2002). Some readers may be skeptical of these as related to the service of editing, noting that there is often little evidence of empathy or helpfulness in editorial decision letters! However, I do believe there must be some elements of these dispositional traits for those who take on the editorial role. An editor has some level of understanding of what authors go through to develop the research based on his or her own research experiences. A good editor will convey empathy regarding challenges (e.g., why an author might not be able to obtain additional data) while at the same time not let empathy override quality standards for publication. Editors who view their role as one of "helping authors create the best possible manuscript" may invest more and provide better service for authors and the profession than those who do not; however, "helping" can become inappropriate overstepping of the boundaries of one's role (see Bedeian, 2003, for a full discussion).

Finally, Penner (2002) suggests that the organization's attributes influence decisions to volunteer. The role of a journal's reputation, values, and practices in taking on an editorship is an important one. A journal with which one feels some affinity in terms of values and standards would be one a person is willing to associate one's name with in a public way. One should also make sure any negative perceptions of the editorial process are addressed and the process is transparent to preserve the integrity of a journal's reputation (see Lilienfeld, 2002; Lundberg, 2002; McCarty, 2002; Newcombe, 2002 as an example).

Having provided some thoughts as to what predisposes individuals to editorial service, the literature on citizenship behaviors is discussed next to provide a basis for understanding why editing is clearly discretionary service behavior.

Editing as professional citizenship

Serving as an editor is a form of professional citizenship. According to Organ's (1988) definition of citizenship behavior, it fits two of the three criteria: it is a discretionary behavior, not an essential part of one's job; and, in the aggregate, it promotes the effective functioning of the organization (in this case, the journal or the profession). However, Organ also states citizenship behavior is not directly or explicitly recognized by the formal reward system. While being an editor may not be a directly compensated role for many, some editors do get an honorarium and editing does provide recognition and is often rewarded in university merit pay systems.

Organ, Podsakoff, & MacKenzie (2006) and Podsakoff, MacKenzie, Paine, & Bachrach (2000) suggest seven citizenship dimensions, and most of these are indeed part of an editor's role. First, *helping behavior*. One goal of editors is to help others publish their work. Second, *sportsmanship*. Editors should be willing to tolerate impositions of the role without complaining (well, maybe I have not entirely embraced this dimension, but one should!). Third, *organizational loyalty*. An editor promotes and remains committed to the specific journal and also to the profession and advancement of it. Fourth, *organizational compliance*. Editors internalize the "rules" of the peer review process as enacted for a given journal (e.g., the standards of quality, the definition of conflict of interest). Fifth, *civic virtue*. An editor recognizes being a part of the whole, as the earlier discussion on professional identification and motivation indicated. Sixth, *self development*. Editors do take on voluntarily improvement of one's knowledge and skills (e.g., I will look up unfamiliar articles referenced by authors and read them; I sometimes seek out advice on the use of less common analytic techniques). The seventh dimension, *individual initiatives*, or engaging in above and beyond, is probably less part and parcel of the editor's role, although one can point to many editors that do this (Feldman's series of editorials in *Journal of Management*, which aimed to educate the readership, would be a good example; Feldman, 2006). Hence, it is clear that serving as an editor covers many of the dimensions of professional citizenship behavior.

Researchers have pointed out potential downsides to engaging in too much organizational citizenship behavior (OCB). One concern for any editor is whether the editorial role detracts from other roles – I am always asked by individuals thinking about taking on editorial roles whether this will affect research productivity. Joireman, Kamdar, Daniels, & Duell (2006) described citizenship behavior as posing a conflict between an individual's short-term self-interest and the long-term collective interests of the organization and suggested such behaviors pose social dilemmas. They demonstrated that OCBs are more likely when individuals adopt a long-term horizon. The editor's role will be less appealing if one is focused on what needs to be accomplished in the semester or two ahead (i.e., classes to prep, grants to manage, papers to get out) than if one is thinking about one's long-term career contributions.

Research on OCBs suggests that citizenship behavior can lead to greater stress, overload, and work–family conflict (Bolino & Turnley, 2005). One needs to acknowledge that adding a role to one's plate is not without cost, although there certainly are ways to reduce or manage the costs. As noted earlier, an individual might negotiate for a change in some of his or her current roles such as a course reduction, change in course composition, or reduction in administrative duties. I would be remiss if I did not acknowledge that there are stresses associated with editing: time conflicts, as authors are waiting for decision letters (and there is always a letter to write) but one needs to attend to research, teaching and life outside of work; strain, as one can worry over making the right decision on a paper; and feelings of overload, as one always has more papers to read. Indeed, in finishing up this chapter I have put aside some decision letters for a few more days – balancing the tensions of how late can I tolerate being with the letters with how late I can tolerate being with the chapter (with the kids off from school for holidays added in) illustrates the overload problem clearly!

One interesting perspective on why individuals undertake more costly OCBs is an evolutionary psychology viewpoint proposed by Salamon and Deutsch (2006). They propose that the handicap principle suggests that individuals will undertake behaviors that are costly if they can be used to signal something unique or scarce about the qualities of the individuals undertaking them. Hence, the ability to bear the cost of the behavior sets an individual apart from others and demonstrating that ability leads to desired outcomes in the long term. The role of the editor can be construed as a costly citizenship behavior, but its undertaking is done in part to signal one's capabilities to manage the costs and can lead to other rewards in the long-term.

Editing as customer service

One literature that gives some food for thought regarding editing as service is the literature on customer service behavior. It is important to realize that in speaking about customer service behavior, we are talking about the actions and activities on the part of the editor meant to influence service quality; certainly, much influences the authors' experience of service that is outside of the editor's behavior (e.g., the downtime on the manuscript submission website; the behavior of reviewers). There are a few select points from the customer service literature that are especially relevant to the topic of editors as service providers: coproduction of journals, customization of service, service recovery in editing, service relationships versus encounters, and job attitudes and service.

First, one distinguishing feature of services is the level of "coproduction" or the extent to which the client is an active participation in the productions of the service (Bowen & Schneider, 1988; Schneider, 1990; Schneider & Bowen, 1985, 1992). For example, a doctor relies on a patient to provide information on medical symptoms, individuals in fast food restaurants may be expected to bus their own tables, and online sales sites expect customers to correctly fill out order information. What does this have to do with editing? As with any service, when the customer and the service provider do not have similar expectations regarding the role of the customer, problems can arise (Kelley, Donnelly, & Skinner, 1990). As with any service, customers must be able and motivated to engage in coproduction (Legnick-Hall, 1996).

As an editor, there is some frustration when an author does not do what is expected – in following journal guidelines regarding style and formatting, in including the standard sections of an empirical piece (e.g., I am amazed at how many submissions will lack a table of descriptive statistics, neglect to have at least a paragraph on limitations in the discussion, or where no one has ever taken the time to check the reference section against the text). This failure, on the part of the author, to take a fuller role in coproduction leaves the editor with pointing out these problems, and there have been a few times where I felt akin to the person cleaning off the tables at McDonald's for those too lazy to do so.

At a less "picky" but still obvious level, though, journal coproduction expectations include that authors will do a thorough literature review rather than a cursory glance, that authors will seek help with analyses when uncertain as to how to proceed, that authors will spend more than a few minutes thinking about alternative explanations for results and directions for future research rather than assuming the editor and reviewers will do these things. Further, the expectation is that authors will work to be responsive to reviewer comments rather than leaving the editor to arbitrate. In general, the literature on customer service behavior and coproduction emphasizes that there needs to be a match between customer and service provider expectations regarding what is the role of each party (Legnick-Hall, 1996). One challenge for an editor is to continually convey service provider expectations – through journal policies, through editorials, through speaking at conferences, through forums such as this book, but most often through each of those decision letters that get written.

On the other hand, if the editor is to provide quality service in a coproduction context, he/she cannot ignore the author's expectations. One common expectation of authors is not just to receive a decision but to receive feedback and guidance. An editor is expected to provide some synthesis of what are the main issues with the paper and how they can be addressed (i.e., if not through revision, what can be done in future research efforts). Not meeting expectations for feedback and guidance is a failure in coproduction on the part of the editor. This need not be overly detailed feedback and guidance – pointing out every grammatical error in a manuscript is not needed, stating that one needs to get a proofreader is fine; providing a tutorial in hierarchical linear modeling is not needed, noting the need to learn about the analytic approach is sufficient. Certainly, if the author's expectation is unwarranted or unreasonable (e.g., reading a very long piece to suggest how to cut it; one week turn around time on a manuscript because the author is up for tenure next week), the editor has to address that.

A second point from the customer service literature that relates to the role of editor as a service provider is the distinction between services that have standard interactions versus customized ones (Bitner, Booms, & Mohr, 1994; Rogelberg, Barnes-Farrell, & Creamer, 1999). Standard types of interactions have a "script" that both the customer and service provider know to follow; customized interactions require greater coproduction and may lead to greater differences in expectations. On the one hand, we can argue that the service interaction of editors with authors is unique and customized – each decision is based on a unique manuscript and the letter produced by the editor is tailored to that paper. However, there are some elements of a standard script as to how the process occurs (e.g., what to submit, what to expect in terms of time, what to expect in a reply, what to do in response). Bitner, Booms, & Mohr (1994) noted that when a customer is unfamiliar with what should occur, his or her expectations are less likely to match up with those of the service provider. Hence, the challenge for an editor is not to let the fact that some authors are naïve regarding the way things should transpire (e.g., in terms of inappropriate correspondence, in terms of not knowing how to reply to revision requests) influence his or her feelings about the manuscript – customer education is required. Editors serve the profession by performing this ongoing educational function.

A third topic from the customer service literature that I wish I had thought about more before becoming an editor is that of service recovery – what do you do when there is a screw up (Chang, 2006), an inevitability as the peer review process involves humans. The literature on service recovery highlights the importance of three attributes: (a) choice of what needs to be done to make up for the failure, (b) compensation for the failure (e.g., offer free dessert), and (c) apology (Mattila & Cranage, 2005). Given the nature of service provision on the part of editors, there often isn't a lot to be offered in terms of choice for the authors or in terms of compensation, but the apology should be provided. Editors are ultimately responsible for any administrative or system screw-ups even if these are errors on the part of others (e.g., misspelled author names and affiliations on a final copy about to go to production; correspondence neglected by administrative assistants), and it is important to get the individuals responsible to apologize and correct the error. That is, the editor bears a great deal of responsibility for service recovery activities for a journal.

However, there is a challenge to service recovery when the poor service is on the part of a reviewer. As an editor I have perhaps too many times had to add near the beginning of my decision letter, "I apologize for the length of time it has taken to get to this decision as we had a non-responsive reviewer and had to seek someone else." Such apologies for poor service may not lead to customer recovery; authors do think about lengthy processes when choosing what journals to target their papers toward. Further, there are challenges to service recovery when a reviewer's poor service is a very weak or superficial review (i.e., getting an additional reviewer would be appropriate service to the profession in ensuring quality standards, but the author may not see that as the appropriate recovery action). Further, if the poor service delivery on the part of the reviewer is related to inappropriate tone albeit correct content, one walks the diplomatic line of signaling to the author and the reviewer that you recognize the "poor service" by the reviewer while at the same time agreeing with his or her substantive points.

Another distinction in the customer service literature that is important to understanding the editor's role is that of the type of relationship between the customer and service provider (Gutek, 1995; Gutek, Bhappu, Liao-Troth, & Cherry, 1999). Service relationships are ones where a customer and the service provider expect to have repeated contacts (e.g., hairdresser); service encounters are single interactions with no expectations of future interactions (e.g., store cashier). Where does the editor fall? While he/she may, in fact, have many service encounters as many authors do not submit multiple manuscripts during an editor's tenure, he/she must approach each interaction as if it is part of a service relationship so that authors wish to publish in the journal in the future. The editor is not just 'editor', but the 'editor of Journal X', and as such represents the journal, not just herself. Approaching with an expectation of future interactions leads one to see providing good service as in one's self-interest, whereas in encounters, those motivations are not there (Gutek et al., 1999).

One final note is that a number of studies have demonstrated a link between service provider job attitudes and customer satisfaction (Schmit & Allscheid, 1995; Susskind, Kacmar, & Borchgrevink, 2003), noting a likely reciprocal causality. Editor's satisfaction with the editing role can influence interactions with authors and reviewers, and the satisfaction of those parties will be affected. Decision letters may not be as thoughtful when an editor feels stressed or the process is not intellectually engaging, compared to cases where the editor enjoys editing. A surprise for me as an editor has been that "service complaints" are far less numerous and "service compliments" far more frequent than I would have anticipated. It is rewarding (and reinforcing) to receive emails expressing appreciation for the service provided from authors who have experienced a negative decision or have been through a demanding revision process.

Editing as servant leadership

In preparing this chapter, I wondered if the concept of "servant leadership" might be important to understanding editing as a vital professional service. There is debate over the conceptualization of servant leadership (indeed the literature has been described as "rather indeterminate, somewhat ambiguous and mostly anecdotal" (p. 145; Russell & Stone, 2002)). However, there are useful heuristics for purposes of this discussion on editing, even if there is empirically much to debate.

Servant leadership is seen as stewardship in that one has trust in managing the property or affairs of another (Reinke, 2004; Russell & Stone, 2002). Editors are given a tremendous stewardship by the profession – the role of ensuring that a journal maintains an unbiased role in the production of knowledge, that high quality standards are maintained, and that knowledge is advanced. Such a stewardship is no light burden for an editor, and most editors can relate a time or two where they worried about whether the standards they were applying for a given decision were the appropriate ones. Stewardship can be thought of as belief that the journal has "a legacy to uphold and must purposefully contribute to society" (p. 308, Barbuto & Wheeler, 2006). As noted above, journal editors take on the professional identity of the journal (e.g., its aims and mission, the intellectual niches it fills) and are stewards of that identity. In choosing to make changes to editorial policy or journal focus, the editor must consider this stewardship.

Greenleaf (1977), who is credited with coining the concept of servant leadership, suggested that the test of servant leadership is whether those served grow as persons. In this sense the editor must pass this test – decision letters should provide the individual with an opportunity for growth in some fashion (e.g., knowledge of how to better present one's work, literature one was unaware of, analytic techniques one should master). Stone, Russell, & Patterson (2004) described servant leadership as "a belief that organizational goals will be achieved on a long-term basis only by first facilitating the growth, development, and general well-being of the individuals who comprise the organization" (p. 355). The long-term goal of the profession is advancing knowledge; editors must keep in mind that achievement of that goal requires authors and reviewers find meaning from their engagement in the process.

The "editor as servant leader" analogy can only be taken so far, though, as authors and reviewers aren't followers and the same goals are not shared by all parties (i.e., at an abstract level all are working toward seeing work published, but for editors and reviewers that would be "work that meets the standards of the journal" whereas for authors that would be "my work"; editors keep an eye on page budgets whereas authors and reviewers feel it essential to add clarification or to mention moderately relevant references).

Implications for authors

An "editing as service" lens has implications for authors. First, recognize that as volunteers performing a professional citizenship role, editors may sometimes be challenged by their workload. As in any other service area, friendly inquiries over delays or what you view as poor service will be appreciated much more than strident demands.

Second, acknowledge your role as an author in the coproduction of the service. Meet the expectations of the journal regarding that role. Familiarize yourself with journal submission guidelines and follow them.

Third, treat the exchange surrounding a manuscript as a service relationship, not just an encounter. Recognize that despite an unsatisfactory outcome in a given instance (i.e., a rejection), you expect future interactions and an ongoing relationship with this editor. Work to make that a positive, professional relationship.

Finally, recognize that your attitudes affect the editor's. Positive experiences with a journal should also be acknowledged so that the editor gets feedback on what she is doing right as well as what she needs to improve.

Implications for editors

How might this lens of "editing as service" lead to cultivating editors? Recognizing the inherent service components of the role is important to ensure that those who take an editorship do so without misconceptions regarding the nature of the position or the rewards one will attain. Considering motives for volunteering and the costs of service are important to making decisions to serve in this capacity. Understanding that leadership of the profession by a journal editor is through service provision can negate misconceptions regarding the nature of editorial influence.

When thinking of editing as service, it is important to keep in mind that authors are not the ultimate target of one's service – the profession is. Judging an editor solely based on "comment cards" from authors would not be the best method of assessing service quality. Instead, the quality of an editor's service is best judged by the standards of stewardship, but not stewardship defined solely as caretaking of the review process. An editor's stewardship should lead to the growth and development of individuals and to advancement of the knowledge base of the profession. Such is the legacy of service journal that editors aspire to create, one that I hope readers of this volume consider as a worthwhile one to pursue.

References

Barbuto, J. E., & Wheeler, D. W. (2006). Scale development and construct clarification of servant leadership. *Group & Organization Management*, 31, 300–26.

Bedeian, A. G. (2003). The manuscript review process: The proper roles of authors, referees, and editors. *Journal of Management Inquiry*, 12, 331–8.

Bitner, M. J., Booms, B. H., & Mohr, L. A. (1994). Critical service encounters: The employee's viewpoint. *Journal of Marketing*, 58, 95–106.

Bolino, M. C., & Turnley, W. H. (2005). The personal costs of citizenship behavior: The relationship between individual initiative and role overload, job stress, and work-family conflict. *Journal of Applied Psychology*, 90, 740–8.

Bowen, D. E., & Schneider, B. (1988). Services marketing and management: Implications for organizational behavior. *Research in Organizational Behavior*, 10, 43–80.

Chang, C. (2006). When service fails: The role of the salesperson and the customer. *Psychology & Marketing*, 23, 203.

Clary, E. G., Snyder, M., & Ridge, R. D. (1992). A functional strategy for the recruitment, placement and retention of volunteers. *Nonprofit Management and Leadership*, 2, 333–50.

Feldman, D. C. (2006). Communicating more effectively with editors: Strategies for authors and reviewers. In Y. Baruch, S. E. Sullivan, & H. N. Schepmyer (Eds.), *Winning reviews: A guide for evaluating scholarly writing* (pp. 236–50). Basingstoke: Palgrave Macmillan.

Greenleaf, R. K. (1977). *Servant leadership: A journey into the nature of legitimate power and greatness*. New York: Paulist Press.

Grube, J., & Piliavin, J. A. (2000). Role identity, organizational experiences, and volunteer experiences. *Personality and Social Psychology Bulletin*, 26, 1108–20.

Gutek, B. A. (1995). *The dynamics of service: Reflections on the changing nature of customer/provider interactions*. San Francisco: Jossey-Bass.

Gutek, B. A., Bhappu, A. D., Liao-Troth, M. A., & Cherry, B. (1999). Distinguishing between service relationships and encounters. *Journal of Applied Psychology*, 84, 218–33.

Joireman, J., Kamdar, D., Daniels, D., & Duell, B. (2006). Good citizens to the end? It depends: Empathy and concern with future consequences moderate the impact of a short-term time horizon on organizational citizenship behaviors. *Journal of Applied Psychology*, 91, 1307–20.

Kelley, S. W., Donnelly, J. H., & Skinner, S. J. (1990). Customer participation in service production and delivery. *Journal of Retailing*, 69, 104–26.

Legnick-Hall, C. A. (1996). Customer contributions to quality: A different view of the customer-oriented firm. *Academy of Management Review*, 21, 791–824.

Lilienfeld, S. O. (2002). A funny thing happened on the way to my *American Psychologist* publication. *American Psychologist*, 57, 225–7.

Lundberg, G. D. (2002). The publishing dilemma of the American Psychological Association. *American Psychologist*, 57, 211–12.

Mael, F., & Ashforth, B. E. (1992). Alumni and their alma mater: A partial test of the reformulated model of organizational identification. *Journal of Organizational Behavior*, 13, 103–23.

Mattila, A. S., & Cranage, D. (2005). The impact of choice on fairness in the context of service recovery. *The Journal of Services Marketing*, 19, 271–80.

McCarty, R. (2002). Science, politics, and peer review: An editor's dilemma. *American Psychologist*, 57, 198–201.

Newcombe, N. S. (2002). Five commandments for APA. *American Psychologist*, 57, 202–5.

Organ D. W. (1988). *Organizational citizenship behavior: The good soldier syndrome*. Lexington MA: Lexington Books.

Organ, D. W., Podsakoff, P. M., & MacKenzie, S. B. (2006). *Organizational citizenship behaviors: Its nature, antecedents, and consequences*. Thousand Oaks, CA: Sage.

Penner, L. A. (2002). Dispositional and organizational influences on sustained volunteerism: An interactionist perspective. *Journal of Social Issues*, 58, 447–67.

Piliavin, P., Callero, P. L., & Grube, J. (2002). Role as resource for action in public service. *Journal of Social Issues*, 58(3), 469–85.

Podsakoff, P. M., MacKenzie, S. B., Paine, J. B., & Bachrach, D. G. (2000). Organizational citizenship behaviors: A critical review of the theoretical and empirical literature and suggestions for future research. *Journal of Management*, 26, 513–63.

Priem, R. L., & Rasheed, A. A. (2006). Reviewing as a vital professional service. In Y. Baruch, S. E. Sullivan & H. N. Schepmyer (Eds.), *Winning reviews: A guide for evaluating scholarly writing* (pp. 27–40). Basingstoke: Palgrave Macmillan.

Reinke, S. J. (2004). Service before self: Towards a theory of servant-leadership. *Global Virtue Ethics Review*, 5, 30–57.

Rogelberg, S. G., Barnes-Farrell, J. L., & Creamer, V. (1999). Customer service behavior: The interaction of service predisposition and job characteristics. *Journal of Business and Psychology*, 13, 421–35.

Russell, R. F., & Stone, A. G. (2002). A review of servant leadership attributes: Developing a practical model. *Leadership & Organization Development Journal*, 23, 145–57.

Salamon, S. D., & Deutsch, Y. (2006). OCB as a handicap: An evolutionary psychological perspective. *Journal of Organizational Behavior*, 27, 185–99.

Schmit, M. J., & Allscheid, S. P. (1995). Employee attitudes and customer satisfaction: Making theoretical and empirical connections. *Personnel Psychology*, 48, 521–36.

Schneider, B. (1990). The climate for service: An application of the climate construct. In B. Schneider (Ed.), *Organizational climate and culture* (pp. 383–412). San Francisco: Jossey-Bass.

Schneider, B., & Bowen, D. E. (1985). Employee and customer perceptions of service in banks: Replication and extension. *Journal of Applied Psychology*, 70, 423–33.

Schneider, B., & Bowen, D. E. (1992). Personnel/human resources management tin the service sector. In G. R. Ferris & K. M. Rowland (Eds.), *Research in personnel and human resources management* (Vol. 10, pp. 1–30). Greenwich, CT: JAI Press.

Stone, A. G., Russell, R. F., & Patterson, K. (2004). Transformational versus servant leadership: A difference in leader focus. *Leadership and Organization Development Journal*, 25, 349–61.

Susskind, A. M., Kacmar, K. M., & Borchgrevink, C. P. (2003). Customer service providers' attitudes relating to customer service and customer satisfaction in the customer-server exchange. *Journal of Applied Psychology*, 88, 179–87.

4
A Letter to Editors

Stephen R. Barley

Dear Colleague:

Congratulations and welcome to the other side! If you thought it was tough being an author, there's often more confusion here and potentially less relief, if for no other reason than that you will have fewer people with whom you can commiserate. You probably recognize that you have just landed a position of some power. What you do not know yet is that your power will be far less than others, and perhaps even you, presume. Like it or not, you have also just become a businessman or businesswoman. Production schedules, costs, income and surely personnel issues will soon be (and should be) as important to you as the quality of the papers you publish. In fact, the intellectual and operational sides of a journal are tightly bound: mess up one and the other will eventually suffer. Finally, you are now a public figure whose actions will draw notice and affect the peace of mind, and possibly the well-being, of colleagues throughout the field.

You may shun or embrace editorial power. You may throw yourself into or buffer yourself from the business. But you cannot escape the reality that your decisions and those of others associated with the journal will shape peoples' lives and, by the theory of what-goes-around-comes-around, the health of your journal too. The reason is simple: your colleagues will hold the journal accountable for what you do and for the type of experience you offer them in a myriad of ways. While serving as the book review editor and then as the editor of the *Administrative Science Quarterly* (*ASQ*), I gradually realized that how one plays the role of editor deserves deliberation. I see editorship as the art of juggling three primary and sometimes conflicting roles: those of ambassador, mentor, and manager. Journals succeed when editors play all the three well.

The editor as ambassador

Most of us become editors with no prior work experience. We show up knowing how to think like authors, reviewers, and readers. Being able to do so is, of course, necessary, because editors need to consider each constituency's perspective in everything they do. But knowing what it means to be an author, a reviewer, or a reader is insufficient precisely because these perspectives are what a field's insiders know. Once you become an editor or associate editor, you essentially step outside the field.

I know this sounds odd, even counterintuitive. Most people would argue that becoming an editor puts you squarely at the center of a field and, sociometrically speaking, they're right. Nevertheless, the experience of editing is singular. Editors do not have the luxury of thinking just like an author, just like a reviewer, just like a reader, or even like all three. Instead, you must keep these perspectives in mind but transcend them to become something more akin to an ambassador while at the same time resisting others' attempts to treat you as an oracle. Here's why.

All fields cleave into camps along substantive, methodological, and philosophical lines. Unless a journal is extremely specialized, it must attract and publish manuscripts from many camps. If the journal is sponsored by a professional association, creating a tent large enough for all camps to gather may even be part of the editor's unwritten job description. Excluding or offending camps, either intentionally or unintentionally, risks more than illwill. Members of a disgruntled camp may decide to send their manuscripts elsewhere. The same is true for being perceived to favor one camp or another, whether the perceptions are accurate or inaccurate. Perceptions of favoritism invite people to act as if favoritism existed, thereby, creating the conditions of a self-fulfilling prophecy. As W. I. Thomas put it, "If people believe things to be real, they are real in their consequences." I cannot emphasize this point enough: it is possible for one or more of your constituencies to act as if your journal discriminates even if it doesn't. Whether you do or don't makes no practical difference.

When members of camps cease to submit, and especially when they do so en masse, they push editors in the direction of either missing deadlines or accepting manuscripts of lower quality to fill issues. The effect is directly proportional to the size of the camp, its level of disaffection, its status within the field and the percentage of high quality manuscripts that its members produce. Missing deadlines or lowering standards to make ends meet reflects badly on the journal. Moreover, missing deadlines because the journal's pipeline is empty will raise your costs because printers usually try to schedule to capacity and often charge penalties when schedules slip.

Any journal's lifeblood is a continuing stream of high quality submissions. To ensure such a stream, editors must become ambassadorial. Being an ambassador means, in part, assuring authors that papers originating from all camps within the journal's purview are welcome and will be evaluated fairly. It is crucial that you make such assurances genuinely, because authors will test your claims. The only development worse than the perception that your journal is biased is the perception that you and your coeditors are not true to your word.

Like an ambassador, editors also receive invitations to attend the academic equivalent of state dinners. Potential authors feel, perhaps rightfully so, that meeting the editor will help them understand the journal's priorities. Some suspect that getting to know the editor might offer an edge, should they decide to submit. Accordingly, having become an editor, you will now find yourself more in demand than before. You will be asked to serve on panels on publishing. Here you will be expected to talk about how journals operate, about being an editor, about being a reviewer, and about being an author. People will ask you for tips on writing. You may even find yourself being invited more frequently than before (and after) to deliver talks on your own work at other campuses and at conferences you don't typically attend.

All such events are opportunities to keep the journal in the public eye, as well as opportunities to do important public service, because many scholars, especially those who are new to the field, do not really know how journals operate. Nevertheless, should you accept such invitations, and you should, it behooves you to remain cognizant that as an editor your opinions and words are no longer your own. Because authors look to editors for indications of what a journal wants to publish and what authors need to do to get published, every word you speak in public may be read by someone as a clue, sign, or signal of your journal's priorities and biases. In other words, whether you like it or not, people will treat you like an oracle. Colleagues will imbue your words with more importance than deserved and sometimes even treat them as if they were *de facto* editorial policy. Thus, as a good ambassador, I urge you to be circumspect about airing your personal likes and dislikes, especially regarding theories, methods, and topics for investigation. Rest assured that the need to self-monitor will eventually end. Your newfound popularity will disappear just as suddenly as it arrived once you hand the editorship to your successor. On that day you can safely return to expressing your opinions with impunity, because once again few will care what you think and you will no longer be in the position to harm either the journal or the field.

The editor as mentor

All manuscripts contain a piece of an author's self. In many instances, the author has spent years doing the research and developing the perspective or theory that the paper presents. Months, if not years, have gone into the writing. Most writers will have thought about and chosen their words carefully. This is true even when readers universally experience the manuscript as haphazardly conceived, inadequately organized, and poorly written. Journals do better when editors keep firmly in mind that no matter how flawed the manuscript, they are handling an emanation of a person's self. Handling an author's self does not mean cutting the author more slack, compromising the journal's standards, or refraining from giving tough feedback. It does mean realizing that the editor's and the reviewer's jobs are fundamentally different.

The *Oxford English Dictionary* (*OED*) suggests that "reviewer" connotes antagonism: "one who criticizes new publications." As anyone who has submitted a paper to a journal can tell you, the reviewer's job is to identify loose arguments, unqualified claims, methodological flaws, and various types of oversights. Especially competent reviewers also sometimes advise authors on how to develop the manuscript as an act of communication. (These are the reviewers who are at serious risk of being asked to be editors.) Nevertheless, most reviewers do not have the skill, proclivity, or time to help authors restructure manuscripts as documents or arguments. The most a reviewer can usually do is suggest an alternative take. Because peer reviewed journals use at least two and often three reviewers, an author is unlikely to profit from the editor adding another critical voice. In fact, when blessed with good reviewers, editors have leeway, if not the obligation, to assume the role of mentor.

Interestingly, the *OED* actually defines editorship as connoting a helpful, developmental stance: "One who prepares the literary work of another person, or number of persons for publication, by selecting, revising, and arranging the material." Editorial mentoring entails synthesizing the commonalities that lie beneath what might otherwise appear as the reviewers' discrepant views, not only to warrant the journal's decision, but to assist the author in making subsequent versions of the manuscript better regardless of which journal receives them. Although editors of journals almost never have the time to edit manuscripts actively, providing authors with even a sketchy rubric for restructuring arguments is far more helpful than simply reiterating the reviewers' points. In my experience, most papers are not rejected because their methods are inadequate or because their ideas are fundamentally flawed, although some papers do suffer from these problems. Instead, journals reject most papers because authors have not yet adequately framed, organized, and communicated their argument, which, in turn, frustrates reviewers making them even more critical.

Why should an editor take the time to mentor when it is more efficient to do otherwise? First, compared with critique, authors are less likely to perceive mentoring as threatening to the self. Second, mentoring increases the author's chance of being published somewhere. Third, and most important, when editors write as mentors, they enhance the probability that authors will submit again. All three are likely to lead authors to speak well of the journal regardless of the paper's disposition, thereby enhancing the journal's reputation as a fair and reasonable place to submit *even if* one's paper is *not accepted*. As an editor, you can hardly ask for more.

The editor as manager

Ambassador and mentor are outward-facing roles; they are the roles most visible to authors and reviewers. The editor as manager is an inward-facing role, seen most clearly by the journal's other editors and staff. Nevertheless, how editors play the role of manager strongly affects how authors and reviewers experience a journal, even if authors aren't fully aware that this is so.

Aside from securing subscriptions and monitoring production, managing a journal involves orchestrating the flow of manuscripts and reviews. Authors and reviewers are strongly affected by both flows. Aside from useful reviews, authors primarily desire and deserve prompt turnaround of their manuscripts. The expectation that journals will handle manuscripts expediently is increasingly important in an era when the pressure to publish both well and frequently seems to be growing. The pressure is particularly acute for untenured academics. Perhaps the only outcome more disappointing to an author than having a manuscript rejected is waiting an inordinately long time to have it rejected. Delay adds injury to insult. Every day that a manuscript sits under review reduced the number of days that the author will have to revise and resubmit the manuscript elsewhere. If the author's tenure clock is ticking, a long review process definitely amplifies a rejection's deleterious consequences for his or her career. For this reason, I firmly believe that every editor has a moral obligation to minimize delays in processing manuscripts.

The review process consists of three phases: (1) the time between the manuscript's arrival and the point when the all reviewers have agreed to do a review, (2) the period when the manuscript is in the reviewers' hand, and (3) the time between the arrival of the last review and the author's receipt of the decision letter. The length of each phase affects turnaround time. Editors directly control the duration of the first and last phases. They only indirectly control the second phase, which is usually the longest. Nevertheless, editors can substantially influence the duration of each phase, including the second.

Before sending a manuscript to reviewers, an editor must decide whether the manuscript is appropriate for the journal and its audience. When I was editor of ASQ, 15 to 20 percent of each year's submissions were inappropriate for the journal. The reasons for mismatch were varied. Many were written for practitioners and contained no research. Others were fine pieces of research, but on topics better suited for journals in other fields. Some were so poorly written or executed that sending them out for review would be to waste reviewers' time. Still other manuscripts were term papers authored by undergraduates or manifestos and rants written by apparently unstable individuals.

Editors do well to adopt a policy of immediately returning such papers unreviewed, along with a letter that clearly and politely explains why the manuscript does not fit the journal. The rationale is twofold. First, returning submissions enables authors to locate a more suitable home for their work with minimal delay. Most authors would rather be told immediately that their manuscript is inappropriate than to wait months before learning they chose the wrong outlet. Second, returning manuscripts wastes no reviewer's time. Reviewers' rightfully resent being asked to handle manuscripts that they should never have received, and resentful reviewers eventually stop reviewing.

Assuming the manuscript is appropriate for the journal, the editor's next task is to choose reviewers. Choosing the right reviewers is paramount for managing turnaround. In fact, it is the primary way that editors can affect the duration of the second phase of the review process. Minimizing the amount of time that manuscripts stay with reviewers requires choosing reviewers from a reviewer's point of view.

Reviewers are volunteers. They receive few rewards for handling a manuscript, except, of course, for being appointed to the journal's board and then being asked to review even more manuscripts. Most people agree to review out of a sense of reciprocity: we review others' papers so they will review ours. Nevertheless, no matter how altruistic the reviewer might be, accepting a manuscript amounts to agreeing to be interrupted and sidetracked. Accepting a manuscript means that reviewers must set aside time for a journal, time that they could have devoted to something else. In this sense, the reviewer's time is a gift to both the author and the journal, and a substantial gift at that! Doing a review often takes a day or more of a reviewer's time. Such gifts are precious and are not to be wasted.

Editors waste reviewers' time by requesting that they handle papers on topics in which they have no interest, that employ methods in which they have no expertise, and that are written from ontological or epistemological perspectives about which they are blissfully ignorant. In the latter case, the request is also unfair to the author, since authors deserve to have their papers critiqued from within the paradigm in which they work. Editors can also abuse a reviewer's time, even if they don't waste it. Abuse occurs when a journal sends a reviewer too many papers in too short a period of time. Ironically, editors are most likely to make this mistake with their best reviewers because it is easy to ask for help from responsive reviewers who write helpful reviews. Unfortunately, even the most willing reviewer may eventually begrudge editors asking for help and, hence, refuse to review the manuscript or, worse yet, procrastinate starting the review. In other words, reviewers are more likely to finish reviews quickly when the journal has not worn out its welcome, when the manuscript is relevant to their substantive interest, and when they feel competent to review the paper on methodological and ontological grounds.

Only with a good database can you avoid wasting or abusing a reviewer's time. The database must be current and ideally it should contain the names of a large number of reviewers. For each reviewer, the database should contain information on what subjects and methods the reviewer feels competent to give help. You should assign manuscripts to reviewers whose interests and competencies match the article. Notice that this also increases the odds that the paper will receive a fair audience. In addition, the database should track which manuscripts have previously been sent to the reviewer, when they were sent, and how long the reviewer had the manuscript in his or her possession. You should use the first two pieces of information to resist calling on the reviewer too soon after having last done so. The last piece of information is valuable in deciding whether or not to use the reviewer in the first place. Because reviewers who take an inordinately long time to complete a review disadvantage authors, I counsel using them infrequently, if at all, regardless of how useful their reviews might be.

In recent years, journals have begun to ask authors to revise their papers two or more times before reaching a decision about whether to publish. Please, resist this temptation. Allowing more than one chance to revise and resubmit frustrates authors, wears reviewers down, and extends the time it takes to publish a manuscript beyond what is reasonable. If at the end of the second round of reviews, you want to neither reject nor accept the paper, then allow yourself only one option: accept the paper provisionally subject to the author meeting the journal's stipulations. This removes the author from undue jeopardy, relieves the reviewers from further duty, and places the onus of responsibility for further developing the manuscript squarely on the editor's and the author's shoulders. My experience is that editors make much cleaner decisions when operating with a "Revise and Resubmit Once" policy. In the long run, all parties benefit.

Because editors write decision letters, they are personally responsible for the lag between the journal's receipt of the last review and the author's receipt of the decision. I urge you to set the goal of having decision letters in the mail less than ten days after the last review is on your desk. If you are unwilling to commit to producing decision letters this quickly, perhaps you should reassess whether you are cut out to be an editor. If you find yourself handling too many manuscripts to write timely decision letters, then it is time to recruit another associate editor!

Sooner or later, every editor, no matter how talented and diligent, reaches the point when he or she begins to resent writing decision letters because they take too much time and effort. This is the first sign of editorial burnout. Unless you are truly an exceptional altruist, it will happen to you. When you begin to have these feelings, interpret them as evidence that it is time to put the journal in someone else's hands. By resigning you will be doing yourself, your coeditors, and your authors a favor.

Why, if the reality of editing is less glamorous than it might appear and is sometimes downright onerous, would anyone in their right mind agree to take on the role? I suspect every editor has his or her unique answer to this question. For me, there has been the satisfaction of knowing that on occasion I made a positive difference in someone's career. I also know that during my tenure, the journals that I edited managed to publish papers that altered the way members of the field viewed topics and that pushed a body of scholarship forward. Because I was an editor, I was able to meet and become friends with individuals that I would not have otherwise met. Finally and perhaps most importantly, I found intrinsic satisfaction in solving the practical problems of the business and producing a tangible product that had meaning to others. I have no doubt that you will enjoy some of these and other satisfactions. Editorship is an important role, and skilled individuals who are willing to assume the role are hard to find. That you have chosen to take it on matters to the rest of us. Thank you!

Part II Effective Editorship

5
Setting up an Effective Manuscript-Review Process

K. Michele Kacmar

My chapter is on journal infrastructure, an important issue for editors and authors alike. How the review of a paper is managed will determine repeat business, the tone, and content of the word of mouth advertising, and the overall reputation of the journal. As authors, we all have been involved in both pleasant and not so pleasant review processes. As the editor of the *Journal of Management (JOM)* from 2000 to 2002, one of my top priorities was to ensure all authors received a developmental, expedient review of their work. To accomplish this goal, I undertook various steps to develop the system we used to shepherd a paper through the review process at *JOM*. In the following pages, I will describe this system and then offer some insights about the review process that every author should know.

When I assumed the editorship of *JOM* in July of 1999, we had a completely paper based, snail-mail review process. Under this system, authors would send four copies of their paper to the journal office. The editor would review the paper and select three reviewers. One copy of the paper and the review forms would be stuffed in an envelope and mailed to each of the selected reviewers who would complete their reviews and mail back the review sheets to the journal office. While this process was not uncommon at this time, it had several disadvantages. First, authors were responsible for copying and mailing their manuscripts. Problems arose in both of these phases. For instance, manuscripts arrived with missing or crooked pages, manuscripts were damaged or delayed during the mailing process, or they simply never arrived. Second, the time it took to mail the papers to reviewers had to be incorporated into the review process. This was especially disconcerting to international reviewers. The international mailing time sucked up so much of the time provided for a review that they had only a few days to conduct a review and get it back into the mail to meet their deadline. Further, reviews lost, delayed, and damaged in the mail were still an issue. Surprisingly, many reviewers mailed the only copy of their review to us; so when asked, they could not produce a replacement copy for us. The final step, getting the decision letter and reviews to the authors, was plagued by the same problems described above. However, one of the biggest disadvantage of this system was that submissions arrived at a single physical location (the journal office), even when the editor and associate editors were not located there. This final issue was a significant problem for me because I was on sabbatical, working at the Bellagio Casino in Las Vegas, during my first year as the editor of *JOM*.

Knowing that I needed the manuscript-review process to be more mobile to support my sabbatical plans, I decided to automate the process. I started with the return of reviews. At the same time that I mailed a hard copy of the paper to a reviewer, I also sent an email to let him or her know that a paper to review was on the way. Attached to that email was an electronic version of the review sheets. Reviewers were asked to complete the electronic review sheets and email them to the journal office. This approach took away many of the disadvantages described above. It provided reviewers more time to complete their reviews as they could return the review via email on the day it was due. It eliminated copying and mailing costs incurred by reviewers. It allowed me to electronically ship reviews to the associate editor, saving time and money. Finally, it allowed me to communicate with authors and reviewers electronically, cutting even more time off the review cycle. Most importantly for me, it provided me with a virtual office as I was able to access submissions and reviews no matter where I was.

With electronic reviews pouring in from all over the world, I needed a manuscript-tracking system in the database to manage them all. I took my problem to my husband, Chuck, a computer genius, and asked him for help. We sketched out what the system needed to do to support an electronic environment, and he implemented our plan. After months of testing, modifying, and experimentation, I had a system so sophisticated that with only a few key strokes I could send a paper and the review forms to a reviewer, a decision letter to an author, and feedback about the disposition of the paper to the reviewers.

With the review process automated, I turned to implementing electronic submissions. Because I knew from the beginning of my editorship that I wanted to automate the review process, *JOM* submission instructions required that an electronic copy of the manuscript be submitted on a disk along with the hard copies. I used the disk version of the papers to test drive the electronic review process with the international board members. These folks were extremely excited about being part of the pilot test because of the slow international mail service.

During the pilot test we ran into some problems, mostly software issues. Mircosoft Word, for example, automatically inserts who originated the document in the properties option. This makes blind submissions impossible. Similarly, those who use the track changes feature sometimes did not remove all of the changes prior to submitting the paper, allowing the reviewers to see the "behind the scenes issues" that they were not meant to see. Those who did not use Word faced even more problems as the translation programs available did not always produce the wording intended by the author. However, after installing a few more database options, I was able to send a clean, blind version of a submitted manuscript to reviewers allowing the vast majority of manuscripts to be handled electronically by the end of my first year as the editor.

Logistical issues are only a part of the manuscript review process. Another main component is reviewers, who also need to be tracked and monitored. Each manuscript submitted to *JOM* was sent to three reviewers. Given that we received about 350 papers a year, that equated to over 1,000 reviews a year. With just over 100 board members, each reviewer received nearly 10 papers a year, not counting the revised papers they reviewed. To keep the board members' task manageable, we enlisted ad hoc reviewers. These are qualified reviewers who volunteered or were recommended but who were not on our board. The internal rule was that an ad hoc reviewer could not be used more than three times a year, or he or she had to be promoted to the board.

Reviewers for a manuscript were selected based on their areas of expertise and prior reviews. Reviewers were given six weeks to complete a review and were not sent a new paper until after the six weeks passed. If they returned the paper before the six weeks expired, they were placed on "vacation" until the six weeks elapsed, so that their efficiency would not result in another paper for review being sent to them. Reviewer names returned to the availability list were listed in order of the due date for their last review. This means that within content area (e.g., agency theory) the reviewer names were ordered in such a manner that the reviewer who returned a review most recently was at the bottom of the list.

In a perfect world, all reviewers would return their reviews in the time allotted. We, of course, live in academia, not in a perfect world. In order to ensure that authors were not kept waiting for a decision on their paper longer than the advertised 60 days, we built into the database reminder emails that were sent one week and again one day before a review was due. As you might suspect, some reviewers did not even know I sent reminders as their reviews always arrived prior to the first scheduled reminder. However, others received reminders on every paper they were sent to review. The fastest *JOM* reviewer averaged an eight-day turnaround on the 26 papers he reviewed during my editorship. The slowest reviewer averaged 49 days, which is seven days *longer* than the 42 days reviewers were provided, on the eight papers he reviewed. This statistic does not include the three papers he held for over 60 days, without *ever* returning a review, forcing a decision on a paper with only two reviews. As you might suspect, about 20 percent of the reviewers caused about 80 percent of the problems. What you might not guess is that the 20 percent were all experienced reviewers who had served on editorial boards for many years.

Even the most sophisticated manuscript-review process in the world is only as fast as the reviewers who participate in the process. This means that the editor must manage and control the reviewers. To ensure that *JOM*'s response time to authors did not exceed what we advertised, we continually monitored the quality and timeliness of reviewers. When faced with unresponsive or unconstructive reviewers, we put them on permanent "vacation" and replaced them with efficient, motivated ad hoc reviewers. At the end of my three-year term, the average response time for a first-time submission was 42.7 days. This enviable turnaround time can be attributed to *JOM*'s committed, qualified editorial board, which is exactly what every editor wants.

So let's recap what the review process at *JOM* entailed. An author electronically submits a paper to the *JOM* office. The paper is received and logged into the manuscript-tracking database. The database automatically generates an email to the author indicating the paper's arrival and tracking number. The paper is forwarded to the appropriate action editor (AE) based on whether the paper is micro or macro in focus. The AE has two choices. One option is to desk reject the paper. A desk reject indicates that the paper is not suited to the journal. This can be due to either content (e.g., too applied or outside the journal's mission) or format (e.g., 150 pages long or not formatted for a management journal). When an AE desk rejects the paper, he or she writes a letter to the authors explaining the decision and offering alternative journals that might be more receptive and forwards this to the *JOM* office to be shared with the authors. The second option is to place the paper into the review cycle. To do this, the AE selects three reviewers from the available reviewers in the database and forwards these names to the *JOM* office. The reviewers are assigned to the paper in the database. This removes them from the available list and generates an email review request that includes a blind version of the paper and the review sheets. If a reviewer declines the request to review, which happens once about every 25 review assignments, the AE is informed and an alternative reviewer is selected. The alternative reviewer is assigned to the paper and the original reviewer is put back on the available list.

When a completed review arrives, it is logged into the database and the reviewer is put on vacation until their six weeks are up. If the review does not arrive within five weeks, the first reminder message is sent. If the review is still not received by the day before it is due, a second reminder notice is sent. If the deadline passes and there are two reviews returned, the reviewer who has yet to respond is sent an email indicating that the editors are moving on without him or her. If there are not two completed reviews, the editor phones the reviewer and requests a date for when to expect a review. Once at least two completed reviews are received, they are forwarded to the AE. The AE is given a week to read the paper, synthesize the reviews, make a decision, and write the author's letter. The letter is electronically forwarded to the *JOM* office and logged into the database. The letter and reviews are then emailed to the authors and the reviewers, and the manuscript is marked as closed in the database.

Implications for authors

Now that you are familiar with the manuscript-review process, allow me to offer some insights that every author should know. If you have never reviewed for a journal, volunteer to do so or ask someone you know who is on the editorial board to recommend you. This is as easy as sending a cover letter indicating the areas in which you feel competent to review and attaching a copy of your vita. Most editors will only select ad hoc reviewers who have published in a refereed journal, but not necessarily in their journal. Select a journal to which you frequently submit. Not only will this allow you to see what goes on behind the scenes, but it will expose you to the content of the review sheets and reviewer guidelines that outline how your submissions are judged by the reviewers. When you receive a paper to review, immediately contact the editor and indicate your willingness to review the paper. Then, dig in.

Create the review you would like to receive. It should be constructive, informed, and to the point. Providing more than a three-page review is overkill. Be sure to number your points so that the AE can easily refer to your suggestions in his or her decision letter. Most importantly, beat the deadline. Your goal should be to not receive an email reminder, which means you need to return your review a week to ten days prior to the stated deadline. If it is your first review, ask a seasoned colleague to "peer review" it for you prior to submitting it. When the decision letter arrives, read it to see if the AE mentioned any of your points in the letter. Compare the issues you raised to those raised by the other reviewers to see how closely they align. Then sit back and wait for the next review request to arrive.

Prior to submitting your work to a journal, secure the most current copy of the submission guidelines and read it carefully. Follow the requirements to the letter. This is one of the very few things you have complete control over during the review process. Use it to your advantage. You would be surprised by how many papers arrived at *JOM* that did not follow our submission guidelines. All this did was delay the review process and aggravate the editors and reviewers. Why go there? You also need to use the submission guidelines to determine the appropriateness of your submission. Taking this step will limit the number of desk rejects you receive. Another way to limit desk rejects is to ask a colleague familiar with your target journal to peer review your paper for you prior to submission. Experienced reviewers and authors can quickly determine its fit with your target journal and find correctable problems that will make your paper look better to the reviewers assigned to read it.

Another interesting fact that I did not know until after I served as an editor is that there are better and worse times to submit a paper. One of the worst times to submit is during the summer. The reason for this is that nearly a third of my editorial board took the summer off. What this means to you as an author is that a paper submitted during the summer may be reviewed by someone less directly involved in your research area or someone who is being called upon quite heavily to make up for other vacationing board members. Similarly, submitting a paper in December is a bad choice as many reviewers are away from their offices for an extended period of time prolonging the review process. A good time to submit a paper is in September or January when all of the vacationing reviewer have returned rested and ready to review.

As a former editor, one of the most frequently asked questions I get is, "may I contact the editor?" My answer is always the same – depends upon why you want to contact him or her: If it is simply to whine about a set of reviews you received, then the answer is no. Use colleagues, friends, and family for this. If there was a problem with the reviews (you got some for the wrong paper or some were missing), by all means. If you submitted your paper and have not heard back from the journal office after three weeks, sure. If you have heard back from the journal office but have not received your reviews by the advertised time, no. To do so will only remind the editor that he or she is not doing a good job, and no good will come from that. It also may force the editor to make a decision with only two reviews, which may not be to your advantage. My advice is that rather than focusing on what is under review, focus on what you need to get under review. Whenever you do decide to contact the editor, email first to set up a time to chat. This will allow the editor time to pull the paper and get up to speed prior to talking with you. Remember, the editor is responsible for over 50 papers, not just yours.

Implications for aspiring editors

So you think you want to become an editor? Before saying yes, consider the following. To excel as an editor you must be organized. First, you must be able to prioritize and complete tasks on a daily basis. Implementing an effective submission and review system will help a great deal with this. Develop a system with built-in reminders of what you need to be doing (e.g., reminding reviewers, reading reviews and the paper to develop a letter) to keep the review process for each paper on track. Second, you must be able to see the big picture as well as the very small details. Again, your system can help with this. For example, tracking and using historical data about the number of papers accepted, rejected, and still in play will allow you to predict and control your journal's "in press" time. Third, you need to be a good matchmaker. That is, you need to be able to match reviewers to papers. Developing a system that can match available reviewers to papers requires a great deal of work up front, but will definitely be worth it on the long run. Finally, you and your system must be agile. While the review process can be described as a series of steps to follow, not every paper you receive will follow these steps. For instance, some reviews will never show up or some reviews will be so poor or nasty that you will not want to share them with the authors. What will you do in these cases? Ask for another review or go with what you have? Building flexibility into your system will allow you to effectively deal with the unexpected.

Even with all of the trials and tribulations involved in running *JOM*, serving as its editor was one of the most rewarding professional experiences of my life. I met many wonderful people in the field, I read many papers that I would not otherwise have read, and along the way I learned how to be a better reviewer and author. However, I'd be lying if I said I'd ever do it again. Being an editor takes over your life and reduces your own research productivity substantially. These are two things I'm not sure I'll ever be ready to give up again.

6
Communicating with Authors
Sara L. Rynes

As editor of *The Academy of Management Journal* (*AMJ*), I am often asked whether or not I like the job. Almost without thinking, I say: "I like it much better than being a reviewer. It's much more positive and creative."

Why do I feel this way? As I reflect upon my enthusiastic reaction toward the editorial role, it seems a bit puzzling. How can I think of the role as "positive and creative" when approximately one-third of the manuscripts we receive at *AMJ* are desk-rejected (i.e., rejected without sending them out for review), or when only 8–10 percent of the manuscripts we receive are ultimately accepted?

In part, I think the answer lies in selective perception and retention: what sticks in my mind when I think of editing are mainly the positives and the successes. Alan Meyer, writing about his experiences as a veteran reviewer, beautifully describes the feeling of a successful review process:

> Now and then – out of the tedium of routinized, ritualized manuscript review cycles – a bona fide high-performing system emerges. On five occasions I have seen a seriously deficient or highly preliminary paper somehow pique the reviewers' interest, and trigger a set of especially thoughtful and constructive comments. Usually the reviewers' objections appear irreconcilable and their demands seem impossible, but instead of giving up the author rises to the occasion … When the revision is resubmitted, the author's unexpected improvements delight and energize the reviewers, eliciting creative ideas for further sharpening the analyses, extending the argument, and enlarging the contribution. It is an exhilarating experience when a distributed network made up of blind reviewers linked to an anonymous author by a harried journal editor jells in this way.
> (Meyer, 1995, p. 264)

In Meyer's description, the author and reviewers play the heroic roles. The "harried editor" seems almost an afterthought, an administrator whose main function is to link the unknown parties to one another. Perhaps not surprisingly, however – (cognitive dissonance reduction is alive and well!) – I believe that editors often play a significant role in the creation of such peak reviewing experiences.

First, it is the editor who assembles the particular set of actors, carefully selecting a group of reviewers who, taken together, should be capable of responding thoughtfully to the major substantive and methodological features of the paper. Second, because the editor has the advantage of seeing all the reviews prior to reaching a decision, the editor often spends considerable time thinking about how to reconcile those "seemingly irreconcilable" views before he or she communicates with the author and the reviewers. Third, in writing the decision letter, editors can also help authors to feel that seemingly impossible demands are "doable" by winnowing through many pages of reviewer comments to focus on a few key points. Fourth, they can motivate authors toward peak performance by suggesting that they are dealing with a "difficult but potentially attainable" goal (Locke & Latham, 1984).

As I leave the world of editing later this year, I suspect it is the peak experiences that I will remember most. However, as Meyer's quote suggests, most of the editor's job consists of dealing with far more "ritualized, routinized review processes," 90 percent of which result in rejections rather than peak experiences. Communications with authors in these cases are generally shorter and, indeed, more routinized. For example, in the case of seriously deficient submissions (e.g., nonempirical essays submitted to *AMJ*, which is an empirical journal), the rejection letter may consist of one or two paragraphs stating the reason for the rejection and referring the author to the journal's "Information for Contributors."

Thus, communications to authors are highly varied. Ideally, they are matched to the precise situation, which includes such features as the quality of the submission, experience level of the author, and phase of the review process. Because of this variety, it is a bit difficult to state general principles for communicating with authors, or to organize them in a meaningful way. Nevertheless, here are some general pieces of advice based on my experiences to date. I begin with one that applies mostly to editors-in-chief rather than associate editors, and that addresses authors in general rather than authors who have submitted a particular manuscript. Subsequent suggestions are more tailored to specific authors and their manuscripts.

1. *Communicate proactively with general audiences to maximize the chances of receiving promising submissions.* At a time when authors from anywhere in the world can submit manuscripts with the click of a mouse, there is considerable potential for receiving manuscripts that are not a good fit with a particular journal's mission or that do not meet its standards. As such, most editors use a variety of proactive communications to try to minimize the number of such submissions. These communications are posted on journal Web sites, as well as published in printed issues.[1]

For most journals, two of the most important proactive communications are the mission statement and some version of "Information for Contributors." Mission statements are inevitably somewhat general. For example, *AMJ*'s mission is "to publish empirical research that tests, extends, or builds management theory and contributes to management practice. All empirical methods – including, but not limited to, qualitative, quantitative, field, laboratory, and combination methods – are welcome. To be published in *AMJ*, a manuscript must make strong empirical and theoretical contributions and highlight the significance of those contributions to the management field. Thus, preference is given to submissions that test, extend, or build strong theoretical frameworks while empirically examining issues with high importance for management theory and practice. *AMJ* is not tied to any particular discipline, level of analysis, or national context."

Because most mission statements leave considerable room for interpretation, it is important to provide additional "Information for Contributors" that gives more specific guidance to authors about how the journal's mission is operationalized in practice. In *AMJ*'s case, our Information for Contributors begins with the mission statement, continues with our criteria for publication, discusses article length and preferred writing style, and indicates the preconditions for submitting a manuscript to *AMJ* (e.g., results not previously published, article not previously rejected by *AMJ*, notification of related publications from the same data base). It also discusses desk rejections, normal review processes, and typical timelines for processing reviews; refers authors to our style guidelines, and makes explicit our expectation that those who submit manuscripts to *AMJ* will also be willing to serve as reviewers.

Because both the mission statement and Information for Contributors can have a considerable impact on what is actually submitted, I would advise every new editor to scrutinize their contents to see whether they are up to date or if policies or practices need to be modified. For example, in the case of *AMJ*, we modified the mission to make it clearer that we welcomed qualitative and theory-building studies in addition to quantitative, theory-testing research. We also modified our Information to Contributors to eliminate research notes and to move to a "length-to-contribution" ratio as the standard for determining manuscript length.

In addition to the mission statement and Information for Contributors, *AMJ* also posts its style guide for authors, a list of previous *AMJ* "best paper" winners, and semimonthly "From the Editors" columns that comment on various aspects of the publication process. These fall into two categories: the general publishing and review process (e.g., essays on what it means to make a "strong contribution" or how to get more out of the review process) and special topics (e.g., international research in *AMJ* or ways to improve qualitative submissions). Over time, these "From the Editors" columns have become more extensive and cumulatively offer considerable guidance to prospective authors about how to improve their chances of successful submission (or when their manuscript might best be sent to another journal).

These proactive forms of communication are aimed at all potential contributors to *AMJ* and, more generally, to the scholarly community at large. They are designed to maximize the potential fit between manuscripts submitted to the *Journal* and its mission, as well as to improve the quality of manuscripts in general (see Bartunek, Rynes, & Ireland, 2006; Gephart, 2004; Suddaby, 2006). In this way, they are different from the rest of an editor's communications, which are directed specifically toward the authors of particular manuscripts.

2. *Prepare templates for desk-rejection letters.* Given that I had been an associate editor at *AMJ* for three years before becoming its editor, I thought that I was highly experienced in all aspects of the job except selecting reviewers. Was I ever wrong! The biggest shock in my first few weeks as editor concerned the large number of submitted manuscripts that had no chance of making it successfully through the review process, and seeing just how far "off" some manuscripts can be. This was an aspect of the job that the previous editor had handled entirely on his own. As such, the other associate editors and I were blissfully unaware of the existence of this "dark underbelly" of the submission process.

During my term as editor at *AMJ*, the proportion of manuscripts that have not been sent through full initial review has ranged between 30 percent and 40 percent. While this number may seem shockingly high to those who have not served on editorial boards, it is not at all out of range with the number of desk rejections at other top management journals such as *Administrative Science Quarterly, Academy of Management Review,* or *Journal of Organizational Behavior.*[2]

Desk-rejection letters are usually shorter than rejection letters written after a full review process. Usually, the idea is to convey the main reason (or two) for the rejection, without soliciting two or three additional opinions. Because the number of desk rejections is fairly high and the number of basic underlying reasons quite limited, most editors develop a set of "templates" for these types of decision letters. The introductory and ending sections of such letters are fairly standardized, with the middle being tailored to the individual manuscript. These middle sections can be either quite perfunctory or occasionally quite elaborate.

For example, *AMJ* receives quite a few manuscripts that present descriptive data regarding some phenomenon (e.g., demographic differences in job satisfaction, international differences in management opinions, employee reactions to organizational change) but do not address any broader theoretical issue. Because most such manuscripts do not offer any promise of meeting *AMJ*'s "strong theoretical contribution" requirement,[3] there is no need for a lengthy letter. Rather, the editor can acknowledge that although the manuscript addresses an important practical issue, the journal's policy also requires a strong theoretical contribution.

Wherever possible, it is also helpful to suggest alternative outlets that might be better-suited to the paper, especially when the main issue is lack of fit with the journal's mission and when the manuscript seems to have some promise for alternative journals. For example, *AMJ* does not publish methodological or scale development articles unless they also offer supplementary analyses that make a theoretical contribution (e.g., establishing a new construct in a nomological net). Such papers might well be competently executed and potentially suited for top-tier outlets other than *AMJ*. In these cases, we often refer authors to other highly regarded journals such as *Journal of Applied Psychology, Organizational Research Methods, Organizational Behavior and Human Decision Processes,* or *Strategic Management Journal*.

In other cases, a manuscript may appear destined for rejection if sent through the full review process, but the editor sees some potential for success if the manuscript is revised. For example, sometimes we receive manuscripts from authors whose training is in an area other than management (e.g., economics or operations research). In such cases, a potentially strong empirical manuscript may need considerable reworking to make a theoretical contribution that is relevant to management or organizational theory. In these cases, the editor may choose to "desk edit" the manuscript – that is, to write a full review on his own, or perhaps with the assistance of a single expedited review. These letters are typically highly developmental and take as much time to write as a "revise and resubmit" letter for a manuscript that has gone through the full review process. However, the editor takes the time because he or she sees promise in the research (or researcher), responding with a letter that acknowledges the quality of the research, but also the limited prospects for success unless the manuscript is revised before being sent out for full review.

3. *Don't overwhelm authors with excessive detail in decision letters.* I will never forget one of the most discouraging review processes I have ever participated in as an author. In the first round, my coauthors and I received six single-spaced pages of reviewer comments, which were summarized by the editor in two single-spaced pages. In addition, however, the editor added two more single-spaced pages of his own comments, listed from "a" to "z" and then from "aa" to "ff." Yes, 32 specific comments in addition to his general comments, as well as all the specific comments offered by the original three reviewers. Of course, like many authors who try to do a conscientious job of revising and responding to reviewers (see Agarwal, Echambadi, Franco, & Sarkar, 2006), we addressed each and every comment in our resubmission letter (and most in the manuscript as well). In response to our efforts, we received a five-page, single-spaced letter from the editor, which included 37 specific comments (all the way to "kk") in addition to those provided by the reviewers. Again, we responded to all reviewer and editor comments. In round three, we received another four-page letter from the editor, with 11 specific editor comments in addition to those provided by the reviewers, and – the crowning glory – a rejection!

Having to respond to many points from two or three reviewers – plus the editor – seems to have become a "normal" part of an author's experience. For example, at *AMJ*, three reviewers' comments typically add up to somewhere between 6 and 12 single-spaced pages.[4] In addition, reviewers often disagree on their overall opinions about a manuscript's merits, as well as the specific features that should be highlighted, downplayed, or revised. That is a lot of information for an author to digest and respond to, both practically and psychologically.

I believe that an editor can be of great help to an author in dealing with this information overload. In the face of all this commentary, most of it critical, the editor can bring into focus a limited number of *main* issues requiring serious attention. The logic behind this belief has been well-expressed by Elaine Romanelli, writing about "lessons somewhat painfully learned" as a reviewer:

> The rule of thumb I use (as a reviewer) goes as follows: If revisions to improve the fundamental problems in the paper would clearly eliminate associated problems, I spend little time on the associated problems. I think this is also fair to the author. Nothing annoys me more, as a writer, than a reviewer who nitpicks his or her way through every detail of a manuscript after already calling for a "complete overhaul." Not only may I have to respond to all those comments, even though they may no longer be relevant, I feel somewhat humiliated. I would like a reviewer to give me a little credit, and a little room, to revise my paper myself.
>
> Which brings me to collegiality; collegiality saves time because it assumes that the author is a competent professional who can probably revise a paper given some good, general guidelines. Less detail about minor problems can mean more focus on the broad strokes that most revisions require.
>
> (Romanelli, 1995, pp. 201–2)

Now, we have some editorial board members at *AMJ* who believe that it is always their duty, even on the first round, to point out relatively minor issues relating to exposition, analyses, and the reporting and discussion of results. Many of them feel that they "owe" this to the author, particularly if they suspect that the author might not have received the highest-quality training. I respect and appreciate them very much for their conscientiousness in fulfilling this mentoring role.

On the other hand, I think that Romanelli's sentiments are reasonable, and that they are particularly appropriate from the *editor's* perspective. The wisdom of her remarks became clearer to me during an "aha!" moment at the 2006 Academy of Management meetings in Atlanta. I was participating in a professional development workshop where another editor indicated that he was frustrated with authors who spent more time answering detailed reviewer comments than fixing the major problems with the manuscript. He then turned to me and asked whether I had had the same experience. I indicated that yes, I had, but that I also had a lot of sympathy for authors because I thought that we, as editors, were not sufficiently relieving authors of the responsibility to address every single comment. (This was certainly true at *AMJ*, as well as at most other journals to which I submitted my work). As such, I speculated that authors were terrified of offending reviewers or being regarded as insufficiently responsive to them.

I left the panel wondering if there was anything that I, as an editor, might be able to do about it. Fortunately, the associate editors and I had a meeting the very next day, followed by a full editorial board meeting the day after that. In both meetings, we immediately began discussing how we might modify the way we asked authors to respond to revise and resubmit (R&R) invitations. Our goal was to maximize time spent improving the manuscript, and to minimize nonproductive time spent regurgitating every detail of the revision process.

Less than a month later, we implemented new procedures for streamlining the R&R process. The essence of the new policy can be seen in *AMJ*'s revised instructions to authors who receive an R&R invitation:

> As you revise your manuscript, please consider each reviewer comment carefully, since even relatively minor comments can sometimes trigger large improvements in a manuscript. However, once the revision has been completed, please focus your transmittal letter mainly on the issues raised in my letter rather than on the specific points raised by each reviewer. Our intent is to have you spend most of your time improving your manuscript rather than documenting in great detail all specific changes that have been made. To that end, please indicate (in approximately 5–7 pages) how you have responded to the points raised in my letter. Because my letter synthesizes both the reviewers' and my own major concerns, addressing these points will generally ensure that the major issues have been addressed.
>
> (Editor's note, *AMJ*, 2006, p. 873)

It is too early to know the long-run implications of these changes, but so far it looks as if authors are taking the new procedures to heart. The associate editors and I are on the lookout for any potentially adverse consequences of these changes and have encouraged the editorial board to submit any relevant feedback. At the moment, the changes still feel very good to me, and I suspect they feel even better to our authors.

4. *Focus on issues, leaving solutions to authors.* Critics of the review process (as well as some editors; e.g., Daft & Lewin, 1990) have expressed concern about over-editing of papers, even to the point where editors or reviewers are accused of "ghostwriting" articles. This is a complex issue, in that there can be strong differences in perceptions as to whether an editor's suggestions

or requests are truly necessary to ensure an article's quality, or whether they represent an inappropriate intrusion of the editor's values or preferences into the author's work.

While the intricacies of this issue go far beyond this essay, I do think that reviewers and editors (myself included) can be overly directive. However, my own experience, both from observing my own editorial and review work as well as the work of others, suggests that the tendency to over-edit is probably greatest among editors and reviewers with less experience. Both Meyer (1995) and Romanelli (1995) indicate that early in their careers as reviewers, they tended to view the reviewer's role solely as "critic." Romanelli says of her first review:

> I had to figure out how to write a review that would impress the editor. In truth, I hadn't a clue. I thought I had to show that I was 'up' on my literature, and that I knew the relevant research methods. No fatal flaw should get by me. In keeping with the instructions to reviewers to 'take into account clarity of writing,' I supposed I should also help the authors to write more clearly. Thus I set out to comment, having now read the paper maybe once, on virtually every aspect of the manuscript … That first review was more than eight single-spaced pages long. I patiently explained problems in each of the sections and, with some pedantry, described how the author could do better. I didn't know then, and I don't know now, who that author was, but I hereby offer an apology.
>
> (Romanelli, 1995, p. 197)

Meyer offers this description of one of his early editorial decision letters:

> I once got carried away and offended a respected colleague. Envisioning a "far better paper" than the manuscript he had submitted, I suggested a complete recasting of the theory and data. I could hardly wait to see the revisions. But my enthusiasm for the project was dashed when the author abruptly withdrew his paper from further consideration at that journal. My colleague later explained that, while he found my ideas for revising "insightful and most interesting," this was not the paper he had set out to write … Since then, I have taken pains to present any recommendations for significant changes as ideas offered for an author's consideration, not as conditions for a favorable recommendation.
>
> (Meyer, 1995, pp. 266–7)

Even after all these years as a reviewer and editor, I suspect that I am still occasionally overly directive with authors. But I consciously try harder not to be, particularly in areas concerning framing or exposition. Given that the tendency to be overly directive is usually greater early in one's editorial career, perhaps new or aspiring editors reading this book can make a conscious effort to write letters that raise issues more than dictate solutions, and to encourage their associate editors to do the same.

5. *Use a personalized writing style.* Early in my reviewing career, I used to talk "about" authors in the third person (e.g., "the authors seem to argue"). However, after reading the reflections of more experienced reviewers (e.g., Daft, 1995; Mayer, 1995; Pondy, 1995; Romanelli, 1995), I adopted their convention of referring to authors in the second person. (For example, Daft's excellent essay is titled, "Why I recommended that your manuscript be rejected and what you can do about it.") I am specific about how I feel about the author's work and try to use language in much the same way (albeit perhaps a bit more formally) as I would if he or she were sitting across the table from me.

However, taking a tip from the voluminous research on performance feedback (e.g., Kluger & DeNisi, 1996), I am also careful to separate the *author* from the author's *work* in the delivery of specific feedback. Because people respond better to critical comments when they are focused on the work rather than the person, I consciously try to use phrases such as, "the way the manuscript is written, it seems ..." or "at present, the discussion section appears to ..." rather than saying, "you don't seem to ..." or even, "your manuscript doesn't seem to ..."

6. *Don't understate the amount of revision necessary.* Earlier in this essay, I indicated that editors can help encourage authors by using language that signals the presence of a difficult, but potentially attainable, goal. While my earlier message focused on the "attainability" segment, this one focuses on the difficulty. One of the most disappointing experiences as an editor (or a reviewer) occurs when the initial manuscript looks quite promising relative to other first submissions, but the second version comes back with only perfunctory changes. Given that most journals try to make a final (or close to final, such as "conditional acceptance") decision in the second round, this situation often results in the manuscript's rejection.

In reflecting on the number of times this occurred to me early in my term as an associate editor, I wondered if sometimes the author had underestimated the amount of effort that would be required as a result of an insufficiently "challenging" decision letter from me. After a few such experiences, I began to err on the side of describing revisions as "high risk" or even "very high risk" in an effort to make sure that the authors did not underinvest in the revision. While this may cause the authors greater initial anxiety, I believe that it increases the chances that authors will rise to the occasion in the next round.[5]

7. *The editor is not a fourth reviewer; the editor is the decision maker.* Making decisions, particularly when the vast majority of them are not what authors want to hear, is difficult. The natural tendency, I think, is to hide behind "the journal" or the reviewers in explaining a decision. In fact, if I had been left to my own devices, I probably would still be writing decision letters using the word "we" instead of "I" to explain the rationale behind my decisions.

However, as an associate editor for *AMJ*, I was strongly socialized into the view that the editor is far more than the person who simply records the reviewers' judgments or tallies their "votes." Rather, he or she takes direct responsibility for the decision rendered. Admittedly, this view gives the editor not only more responsibility, but also more power. While at first blush the idea of a "powerful editor" might seem undesirable to authors, there are several reasons that it can actually work to the author's advantage. Some ideas behind giving editors a fair amount of power and responsibility are (a) they have been selected for their expertise and experience at evaluating manuscripts, (b) at the end of the review process, they have far more information about a manuscript than does any single reviewer, (c) as people whose names appear on the masthead of the journal, they have more of an interest in making good decisions *for the journal* than do most reviewers (Frey, 2003), and (d) since most reviewers view their role as that of "prosecutor," editors often play the role of rescuing or "defending" a manuscript.

In their role as final arbiters, however, editors have certain responsibilities. For example, I believe it is very important that editors notice disagreements or discrepant ideas across reviewers and that they specifically address them in their decision letters (see also Jacobs, this volume). This may amount to simply highlighting the different views and leaving their resolution to the author(s), or it may mean tipping your hand in a certain direction. Secondly, the editor needs to (gently) indicate where he or she believes a reviewer has made a mistake, or where (and how) his or her views differ from those of a reviewer. This can require a fair amount of delicacy on the part of the editor, but it is very important in terms of safeguarding the integrity of the review process.

Final thoughts

I began this essay talking about my positive feelings about being an editor and describing (with help from Alan Meyer's excellent 1995 essay) how uplifting it can be to participate in a successful review process. In closing, I would like to focus more on people than processes.

The range of human behaviors that one encounters as an editor is truly incredible. There are senior scholars who are very well respected academically, but whose long publication records are achieved in part because they do not provide the same services as reviewers that they routinely expect others to provide to them. There are those who resubmit papers that have previously been rejected by a journal but who brazenly check the "no" box when explicitly asked this question during the submission process. There are those who always try to appeal rejection decisions, figuring (I suppose) that the squeaky wheel gets the grease. As one former editor of a prominent journal said to me when I began my term at *AMJ*, "If you sit at a table with other editors, pretty soon it starts coming out. We all know who they are."

They do it to every journal and many of their students behave the same way they do. But I'll shoot you if you ever say I told you so."

So yes, there are people who can "get you down" as an editor. But then there are all the rest! There are reviewers, some just starting their careers and others who have been prolific authors for over 30 years, who astonish me with their dedication to mentoring fledgling authors and to improving the manuscripts they review. There are authors who always go far beyond the "letter of the law" to produce revisions that exceed everyone's expectations. There are reviewers and authors who deliver awe-inspiring performances despite the fact that they have recently lost a parent, spouse, or child or been uprooted by an environmental disaster such as Hurricane Katrina. Finally, there are those authors who, after their manuscripts are rejected, write "thank you" letters that in one way or another tell me that they understand my role as editor and that they have learned something from the process. I swear, sometimes it feels as if these authors are trying to cheer *me* up after I send a difficult rejection letter.

I will never forget these people. If they are just starting their careers, I will root for them from the sidelines and watch what they do with great interest. Maybe, when they do something I particularly admire, I will send them an e-mail, as several of my "personal heroes" have done for me over the years. If they are near the end of their careers, I will attend their retirement parties (if someone remembers to invite me). If I see them at professional meetings, I will always rush up to give them a hug. They inspire me.

I hope you know who you are.

Acknowledgments

Many thanks to Yehuda Baruch, Amy Hillman, Duane Ireland, Kenneth Law, Chet Miller, Nandini Rajagopalan, and Debra Shapiro for comments on an earlier version of this chapter.

Notes

1. At *AMJ*, the Web page is generally the place where prospective authors can find the most up-to-date information about editorial policies. Changes in editorial policies generally take three or four months to find their way into printed issues because of publication lags. The Academy of Management's "in press" Web page is also the fastest way to find papers that have been accepted by the Academy's journals but that are not yet in print.
2. All editors I contacted said their desk rejection rates were at least 20–25 percent. One editor said that his desk-rejection rate was "only" 25–30 percent, but indicated that his associate editors were urging him to increase that number.
3. Occasionally, a manuscript that is completely devoid of theoretical content can be modified, post hoc, to satisfactorily remedy this deficiency. It is rare, however, for this to occur once the data have already been collected, particularly given the vast amount of theorizing that has already been offered in areas such as job satisfaction or organizational change.

4. One might wonder whether longer reviews are necessarily better. Although this is not always the case, in general, a positive relationship does seem to hold. For example, Cummings, Frost, & Vakil (1985) found that the best reviewers played the role of both critic and coach, and that their reviews were significantly more thorough, attentive to technical detail, and substantive. *AMJ* reviewers who receive "best reviewer" awards probably provide, on average, three single-spaced pages of comments, and occasionally more.
5. I do not label a revision as "high risk" if I am quite confident that it can be successfully revised. But I am more likely to err on the side of "high risk" if the outcome seems uncertain.

References

Agarwal, R., Echambadi, R., Franco, A. M., & Sarkar, M. B. (2006). REAP rewards: Maximizing benefits from reviewer comments. *Academy of Management Journal*, 49, 191–6.

Bartunek, J. M., Rynes, S. L., & Ireland, R. D. (2006). What makes management research interesting and why does it matter? *Academy of Management Journal*, 49, 9–15.

Cummings, L. L., Frost, P. J., & Vakil, T. F. (1985). The manuscript review process: A view from the inside on coaches, critics, and special cases. In L. L. Cummings and P. J. Frost (Eds.), *Publishing in the organizational sciences*, pp. 469–508. Homewood, IL: Irwin.

Daft, R. L. (1995). Why I recommended that your manuscript be rejected and what you can do about it. In L. L. Cummings and P. J. Frost (Eds.), *Publishing in the organizational sciences* (2nd ed.), pp. 164–82. Thousand Oaks: Sage.

Daft, R. L., & Lewin, A. Y. (1990). Can organizational studies begin to break out of the normal science straightjacket? An editorial essay. *Organization Science*, 1, 1–9.

Editor's note. (2006). Streamlining the revise and resubmit process at *AMJ*. *The Academy of Management Journal*, 49, 873–4.

Frey, B. S. (2003). Publishing as prostitution? Choosing between one's own ideas and academic success. *Public Choice*, 116, 205–23.

Gephart, R. P. (2004). Qualitative research and the Academy of Management Journal. *Academy of Management Journal*, 47, 454–62.

Jacobs, J. A. (2007). The case for an activist editorial model. This volume, chapter 13.

Kluger, A. N., & DeNisi, A. (1996). The effects of feedback interventions on performance: A historical review, a meta-analysis, and a preliminary feedback intervention theory. *Psychological Bulletin*, 119, 254–84.

Locke, E. A., & Latham, G. P. (1984). *Goal setting: A motivational technique that works!* Englewood Cliffs, NJ: Prentice-Hall.

Meyer, A. D. (1995). Balls, strikes, and collisions on the base path: Ruminations of a veteran reviewer. In L. L. Cummings and P. J. Frost (Eds.), *Publishing in the organizational sciences* (2nd ed.), pp. 257–68. Thousand Oaks: Sage.

Pondy, L. R. (1995). The reviewer as defense attorney. In L. L. Cummings and P. J. Frost (Eds.), *Publishing in the organizational sciences* (2nd ed.), pp. 183–94. Thousand Oaks: Sage.

Romanelli, E. (1995). Becoming a reviewer: Lessons somewhat painfully learned. In L. L. Cummings and P. J. Frost (Eds.), *Publishing in the organizational sciences* (2nd ed.), pp. 195–202. Thousand Oaks: Sage.

Suddaby, R. (2006). What grounded theory is not. *Academy of Management Journal*. 49, 633–42.

7
Building and Maintaining a Strong Editorial Board and Cadre of Ad Hoc Reviewers

Daniel C. Feldman

Some of the most important decisions you will make as an editor – and some of the decisions that will have the greatest impact on the success of your editorship – have to be made before the first manuscript ever crosses your desk or pops up on your computer screen. Whom you choose as your associate editors, whom you choose as your editorial board members, and whom you invite to be ad hoc reviewers determine the quality of the reviewing "service" your faculty colleagues will experience as "customers." Moreover, these choices send important signals to the marketplace about your values, priorities, and preferences as an editor.

Choosing associate editors

Actions speak louder than words, and no action speaks louder for an editor than his or her choice of associate editors. The field will look at the qualifications of your associate editors, their reputations as scholars and as reasonable colleagues, their respective areas of expertise, and even their methodological specialties as strong signals of what kinds of papers you are most likely to welcome and most likely to publish. Moreover, because the associate editors play a big hand in choosing members of the editorial board, their own sets of values and network connections have ripple effects on the composition of the editorial board as a whole.

Perhaps the most critical first step prior to choosing associate editors is identifying what you yourself feel are the most important goals you want to achieve during your term in office. In my case, I had a very clear vision of what I wanted for *Journal of Management*. I wanted to publish articles that spoke to the field as a whole rather than to small cul-de-sacs of research specialists. I wanted to publish articles that addressed real-world problems and not simply articles that were well-executed but minor in scope or irrelevant to management problems. I care deeply about the quality of writing, and did not want to accept turgidly or opaquely written manuscripts that no one would read, care about, or understand. And, because the journal had come to be perceived by some in the field as a micro-oriented journal, I wanted to signal the faculty in strategic management that I really wanted their submissions, too.

The next step is identifying the individuals who share your values and are willing to invest their time and energy into the enterprise. It is not surprising that many editors choose at least one of their associate editors from their current home institution (or from a university at which they had previously been a faculty member). Working side by side a colleague gives you an excellent idea of his or her work habits and work values. Looking at recent winners of "best reviewer" awards at peer or aspirant journals is another way to proceed, with the caveat that what makes a great reviewer does not always make a great associate editor. (Taking three full days to write a great review represents a wonderful dedication of time from a reviewer, but such an investment of time is totally dysfunctional for an associate editor who may have to write 2–3 decision letters per week.) Current and former editors of other journals may also be particularly helpful sources of information in this regard.

There are a few more subtle issues to consider in selecting associate editors. While editors typically get course release and secretarial support, associate editors typically do not, and so you have to ensure that the individuals you choose can devote the time needed to the job at hand. The distribution of associate editors across subfields sends a strong signal to potential faculty authors, and it is thus a good idea to make sure the distribution of associate editors' subfields aligns closely to your preferences for (or expectations of) submissions. You also want to make sure that your associate editors can work well with each other, since on numerous occasions you will have to work together as a team – at editorial board meetings, at conventions, in crafting editorials, in dealing with publishers and marketing directors, in working on special issues and journal awards, and so forth.

Another major decision you face is how many associate editors you should have serving under you. The fewer the number of associate editors, the greater the workload on each – but the greater the level of consistency of editorial decision leniency (or harshness) across action editors. The greater the number of associate editors, the lesser will be the workload on each associate editor – but the potential for disparity in values, timeliness, and harshness across action editors is greater. As a general rule of thumb, I would say that 50 is the absolute maximum number of papers an associate editor could handle per year, so expected submission rates are a critical factor in this decision. Journals with less than 100 submissions per year may not need associate editors, but may instead choose to use "consulting editors," delegate some responsibilities to special issue or special section editors, or utilize some other structure instead.

Finally, there is the question of whether or not editors are using associate editors to groom them for succession to the editor role. Some journals implicitly, if not explicitly, use a strategy of "promoting" one of the associate editors to become the next editor. Other journals throw the nomination process for editor wide open, while still other searches are run in conjunction with publishers or affiliated professional associations. While there is certainly much to be gained in terms of institutional memory by always having the next editor be a former associate editor, that public good is sometimes outweighed by public perceptions of an editorial board that is too "clubby" and an editorial strategy that never seriously renews itself. Moreover, that strategy has the potential to cause subtle conflict, rather than cooperation, among associate editors as well as a divergence of associate editors' goals from the editor's goals.

Choosing an editorial board

Choosing an editorial board is more of a "black box" than choosing associate editors for a variety of reasons. You are dealing with a much larger number of individuals, and you are selecting people as board members from subfields with which you may have little direct exposure. Perhaps more critically, you have less "hard" data with which to make your decisions. Many journals do not have systems that evaluate reviewers, and those that do might not assess reviewer quality in the same way you would. For example, many journals rate reviewers on the number of days required by them for completion of their reviews. I personally care a lot about getting reviews in on time, but I do not assume that the person who handed in the review on Day 14 was twice as good a reviewer as the person who submitted the review on Day 28. Some editors highly value the length of review as a criterion of reviewer performance. While I did not want two-paragraph reviews, I also did not want six pages of single-spaced comments in which every punctuation error was covered in obsessive detail.

Your predecessors as editors can give you considerable assistance here. At the minimum, they can tell you the people you need to "drop" or "keep" from the current board. Your associate editors (especially those not in your subfield) can give you some great leads on potential board members whom they have worked with over the years. Networking with faculty you are definitely appointing (or reappointing) to the board to get additional nominees is also helpful.

One of the big issues currently being debated among scholars in the field is the role that board members' professional reputations and publication records should play in their selection. There is some legitimacy to this concern. Potential authors are angered when their papers are rejected by members of an editorial board who are themselves perceived to lack credible publication records. I am largely sympathetic to that concern, with some exceptions.

By and large, I prefer to have people with more than five years of service in the field on the board – not only because they will have more external credibility, but also because they will have outgrown the need to treat every review as a journal critique in an intro methods seminar. At the same time, there are some research topics and some research methodologies that are relatively new in the field and there are not enough senior faculty members to serve as reviewers. In those cases, having some relatively junior and relatively unknown faculty is not only inevitable but also desirable. Conversely, some new journals have a few senior scholars on their boards to gain institutional legitimacy, but these faculties do a very small proportion of the actual reviewing.

When I was a junior faculty member, the editorial board selection process seemed very random to me and not fully grounded in a meritocracy system. When I was faced with the selection process myself, I realized how many factors come into play besides "merit." First and foremost, the composition of the board has to be proportional to the kinds of manuscripts you expect. Thus, if you don't expect many papers on a particular topic or using a particular methodology, you can't fill up the board with tons of people from these areas, no matter how competent they may be. Second, editors are sensitive to diversity, broadly defined. Editors want gender and racial diversity, for sure, but they also want diversity across geographical regions of the country (and continents) and representatives from both public and private universities. As business schools in Europe, Asia, and Australia become both more numerous and much larger, having an internationally diverse editorial board can lead to greater submissions and journal subscriptions globally. Consequently, editors are reluctant to take more than 2–3 individuals from any one university as board members, independent of the quality of the faculty involved.

New editors also want to add some new board members to revitalize or broaden the journal's constituencies, and thus some long-standing members may rotate off the board even if they have done an excellent job. In several journals, there are preset terms of membership and "term limits" so that the editorial board members will not feel offended when their terms end with a change of editors. There are several benefits of having some carry-over board members; they provide institutional memory and help the new editor learn the norms and culture of the editorial team.

Editors will tell you that the ability to review a variety of topics makes a faculty member a much more highly desirable board member. Some faculty members only want to review papers on one topic (or one very small cul-de-sac of that topic) and/or only want to review papers that use one particular methodology. Editors cannot afford to fill up their boards with "one-trick ponies." For that reason, faculty who are only willing to review a very small subset of articles are much less likely to become members of the editorial board. Junior faculty who want to become board members should write to editors, volunteering to be ad hoc reviewers. Editors always welcome the help, and it's a good way for a junior faculty member to establish his/her own legitimacy as a scholar.

Size, too, is a prominent issue in the composition of the editorial board. My own personal experience, both as editor and as a board member, is that once the board size exceeds 100, the sense of being a member of a "team," even broadly defined, vanishes. If a board member only gets 1–2 manuscripts a year, then the sense of attachment to (and investment in) the journal is quite low. To a considerable degree, the size of the editorial board influences both the cohesiveness of the board itself and the editor's need to rely heavily on ad hoc reviewers.

Maintaining a strong editorial board

Many people have heard the old joke about a man and his boat: The second happiest day of a man's life is the day he buys the boat; the happiest day of his life is the day he sells it. Similarly, many scholars feel honored to become members of an editorial board, but after the initial flush of excitement dies down, they lose enthusiasm and energy over their terms of service.

To the extent that the board size can be kept to a manageable level, board members may engage in less social loafing. When board members know that there are over 200 other individuals who can pick up the slack, they are more likely to be picky about what they will review and when they will review it.

Another way an editor can maintain a strong editorial board is setting strong and realistic expectations among board members when invitations to join the board are issued. Sometimes editors are a little coy or vague about what their expectations of board members are. It is better to be straightforward with potential board members about the number of articles they will need to review, the kinds of reviews you are looking for, and the mission of your journal. In that way, faculty members who do not buy into that vision or cannot accept the workload can opt out graciously. At the same time, editors occasionally have to counsel an editorial board member off the board for consistent or flagrant violation of expectations. Even among professionals, there have to be boundaries that cannot be crossed.

Virtually every journal has now gone to fully electronic submissions and reviews. The efficiency benefits of this system are obvious. However, most journals are now using "canned" acknowledgements and other types of correspondence that have the warmth of a telemarketer's phone message. These messages sometimes do not even bother to include the board member's name or the article name or the name of the sender of the correspondence; they remind me of those wonderful memos faculty occasionally receive from "the dean's office." While high volume journals can no longer personalize each and every piece of correspondence, the failure to do so at all can lead to low commitment among board members. Some occasional personal correspondence thanking board members for particularly good reviews or explaining why you chose not to follow their advice are valued by editorial board members and help increase affective commitment to the board.

Editorial boards do not get together very often; most journal boards only get together once a year. Consequently, how you run that meeting and what you choose to do at that meeting have a significant impact on how faculty members feel about the board as a whole. Over the years, both as an editor and as a board member, there are several tips I picked up along the way in this regard.

First, keep the meetings short (less than 75 minutes). Your board members have lots of other obligations on their minds and you do not want to overstay your welcome. Second, engage the board members in discussions of important strategic issues. The deadliest board meetings I have attended consisted of long, detailed, PowerPoint presentations from the publishers about their marketing efforts and what they are charging libraries for subscriptions. Board members will be nodding off to sleep or aimlessly munching on whatever snacks you have provided. Third, at least for senior faculty, their drawers are full of journal-branded t-shirts, pens, and letter openers. (As an aside: Where on earth can you wear a journal-logo t-shirt without embarrassment?) Think about what board members would like to receive as gifts of appreciation rather than using gifts as "branding opportunities."

Developing a cadre of ad hoc reviewers

Perhaps the greatest amount of uncertainty in the review process comes from the use of ad hoc reviewers. Many senior faculty members are on numerous editorial boards and are disinclined to serve as ad hoc reviewers for other journals. As a result, many ad hoc reviewers are relatively junior in the field and relatively inexperienced as reviewers. Besides your predecessors as editors, the best source of leads for ad hoc reviewers is your editorial board team. If, as discussed above, the board comes from a diverse set of schools and subfields, its members will be a tremendous source of names of junior faculty who would be excellent ad hoc reviewers.

As with the editorial board, it is important to set clear expectations for ad hoc reviewers. These expectations should revolve around the number of manuscript reviews that might be expected per year (e.g., 2–3), the importance of timeliness, and the tone and level of detail you are looking for in reviews. By and large, it is better not to use more than one ad hoc reviewer on any manuscript since the variance in quality and timeliness is higher than the corresponding variance across editorial board members. While editorial boards have very little out-migration, there is a lot of turnover among ad hoc reviewers; some work out and others do not. For this reason, editors typically solicit names of additional ad hoc reviewers from their board members at least once a year.

Some editors may also contact scholars whom authors cite heavily in their manuscripts as ad hoc reviewers. Newer journals, in particular, often ask faculty who have recently published in their journals to become ad hoc reviewers. Several journals now are also asking faculty members who are submitting articles to an outlet to also commit themselves to serving as an ad hoc reviewer for that journal.

It is, of course, harder to build commitment among ad hoc reviewers than it is among board members. However, sending ad hoc reviewers letters of acknowledgement and token gifts helps build a somewhat higher level of commitment. Also, over time, editors do add faculty members to their editorial boards. Some current board members drop off to meet new commitments. As submission rates increase or as certain kinds of manuscripts become more numerous, new editorial board members have to be recruited. I communicated to ad hoc reviewers that those with particularly conscientious service in their current roles would be seriously considered for future openings on the board – and then followed up that promise with action where possible. In those years where I had more than one board meeting, I also invited the ad hoc reviewers to the second meeting. Virtually all journals now publish acknowledgements of ad hoc reviewers once a year.

Conclusion

Being an effective manager is at least as important as being an insightful scholar in your role as editor. You not only have to have an eye for good papers; you also have to have an eye for good reviewers. Thinking carefully ahead of time about your own goals as editor and the qualities you want in your associate editors and editorial board members will save you endless problems over the course of your term in office. It is not only the people you choose, but also how the people you choose align with your vision of the journal, that will determine the success of your editorship.

8
Managing the Editorial Review Process: It's the People That Matter

Angelo S. DeNisi

I served as the editor of the *Academy of Management Journal* (*AMJ*) from 1994 until 1996. I had served on the editorial boards of several journals (including *AMJ*) and I also served as a consulting editor under Mike Hitt's editorship, prior to being appointed as the editor. I thought I understood the review process pretty well because of these earlier assignments, as well as because I had submitted a reasonable number of papers to journals myself, and had a variety of experiences with those papers. But, it was only when I actually took on the job that I came to realize how complicated the job of a journal editor really is. Sometimes people believe that being an editor for a professional journal is the ultimate in power in the field – they are mistaken. I don't know what it is like to be the editor of *Time* or *The N.Y. Times*, but I have learned something about the job of journal editor. The most important thing I learned is that the key to being a successful editor is the ability to balance the needs and concerns of *all* the individuals who are involved in the editorial process. There are actually more parties that have a stake in what happens during this process than many people realize, and an editor must be a successful manager of various groups, all with different and potentially conflicting interests in the editorial process. Anyone contemplating accepting the job of editor must understand this situation, and so the focus of this chapter is to identify the relevant parties and to discuss some of the issues involved in managing them throughout the editorial process.

So who *are* the relevant players in the editorial process? First and foremost, of course, there are the authors of the manuscript that has been submitted for possible publication. These individuals have the most to gain or lose by the decision-making process and, quite often, they view themselves as the only people who have some stake in the outcome. But they are wrong. The reviewers of the manuscript (including any consulting editors that may be involved) have a stake in the process, and they must be managed as well. In addition, editors must also be concerned about the publisher of the journal and the ultimate consumers of the journal – the readers and the scholarly community. Effectively managing the process means effectively managing all of these groups of participants. Each has some stake in the process and the outcome of the process but, as I will discuss later, each group has its own set of goals for the process, and those goals can conflict with each other. I will discuss some of these conflicts as I go through the issues involved with each group, beginning with authors and the reviewers, since these are the groups that require the most attention.

Dealing with authors

Authors submit their work to a journal in the hopes of getting it published. Therefore, it is easy to think about the authors as a group of passive consumers who simply want something from the journal and the editor – they would ultimately like their paper to be published in the journal. Of course, very few papers are accepted after the initial round of reviews, and so, in the short run, they want useful feedback that will enable them to strengthen their paper, and they want the opportunity to make those changes and revise the paper.

But I believe that we are wrong to think about authors in this way only. Instead, I believe we must begin by thinking about the set of all journals in a field as constituting a competitive environment. In this environment, the authors hold the ultimate power because they can select *where* to submit their work. If an author has a good piece of research (ignoring for the moment how one defines that), any editor wants that author to submit that paper to his or her journal, and to submit it there as their first choice. A journal can be no better than the papers it publishes, and those papers can be no better than the papers that are submitted. Therefore, most journals in a field are competing for the same set of "good" papers (there are always a few more specialized journals that follow more of a niche strategy, although even here there can be competition), and that means competing for the attention of the authors *before they actually submit their papers.*

How? By providing good reviews from good reviewers. The more obvious solution of accepting everyone's paper won't really work in the long run. Authors want their papers to appear in prestigious journals, and one way to increase prestige is to have and hold to high standards. Thus, making it difficult, but not impossible, for a wide variety of authors to publish their work is the first step in attracting good papers. Journals that are perceived to have strong ties to certain Universities or groups of Universities (whether or not those perceptions are correct) will limit the range of papers that are submitted, as well journals that are perceived to favor certain approaches or methodologies (of course, some journals *do* favor certain methodologies as part of their niche strategy). Authors want to believe that, whoever they are, and wherever they work, their work will be judged on the basis of its merits only.

But the editor can have the greatest impact upon authors' preferences for different journals by effectively managing the review process. A journal's reputation for fair, thoughtful, and timely reviews is the best competitive weapon an editor can have. Authors who have never submitted a paper to a particular journal will consult with friends and colleagues and seek information about their experience with a given journal. Of course, if a colleague had a paper accepted at a given journal, he or she is likely to say good things about the process, but since everyone recognizes that a substantial number of papers submitted to a top journal will be ultimately rejected, it is most important that the editor effectively manage the process for rejecting papers.

No one enjoys having one's papers rejected. But research on perceived justice, in its various forms, suggests that rejected authors will feel better about their rejections if they feel the procedures followed were fair, and if they are treated with respect throughout the process (See, for example, reviews by Bies & Moag, 1986; Brockner & Wisenfeld, 1996; and Colquitt, Conlon, Wesson, Porter, & Ng, 2001). At the most basic level, this means providing authors with reviews that are fair, informative, developmental, and timely. Note that all of these conditions must be met in order to manage the process effectively, and this is difficult to do in a form letter. I know, from personal experience, that a letter simply stating, "the reviewer comments are enclosed and are clear" just isn't very satisfying. Many years ago, I sent a paper, based on the conceptual part of my dissertation to *Psychological Bulletin* and was told in the cover letter that there was much about my paper that was interesting and that my paper was good, but "not good enough for *Psychological Bulletin*." During my tenure as editor at *AMJ*, I made all the editorial decisions and so wrote several thousand letters. I never used a form letter and always tried to be encouraging, especially when it was clear that a paper was based on a dissertation. I even noted that I understood what it meant to have papers based on your dissertation rejected, as that was exactly what happened to me.

In addition, if we want people to feel they are being treated fairly, an editor must identify reviews who do not have a vested interest in seeing a paper rejected (or accepted), or have an agenda that they intend to carry out through the review process. Providing thoughtful reviews means identifying reviewers who have some perspective on the field such that they can determine which papers actually have the potential for making a contribution. Providing informative reviewers means identifying reviewers who can point authors towards other bodies of literature that might be useful, or other analytical techniques that might be more appropriate. Providing developmental reviews means identifying reviewers who can help the author to see how a paper can be improved and how the paper could be framed in order to make its potential contribution seem clearer.

Finally, providing timely reviews means following up on late reviewers and establishing a norm that reviews should be submitted on time. This is not the case for all journals, and review processes that extend over a year are not uncommon at some journals – to the detriment of the journal. Most major journals actually publish these statistics in the journal, at least once a year.

Typically, journal editors aim for a two-month turnaround, and many meet this goal. That is, from the time a paper is received by the editor, to the time an initial decision letter goes to the author, on average, is roughly 60 days, and *AMJ*, for example, has hovered around that average for a number of years.

One last observation on the issue of perceived fairness relates to the comments sent to the editor versus those sent to the author. Several years ago, an editor informed the editorial board that he/she was intent on providing developmental feedback to authors. Therefore, the board members were sure to provide feedback about how a paper could be improved and to be as positive as they could be – in their comments to the authors. But, as I shall discuss below, the reviewers' job (especially those on the editorial board) is to help the editor make a decision. Therefore, there are always two sets of comments – one for the editor and one for the author. This editor was almost insuring that, for any paper that would be rejected, the feedback received by the author would be much more positive than the comments and recommendations received by the editor. There were several reviewers who did this on their own when I was editor, and it can cause a problem. The author cannot understand why his or her paper was rejected because the comments she or he received are generally positive. The editor, of course, has the additional information supplied by the reviewer, and that is the basis (in part) for the decision. Although I believe that positive and developmental feedback are good, I also believe that the reviewer should make it clear – to everyone involved – why he or she believes the paper should be rejected, or what exactly needs to be done if there is to be a revision.

In general, then, the role of the reviewer is to help the editor make an informed decision. Therefore, if a reviewer recommends that a paper be rejected (recommends to the editor, not to the author), he or she should state, in clear language, why the paper should be rejected and what, if anything could be done to improve the paper. If this decision is based on poor fit with the mission of the journal, this should also be made clear to the author (by the reviewer or the editor), and an alternative outlet might be suggested. It is also important that, throughout the process, the authors are treated with respect and, as noted earlier, this means telling the author with something more than a form letter, that a paper has been rejected. It means, instead, making it clear that the editor read the paper, read the reviewer comments, and arrived at an informed decision after some consideration. Given the recent trends of telling authors of decisions via e-mail, this "personal touch" is even more critical. If an editor follows these guidelines, authors will feel more positive about the process, which, in turn will lead them to recommend the given journal to other potential authors. Thus, fair treatment of authors is important not only in its own right, but as means of competing better for the best papers in the field.

Much of what I have suggested requires careful management of the reviewers, and I will come to that group shortly. But first, there are some other issues that must be addressed concerning the treatment of authors. There are, of course, three likely outcomes to the review process for a paper – rejection, acceptance, and a request for a revision. Of these, rejection is the most common in top journals, which is why it is so important to treat authors whose papers have been rejected with respect. As I have mentioned, personal letters (or personalized e-mails), especially letters acknowledging the merits of the paper and acknowledging the disappointment experienced by the author, are an important part of this process. I can recall writing a rejection letter for a person who had been a student at my former University (not my student, but I knew the person well). I also knew that this person was coming up for tenure and that this rejection would probably mean the person would be fired. That was the most difficult letter I wrote as an editor and, although I tried to sound encouraging, and to talk about the good points in the paper, I never felt good about the letter. I cannot imagine how anyone could hope to deal with this kind of situation with a form letter.

Furthermore, in many cases, when a journal rejects a paper, the editor will not consider a resubmission. If that is the case, it should be made very clear in the rejection letter. If it is not clear, the editor will be swamped with requests to consider a resubmission because most authors believe that the problems identified by the reviewers are "fixable". I should note, however, that it is my personal view that, if an author truly believes she or he can address the issues raised by the reviewers, and is willing to make this case to the editor, it should be all right to allow some of these authors to resubmit.

The next most likely outcome, however, is a request for a revision. This outcome means that there are issues with the paper in its current form, but that it *may* be possible to resolve these with a revision. The likelihood of a successful revision varies, obviously, and it is important to let authors know what they are facing of they decide to resubmit. It is unfair to *encourage* an author to revise and resubmit a paper with little possibility of success, although an author, understanding the probabilities, may choose to submit such a revision if the opportunity is offered. In any case, the editor must tell the author, in as clear terms as possible, exactly what he or she must do in the revision. This is especially important when different reviewers are requesting conflicting sets of changes. If new data or additional analyses are required, then that should be told to the author. If other literature needs to be consulted and integrated into the paper, then that too should be communicated clearly. Clearly, it requires a reviewer with expertise in the field to identify the potential contribution when a paper suffers from problems. It is much the same talent as some people have when they look at an empty house and are capable of seeing its potential as a home.

Once a revision is submitted, it typically goes back to reviewers, and, once again we have three possible outcomes – rejection, further revision, or (conditional) acceptance. I will not comment on policies allowing only one revision, since such policies have both advantages and disadvantages that go beyond the scope of the present discussion. Requests for further revisions should follow the same principles as above, and conditional or outright acceptances are always welcome. Rejections of revised papers, however, present special problems, and the more revisions the paper has gone through, the greater the problems when it is rejected.

Rejecting a revised paper requires a great deal of tact and diplomacy. Even when the reviewers feel that the revision was totally inadequate, the author has made a substantial investment and is likely to be very disappointed. Furthermore, if there have been multiple revisions, the paper may have changed in its focus and it may now be less suitable for submission elsewhere (although any advice the editor can give the author about resubmission elsewhere can help ease the pain). Therefore, the need to explain the decision in clear terms becomes even more important when we are dealing with rejecting a revised paper. During my term as editor, this was the situation that was most likely to result in a phone call from an author, although I am happy to say that only a few of these conversations got really ugly. Every now and again, an author whose paper is rejected will get angry and berate the editor. This is a painful time for the author, and the editor must resist the temptation to get angry in return – even if that is easier to say than to do.

One final note about treating authors relates to a more positive outcome when a revision is initially requested or a further revision is called for. Editors should resist the temptation to tell the authors how to rewrite the paper. I have received reviews where the editor simply made changes in the manuscript that he or she felt would improve the paper, and I was simply to accept them or not (I accepted them). The paper is the intellectual property of the author (see Bedeian's chapter, this volume, for elaboration). The editor can decide to reject it or publish it, and she or he should always provide suggestions on how to improve a paper, but it is the authors' paper and she or he must have ultimate control over what it says.

A number of years ago, I (along with two colleagues) submitted a paper to the *Journal of Personality and Social Psychology* (*JPSP*). We received a letter from the editor suggesting that we could revise and resubmit the paper, but that he was not very optimistic, given the reviewer comments, but he urged us to take each comment seriously because he said that he believed the comments would all serve to improve the paper. He did not instruct us to do anything else, and he really provided very little in the way of true direction.

The reviewer comments were quite extensive and suggested additional literature that might bolster our theoretical arguments, as well as additional analyses, which might bolster our empirical results. We spent a great deal of time reading some new lines of research, and found that they were directly relevant to the points we were making and helped to support our case.

We ran the additional analyses, and each set of results strengthened our case and helped us to rule out alternative explanations for our results. In short, every comment we received helped to improve the paper. When we read the revised paper we could easily appreciate how much better it was and we realized that we would never have arrived at that point without the reviewer comments. No matter what happened next, we knew we had a better paper. Fortunately, so did the reviewers, and the paper was accepted.

That editor was fortunate enough to have assigned very good reviewers (more on this later), but he was also wise enough to realize that all he needed to do was to point us in the right direction. If we didn't see how that would benefit us, it was our problem. Furthermore, if the additional work weakened the paper rather than strengthened it, this would suggest that there was not much of a contribution there to begin with. Letters such as this are part of dealing with authors respectfully, while trying to help them improve their work. This is not only the right thing to do, but it is also the smart thing to do in a competitive environment where you want authors to submit their work to your journal.

Dealing with reviewers

Dealing with reviewers may require better management skills than dealing with authors. If an editor does not manage the reviewers properly, the authors will not perceive that they have been treated fairly and, in fact, the journal will run the risk of rejecting worthwhile papers and publishing less meritorious papers. Why are reviewers so difficult to manage? The biggest reason is that they are contributing their time and expertise for virtually no compensation. An acknowledgement at the end of the final issue of a volume, or even a name on the journal masthead, is not fair recompense for the time and effort required to be a good reviewer. Perhaps we should pay reviewers but, short of that, editors ask reviewers to take time from their own work to read papers, offer helpful comments, and make a recommendation to the editor. Yet, without this input, the review process cannot continue.

The first thing for an editor to do is to identify "good" reviewers. I have already made reference to several characteristics that I think are important for good reviewers. Editors talk to other editors, and especially their predecessor at a journal, to gather information about who is good. What makes a reviewer a "good" reviewer? A good reviewer helps the editor to make the right decision. Reviews that list shortcomings of a paper, or praise its merits, are not necessarily the most useful. A good review outlines what is good about a paper and what needs to be done to make it acceptable, along with some estimation of the likelihood of a successful revision. A good reviewer provides this type of information in a timely fashion. Furthermore, while all scholars have biases and preferences for methods or ways to treat a topic, a good reviewer will not allow these biases and preferences to get in the way. In other words, a good reviewer can see merit in an approach even if it is not the approach that she or he might choose. Therefore, good reviewers neither suggest rejecting or accepting every paper they review.

This then brings me to the potential conflicting goals of reviewers and editors. Most of us begin trying our hand at reviewing papers in doctoral seminars when we are in graduate school. In order to seem clever and to impress the professor and our fellow students, it is often useful to find as many things wrong with a paper as we can. Many reviewers seem to carry some vestige of this when they review papers for journals. Furthermore, given the time demands of doing reviews (and, for most good reviewers, this will be multiplied by several journals), it is in the reviewers' best interests to find enough that is wrong to be able to reject a paper, since requesting a revision will mean reviewing that paper again. I am not suggesting that most reviewers consciously want to reject papers, or that they don't wish to be developmental, but, at the margin, the best payoff for reviewers comes with a recommendation to reject.

The editor, however, is looking at a much different set of incentives. If the editor rejects every paper, there will be no papers to publish, which is why the biggest source of stress for editors is "white space" or the lack of papers to publish. Therefore, the editor must sift through the comments of the reviewers and determine if there is some potential for a contribution buried under the reviewer's criticisms. A good reviewer, then, also gives the editor something to focus on in asking for a revision, and must be open to the possibility that a paper *can* be successfully revised.

Let me return to those reviewers from the *JPSP* paper. What made the reviews they supplied so useful? First of all, there were no gratuitous comments from any of the reviewers, and no one made comments just to show off how much they knew. Next, no one told us what would they do in a similar situation, but simply provided information about how to improve the paper. Also, each suggestion was very specific and included the reviewer's rationale for making the suggestion. Finally, as it turned out, each comment or suggestion made the paper better. These are the characteristics of any good review. The purpose of the reviewer comments should not be to make the reviewer look good (or, worse yet, look better than the author) or to get the author to read the reviewer's own work (unless it really is relevant), and reviewer comments should be as specific as possible so that they actually help the author – since that is the real reason for those reviewer comments.

If a reviewer does not provide high quality reviews to the editor, he or she should not be used as a reviewer. This includes the case where the reviewer is always late or where the reviewer rejects literally everything. Eventually, all editors learn that some very well-respected people in our field are poor reviewers and some lesser-known individuals are great reviewers, while also learning that there are some prominent individuals that could always be counted upon to provide helpful reviews in a timely fashion – as long as you didn't count on them *too* often!

Some reviewers may not do a good job initially, but they learn and improve their skills by reading other reviews and decision letters, and by getting feedback from the Editor. But, in the end, the Editor must understand how important it is for the reviewers to provide the kind of feedback that can help authors – either to revise the paper or to submit it elsewhere. Good reviewers are critical for good decisions on the part of the editor, and they are critical for the quality of the experience for the author, which will help enhance (or hurt) the reputation of the journal as a desirable place to submit one's work.

Before closing this section, I should add something about dealing with members of the editorial board. These are reviewers who have (hopefully) demonstrated some expertise in the past, and have shown that they can provide useful reviews. In some cases, these may be individuals who have some specialized knowledge that is rare in the field but, in general, these are also individuals who, when they accepted a position on a board, agreed to review on a regular basis. Editorial board members should be chosen with great care because it is quite uncomfortable when they have to be "fired." I did ask one board member to leave the board because he or she was always several weeks late with reviews, but it was not a pleasant experience. The editor has more good will with board members and so they are generally more willing to accept guidance and feedback, but they are fairly intolerant of editors who consistently ignore their recommendations. Thus, although board members are often the most valuable reviewers, they also require an extra level of diplomacy when dealing with them.

Dealing with the other participants

Authors and reviewers constitute two critical constituent groups involved in the editorial process, but they are not the only participants. Unless the editor owns the journal, there is some oversight of the entire process from a publisher. Professional organizations (such as American Psychological Association [APA] or the Academy of Management [AOM]), or private publishers (such as Blackwell or Wiley) have a real interest in what appears in the journal and how well the process is managed. The interest in content usually does not extend beyond the notion of wanting to publish "good" papers that are "interesting," and the interest in the process is just to make sure that potential authors remain willing to submit to the journal. Yet this group also requires attention.

Private publishers are usually for-profit firms and so they are interested in cost containment and how budget dollars are spent. They may view fewer issues of the journal, with more articles, as more cost-effective than more issues with fewer articles, but this puts more pressure on the editor to build a good pipeline of papers ready to be published. Professional organizations may be more concerned with their own reputation and so may insist upon certain codes of ethics for submission and publication. For example, the (APA) will not publish any paper that has appeared in another outlet that has an ISBN number. This includes proceedings from most meetings such as the AOM meetings. This insistence can cause problems with authors if, after submission, it turns out the paper was published in a proceedings volume somewhere. Professional associations may also have ethical guidelines concerning who should receive author credit, and even policies about whether or not editors should be able to submit to their own journals. All of these issues must be considered by the editor.

Finally, the editor must always consider the impact of her or his decisions and policies upon the readership of the journal. Depending on the journal in question, this group may include the leading scholars in the field, the most innovative instructors, or business leaders. In any case, the readership has certain expectations about what they will find when they open a copy of the journal. They may expect to find the latest in statistical techniques used to analyze data, or the most recent statement of a cutting edge theory, or they may expect to find practical information that can help them in the classroom or in the boardroom. If the readership is repeatedly disappointed with what they find, they will stop subscribing to, or reading, the journal, and they will be less likely to cite papers from the journal. Over time, this will affect the prestige of the journal and so, eventually, the willingness of authors to submit papers to the journal.

Obviously, the expectations of the readership depend upon the journal, but the editor can never lose sight of these expectations. The readership for a practice-oriented journal does not expect to find a lot of theory in the papers they read, nor do they desire complex statistics. The readers of management journal may not expect to find paper too heavily steeped in economics or psychology, and they may not expect to see too many laboratory experiments. Consistent adherence to these expectations will result in authors selecting themselves out of certain journals, but that is simply a cost of doing business. Readers looking for strong theory (for example) cannot be repeatedly disappointed when they open a journal or they will go elsewhere to read the research that will influence their own work, and will likely submit that work elsewhere as well.

Implications for authors

The discussion, to this point, has really focused on the issues from the perspective of an editor or a prospective editor. But potential authors also need to be aware of these (and other) issues because every problem that faces the editor will eventually trickle down to impact an author as well. So what can a potential author learn from this discussion?

The first and the most important implication is that there is no one person who has absolute control over what happens to a paper. In the case for almost all journals, reviewers are anonymous, while editors actually sign decision letters. Therefore, it is easy to focus on the editor as the power behind the decision. But, although the editor must take ultimate responsibility, I tried to explain how the editor is also trying to balance the needs of different critical constituencies in the review process, and so he or she cannot always reject, or dismiss, the opinions and recommendations of the reviewers. This means that, as an author, who might be responding to reviewer comments in a revision, it is important to respond to *every* one of the reviewer comments. It is not necessary that an author do everything that is suggested, but it is important that the author acknowledge each comment and recommendation – even if they seem frivolous. The editor will have no choice but to ask for further revisions if a reviewer is not satisfied with a revision, and depending on how dissatisfied the reviewer is, you might not get another chance. Of course, it is always possible that the editor is not willing to listen to a reviewer, but the author doesn't know this, and there is no reason to take chances.

This may sound as though I believe that an author has few rights or routes of appeal during this process. I do not believe that at all. As I noted earlier, the paper is the property of the author and she or he can withdraw it from the process at any point. But beyond that, there are surely occasions where the reviewers are simply wrong in their criticisms of a paper, and the editor is wrong to go along with the reviewer's recommendations. Perhaps it is simply a matter of whether or not an issue can be addressed with a revision, but it can go beyond that. What can an author do if he or she believes that the reviewer missed the point of the paper? In most cases, she or he can contact the editor and appeal the decision. I say, in most cases, because I know that some editors try to discourage this type of appeal, but I personally believe that anyone can make a mistake and it is no great sin to admit it.

I can recall a paper that I received during my tenure as an editor, which I duly sent out to three qualified reviewers, who generally believed that there were problems with the paper and that a revision would not help. I read the paper and the reviews (the paper was outside my own areas of expertise), and felt that the reviewers were reasonable and so I rejected the paper. The author called me to say why she or he believed the reviewers were incorrect in a number of places. We talked for a while, and I told the author to write a response to the reviewers, pointing out where he or she believed there were errors. I suggested that this letter accompany a revised manuscript where the author dealt with those issues she or he believed were valid and could be addressed. The author was persuasive, the paper was improved, and it was eventually published, but that was because the author handled the entire process so well – the story does not always have a happy ending.

The first thing an author must remember when appealing a decision is that this is not something that should be done frequently. The author must feel very strongly about the paper and the positions taken, and should also be convinced that this outlet is the best for the paper. Next, the author must also remember that the reviewers will see *all* the correspondence about the paper. Therefore, if an author is going to take issue with something a reviewer said, this must be done tactfully. Insulting a reviewer is never a good strategy, but in this case it is especially a poor strategy. The author must acknowledge the reviewer's points, but then present additional data or information which supports a different decision. Notice that I said the author must present additional data or information – this does not mean to simply argue the point again. The reviewer clearly came to a different conclusion than the one the author hoped for, and now the author must show that there are other issues to consider, or more recent work done in an area, or simply that the author has more data that all support the author's position.

But these implications for the authors have focused upon the review process. What can an author learn about how to write that brilliant paper that everyone wants to publish? This is probably the most common type of question that editors (and former editors) receive. Honestly, if there are "five easy steps" to writing a successful journal article, I don't know about them, and I still get papers rejected at the same rate as before I was an editor. I have picked up a few pointers, though, that might help.

First of all, everyone enjoys reading a paper written with enthusiasm. If you, as an author, don't believe in a paper, you probably won't convince anyone else to publish it. Second, although there are many scholars who have built substantial reputations by simply doing the next logical study in a research program, reviewers and editors are excited about new ideas, or old ideas approached in new ways. This may require a level of creativity that not everyone possesses, but the more broadly a person reads the literature, the more likely she or he is to stumble upon new ways of dealing with old problems or new problems entirely. A third thing I've learned is the importance of being simple and clear. High powered statistical techniques may help us answer questions we could not answer before, but, in many cases, there are simpler techniques that work just as well. Furthermore, they are easier to explain and easier for reviewers to deal with. Whenever I received a paper with a very specialized analytic technique, I always sought out the expert (or experts) on that technique to serve as a reviewer. These reviewers tended to be very critical of authors who did not fully understand the technique, and so authors actually fared worse in the review process than they would have if they had used simpler techniques.

In any case, it is important to communicate clearly, exactly what you have done and why. When a reviewer cannot understand what happened or why something was done, he or she often attributes this to an attempt by the author to cover up a problem. Authors do no want reviewers (or editors) reading their papers with that kind of mindset. Also, it is amazing how many papers are submitted where there is not a simple statement of hypotheses (assuming an empirical paper), the theory upon which they were based, and whether or not they were supported. These basic messages, if missing, or inaccessible to the reviewer, will cause problems.

These observations are not meant to serve as the keys to successful publications, but they can help authors avoid problems. The process obviously begins with the paper itself, and the author must write the best paper he or she can, explaining what was done and telling the reviewers why it is important. The author must then decide where to submit the paper. I discussed some of the ways an editor can try to attract good work, but the author must be realistic about the strengths and weaknesses of any paper, as well as if the paper really "fits" the mission of the journal. Once a paper is submitted, there is nothing an author can do until the reviews come back, and I discussed some ideas for dealing with reviewers earlier.

But, when I was asked to write this chapter I really wasn't thinking about authors as much as I was thinking about potential editors. Agreeing to serve as the editor of a major journal is a serious commitment of time and energy. It is not a decision that should be taken up lightly. Even if time is not an issue, there are still other considerations, and I tried to discuss some of these in this chapter. Journal editors are not omnipotent. They cannot simply reject or accept papers on a whim. There are too many constituencies involved in the process for the editor to truly have the power that some people believe they possess. A journal editor must balance the needs and concerns of these different groups while trying to publish the best work possible. Therefore, the job of editor is not for people seeking power or control. Instead, it is for people who look at the editorial process and believe that they can do as well as (or better than) some others, and that they can make a significant contribution to the field by allowing interesting and provocative research to be made available to others in the field. Editorial jobs are not for those who wonder what they will gain from such a position – they are for those who can imagine what they can give to the field by accepting such a position. I hope this chapter will help make that distinction clearer.

References

Bedeian, A. This volume, chapter 14.
Bies, R., & Moag, J. (1986). Interactional justice: Communication criteria of fairness. In R. Lewicki, B. Sheppard, & M. Bazerman (Eds.), *Research on negotiations in organizations*, Vol. 1. Greenwich, CT: JAI Press, pp. 43–55.
Brockner, J., & Wisenfeld, B. (1996). An integrative framework for explaining reactions to decisions: Integrative effects of outcomes and procedures. *Psychological Bulletin*, 120: 189–298.
Colquitt, J., Conlon, D., Wesson, M., Porter, C., & Ng, K. Y. (2001). Justice at the millennium: A meta-analytic review of 25 years of organizational justice research. *Journal of Applied Psychology*, 86: 425–45.

9
Being an Ethical Editorial Board Member and Editor: The Integral Role of Earned Trust

Debra L. Shapiro and Jean Bartunek

Can authors, especially aspiring authors whose work is not already well-known, trust the reviews they receive from major journals? Can they trust that editors will act fairly towards them? These are crucial questions that speak to the trustworthiness of a field and the sources of its scholarly development. In this chapter we will discuss why editorial trustworthiness is so important and what it means in practice. We will attempt to provide some reassurance for aspiring authors that their submissions will often be read by people who care about both their manuscript and the larger field towards which it may contribute. Finally, we will suggest some ways that authors can signal that the work they submit is trustworthy.

The primary purposes of publication in academic journals are knowledge creation and dissemination. However, authors do not simply publish their papers on their own; journal editors, associate editors,[1] and, to a lesser extent, editorial board members are "gatekeepers" in academic disciplines, who ultimately determine the publication-fate of manuscripts submitted to their journals. Thus, their trustworthiness has considerable impact on the knowledge that is created and disseminated, and on the careers of would-be authors.

Because journal publications are integral in determining the tenurability and promotability of professors, journal editors therefore have not merely "publication fate-control," but also "career fate-control." The inseparability of these two types of controls is represented by the expression "publish or perish," which is understood all too well by academics who have yet to be tenured, and especially by those who have not had frequent publication experience (Baruch & Hall, 2004; Caplow & McGee, 1958). This concern suggests that the responsibility of journal editors and editorial board members is very large: to "review fairly or kill" individual scholars (Shapiro & Sitkin, 2006).

But affecting the fate of individual scholars is only one part of editors' and reviewers' responsibility and impact; additionally, the responsibility and impact of editors and reviewers regards the development of a scholarly field. That is, reviewers and editors have a dual role. As Shapiro and Sitkin (2006) note, they are responsible to both paper-authors (as developers) and the professional community (as gatekeepers to ensure the advancement of high-quality scholarship). The gravity of this dual responsibility is the reason why it is critical for the individuals who serve in these roles to be accomplished in all dimensions essential for earning and keeping trust, namely

(1) in their demonstrated *competence*, or ability to produce high-quality scholarship and high-quality reviews;
(2) in their demonstrated *benevolence*, or devotion towards developing (not destroying) newer scholars and the professional field; and
(3) in their demonstrated *integrity*, or consistency as producers, evaluators, and mentors of high-quality knowledge.

These three dimensions comprise the antecedents to trust identified by Mayer, Davis, & Schoorman (1995). Similarly, we believe that excellence on these three dimensions is essential for journal editors to be fully trusted to serve as gatekeepers of our field. These qualities should be reflected in reviewers as well, especially reviewers on the editorial boards of major journals.

This chapter proceeds as follows. First, we elaborate on what should be the evidence to determine whether scholars have adequate competence, benevolence, and integrity to serve as editorial-review board members for a particular journal. Then we provide reasons for why it is imperative that trust standards and selection procedures for journal editors (and especially editors of our field's top-ranked journals) must be even more stringent than for board members. Based on experiences as associate editor at the *Academy of Management Journal* (*AMJ*; 2004–7; Debra Shapiro) and past president of the Academy of Management (AOM; 2001–2) and chair of the advisory committee for *AMJ* from 2004–2007 (Jean Bartunek), we describe the initiatives taken at *AMJ* that aim to ensure that trust-related scrutiny in selecting the editorial board members. In chapter 23, Wayne Cascio describes processes used to choose the editors of AOM journals.

We hope our thoughts and description will sensitize authors to the responsibilities required of editorial board members, and especially journal editors, and illuminate some procedures currently used to help ensure that such responsibilities are delegated to those whose records demonstrate they can be trusted to act in a trustworthy way. In so doing, we also hope to heighten appreciation for the many editorial board members and journal editors who continually strive to act with competence, benevolence, and integrity.

What precisely does the evidence of "competence" require?

A prerequisite for membership on an editorial board is competence as a scholar. "Competence" by itself means nothing; it must be contextually oriented if this word is to carry meaning. In the context of scholarship, competence typically refers to one's skill, or ability: (1) in conceptualizing value-added ideas regarding how and *why* relationships of interest occur and/or *when* relationships of interest are more, versus less, likely to occur; and/or (2) in testing such value-added relationships. External indicators of scholars' competence typically include, among other things, publications in refereed journals, especially those that are ranked by the *Financial Times* or highly rated in the *ISI Journal Citation Reports* (Rindova, Williamson, Petkova, & Sever, 2005), and the frequency with which their work is cited and used to inform the work of other scholars.

While competence as a scholar is necessary, it is by no means sufficient for serving as an editorial board member. The skills needed to be an effective editorial board member include, in addition to scholarly competencies, a broad and continuing knowledge of the field and its literature, expert knowledge about how to find flaws in and improve a paper, and the ability and willingness to help scholars improve the logical coherence, accuracy and value-added clarity of their text's theoretical and/or empirical substance. To do this, editorial board members must understand what is "old news" in order to help clarify what insights in a submitted manuscript are really new. Additionally, editorial board members must be current in their knowledge regarding optimal analytical methods (if the paper is empirical) since improvements in methods as well as conceptual understandings are continually evolving within scientific communities. There are many fine scholars who do not have the reviewing competency necessary to serve as editorial board members of prestigious journals.

Demonstrating competence as a scholar and as a reviewer is important in determining a scholar's appropriateness in serving as a member of an editorial board. However, it is only one of the three essential antecedents to determining whether a scholar can be fully trusted to serve as a gatekeeper for the field on an editorial board.

What precisely does the evidence of "benevolence" require?

Benevolence refers to "the extent to which a trustee is believed to want to do good to the trustor aside from an egocentric profit motive" (Mayer et al., 1995: 718). In the context of scholarship, benevolence would thus be illustrated whenever a scholar behaves in a manner that serves rather than hurts the interests of others. In the context of reviewing, benevolence is illustrated by serving, rather than harming, the relevant stakeholders to a scholarly journal, including the submitter, the journal, and the larger professional field.

At first glance, individual submitters may see benevolence as illustrated by readily accepting another's submitted work by granting it "acceptable for conference presentation" or "acceptable for publication," depending on which kind of acceptance the submitter seeks. However, these outcomes may be judged *not* benevolent if the quality of the submitted work is below the standards of the submitter's professional community. Additionally, if the submitted work that is below standards is readily accepted by a reviewer wishing to be "kind," in the long run false praise will likely harm the submitter's interest since it will rob him/her of the opportunity to strengthen skills that, in actuality, are in need of being built up.

Because editorial board members are accountable to their field as well as to individual submitters, they are generally required to critique, not just praise, authors' submissions. Benevolence in the context of reviewing thus, more often than not, is demonstrated in the manner in which criticism is communicated, especially the extent to which it is developmental. Shapiro and Sitkin (2006) identify the communication qualities needed for criticism to be developmental in character – namely, the need for feedback to be (1) timely, (2) interpersonally sensitive, (3) consistent with criteria for paper-acceptability that have been publicized or stated by journal editors and/or by reviewers in previous communications, and (4) selfless (e.g., open-minded, or willing to give consideration, to new ideas that may challenge those previously articulated by the reviewers). Shapiro and Sitkin note that such qualities essentially exemplify what organizational-justice scholars have called "interactional justice" (see Shapiro & Brett, 2005, for a review). Not surprisingly, then, editorial board members demonstrate benevolence towards authors when they treat them with dignity and respect and when they hold them to quality standards that are valued by their scientific community – that is, *when they behave fairly* in interpersonal and procedural ways (see Shapiro & Sitkin, 2006, for an elaboration of this point). They demonstrate benevolence towards their scholarly community when their feedback to authors includes respectful (rather than ridiculing) reference also to the concerns of the reviewers and to the procedural standards that are commonly used to assess the value-added nature of papers' stated contributions. Delivering feedback in dignity-enhancing ways is the ethical, not just benevolent, thing to do – for *all* stakeholders associated with a manuscript under review.

Although it is important when determining a scholar's appropriateness as an editorial board member to examine that scholar's benevolence in the ways noted here, this is, again, only one of three essential antecedents to determining whether a scholar can be fully trusted to serve as a gatekeeper in the field. A scholar who is competent and benevolent still may *not* necessarily be trusted in the role of gatekeeper. Why? Because, as we will argue next, these two characteristics must also be demonstrated consistently over time for the scholar to be fully entrusted with gatekeeping responsibilities.

What precisely does the evidence of "integrity" require?

"Integrity" refers to "the trustor's perception that the trustee adheres to a set of principles that the trustor finds acceptable" and does so *consistently*

(Mayer et al., 1995: 719). In the context of reviewing, integrity would thus be illustrated whenever a reviewer's competence and benevolence are demonstrated consistently, or in a sustained manner over time and across manuscripts. The importance of sustained competence and benevolence is that the continuance of each of these characteristics are required if editorial board members are to be considered trustworthy in serving the interests of the scholarly community as well as authors. Scholarly advancement (for either individual authors or a field) is not a one time/short-term event. Providing top-notch gatekeeping and developmental contributions with consistency is essential for the advancement of management and behavioral science (indeed any science) to occur.

Evidence of reviewers' integrity as indicated in their ad hoc reviews is often reflected in their selection for editorial boards. Sometimes it is reflected for editorial board members in "Best Reviewer Awards." Such honors are typically extended to reviewers who have demonstrated in their reviews, in a repeated manner, competence and benevolence (as defined earlier). Identifying reviewers who meet this description has been eased by metrics of reviewers' performance-quality (e.g., in terms of timeliness, substantive helpfulness, and constructiveness) that are kept by journal editors and/or electronic systems such as "Manuscript Central" being used by an increasing number of management journals such as (as of early 2007) *AMJ*, *Academy of Management Review* (*AMR*), *Organization Science*, *Human Relations* and the *Journal of Organizational Behavior*. Even for journals that receive a smaller number of submissions and that do not have extensive records of individual reviewers' integrity in any given year, it is possible to keep records dating over several years about the quality of reviews conducted.

Our point to now has been that journal editorial board members must demonstrate all three dimensions – competence, benevolence, and integrity – if they are to be appropriately entrusted with the responsibility of gatekeeping. For this reason, for example, a scholar with more seniority or citation counts is not necessarily the best person to be on an editorial board. Instead, this role should go to a scholar with more combined evidence of competence as a scholar and an ad hoc reviewer *and* benevolence *and* integrity (all else equal). We are assuming, of course, that the needed content-related expertise (hence competency) is present in the scholar chosen via the latter criteria. Sometimes highly specialized papers require finding scholars with specialized knowledge who may score lower on the other dimensions. Over all, though, finding and selecting reviewers whose records *demonstrate* evidence of all three trust-antecedents promises to place the publication, the career-fate of authors, and the advancement of the scholarly field in the hands of those who can be more fully trusted to advance scholarly work of scientific merit, to treat authors with dignity and respect, to develop authors into stronger scholars and, as a result, to act ethically.

The trust needed in editors versus reviewers: More or less?

Is the trust needed in the editor similar to that needed in editorial board members, or is it greater? In one sense, the trust needed in editors is equal to that needed in editorial board members in general; after all, the editor is him/herself a reviewer! And thus, surely, editors must demonstrate competence, benevolence, and integrity.

However, the level of integrity required of editors exceeds that which is required in editorial board members. This is because the *zone of authority* held by editors (including associate editors) is greater than that of reviewers; editors' authority essentially enables them to control the Fate-controllers. Why? Because editors are empowered to change who sits on their editorial boards, who receives submitted manuscripts for review, what the "template" for evaluating submitted manuscripts will be, and, ultimately, how the reviews will be taken into account in decision making about manuscripts. If a reviewer makes a mistake or is not trustworthy, an editor can rectify it, but if the editor is not trustworthy there will be no recourse.

Editorial empowerment is important if editors are to be enabled to potentially improve upon past editorships, for example, by encouraging manuscript submissions from scholars who may have felt underrepresented during previous journal editors' leadership or by changing the domain and/or approach of a journal (e.g. expanding or decreasing the number of scholarly methodologies seen as appropriate). We liken the process of selecting journal editors to the process of selecting judges, where intense scrutiny is needed for evaluating candidates' *character* as well as *competence*.

Particularly in the AOM, where journal editors are often viewed as representatives of the Academy and its policies, the trustworthiness of the editor is crucial. Consistent with this, the standards and the review process for selecting journal editors are stringent. Characteristics taken into account in this selection include candidates' scholarly record, their vision for (the development of) the journal, their administrative skill as well as the practical issue of the ability of their university to support the editing of a journal, the quality and timeliness of their reviews when they have served on an editorial board, and the competence, benevolence, and integrity they have demonstrated when they have been in an editorial role (e.g. for a special issue of a journal or as an associate editor). Particular attention is paid to the quality and timeliness of the editorial letters they write, as well as especially how developmental these are for authors. Chapter 23, by Wayne Cascio, describes the careful selection process the AOM uses for the editors of its journals.

An illustrative way of choosing trustworthy editorial board members

To illustrate our points, and to indicate how some of what we have described is enacted by *AMJ*, we would like to indicate some of what *AMJ* does to ensure the trustworthiness of its editorial board members. Some of this material is taken from Rynes (2006).

One of the first criteria that *AMJ* uses for selecting board members is that individuals have strong publication and citation records. In addition, however, potential editorial board members need to demonstrate that they are able and willing to provide high-quality reviews and to do so in a timely fashion. Starting with Janice Beyer's 1985–7 editorship, editors have rated both the timeliness and quality (including how developmental they are) of all reviewers' reviews of virtually all of the manuscripts received. *AMJ* typically uses six to eight "work samples" of ad hoc reviewers to determine whether they should be invited to join the editorial board. Thus, invitations to join the *AMJ* editorial board are based on considerable experience of reviewers' competence, benevolence, and integrity, their ability to do high quality, developmental reviews and to do them consistently. Many journals do not have the volume of manuscripts or number of possible reviewers or editorial board members that AMJ does. All journals, however, have the responsibility for assessing the dimensions of trustworthiness present in their editorial board members in ways that are appropriate to the journal's own situation.

Advice for aspiring authors, reviewers, and editors

How does the integral role of earned trust in the selection of editorial board members and journal editors apply to aspiring authors, reviewers, and editors? For all of these stakeholders, earning trust means acting in the three ways identified in our chapter. For authors, this means maximizing ways to demonstrate competency, including (at a minimum) knowledge of the format requirements and content relevance associated with the journal to which they are submitting work. For authors, earning trust also means maximizing ways to demonstrate benevolence, including (at a minimum) *expressing appreciation and open-mindedness* rather than disgust in response to constructive criticisms they have received from their reviewers and editor. Additionally, authors can demonstrate benevolence by *acting ethically* (i.e., *not* plagiarizing others' or even their own work). Any time authors lift text from another paper, including their own that may have been published elsewhere, and use it uncited in a paper, they are plagiarizing – a "crime" that risks instant rejection of their paper if it is under review or worse (e.g., being reported to the AOM's Ethics Committee). Additionally, authors can demonstrate benevolence by *acting in ways that serve others* in their professional community (e.g., by agreeing to serve as reviewers when requested by editors), and not in ways that suggest they wish to serve only themselves (e.g., by generally declining to review papers for journals where they regularly submit their own work; see Sara Rynes' chapter in this book for an elaboration of this point). Finally, authors can earn the integrity-based aspect of trust *by consistently, over time, demonstrating competency and benevolence* in the ways described here.

The points just made for aspiring authors include a reminder that authors are also often reviewers. As such, they can earn trust by doing the things just noted – namely, by *expressing open-mindedness in their reviews* to ideas by authors that may oppose previous theories, methods, and/or paradigms that they as well as other scholars may have personally endorsed in the past; by *acting ethically*, for example by exposing plagiarism or other unethical acts (such as a "dual-submission," which occurs when authors submit a paper to two or more journals simultaneously). Additionally, aspiring reviewers can earn trust by *acting in ways that serve others*, which they do when they act benevolently and ethically in ways described here. *Doing all of these things consistently* will in turn increase aspiring reviewers' perceived integrity too.

How does the integral role of earned trust in the selection of associate editors and journal editors apply to scholars aspiring to become either or both of these gatekeepers? Again, we believe the implication is that *earning trust is essential*. As associate editors or editors, this means *expressing open-mindedness to the content of reviews, but remembering that their role is – not "vote-counter" but – Judge*. It is thus possible that an associate editor or editor may view a paper whose reviewers advise rejection as one that is worthy of at least one revision opportunity. The developmental role of the associate editor and editor may enable scholars in such roles, perhaps more than an individual reviewer, to recognize a "diamond in the rough" more readily. Ideally, however, all reviewers will err on the side of offering ways to strengthen a submitted manuscript before assuming that there is no way to do so.

Acting ethically is another way for associate editors and editors to earn trust; as we noted earlier, this can be done by exposing plagiarism or other unethical acts (such as a "dual-submission"). *Being consistent in their ethical conduct towards all authors*, regardless of whether they know authors personally as well as professionally, is essential if editors and associate editors are to earn perceived integrity.

In summary, we believe that the importance of earning trust in the three ways identified in our chapter provides fundamental "prescriptions" for aspiring authors, reviewers, associate editors and editors. Everyone's willingness to maximize the ways needed to earn trust promises to create a community of generous, creative, and ethical scholars who, together in these ways, can significantly advance behavioral science!

Conclusion

We have discussed the importance of trustworthiness – as illustrated by competence (in both scholarship and reviewing), benevolence, and integrity – in the editorial-review process, and have described how *AMJ* chooses editorial board members based on their performance according to these dimensions. We have also suggested ways that aspiring authors, editorial board members, and journal editors may demonstrate their trustworthiness. We hope our thoughts and description will (1) sensitize readers, especially new authors, to the responsibilities required of everyone involved in the editorial process, (2) illuminate procedures currently in place to help ensure that such responsibilities are delegated to those whose records demonstrate they can be trusted to act ethically, and in so doing, (3) heighten appreciation for journal editors who rarely receive thanks for their efforts to serve our field, and (4) inspire scholars who welcome the opportunity to improve how management and behavioral sciences march forward to build records that will earn them the trust needed to, one day, responsibly serve as editorial board members and, perhaps, as journal editors.

Notes

1. At some journals, such as *AMJ*, the associate editors are delegated full decision-making authority regarding the fate of manuscripts received by them. For this reason, we refer to associate editors as well as editors as gatekeepers. Hereafter we refer to only editors, due to the fact that not all journals delegate fate-control to associate editors and due to this book's focus on issues of "editorship."

References

Baruch, Y., & Hall, D. T. (2004). The academic career: A model for future careers in other sectors? *Journal of Vocational Behavior*, 64: 241–62.

Caplow, T., & McGee, R. J. (1958). *The academic marketplace*. NY: Basic Books.

Mayer, R. C., Davis, J. H., & Schoorman, F. D. (1995). An integrative model of organizational trust. *Academy of Management Review*, 20: 709–34.

Rindova, V. P., Williamson, I. O., Petkova, A. P., & Sever, J. M. (2005). Being good or being known: An empirical examination of the dimensions, antecedents, and consequences of organizational reputation. *Academy of Management Journal*, 48: 1033–49.

Rynes, S. L. (2006). "Getting on Board" with *AMJ*: Balancing Quality and Innovation in the Review Process. *Academy of Management Journal*, 49: 1097–102.

Shapiro, D. L., & Brett, J. M. (2005). What is the role of control in organizational justice? In J. Greenberg & J. Colquitt (Eds.), *Handbook of organizational justice* (pp. 155–77). NJ: Lawrence Erlbaum.

Shapiro, D. L., & Sitkin, S. B. (2006). Fairness as a key criterion in reviewing. In Y. Baruch, S. E. Sullivan, & H. N. Schepmyer (Eds.), *Winning reviews: A guide for evaluating scholarly writing* (pp. 79–88). Basingstoke: Palgrave Macmillan.

10
Using Technology to Improve the Editorial Process
Martin Kilduff

I was talking to the managing editor of one of the leading management journals recently concerning the reluctance to move to Web-based publishing. "The authors and the reviewers told us it's far too much trouble to go through all those steps of uploading manuscripts or reviews when you can just put something in the mail or send an e-mail," was her take on the question of technological change. I remembered that not too many years before this, as a reviewer for this particular journal, I was one of those Luddites resisting the introduction of paperless technology in the journal submission and review process. At the board meeting a young scholar had championed e-mail technology as permitting a reduction in the use of environmental resources as the main advantage over sending submissions to reviewers in the mail. But I, in common with most reviewers, always read print copies of papers, so switching to e-mail would involve transferring the cost of printing from the journal to the reviewers, as far as I, and the others, could see. There was no particular advantage in terms of saving the Earth! Thus, so long as the argument was made to move to new technology because it would save paper and other resources, this argument appeared to be flawed.

On being appointed incoming editor of *Academy of Management Review* (*AMR*), I led the charge to move the Academy journals into the Web-based era. Did my mind change concerning the possibilities of new technology reducing renewable resources? The answer is no – I doubt whether either e-mail or Web-based solutions save much in the way of renewable resources, given the energy-hungry computers and servers necessary for electronic transmission on top of the necessity of printing out copies of documents. But new technology is being embraced for quite different reasons: time saving, efficiency, system reliability, and global accessibility.

For a journal receiving 200 or so manuscripts per year, the task of sending everything by ordinary mail may still be feasible, given a well organized and stable office staff, together with little outside pressure for ever-faster decision cycles. This was the situation with *Administrative Science Quarterly* (*ASQ*) during my time there as associate editor, during which the possibility of moving to e-mail submission was discussed and then rejected. (*ASQ* has, more recently, moved toward e-mail submission, however.) But at *AMR*, submissions number 500 or more per year, the office traditionally moves every three years to another location, and there is pressure from the Academy to reduce review times. Under these circumstances, *AMR* had moved in the late 1990s toward a system of e-mailed manuscripts, reviews, and decision letters.

My experience as an associate editor at *AMR* showed me that a reliance on e-mail transmission of manuscripts, reviews, and decision letters had some benefits in terms of faster processing of manuscripts, but suffered some dire potential consequences in terms of overworked staff. I remember visiting the *AMR* office in New Orleans in the spring of 2005. The levies had already overflowed in that particular office – each day a veritable flood of routine e-mail had to be cleared by the managing editor just to keep the operation from sinking under the burden of reminding late reviewers, responding to authors' requests, sending new submissions to reviewers and editors, and so on. If the managing editor took a few days off, then the process of managing the journal threatened to become mired in a permanent backlog of queries and tasks. Thus, the move to a Web-based system represented immediate benefits in freeing up central office-staff time. Web-based systems tend to be expensive and are probably infeasible at present for stand-alone journals that do not have the support of professional associations. However, as we move forward into the electronic publishing era which will doubtlessly see the end of print journals, we can anticipate that everything will be Web-based.

At present, I think there is a tipping point somewhere around the 250 plus annual submission range at which the benefits of routinizing many operations such as e-mail transmissions through a Web-based system outweigh the costs in terms of staff, editors, authors, and reviewers learning the system. It was clear to me after my visit to New Orleans that I would either have to hire two or more full-time staff, or I would have to radically change the way that *AMR* was run. Fortunately, there was a long-standing commitment on the part of the Academy to move toward a more efficient, Web-based system for all its journals. *AMR* was scheduled to come on line sometime in the middle of my term as editor. But this would mean I would have to start out with one system, which was patently inadequate, and then introduce another parallel system half way through my editorship. I recall David Harrison, the editor of *Organizational Behavior and Human Decision Processes*, a journal that already utilized Web-based submissions, strongly advising me, on the basis of his experience, to make the transition from the very beginning of my term rather than trying to juggle an ongoing system while introducing another system.

Thus it was that I made the decision shortly after visiting New Orleans to move the whole *AMR* operation from e-mail to the Web, with a start date of

July 1, 2005, when new manuscripts would officially begin flowing toward the Penn State office. I considered the Web-based system to represent the equivalent of a full-time, experienced additional managing editor in charge of routine tasks such as notifying authors that their papers have been received, contacting potential reviewers concerning their willingness to review and providing them with access to relevant manuscripts, and so on. All of this could be handled relatively automatically by an automated Web-based system, thus freeing up office staff for the more important tasks of manuscript management and relationship management.

I had not anticipated the amount of work that it would take to fully customize the Web-based system for the needs of a distinctive journal such as *AMR*, a journal that had achieved a preeminent place in terms of the publishing of conceptual and theoretical papers in the field of management and organization studies. I was not prepared to just take an off-the-shelf system, but devoted many tedious weeks to carefully going over every aspect of the system to make sure that it fully represented the values I had come to associate with *AMR* at its best. Thus, all the preformatted decision letters had to be completely rewritten to represent *AMR* norms of civility rather than the rather abrupt norms apparently characteristic of the more basic sciences usually served by the Web-based system the Academy was purchasing.

I also faced the possibility of fairly radical change in the management of this illustrious journal. Historically, *AMR* had been run with a tight control from the editor, who made all decisions concerning reviewer assignment. The switch to a new technology opened up possibilities for deliberately altering relationships of authority – new technology, as Barley (1986) reminded us, provides opportunities for structuration. Thus, it was possible for the new technology to handle a larger number of associate editors than was possible under the previous system. It was also possible to delegate more decision-making authority to these experts, rather than hoarding all the authority to myself in the central office. Further, it was possible to involve the authors more directly in the process by offering them the opportunity to nominate reviewers. I enthusiastically took advantage of these opportunities for beneficial change. The number of associate editors increased from four to seven, and, after extensive discussion with my new team, we decided on a new system of delegated authority with respect to the choice of reviewers that would combine efficiency and effectiveness.

Briefly, for each paper submitted the editor-in-chief (myself) would pick a set of names of reviewers from which the managing editor would choose three who were available (including at least one board member for each paper). At this point, the action editor would have three days to make changes to the assigned reviewers in collaboration with the managing editor. The default was that the editor-in-chief's reviewer picks would be acted upon unless the action editor intervened. Thus, papers would be processed efficiently rather than sitting waiting for attention, but the expertise of action editors would always be available to improve the effectiveness of reviewer allocation. This was the innovative solution to how to balance desirable delegation of authority and centralized control of efficiency.

After much simulation of submission and review processes, the system was launched on July 1 with few hiccups. Submitted papers received automatic acknowledgments even when no one was in the office. Reviewers were asked to decide on whether to review a paper or not based on the e-mailed receipt of the abstract alone – this tended to speed up the decision making compared to the previous system of either e-mailing complete papers or mailing manuscripts. Once reviewers agreed to review a paper, reminders concerning overdue reviews were generated from the system rather than being the responsibility of the managing editor. The system was accessible anywhere in the world by editors, reviewers, and authors, thus facilitating the internationalization of the journal, including the location of one associate editor outside the US.

There were still unexpected hiccups and continuing problems following the launch of the system. For example, we still haven't figured out how to change the system so that it automatically sends reviewers copies of decision letters and reviewer comments without disclosing other reviewers' e-mail addresses. So, this repetitive process has to be performed manually for every single manuscript decision.

A primary benefit of Web-based systems was revealed after the Katrina disaster shut down the Tulane office that had continued to process manuscripts submitted prior to July 1, 2005. For several months, there was no access available to the files housed on the Tulane computers. The wisdom of having a dispersed, Web-based system suddenly became quite apparent when faced with the limitations of a locally based e-mail system housed on vulnerable servers. Unlike an e-mail-based system customized to the particular circumstances of the institution which houses the *AMR* office, the Web-based system would be inherited by each new editor, ensuring the transfer of memory concerning manuscripts, reviewing patterns, and prior decisions.

A further benefit of the Web-based system became apparent when several of the editors, including myself, decided to move schools. On moving from Penn State to the University of Texas, I arranged for the *AMR* office to remain at Penn State. This meant that I could no longer walk down the corridor with my recommendations for reviewers scribbled on the form that accompanied my copy of the manuscript provided to me by the managing editor. Instead, we had to take greater advantage of the capabilities of the Web-based system. Even more so than before, this system became the mediating database into which I contributed advice and decisions and from which I extracted papers, reviews, and information. My suggestions for reviewers were now incorporated in a note attached to every set of manuscript files. Thus, instead of just the managing editor being privy to these suggestions, they were available also to the relevant action editors. This greater reliance on the Web-based system considerably facilitated the management of professional relationships among a distributed team. We have tried to avoid the isolation perils of distributed technology (discussed by Baruch, 2001) by keeping in touch through telephone and through personal meetings.

This is not to say that a Web-based system is likely to be fully adjustable to all the demands of modern journal publishing. In the case of *AMR*, book reviews that *AMR* solicits and publishes bypass the system completely, and the dialog submissions are handled somewhat clumsily within the system, given that such commentaries on published papers do not go out for review. Further, papers without abstracts or in some other ways not ready to be sent for review have to be "unsubmitted" in order to permit the authors to go through the whole process over again. Reviewers agree to review papers on the basis of abstracts (the complete papers are not available until reviewers agree to review), and sometimes these abstracts mislead concerning the actual content of papers, causing reviewer discontent. These are just a few of the rigidities experienced on a day-to-day basis.

In general, however, the task of taking over the editorship of *AMR* should in the future be much less of an onerous undertaking compared to the past. The Web-based system can accommodate changes of personnel without suffering interruptions resulting from the movement of the *AMR* office from one location to another. Indeed, there is no need to saddle the editor of a major journal with the task of hiring staff – it would seem much more sensible to have a permanent journal office and one location with a permanent managing editor who could thus retain the institutional memory so important to the smooth running of any organization. As we have discovered, given the movement of three of the top editorial team at *AMR* to new schools during my editorship, the Web-based system is truly global in being available anywhere where there is an Internet connection. The internationalization of editing and reviewing can be better accomplished through a Web-based system than through paper-based or e-mail systems.

So what does all this mean for authors? First, it means that, besides striving to structure arguments clearly and concisely (see Bem, 1995, and Kilduff, 2006, for advice on writing for journal publication) authors have to master the process of uploading their papers on to a website, scheduling enough time for this to be done without errors. On top of this, a new user ID and password must be remembered. In the past, exhortations were given concerning the importance of preparing paper manuscripts for submission. Now, the exhortations are similar in terms of checking apparently minor details and making sure the paper is professionally prepared for electronic submission.

Something new about Web-based submission is the importance given to the abstract. Thus, the second implication for authors is to make sure abstracts are carefully written to communicate the major point of the paper in the context of the relevant theoretical framing. Would-be reviewers first receive the abstract, and it is on this basis that reviewers agree or decline to review a paper. Poorly written or uninformative abstracts are likely to provide poor first impressions. No longer can the author assume that reviewers will simply skip over the abstract – the abstract has become one of the most closely read parts of a paper submitted to a Web-based journal. For this reason, many Web-based journals require authors to craft "structured abstracts" that include such vital details as the background, purpose, sources of evidence, main argument, and conclusion of the paper being submitted. The abstract must be as carefully written as every other aspect of the paper.

Third, authors should remember they have the opportunity to signal the distinctive areas and theories to which they hope to contribute with their work. The choice of theories and topic areas is information available to editors in the choice of reviewers: within the Web-based system it is possible to search for reviewers using the keywords provided by authors. Fourth, authors can nominate reviewers. Although there is no promise that author recommendations will be acted upon, such nominations can be helpful in signaling the kinds of experts that might be relevant for the paper. Authors should be cautioned, however, to use the, option wisely. There is no point in nominating uncritical fans of your work or people who have already contributed significantly to the development of your paper.

Fifth, authors should make sure their papers are in the very best possible shape in terms of establishing clear contributions to theory and research. Submissions that are clearly inappropriate for *AMR* or that make no significant contribution to theoretical understanding beyond what has already been published in prior work are likely to be declined by the editor without review. The very efficiency of the system facilitated by the new Web-based submission and review process also improves the effectiveness of the system in terms of providing more time for the careful prescreening of manuscripts.

Under my editorship, *AMR* took a major leap toward reliance on Web-based technology. With the editorial office at Penn State, the editor at the University of Texas, and the associate editors widely dispersed across two continents, the new technology has really been put to the test. Overall, it has performed well. There are still some processes that need to be better automated. Further, the technology that powers the *AMR* Web-based system is subject to frequent downtimes lasting one or more hours. In the aftermath of the disruption caused by the Katrina disaster to the e-mail-based prior technology, however, these problems with the new technology seem manageable. Unlike the previous system, with the new system I can access manuscripts, reviews, decision letters, and other information from any computer anywhere in the world. In actual fact, I rely completely on voice recognition technology or graphical interface technology for all my textual production on computers, so I tend to travel with my own customized machine. That, however, is a technology story for another day.

References

Barley, S. R. (1986). Technology as an occasion for structuring: Evidence from observations of CT scanners and the social order of radiology departments. *Administrative Science Quarterly*, 31, 78–108.

Baruch, Y. (2001). The autistic society. *Information and Management*, 38, 129–36.

Bem, D. J. (1995). Writing a review article for Psychological Bulletin. *Psychological Bulletin*, 118, 172–7.

Kilduff, M. (2006). Publishing theory. *Academy of Management Review*, 31, 252–5.

11
Moving a Journal up the Rankings

Gerard P. Hodgkinson

Reflecting on ten years' editorial experience at the *British Journal of Management* (*BJM*) – two years as an associate editor (1996–8), followed by eight years as the Editor-in-Chief (1999–2006) – in this chapter, I map out what I consider to be the critical factors that ultimately determine the standing of academic journals in the global marketplace of scholarly excellence within the field of management and organization studies and address the question regarding what steps might be taken in order to improve a journal's performance in that context. Now in its nineteenth year of publication and consistently ranked among the top ten European journals in both the business and management studies listings of the Social Sciences Citation Index (SSCI), the *BJM* constitutes a highly suitable case study for the analysis of these issues.

The chapter is structured in three major sections. First, I reflect broadly on the responsibilities of editorship and the motivations that led me to undertake my roles at the *BJM*. Next, I consider the various factors I believe underpinned the journal's success during my period of office as its Editor-in-Chief. In conclusion, I distil a number of general implications for editors and would-be editors seeking to raise the standing of scholarly journals in what is undoubtedly a diverse and eclectic field.

The responsibilities and motivations of editorship

No one truly worthy of an editorial role with a major scholarly journal takes on their duties without first considering its implications, both communal and personal. At the communal level, the various stakeholders of the journal, chiefly the past and current members of the editorial team and wider editorial advisory board and reviewers, accomplished and aspiring authors, and its subscribers, are watching with keen interest to see who takes on the role and in what ways they might be seeking to develop the journal. The more established the journal the keener the interest, because more is at stake. At minimum, an effective incoming editor is expected to maintain if not improve the standing of the journal in the eyes of the scholarly community they serve. If the journal's reputation is maintained, all well and good; if it is enhanced, so much the better. However, should the journal's standing deteriorate for any reason, this is bound to be attributed to the personal shortcomings of the new editor and the greater the extant reputation of the journal, the greater the concomitant decline in the standing of the incumbent.

In short, the personal reputation of editors is inextricably tied to the relative and absolute performance of their journals. Inevitably, key stakeholders will make comparisons with past editors and competing journals to draw conclusions based on their assessments. A welter of theory and empirical evidence from the field of social psychology concerning the attribution of human behaviour (reviewed in Martinko, Douglas, & Harvey, 2006) teaches us that in their quest for causal understanding, individuals are marked by an overwhelming tendency to apportion blame for poor performance to their environments (including the actions of significant others), while success is typically attributed to the actions of self. Hence, in the case of high performing journals success will likely be seen by the relevant scholarly community as reflecting the actions of a number of stakeholders, not least contributing authors, publishers and reviewers, whereas failure, in the main, will reflect upon the actions of the editor-in-chief and, to a lesser extent, his or her wider editorial team.

It was thus with the feeling of a deep sense of responsibility to ensure that under my stewardship, the *BJM* would continue on the trajectory of continuous improvement set in motion by its founding editor, David Otley, some ten years earlier, that I began to contemplate the possibility of my becoming its second General Editor (latterly entitled Editor-in-Chief). Having first served as an associate editor, it was already clear to me that what might loosely be termed "the enabling conditions" to ensure the continuing success of the journal were well in place, with sufficient potential in the new role for me to take the journal forward to a new stage of development. First, the support system and accompanying routines established by my predecessor, reflecting his impeccable organizational capabilities, were such that I judged I would be able to grow into the role rapidly, without becoming encumbered unduly with a mountain of basic administration. Second, the steady stream of 70–75 manuscripts per annum, roughly twice the number published, was adequate to ensure a healthy flow of copy, while taking the necessary steps to attract larger numbers of submissions of increasingly better quality.[1] Above all, I perceived the Council of the British Academy of Management (BAM), the governing body of the learned society under whose auspices the *BJM* is published, was strongly united in its support of my candidature, a factor that would prove crucial in securing the resources required to expand the editorial team and promote the journal effectively on the international conference circuit, especially in North America and throughout continental Europe.

The primary motivation that led me to first become an associate editor of the *BJM* and subsequently its Editor-in-Chief was the basic desire to help BAM develop into a learned society of comparable standing to the leading UK learned societies that represent the major social sciences (e.g. the British Psychological Society, the Royal Economics Society, and the British Association of Sociology) underpinning the comparatively immature field of business and management studies (broadly conceived), with a view to ensuring that it evolves its research and scholarship to a level in keeping with its strong teaching presence in higher education. Rightly or wrongly, I considered the development of the *BJM* into an internationally ranked journal to be central to this fundamental strategic objective of BAM. Having published a number of articles of my own in journals of the standard to which I was hoping the *BJM* might eventually evolve, I had realized that in the long run all articles, however influential, eventually fade into the background, but the outlets in which they are published, provided they are of good standing, endure, serving as the primary mechanism through which the field more generally is advanced. Hence, I considered that serving the academic community through taking up the editorship of the *BJM*, although potentially costly in terms of my own writing and publication, could potentially yield a greater return for the management and organization studies field as a whole, and so with a considerable degree of trepidation I agreed to take on the role for an initial period of three years, to be extended to a maximum of five years, subject to satisfactory performance.[2]

Factors that drive the performance of scholarly journals

Arguably, the strongest indication that the *BJM* is on the ascendancy is its entrance into the SSCI. Rightly or wrongly, inclusion in this database and the relative ranking of journals within it, as determined by overall impact factor, are increasingly being seen as prima facie evidence of journal quality by business school deans and wider policy makers, in what has become an extremely crowded marketplace. One of my first editorial tasks in a strategic capacity, therefore, was to step up the lobbying of Thomson Scientific, under whose auspices the SSCI is administered, with the intention of securing the *BJM*'s entry as quickly as possible, a process that my predecessor had begun via Blackwells, our publisher of the journal.

Following a three-year evaluation period, the *BJM*'s entry to the SSCI was finally granted in 2002. Our first impact factor of 0.746, which was officially published in 2003, placed us at number 31 in a table comprising 67 management journals, and in 2004, with an impact factor of 1.483, the journal rose to number 14 in the management listing and joined the business listing at number 13. Unfortunately, impact factors are highly unstable and in common with many SSCI-listed journals ranked outside the top eight to ten in highly heterogeneous fields like business and management studies, at the time of writing this chapter (early 2007) the *BJM* is ranked 35/71 in management and 29/61 in business. Nevertheless, considering the fact that there are several thousand scholarly management journals, this is an excellent performance record and certainly well in line with the targets I had set for myself upon assuming the role of Editor-in-Chief. What, then, are the factors that might account for this improvement in performance?[3]

For present purposes it is useful to delineate two broad classes of factors, strategic factors, driving the development of the editorial mission and competitive position of a journal, including its resource capabilities, and operational factors, especially the internal support mechanisms underpinning its basic administration. In the remainder of this section I consider each set of factors in turn.

Strategic factors

As noted above, in the case of the *BJM* the work of my predecessor had ensured that many of the operational factors were already firmly in place. Equally crucial, however, was his strategic vision of a general management journal that could publish within a unified collection academic articles drawn from the entire spectrum of subfields represented in the typical business school environment, ranging from accounting and finance, marketing and corporate strategy to human resource management, business economics, public sector management, management development, R&D management, and research methods. By the time I assumed the role of General Editor, the *BJM* had emerged with a clear identity as a general management journal, upon which I was able to build. In my opening editorial (Hodgkinson, 1999, pp. 1–2), I stated:

> My chief aim is to continue the development of the journal into a truly international outlet for the publication of high quality research across the full range of sub-fields of management inquiry. In practice this means that our editorial policies must evolve so as to ensure that the *BJM* not only attracts the very best offerings from within the UK but also is considered an outlet of choice for scholars from other countries throughout the world.

Consistent with this agenda, I immediately expanded the editorial team and the wider editorial advisory board, changing both markedly in composition, in a push to further internationalize the profile of the journal, while ensuring that it continued to develop apace across all the major management subfields. Martin Kilduff was appointed as the *BJM*'s first associate editor explicitly charged with a major international role. As its chief ambassador in the USA, Martin sought to actively raise the standing of the *BJM* in the eyes of the North American management research community, for example by representing the journal at the Academy of Management (AOM) meetings and encouraging leading and up-and-coming US scholars to submit articles and review manuscripts. At the end of his term, he went on to serve as an associate editor of *Administrative Science Quarterly* and the *Academy of Management Review*, prior to becoming the main editor of the latter. Celeste Wilderom was appointed an associate editor to perform a similar international enhancement role. Her remit was to help expand the *BJM*'s international reach throughout continental Europe. That this strategy of expansion and internationalization of the editorial team was a success is evidenced by the changes witnessed in the profile of submissions to the journal over the period of my tenure. As noted in my penultimate editorial (Hodgkinson, 2005), it was gratifying that the *BJM* had witnessed a steady increase in the growth of manuscripts submitted from overseas in general, but especially from the USA and continental Europe, amid growing competition from a number of rival journals. At the end of 2004, six years into my term:

- the quality and quantity of manuscripts submitted to the *BJM* from across virtually all of the management subfields had risen markedly (the overall volume of manuscripts per annum had approximately doubled over the past six years, excluding submissions to special issues, which had witnessed equally dramatic increases);
- the number of manuscripts submitted from outside the UK had risen sharply, to a point where UK submissions were now less than 50 percent of the total per annum;
- a series of special issues on topics at the leading edge of management research had been introduced and was now well established;
- the rejection rate had risen from approximately 50 percent at the outset of my term to around 92 percent, excluding special issues;[4]
- as noted earlier, having recently joined the SSCI, the *BJM* was showing a dramatic upward trajectory in its impact factor.

I believe the introduction of special issues (replacing the BAM Annual Conference Issue) was one of the major factors that enabled the *BJM* to rapidly climb the SSCI league table. Several of these publications (most notably the 2001 special issue on the nature and purpose of management research) have been cited both frequently and widely, within and beyond the field of management studies per se, thus greatly strengthening the international profile and standing of the journal.

As noted at the outset, in the early days of my editorship the *BJM* averaged around 70–5 submissions per annum. However, by the time my term of office drew to a close (September 2006) this figure had more than doubled.[5] Understandably, this led to increasing pressures from Blackwells, the *BJM*'s publisher, and contributing authors to expand the number of printed pages per volume, pressures which my team and I resisted most strongly. As I explained elsewhere (Hodgkinson, 2005), holding constant the number of pages at a time of significantly increased submissions is one of the several key mechanisms for ensuring that the overall quality of the papers selected for publication continues to rise year-on-year. Again as explained in Hodgkinson (2005), the increasing number of manuscripts submitted enabled the editorial team to raise concomitantly first the methodological, and latterly the theoretical, rigour expected of articles selected for eventual publication, another factor that has undoubtedly contributed to the overall increase in the *BJM*'s standing over recent years.

Operational factors

The importance of having effective mechanisms to support the basic administration of the *BJM* was noted earlier. From my point of view the most important of these mechanisms was the various administrative support staff I employed during my eight-year term. As the journal expanded its operations, the role of the administrator developed accordingly, from one of basic clerical support in the initial processing and tracking of submitted manuscripts, to the management of all aspects of the editorial office, including the development of supporting electronic infrastructure and representing the journal at various academic conferences. In this connection, I was fortunate to procure the services of Liam Irwin. Appointed initially in a short-term clerical role, Liam rapidly developed the back-office support function of the journal's operations, using a range of software systems in readiness for the rapid growth in manuscript submissions that was to follow. He also played a vital support role in the implementation of the *BJM*'s internationalization strategy, not least by organizing a series of highly successful receptions over four successive years (2003–6) at the annual meetings of the AOM and ensuring a continuous presence on the *BJM* publisher's stand.

As various of the chapters in this volume demonstrate, the responsibilities and requisite skills associated with editorship are many and varied, from the setting up of an effective editorial board and manuscript-review process (chapters 5 and 7) to communicating with authors and guiding and supporting them (chapters 6 and 7), while seeking to balance the (potentially conflicting) recommendations of reviewers against the rights of authors to report their work in a manner that does not stifle unduly their own voice (chapters 12, 13, and 14), with due regard to the ethical dilemmas that can arise throughout the various stages of the decision process (chapter 9). Furthermore, authors and reviewers alike expect decisions to be made and communicated both fairly and expeditiously (chapters 6, 8, and 10). The failure to ensure that any one of these component tasks is undertaken with the utmost skill and dedication can potentially yield disastrous consequences. The development of an appropriate administration system is vital to ensuring that these tasks are undertaken efficiently and effectively. Throughout my period of office I was supported by a number of highly competent clerical staff, each of whom ensured that submitted manuscripts were processed as quickly as possible and oversaw the chasing of delinquent reviewers, and occasionally delinquent members of the editorial team (myself included), but Liam Irwin, having worked previously in an IT-operations environment with a strong customer-focussed ethos, offered unparalleled support and much of the *BJM*'s continuing success is down to his superior organizational capabilities, to say nothing of his dedication, loyalty, and commitment.

One other operational factor that needs to be mentioned before concluding this discussion is the role played by the *BJM*'s publisher, Blackwells. Throughout my term, Blackwells played a major role on two fronts:

- ensuring the journal was produced to a high standard and that it appeared on time;
- ensuring an increase in awareness of the journal and sales overseas, especially sales to leading North America academic libraries

A series of marketing campaigns targeted at opinion leaders in top North American business schools was launched over successive years to reinforce the messages sent out at the *BJM* receptions and meet the editors' sessions at the Annual Academy Meetings. Raising the visibility of the journal in this way was a primary mechanism for attracting higher quality international authors, editorial board members and ad hoc reviewers. In addition, within my term of office, Blackwell Publishers:

- introduced a number of electronic systems to support the production and distribution of the journal,
- played a major role in the redesign of journal's image, and
- increased substantially its financial package to support the work of the editorial team

Undoubtedly, the nature and level of support offered by Blackwell in all of the above respects was enhanced by virtue of BAM's policy to offer publication of the *BJM* to competitive tender from time-to-time. Within my term of office the contract came up for renewal twice and on both occasions BAM was able to enhance significantly its business arrangements, thereby creating much-needed additional resources to further its wider strategic goals.

Conclusions and implications

In this chapter, I have outlined what I consider to be the crucial factors that enabled the *BJM* to improve its competitive position as an internationally ranked scholarly journal in the field of business and management studies. Moving from the particulars of the *BJM* case, I believe that it is possible to distil a number of generic lessons for editors and would-be editors of good quality journals more generally in this diverse and eclectic interdisciplinary field, as follows:

Requirements for editorship

Before embarking on a major editorial role, consider carefully the personal and communal motivations for undertaking such a role. In taking the responsibilities of editorship seriously, what additional opportunities will this role preclude? For example, to what extent and in what ways will editorship impact on the individual's personal research and scholarship? To what extent will this role enhance or detract from the realization of their longer-term career goals and aspirations? At the communal level candidates for editorship need to consider the extent to which the journal in question has the potential for further development under their stewardship and the extent to which they are in a position to assemble the necessary team to fulfil that potential, bearing in mind the potential costs and benefits to their personal reputation and that of their sponsoring institution.

Strategic requirements

All successful scholarly journals, regardless of whether they are general management journals such as the *BJM* or of a more specialist nature, enjoy a distinctive identity and occupy a clear niche in the marketplace. Hence successful editors and their teams must be capable of articulating and communicating a clear vision of what it is that they are seeking to accomplish for their journals. In my own case, my aim was to help enable the *BJM* to occupy a premier position as a general management journal covering the full spectrum of subfields but favouring, for publication, pieces that transcended the component subfields to make a discernible contribution to theory development and testing, and with an eye also to practice wherever possible (cf. Anderson, Herriot, & Hodgkinson, 2001; Hodgkinson, Herriot, & Anderson, 2001). Open to a wide range of perspectives and methods from both the USA and European traditions, my ultimate ambition for the journal was to see it gain recognition internationally for publishing from around the globe the best possible work consistent with this vision.

Successful academic journal editors champion relentlessly theoretical and methodological rigour. For the *BJM* to become ranked among an elite group of internationally recognized peer reviewed journals operating out of Europe, it needed to strengthen its offerings in both of these respects. In taking the *BJM* forward, a prime requirement was to ensure that in keeping with its main competitors, articles published addressed issues from a strong theoretical base, i.e. empirical articles reported studies using theory to explain managerial and organizational phenomena and ideally considered the implications of findings for theory development and that nonempirical articles made a substantial contribution to theory development, not just providing a summary of the extant literature. In methodological terms it was paramount that the methods adopted were appropriate to the research question(s) addressed, and irrespective of whether those methods were quantitative or qualitative they had to be executed rigorously. Inevitably, the enactment of this strategy entailed a difficult balancing act, but by no means impossible, as borne out by the quality improvements and rising standing of the journal evidenced above.

Operational requirements

At the operational level aspiring editors need to consider the extent to which the enabling administrative infrastructure is already in place or needs to be developed in order to support the enactment of their strategic vision for the journal in question. As we have seen, in the case of the *BJM* strong support mechanisms were already well-developed – through BAM, the learned society under which auspices the *BJM* is published – and these were further strengthened through the procurement of additional resources from the journal's professional publisher, made possible by operating the market mechanism of competitive tendering. In the case of the *BJM*, the backing of an internationally recognized academic publisher and a strong learned society are undoubtedly two of the most important operational factors that enabled the extension of its international reach, thereby realizing its core strategic objectives.

No less important are the teams of day-to-day support staff at both the editorial office and publishers who ensure the smooth running of all aspects of a journal's operations, from the processing of manuscripts to final production and the marketing campaigns underpinning its competitive positioning strategy. As observed above, the *BJM* has been most fortunate in all of these respects. Throughout my period of office I was equally fortunate to have the backing of a strong editorial team that was wholly committed to the service model and strategic vision I have articulated, and in this chapter editorial board and ad hoc reviewers who for the most part delivered high-quality reviews of manuscripts on a timely basis.

In the final analysis, the successful operation of any journal requires the support and enthusiasm of a diverse array of accomplished and committed colleagues. Serving in both strategic and operational capacities, they are its lifeblood.

Acknowledgment

The financial support of the UK ESRC/EPSRC Advanced Institute of Management (AIM) Research in the preparation of this chapter (under grant number RES-331-25-0028) is gratefully acknowledged.

Notes

1. As discussed later, the number of submissions more than doubled under my editorship and the rejection rate rose from roughly 50 percent to well over 90 percent, two of a number of indicators that the strategy I evolved with my team to improve further the *BJM*'s standing was successful.

2. As events transpired, I was persuaded by the BAM Council to continue my role for a further three-year term. This was made possible, in part, through the award of a senior fellowship of the Economic & Social Research Council/Engineering & Physical Sciences Research Council's Advanced Institute of Management (AIM) Research, which enabled me to extend my term as part of my contribution to AIM's capacity building agenda, in conjunction with BAM.
3. However imperfect, impact factors provide a broad indication of the extent to which the articles typically published are being cited in the listed journals, widely regarded as the core journals of the field. Alternative metrics (e.g. peer evaluations by panels of leading researchers and the number of times articles are downloaded within a finite period) are in any case typically highly correlated positively with impact factor rankings (see, e.g., Brody, Harned, & Carr, 2006; Geary, Marriott, & Rowlinson, 2004; Perneger, 2004). The SSCI is thus a useful objective barometer against which to adjudge the overall standing of a journal and in this connection it is clear that the *BJM*'s entry to this database is an indication that the journal has risen in standing over recent years.
4. The corresponding figure for 2005, the most recent figures available at the time of writing this chapter, was 93.5 percent.
5. In 2005, the most recent year for which complete figures were available at the time of writing this chapter, the number of regular articles (including research notes) submitted was 156. As my term of office drew to a close (September 2006) 158 manuscripts had already been submitted, with a further three-month period remaining to the year-end.

References

Anderson, N., Herriot, P., & Hodgkinson, G. P. (2001). The practitioner-researcher divide in industrial, work and organizational (IWO) psychology: Where are we now and where do we go from here? *Journal of Occupational and Organizational Psychology*, 74, 391–411.

Brody, T., Harnad, S., & Carr, L. (2006). Earlier web usage statistics as predictors of later citation impact. *Journal of the American Society for Information Science and Technology*, 57, 1060–72.

Geary, J., Marriott, L., & Rowlinson, M. (2004). Journal rankings in business and management and the 2001 Research Assessment Exercise in the UK. *British Journal of Management*, 15, 95–141.

Hodgkinson, G. P. (1999). Editorial. *British Journal of Management*, 10, 1–3.

Hodgkinson, G. P. (2005). Editorial. *British Journal of Management*, 16, 1–3.

Hodgkinson, G. P., Herriot, P., & Anderson, N. (2001). Re-aligning the stakeholders in management research: Lessons from industrial, work and organizational psychology. *British Journal of Management*, 12 (Special Issue), S41–S48.

Martinko, M. J., Douglas, S. C., & Harvey, P. (2006). Attribution theory in industrial and organizational psychology: A review. In G. P. Hodgkinson & J. K. Ford (Eds.), *International Review of Industrial and Organizational Psychology – Volume 21* (pp. 127–87). Chichester, UK: Wiley.

Perneger, T. V. (2004). Relation between online 'hit counts' and subsequent research citations: Prospective study of research papers in the *BMJ*. *British Medical Journal*, 329, 546–7.

12
The Developmental Editor: Assessing and Directing Manuscript Contribution

Donald D. Bergh

Making sense of a submission's contribution is oftentimes the dominant issue in a publication decision. However, contribution is often perceived as subjective and prone to disagreement between authors, reviewers, and editors. Fortunately, contribution has objective properties that once identified can help focus attention and resources toward the same objective. This chapter presents a process and logic to help capture contribution and provide direction for its development.

Before I present my thoughts on contribution, it is important to disclose that I advocate the 'active editor' model. Overall, the editor has a stake in the dissemination of knowledge in the field, an opportunity that requires an engagement in the review process. In addition, reviewers probe the nooks and crannies of manuscripts and may miss the larger perspective necessary to balance out the strengths and weaknesses of a particular manuscript's advance. An active editor can work with authors and reviewers to position manuscripts within appropriate conversations and more fully develop knowledge within the field. A manuscript's contribution depends on recognition by members of the field, and editors can help develop that advance by assisting authors in revising their manuscripts so they have the highest likely degree of influence and impact.

In general terms, this active editor is a manager of two jobs. One, s/he manages an evaluation system that leads to a publication decision. Two, the editor guides manuscript evolution, regardless of the outcome (s/he can provide suggestions for how the authors can further develop their manuscript, perhaps where to submit elsewhere, and can guide the dialogue and negotiation between authors and reviewers). The editor is in a unique position (not some mega-reviewer), and can create value by focusing authors and reviewers on the sources, types, and boundaries of a manuscript's primary contribution. Put simply, the editor becomes a partner in the development of knowledge.

Learning how to manage contribution development can be a trial by fire process and the potential of error is a source of serious concern. I experimented with different contribution-capturing models that would help improve publication decisions and provide useful guidance to authors and reviewers. After several iterations, I arrived at a process and typology that helped reduce a complex and subjective matter to a simplistic framework. Other editors certainly have alternative models and I encourage the reader to find the one that best guides his/her thinking.

When I read a submission, I use a process that concentrates on three dimensions of contribution: Origin, Type, and Development. My editing experience is mostly with *empirical* manuscripts, though many of the observations pertain to conceptual ones as well.

Contribution origin

The first step is to identify the contribution and its origin. This is a bit like a treasure hunt. I normally pay little attention to the overall language used; my feeling is that the language, grammar and paragraph structure and organization can be changed. What matters more is honing in on what is new and valuable in terms of motivation, theory, topic, and evidence. The questions that tend to guide me are: What is the defined contribution, and what is its proposed value? What is the structure of the model? I draw a picture of the theoretical model and try to understand what is new about it. Next, is the evidence as presented the basis for new knowledge about a topic, behavior or theory? Is it clear how that contribution adds to understanding?

I carefully go through the manuscript evaluating the research question, theoretical model, research methodology, and overall conclusions to see what is unique, rare, and valuable. In this way, the paper is viewed as competing in a marketplace of ideas (see Bergh, 2003, for additional explanation). Authors are typically up-front about what they think the contributions of their manuscripts are and specify them in the introduction and discussion sections. The order of points made in the discussion is typically a good hint as to the importance the author(s) pay(s) to the intended contributions. This Origin stage is not the time to look for reasons that lead to an editorial decision. Rather, what is/are the author(s) trying to offer our field? (I also look to see if the author(s) might have downplayed or missed something.)

The objective is to describe fully the intended contribution and where it comes from, whether in terms of a new theory, concept, argument, measure, sample, level of analysis, analytical method, or finding. The reviewer comments play a big role in this stage of the process, but I save their remarks until after my own evaluation.

Contribution type

The next step classifies the type of advance; I created a matrix to help guide my thinking here. This matrix has two dimensions; one for theory and one for topic. This 2 x 2 model (Table 12.1) helps me characterize the

Table 12.1 Contribution typology

Topic \ Theory	
New Theory and New Topic (1)	Current Theory and New Topic (2)
Strengths: raise new research questions, open new fields; change the way we think about a theory and topic;	Strengths: test viability of perspectives, develop knowledge and understanding, logic is conventional;
Weaknesses: requires new thinking, risky, the liability of newness.	Weaknesses: novelty and impact. Does testing an existing theory open up new insights?
New Theory and Current Topic (3)	Current Theory and Current Topic (4)
Strengths: Topic is accepted, importance may be sufficient for justifying research, cumulative development of knowledge on topic;	Strengths: Provides replication potential, test viability of methodological differences, provides confirmation of logic and topic;
Weaknesses: New theory may overlap with others, may be resistance to new theory.	Weaknesses: May not open new insights or research arenas. May be seen as a redundant contribution.

theoretical contribution and the advance for the topic. The essence of this stage is to categorize the proposed advance and make sense of what the manuscript is trying to offer.

The vertical axis is Topic; the top boxes being New and bottom boxes being Current. The horizontal axis is Theory, with the left-hand column being New and the right-hand column being Current.

1. **New Theory and New Topic quadrant** (upper left hand, #1): These contributions add to or revise existing theoretical logic and present different evidence on a topical area. The motivation for the research questions tends to focus on limitations in explanations and deficiencies in knowledge about the topic. The theoretical models contain new concepts, models, logic, or perhaps an extended framework. They have new hypotheses. One acid test is the structure and content of the model; are the concepts and the logic an existing perspective or are they new? What is the theoretical basis for the extension or revision? The methodology tends to capture new behaviors, organizational types or constructs that reflect different aspects of an existing topic. The discussion section explains how the findings add to theoretical explanations and knowledge of the topic. These manuscripts offer several strengths: they tend to raise new research questions, guide development of subsequent research, and can change the way we think about a theory and topic. But, these

manuscripts are also risky, require new ways of thinking, and suffer from liabilities of newness.

2. **Current Theory and New Topic quadrant** (upper right hand, #2): These advances apply existing theoretical logic to a new topic or unstudied behavior. Typically, the manuscripts take theoretical arguments that have appeared elsewhere and import them as the basis for the hypotheses. Thus, the underlying reasoning is not new. The methodology usually serves as the basis for the contribution; so the focus is on whether the empirical model adds clarity or development to the knowledge base of the topic. A common example is a manuscript that tests a relationship with pooled cross-sectional longitudinal data when other studies used single-year cross-sectional data. Many of these manuscripts are motivated by a gap in empirical findings of a topic and propose adding a different variable or sample of firms as adding new knowledge. The concern is whether the empirical contribution is significant or another pebble on a pile of rocks. Also, one wonders whether the empirical findings might reveal new insights into a taken-for-granted assumption in the theoretical model. Might the authors be able to use the findings to revise the theory and reposition this paper toward the first quadrant? The strengths of these manuscripts include: testing the viability of perspectives, helping develop knowledge and understanding of existing topic, and providing further insights into conventional logic. The weaknesses concern novelty and impact. Does testing an existing theory produce new insights?

3. **New Theory and Current Topic quadrant** (lower left hand, #3): These manuscripts involve a new model or the importation of a theory from another field to help explain a current topic. They tend to use a new theory to raise different questions and insights. But, the challenge for the author, reviewers, and editors becomes one of defining whether the proposed contribution is different and meaningful from others that currently exist. Manuscripts in this cell tend to add another explanation but one that does not add new knowledge to the topical area or relationship. For example, a theoretical model can be developed from the marriage literature that might provide insights into the management of relationships among acquired and acquiring companies. Unfortunately, many of the concepts that exist in the two literatures are nearly identical, as are the empirical findings. The reviewer and editor might be intrigued by a proposed new perspective, but then become concerned when the same or highly-similar predictions already exist. Key questions center on whether the new theory advances our explanations of the topic and phenomenon, and what becomes clearer or more developed as a result of the new model? The strengths of these contributions include the importance of the topic, which may be sufficient for justifying research and adding to knowledge on the topic. Weaknesses include an overlap of theory with existing logic and whether there might be resistance to the new perspective and its proposed insights.

4. **Current Theory and Current Topic quadrant** (lower right hand, #4): These advances often have an incremental nature, as they typically apply existing logic to a topical question that has already been examined. The manuscripts may include replications with new data, test existing logic in a different context (e.g., the behavior in a different country) or may try to demonstrate a different methodological approach. The logic is typically not new, or the proposed methodological novelties are of such a nature as to represent minor incremental advances at best. The research question is generally one that has already been studied, perhaps not as specifically as offered in the current paper. The challenge with these types of contributions is to reflect on whether the methodology might uncover new aspects and nuances of the theory. Perhaps the theory might lead to a positive and linear relationship, but additional testing might demonstrate a curvilinear relationship. One book worth its weight in gold for uncovering second-order relationships is Aiken and West (1991). The strengths of these contributions are that they test the viability of methodological alternatives, as well as provide confirmation of extant logic and topics. Weaknesses include not opening new insights or research arenas and may be criticized as a redundant contribution.

Overall, the framework helps guide one's thinking to the type of contribution that a manuscript presents and also helps one think about what changes would be necessary to reposition a manuscript to a different cell in order to fit with the overall mission of the journal. For example, journals such as the *Academy of Management Journal* (*AMJ*) specifically require both a theoretical and empirical advance, so manuscripts need to have the potential to be a quadrant #1 article in order to progress through the review process at that outlet. But, not all journals require those qualities. The field benefits from articles that fall into the other categories, as each serves an important purpose. Those that test existing theory to provide insights into a new topic or behavior help further develop empirical knowledge (quadrant #2). Articles that offer new theoretical insights into an existing behavior (quadrant #3) serve an important role by describing new dimensions or by developing new concepts and relationships. Finally, articles that apply current theories to current topics contribute by testing replication potential. Considered collectively, all four types of contributions are needed for a strong foundation of understanding and knowledge.

Once a manuscript's contribution has been profiled, it is instructive to turn to the reviewer's comments to see what they thought about it. Their observations provide an insightful basis for assessing whether the contribution had been defined correctly and completely. They tend to identify the bricks and mortar of the foundation of the advance, and, with your own view as the editor, create a comprehensive understanding of what the contribution is and what it means. Also, considering their assessments after deriving ones of your own preserves your independence as a decision maker. Note that some reviewers only point out limitations and flaws. Their comments may support an editorial decision but not help much with directing the manuscript's contribution.

It is helpful at this stage for the editor to "see the forest and not just the trees." The active editor can help direct the contribution by recognizing the type of concerns the reviewers provide and reconcile them with a generalized framework that helps define the overall contribution type. Bridging levels of concerns and directing development is an important way that editors contribute to improving the quality of the submissions to his or her journal.

Contribution development

This final step is oftentimes neglected. By this point, an editor has identified the manuscript's intended contribution, its source and how its type fits the journal's mission. The editor may have made sense of the reviewers' reports and is now eager to finish up the review process. Despite this momentum, editors are encouraged to go another step to identify a developmental path that will move forward the manuscript's contribution. Doing so helps identify those contributions that might be 'diamonds in the rough' that would otherwise be rejected. In addition, the feedback creates goodwill for the journal by making the authors feel that their submission has some hope while helping to educate reviewers to think in developmental ways rather than just looking for flaws and shortcomings.

Developing a contribution requires hard work, creativity, and some negotiation. For example, a review process described in some recent (2006) From the editors' articles shows how the authors and reviewers worked diligently to develop the paper to the level where it achieved the prestigious Best Article Award (Agarwal, Echambadi, Franco, & Sarkar, 2006; Bergh, 2006). This process involved open-minded authors and reviewers, all of whom worked hard and cooperatively to improve the manuscript.

The creative aspect entails considering how the manuscript can be made as interesting as possible. First, I assess the research question using Davis's (1971) classic article on whether the manuscript is offering an interesting contribution. In addition, some articles published in a recent *AMJ* forum titled "What Makes Management Research Interesting, and Why Does it Matter?" provide an excellent foundation for assessing the interesting coefficient (see Barley, 2006; Bartunek, Rynes, & Ireland, 2006; Dutton and Dukerich, 2006). I also use Sara Rynes' (2002) suggestions about assessing contribution and how it can be improved. The goal is to identify ways in which a manuscript can be repositioned to make the most unique advance possible.

Second, I evaluate the structure and content of the theoretical model using the frameworks from Whetten (1989) and Kilduff (2006). Both provide guidelines that can put authors on paths to engineer the conceptual models in the manuscripts, the underlying engines of a strong contribution. In addition, these readings identify barriers that limit a manuscript's theoretical advance. I compare their requirements of good theory with what I see in a submission and try to offer some specific thoughts that can help the authors bridge the differences.

Third, the manuscript's study can be a gold mine of ideas for developing its value-added. For instance, the correlations might suggest an alternative model that has not been tested and might represent an additional explanation that might be added to the conceptual model. In addition, what other variables would extend the proposed theory? For example, would including an implications variable offer a more comprehensive test of the proposed theory? How about a moderator or mediator? Ask whether there is more that can be squeezed out of the data. You might be surprised.

Finally, the discussion section needs to provide a clear and concise narrative on what is new about the manuscript, why that addition is important (justification), and a demonstration of what it adds to explanations and/or knowledge. Many authors repeat their findings without considering what those mean for extending understanding. The editor can help by suggesting that they identify the most important merits of their findings and then provide a rationale for what they offer, such as explanations of the phenomenon and what we did not know before the study was conducted.

Implications for authors

I have several recommendations for authors. First, the contribution of your manuscript should be obvious and involve no guesswork. Similar to a political debate, do not let your opponent (e.g., the reviewers) define you and your position. You have an opportunity to shape what the reviewers will think about your manuscript's advance and I strongly advise you to focus on what you are trying to contribute. Take the initiative, be as clear as possible, but beware of overselling. A manuscript that defines and justifies its contribution creates a positive first impression and encourages a reviewer to become constructively engaged.

Some ways to do this are to read the introduction sections of award-winning articles to see how the authors defined and positioned their article's advances. Also, evaluate the contribution relative to Davis's (1971) "That's Interesting" typology. Take a positive view of the literature and carefully explain what you are adding to it.

Second, critically evaluate the discussion section of your manuscript. Does it explain what is new and valuable about your findings? Does it justify the importance of the contribution? I do not believe that there is a magic formula that a discussion has to have, but there are some necessary ingredients: it must define the contribution, demonstrate how the advance builds upon previous knowledge or explanations, clarify its boundaries (e.g., strengths and limitations), develop its application and justify its overall value. I sometimes read the discussion section first when I get a submission in order to get a sense of what authors think their findings offer and mean. It is my belief that a strong and compelling discussion can stand alone and convey the contribution and its value.

Third, an important signal of the quality of a contribution is to consider the suggestions for further study. One way an author can convince the reviewers that their manuscript makes an important advance is by linking their study's findings or arguments with new research questions and areas for further study. I sense that many authors treat this almost as an afterthought. But, it is an important indicant of the quality and characteristics of a contribution. The new paths for further development illustrate not only how a manuscript extends or revises prior knowledge but also where we should go from there. Whether a contribution can produce new ideas, concepts, and directions is an important litmus test of the overall value of that proposed advance.

Implications for prospective editors

Editing is a contact sport. It requires that editors become engaged and involved in the review process. It involves an appreciation of conflicting perspectives. It also entails adopting a broader viewpoint of serving a journal. These different orientations create significant challenges. I have some suggestions for how editors can navigate the publication review process.

First, avoid taking sides. Be even, fair, and unemotional to authors and reviewers. Both can interpret issues quite differently and the rhetoric can escalate. Recognize that areas of disagreement can become resolved through guidance, transparency, and development. Focus on issue identification and explanation. By not taking sides and explaining decisions in terms of issue resolution, you can make more rational decisions and ones that feel like the right ones.

Second, most submitted manuscripts are works in progress. Because we have social-science methodologies and theories, we have no perfect studies or manuscripts. Issues and problems exist in all submissions. The net result is the creation of uncertainty in the editorial publication decision. My advice is for editors to ask for revisions when a contribution has promise yet they are uncertain about whether it can be realized. Some manuscripts are submitted so prematurely that resolving the issues will likely produce an altogether different manuscript. Others have fewer concerns, but the reviewers do not have clear consensus. Alternatively, reviewers may offer opposing recommendations and opinions, and they may key on different issues altogether. When in doubt, ask for a revision. You can always say "no" when you have more complete information. But, you cannot say "yes" later, after you reject the manuscript.

Third, concerns have different weighting and priority. An important task for an editor is to sort out the problems and prioritize them. Also, there are some matters that cannot be resolved and we have to decide whether we can live with them or not. I suggest asking whether the overall contribution is significant enough to justify accepting the problems and limitations that coexist. This is a trade-off; managing idealism and reality. It is important that editors publish the work that meets their journal's mission and vision and that they worry less about the unattainable goal of publishing the best work ever done in the history of the field.

Some revision processes are akin to an elimination activity; concerns are raised and addressed through iterations between authors and reviewers. At some point, the editor decides whether enough progress has been made and whether to accept or reject the submission. That model can take a long time to complete and the eventual manuscript may reflect the reviewers' thoughts just as much as the authors. An alternative approach is to concentrate on the most salient matters and give the authors a revision or two to see if they can resolve the problems. Once accepted, the less serious concerns can be left for the authors. Most will make an effort to alleviate those additional matters.

Finally, consider the potential contribution of the manuscript. Is there more that it can try to accomplish? Is there any difference between what the manuscript is currently proposing and what it might be able to realize worth the additional work? For example, would adding another concept to the model provide a significantly improved contribution? Also, consider what barriers exist to the realization of the proposed advance. Is there a need for more theoretical argumentation? Is another variable needed? It is my experience that authors frequently submit narrowly defined manuscripts that could be strengthened considerably through broadening their models and data. These enhanced manuscripts usually fare better in the market of ideas than those that offer smaller overall advances (Bergh, Perry, & Hanke, 2006).

Summary

Overall, I have several suggestions for all involved in the editorial review process. First, it is important that all members divest themselves of attachments to personal rights and view the manuscript as an independent entity. Similarly, having open-minded authors and reviewers can facilitate creativity and innovation that is necessary to move forward the field. Second, editing is more than word-scrubbing or tallying polls of reviewer recommendations. It also carries the responsibility of participating in the conversations in the field. This added task requires an active and engaged editor who makes the effort to assess and develop contributions. Third, identify both the current and potential levels of a manuscript's contribution. From my experience, almost every manuscript can be further improved as a result of the interaction between reviewers and authors. The editor's role in managing the communication process is critically important. Finally, the match between a manuscript's type of contribution and the mission/vision of the journal can be an evolving process. Look for ways the manuscript can be revised to make the type of contribution that is important for your outlet. The challenge is to identify the content and bounds of a proposed advance and then direct the author to pursue the appropriate outlet. Helping an author succeed with their manuscript, whether it is in your journal or not, is a powerful reward and makes all of the hard work and devoted time well worth the investment.

References

Aiken, L. S., & West, S. G. (1991). *Multiple regression: Testing and interpreting interactions.* Sage: Thousand Oaks, CA.

Agarwal, R., Echambadi, R., Franco, A., & Sarkar, M. (2006). REAP rewards: Maximizing benefits from reviewer comments. *Academy of Management Journal*, 49: 191–6.

Barley, S. (2006). When I write my masterpiece: Thoughts on what makes a paper interesting. *Academy of Management Journal*, 49: 16–20.

Bartunek, J., Rynes, S., & Ireland, R. D. (2006). What makes management research interesting, and why does it matter? *Academy of Management Journal*, 49: 9–15.

Bergh, D. D. (2006). Editing the 2004 *AMJ* best article award winner. *Academy of Management Journal*, 49: 197–202.

Bergh, D. D. (2003). From the editors: Thinking strategically about contribution. *Academy of Management Journal*, 46: 135–6.

Bergh, D. D., Perry, J., & Hanke, R. (2006). Some predictors of *SMJ* article impact. *Strategic Management Journal*, 27: 81–100.

Davis, M. S. (1971). That's interesting! Towards a phenomenology of sociology and a sociology of phenomenology. *Philosophy of the Social Sciences*, 1: 309–44.

Dutton, J., & Dukerich, J. (2006). The relational foundation of research: An under-appreciated dimension of interesting research. *Academy of Management Journal*, 49: 21–6.

Kilduff, M. (2006). Editor's comments: Publishing theory. *Academy of Management Review*, 31: 252–5.

Rynes, S. (2002). From the editors: Some reflections on contribution. *Academy of Management Journal*, 45: 311–13.

Whetten, D. (1989). What constitutes a theoretical contribution? *Academy of Management Review*, 14: 490–5.

13
The Case for an Activist Editorial Model

Jerry A. Jacobs

We have all heard complaints about the journal review process. One common grievance is about a reject decision after multiple rounds of review. "My paper was under review at that journal for three rounds of reviews stretching out over two years before it was finally rejected. It was nearly enough to make me want to hit the bottle." A more frequent, if somewhat less exasperating, refrain from authors is the lack of clarity in how to respond to reviews. "I received four reviews from the journal. The comments were mostly thoughtful but they led in many different directions. Unfortunately, the editor provided no guidance in how best to address these comments." The question I pose in this essay is whether these experiences are inevitable or whether there are editorial models which reduce the likelihood of these and other problematic situations.

The peer review process serves at least two functions: a) to help select among the many manuscripts submitted; and b) to suggest improvements to authors. In this essay I would like to focus on the second of these functions, namely offering constructive advice in the context of a decision to invite the authors to "revise and resubmit" (R&R). I outline a model in which the R&R decision is central to the editorial process. In this approach, the editor plays an active role in guiding the manuscript through the process of revision. Among the goals of this model is the reduction of the number of unsuccessful revisions. I also discuss additional revisions that may be suggested at a second decision point, namely the "conditional accept" stage.

Revisions are ubiquitous

As a practical matter, editors rarely accept a paper on its initial submission. In the three years that I served as editor of the *American Sociological Review* (*ASR*), I accepted one paper after the first round of review out of more than 1,250 new submissions, and even in this case the acceptance was conditional on a number of suggested revisions.

Papers typically arrive in less than perfect shape. Problems range from the need to improve the conceptual clarity of the paper to questions about the data, questions about whether the analyses presented fully match the theoretical claims, gaps in the presentation, and so on.

Why do papers need revision? In some cases it is due to the pressures on our system of careers. Assistant professors find themselves under tremendous pressure to publish. Indeed, publications by graduate students are now the norm among those competing for the most sought-after positions. Less-than-perfect submissions, then, can be understood as a by-product of the pressure to fill out curricula vitae.

But there is another, deeper reason, namely that cutting-edge work is by its nature uncertain. Authors may not fully apprehend the true nature of their innovations or the full implications of their findings. In ideal circumstances, the collective wisdom of editors and reviewers can help authors develop their contributions most effectively without overstating their claims.

A final consideration is that the social sciences are characterized by multiple and competing paradigms, and that successfully addressing disparate audiences is a fundamentally challenging endeavor.

As a general rule, I suspect that the more ambitious the paper, the more fundamental the contribution, the more likely that revisions can be helpful. In other words, straightforward research reports are less likely to require as much time and energy to revise as papers that are more ambitious conceptually and empirically.

In my experience, manuscripts may warrant an R&R decision in four situations:

a) the paper has promise but there are various concerns about the presentation and the evidence presented;
b) there are questions about whether the central claims of the paper are adequately supported;
c) there are conceptual ambiguities which need to be resolved before the paper can be published; and
d) the paper is basically acceptable, but there is room for a variety of improvements.

In some cases, the revision process is really about whether the paper can overcome certain challenges. Can the author really more effectively prove the central point? Can the argument succeed at the conceptual level? The course of the revision process will depend on the nature of the issues that need to be addressed.

In a relatively small number of cases, while papers are publishable as submitted, reviewers with expertise in the subject matter at hand are often in a position to suggest a variety of substantive enhancements, large and small. These may include the correction of factually inaccurate statements and the incorporation of neglected references, or they may represent conceptual or methodological improvements. An editor may feel that the author is likely to take the opportunity to revise more seriously with an R&R decision, where the final acceptance of the paper remains uncertain, than with a "conditional accept" decision. Thus, an R&R decision can serve as insurance against an author who might resist requests for further work once the paper has been accepted. In a small number of cases, then, an editor may opt for an R&R decision even when the paper makes a significant scholarly contribution in its current state.

The first R&R as the key decision point

In the editorial model I am suggesting, the first R&R decision is the key decision point. In this approach, the editor reads the paper and the reviews carefully at this stage before making a decision. The editor should be satisfied that the reviews are informative, cover the main issues, and are not limited to one aspect of the paper or one angle of vision. The editor provides detailed advice on what is expected in a revised paper. The goal is to minimize false positives, that is, encouraging authors to revise papers that ultimately will be rejected. Having one's paper rejected, after revisions have been undertaken, is painful for authors. It also takes up a lot of scholar's time, can generate substantially more work for reviewers who are asked to assess multiple revisions, and can considerably delay the eventual publication of a paper.

The other advantage to this approach is to maximize the chances of publishing significant contributions. As a result of a careful review at the R&R stage, the editor is likely to see more clearly what the potential of the paper is likely to be and will also get a sense of how best to advise authors. In other words, this approach benefits the journal as well as reducing the risks to the authors.

It may be useful to contrast this approach to other ways of managing the review process. As an author, I have received decision letters from editors with very little guidance other than that indicated in the reviews. Unfortunately, this approach is quite common. It no doubt reflects the time pressures faced by editors, resulting from the constant flow of manuscripts across their desks. The problem with this approach is that authors are often uncertain about how to proceed. As I discuss in more detail below, it is not uncommon for reviews to disagree on many key points. The lack of clarity from the editor can lead to extra time, extra guess work and, in many cases, unsuccessful revisions.

Another way that my approach differs from common practice is that I often did not solicit a second round of reviews. There are many potential issues that can arise in a second round of reviews. Sometimes one or more of the original reviewers is unavailable. Sometimes new reviewers raise entirely new sets of concerns. A second round of reviews inevitably delays the decision for at least a month and often much longer. In my approach, if I had studied the paper and the first set of reviews carefully, if I had a clear vision of what the contribution of the paper is, or could be, and what I am expecting a revised paper to look like, I was usually in a position to assess whether the revisions have been successful. I sometimes solicited a prompt second opinion from a deputy editor, but this would often be on an expedited schedule. If the revisions seemed to me unsatisfactory or superficial, I would often solicit one or more reviews in order to help justify the decision to the authors.

I came to this approach fairly quickly in my term as editor, based, in part, on my prior dealings with editors and, in part, on mistakes I made early on. For example, there was an occasion in which I commissioned an R&R without reading the paper carefully enough at first submission. The result was that I discovered serious issues with the paper only after the revisions had arrived. I then found myself in a quandary: was I obligated to publish the paper because the authors had addressed the issues that had been raised by the revisions, even though I had serious qualms about the revised product? Had I read the paper more carefully at the R&R stage, it is likely that I would have noticed some of these problems earlier.

The difference in stance between the editor and the reviewer needs to be understood. The reviewers are trying to make a case for their particular understanding of the paper. They don't know what the editor might think, and they don't know who the other reviewers might be. The editor has a clear advantage in seeing a set of reviews so that he or she can weigh the common concerns as well as the issues raised in a more idiosyncratic way by individual readers. Thus, there is a difference between the role of a reviewer and the role of an editor in establishing the direction for the revisions.

Guiding the review process

Given the centrality of revisions to successful journal publication, the process of revision is one of the central academic dramas. What does the editor really expect? What issues need to be addressed head-on and which can be finessed? In my view, the more clarity that editors can provide, the more this process is likely to be constructive and the less likely that authors and reviewers would find themselves in intense conflict.

It is often the case that reviewers diverge in their assessment of a paper. Sometimes, it is not possible to follow the advice of all of the reviewers because disagreements between them on the value of the study are evident. An urgent concern here results when two or more reviewers feel the paper has considerable promise but disagree on the direction that the revisions should pursue. For example, one reviewer may see the key contribution as empirical while another reviewer feels that the central advance is more conceptual in nature. In other cases, all agree that the empirical contribution is key, but differ on what the key conclusions are and what features of the analysis should be highlighted. What is the poor author to do when confronted with such conflicting advice?

Some editors resolve the matter by urging the author to pay special attention to the comments of a particular reviewer. This kind of editorial intervention is certainly helpful in providing guidance to the author. My suggestion is that the editor (or a deputy editor) write a letter outlining the key issues that need to be resolved. An editorial letter outlining a specific roadmap for the author to follow in revising the paper draws on the reviewers' concerns but often raises additional issues that may be seen from an editorial vantage point. I ask questions about issues that don't make sense to me. I point out gaps in the argument, additional analyses that might be useful, and stylistic suggestions that seem appropriate. I feel that I can stand for the general reader, and whatever I might lack in detailed knowledge of the author's specialty area I make up in experience in reading a wide range of papers.

The goal is to give the author a clear set of directions for revising. This does not mean that the author is obligated to write the paper that I would like to see written. It is often the case that authors respond in a memo that they feel I am leading them astray on one or more points. But the more common reaction is appreciation for the careful reading of the paper. If my queries and suggestions are not always on target, more often than not, they highlight areas of ambiguity where more careful writing is in order.

Despite this editorial guidance, not all authors successfully revise their papers. There is considerable variability in the ability of authors to apprehend the points being raised by the reviews and the editor and to respond to them effectively.

In my experience, disagreements about the conceptual framing of the paper are the most challenging issues. In most cases, there is a lack of precision in the manuscript that allows different readers to literally see different papers in the same manuscript. In some cases, this really represents the reviewer's desire that the author make a different point. It is difficult to discern what the empirical core of the paper should look like when there is uncertainty about the conceptual framing. Perhaps for this reason, papers requiring significant work on the conceptual issues are often at the highest risk for failing at the revision stage.

Careful reading of papers at the R&R stage takes a considerable amount of time. There are at least two ways to keep these demands under control. The first is to limit the number of R&R decisions. In the approach I am suggesting, an R&R decision represents a significant investment of time on the part of the editor, and a degree of commitment to the authors. The yield, or rate at which R&Rs are converted into actual publications, should be quite high. For example, there were 431 new manuscripts submitted to the *ASR* during 2004. I invited 56 R&Rs, for an R&R rate of 13 percent. Of these 56, 38 have been accepted and published, 11 were subsequently rejected, and seven had not been resubmitted when my term as editor ended. If you view 38/56 as the yield rate, the fraction is 68 percent of R&Rs that were eventually published. If you compare 38 accepts to 11 rejects, the yield is 38/49 or 78 percent. The overall acceptance rate was 38/431 or 9 percent.

Second, this task can be delegated to deputy editors. However, this requires willingness to delegate and availability of deputy editors with common vision. In some cases, I took the unusual approach of designating deputy editors for a single paper. In other words, an editorial board member (or simply a prominent scholar with expertise on the topics addressed in the manuscript) can be asked to synthesize the reviews and provide the author with an outline of the key revisions that need to be undertaken in order to successfully revise the paper. In one case, a "designated deputy" had recently edited a book on the topic in question. Sometimes I asked the reviewer with the clearest insights and most useful comments to write a synthesis of the reviews.

Edits at the conditional accept stage

I tried as often as possible to read the revised manuscript as soon as it arrived. Having read the manuscript closely at the R&R stage, and having weighed the comments of the reviewers, I generally had a good idea of what would constitute an acceptable revision. If the revision was acceptable, we would move to the conditional accept stage pronto. If there was some uncertainty about the verdict, I would solicit a second round of reviews.

I read the revised manuscript closely, and often had a number of suggestions (or requirements) for the third and final draft. These would be incorporated into a "conditional accept" letter. Since authors often received the conditional accept right after the revision was submitted, they were often happy to do one more round of polishing. The authors were often in a position to maintain their intense focus on the paper. Their revisions often went through several iterations, and my prompt feedback simply represented a final iteration in the evolution of the paper.

One issue frequently addressed at this stage is the length of the paper. At the R&R stage, I sometimes explicitly told authors not to worry about the length of the paper "for now." The concern here is that the author will guess wrong and cut out things that should be left in. In other cases, I explicitly advised the authors to lengthen the paper. This allowed me to see whether the substantive issues could all be addressed in one place at one time. It is far easier to suggest cuts in length once the substantive contributions of the paper are clear. Once the paper has been conditionally accepted, I tried to be as explicit as possible about the extent and the location of cuts.

Suggestions regarding the title of the paper are sometimes an issue at the conditional accept stage. Long, awkward and uninviting paper titles are all too common. Titles should make it clear what the paper is about, but succinct, inviting, and intriguing titles increase readers' interest in the journal. Again, recommendations regarding the title are most likely to be successful once the key contributions of the paper are fully established.

I often encouraged authors to write the most user-friendly abstracts possible. In other words, authors typically seek to explain the essential contributions of a paper in an abstract. However, it also makes sense to try to entice as many readers as possible with the abstract, which is likely to be read by many more people than the paper itself. Thus, there can be some tension between speaking precisely to an audience of specialists and speaking clearly to a wider audience of general readers. This tension may be more acute for a generalist journal such as *ASR*, but I suspect that the same issues are likely to arise for specialist journals as well.

The conditional accept stage is when I review the tables closely. Are there tables that could be condensed or eliminated? Are there too many figures? Are those that remain used to optimal effect? Again, these are issues of polishing the final draft that only make sense to address once the contributions of the paper have been established and the overall form of the paper is clear.

During my tenure as editor of *ASR*, we instituted the practice of making supplemental material available on the *ASR* website. The idea here is to make the articles more accessible to the general reader while still providing the detailed information needed by the specialist reader. Data appendices, supplemental tables and figures, and discussion of side issues can be made available to readers in an electronic form. This makes this material more accessible and more permanent than the traditional approach, where authors indicate that additional results are not shown but available from the author. We currently have a ten-page maximum length on website supplements so that authors are not tempted to use this as a space for dumping large quantities of unedited computer output.

Another standard item on my checklist at the conditional accept stage is examining the footnotes. It is common for papers to have too many long footnotes. In many cases this material can be incorporated into the text; in other cases the material can be eliminated.

I often encouraged an author to more fully develop one or two additional issues, typically in the conclusion. The goal is to invite the author to take their argument to the next level, to make the paper the best that it can be. These are sometimes couched as "suggestions" but in some cases they really are conditions. I have had occasion to go back and forth with an author more than once at the conditional accept stage over such issues.

This extra attention at the conditional accept stage means that the copy-editing stage should go smoothly. In other words, the tables and figures are largely set, the author has had the chance to read the paper over and to address matters of presentation and substance, and thus there is less justification for authors to rewrite the paper at the copyediting stage.

Objections considered

It may be helpful to consider several objections to this approach in order to clarify its strengths and potential pitfalls. The first possible objection is that an "activist" editorial model will result in overediting. One might suspect that the editor's ego can become involved in the process. There is always the risk that the editor will insist on the paper taking the form he or she prefers rather than the one that makes the most sense to the author.

While I certainly recognize this as a possibility, in the end I suspect that there may well be less editorial meddling in the activist approach than in a more laissez-faire model. One example comes to mind that is consistent with this reasoning. One paper had undergone two rounds of revisions before it arrived on my desk. At that point, the paper looked like it had been written by a committee. There had been three reviewers' comments plus deputy editor's comments on two rounds of revisions, and the authors had been at pains to try to satisfy all of these reviewers as best they could. I worked closely with the authors to streamline their argument. This example demonstrates how authors who are anxious to address every reviewers' concern may end up rewriting much more than is necessary or desirable. A clear editorial voice is likely to result in less editorial interference, not more. This is especially true if clarity at the R&R stage reduces the risk of second and third rounds of revisions.

The editor should not require that every manuscript be all things to all people. Editors have to have a clear sense of what is possible with the data at hand, how many issues can be covered in the space of one paper, what the authors are capable of doing, in short, to make sure that the perfect is not the enemy of the good. Clarity on these issues will likely result in clearer papers and less editing designed to satisfy all reviewers than is the case with a more minimalist editorial model.

A second possible concern is that setting the bar high at the R&R stage will result in discounting good papers. The argument here is that authors are entitled to the chance to revise if their paper holds promise. A variant of this objection is that the most ambitious papers often need the most revision, and too stringent a policy at the R&R stage will result in the publication of only the most routine research reports.

The intent of taking the R&R decision seriously is not to dismiss promising work but rather to increase the chances that this work will make its way to publication. Barring policy changes such as increasing the number of pages available to the journal, in the end the same number of papers will be published. The editor typically does not control the number of pages available, but he or she does have control over how many R&R decisions are made. The question is whether it is in the general interest to have many scholars revising papers and many reviewers re-reading these papers when the likelihood of publication is low. A tremendous amount of time and effort is put forth by scholars in revising their work and in reviewing revised papers. If too many of these are doomed to failure, then much of this work may be for naught.

Editors must, of course, be on the lookout for promising work that is not yet fully formed. But there is a danger here as well. It is often difficult to discern what the final product will look like when the first draft lacks theoretical clarity. Here again, I see virtue in an activist orientation. Indeed, papers requiring substantial work need an especially strong editorial hand. These are the papers that are most likely to provoke divergent reviews. In such situations, there is all the more reason for the editor to give the author a clear roadmap for revisions.

A more serious risk is that the editor might set the bar so high at the R&R stage that there are not enough papers remaining to fill the journal. Not all authors will revise their papers on a timely schedule; not all will be able to overcome the challenges laid out by the reviewers and the editor. It is unrealistic to shoot for a yield of 100, that is, a ratio of 1.00 between R&Rs and published papers. As noted above, in my experience, a yield of 2/3rds or 3/4ths is more realistic. Thus, the editor must make sure that enough R&Rs are commissioned to insure an adequate flow of papers.

A fourth concern is that this approach might takes too much of the editor's time. It is undoubtedly the case that reading papers closely at the R&R stage and providing detailed feedback to authors is a time-consuming endeavor. Some of this work can be delegated to deputy editors, but there are clearly limits to how much delegation is practical. On the other hand, getting stacks of revised papers that are not destined to succeed generates substantial work as well. Thus, the activist editorial model, while demanding, may not involve that much more work in the end than the more laissez-faire approach.

Conclusion

I have endeavored to make the case for an "activist" editorial model that focuses considerable time and attention on the initial decision to invite a revised version of the manuscript for consideration. I contrast this approach to a more laissez-faire or minimalist approach to editing.

The essay began with two common complaints from authors: one in which a paper is rejected after multiple rounds of review, and a second where the author is at sea with respect to the best way to address a variety of conflicting advice of variable quality. I maintain that clear and specific guidance from editors at the R&R stage is likely to reduce both of these common ailments in the peer review process.

I also suggest the virtues of a careful reading of the paper at the "conditional accept" stage, since many important matters of style and presentation can be enhanced at this stage in the process.

The editorial model suggested here is quite time intensive. The editor reads papers carefully at least twice. In order to pursue this approach, the editor needs sufficient release time from teaching. The editor needs to select deputy editors with same general vision regarding the importance of guiding the review process. Editors need a solid manuscript-tracking system and a strong staff so that they do not spend all of their time managing the review process. If editors can focus on key task of selecting papers with most potential and working with the authors to bring out the best in these papers, they will find the role to be richly rewarding.

14
Balancing Authorial Voice and Editorial Omniscience: The "It's My Paper and I'll Say What I Want To" versus "Ghostwriters in the Sky" Minuet

Arthur G. Bedeian

As its title indicates, the purpose of the present volume is to "open the black box of editorship." My concerns about the integrity of the manuscript-review process as practiced by the management discipline's leading journals are well documented. These concerns, as they relate to the review process as a means for judging the quality and, thus, the credibility of scientific papers submitted for publication have addressed the social construction of knowledge (Bedeian, 2004); the proper roles of editors, referees, and authors (Bedeian, 2003); and ghostwriting by editors and referees (Bedeian, 1996a & b). In the remarks that follow, I will briefly summarize a few of these concerns and extend my previous thoughts by commenting on reservations I have about how the review process has evolved over the past fifteen or so years and how it may be improved.

Self-management and peer review

One aspect of the manuscript-review process that has always struck me as unique is the degree of self-management that exists within academia. This self-management is, perhaps, no more evident than in the matters of tenure and the peer review of scientific manuscripts submitted for publication. As Biagioli (2002) notes, peer review (in particular) "sets academia apart from all other professions by constructing value through peer judgment, not market dynamics" (p. 11). Whereas most professions are subject to government regulations, certifications, and even audits, we in academia are, for the most part, exempt from such constraints. Rather, through peer review, we supposedly regulate ourselves by engaging in "a series of rational judgments and decisions" (p. 35). In effect, by construing value based on peer judgments and not market dynamics, we have elevated peer review, as a quality-control mechanism, to a special status.

As a consequence, much like the depersonalized economic marketplace, the scientific marketplace of ideas, as enshrined in peer review, is portrayed as a well-behaved and disciplined entity that ensures the public of good science. As every academic doubtless knows, the actual reality of peer review is starkly different. Indeed, the ideal image of peer review as an objective arbiter of scientific merit is, as argued by Biagioli (2002) and others, little more than ritualized fiction for gaining public confidence and, thus, guarding the autonomy and authority we enjoy as academics (Bedeian, 1997).

Ghostwriting

My initial concern with the reality of the manuscript-review process, and how it has evolved in recent years emanated, from my own experience as an author. In revising and resubmitting a manuscript for a special issue of one of our discipline's premier journals, I encountered a guest editor who strongly felt that I should incorporate material suggested by a referee, but with which I philosophically disagreed. In two exchanges, I expressed discomfort at having the material appear under my byline and (before the notion of "ghostwriting" had occurred to me) indicated that I felt I was caught in a situation of "reverse censorship," in that, I was being told that if I wished to have my manuscript published, I would have to include material which I found offensive. The guest editor responded with a fury, upset with the idea of being associated with any kind of censorship – reverse or otherwise. Not surprisingly, the revised manuscript (after two rounds of reviews) was summarily rejected.

Rejection is, of course, a common experience in academic writing. What I find disturbing (among other things) is that it has been estimated that one-third of the authors who have a manuscript rejected not only abandon the manuscript, but "the entire line of research on which it was based" (Belcher, 2006b, p. 1). This is unfortunate because data indicate that many Nobel Prize wining authors have had their award-winning work initially rejected (Shepherd, 1995) and that, on average, over half the manuscripts initially rejected are ultimately published elsewhere (Weller, 2001, p. 64). This especially seems to be true for manuscripts reporting creative and unorthodox research (Frey, 2003). For such manuscripts, referee recommendations are evidently of limited value in judging the merits of unconventional knowledge-claims.

In this connection, whereas the most prestigious journals may receive more "good" manuscripts than they can publish, their ability to select from the "best of the best" is, regrettably, suspect. Miner (2003) has speculated on this very point. He contends that the peer-review process as currently configured "rejects a substantial number of articles that are just as good if not better than what is published." He explains, "This occurs because when we get down to something similar to a 10 percent acceptance rate, it is impossible to discriminate effectively" (p. 341). In support of Miner's contention, Starbuck (2005) has shown that articles published in top-tier journals do not necessarily exhibit significantly higher quality (as measured by the average number of citations they receive) than articles published in second-tier and third-tier journals.

The case of my rejected manuscript, however, ends well. I am one of the two out of three authors that studies suggest do not give up on manuscripts easily. Without hesitation, I submitted my original manuscript – saying what I wanted to say and not what the guest editor and anonymous referee wanted me to say – to another journal where it was accepted and, ultimately, selected to receive a Best Paper of the Year Award. To be honest, despite an invitation to attend an award banquet in London and being presented with an attractive plaque, I would still have opted to have had my manuscript published in the journal that was my first choice.

Rejecting rejection and crossing the line

My experience highlights the vagaries of the review process and what some have come to call the "luck of the reviewer draw" (Bedeian, 2004). This situation is captured in one aspiring author's observation that the best career advice she ever got came at a seminar on publishing. She was told, when she was ready to submit a manuscript for review, to prepare three envelopes addressed to three different journals. "Send it to the first – if it gets rejected, then send it to the second. If it gets rejected again, then send it to the third." The point being that "the process is so subjective that you need to give your work the benefit of the doubt a few times before pulling the plug on it" (Belcher, 2006a, p. 2).

The painful validity of this anecdote is familiar to all those who have revised a manuscript as requested only to have it rejected and then, abandoning the revised manuscript, submitted their original manuscript for publication elsewhere and – lo and behold – had it accepted. A colleague and I still joke about one of his manuscripts that had gone through three rounds of reviews at the *Academy of Management Journal* (*AMJ*) only to be bounced. Frustrated, he submitted his original manuscript to the *Journal of Applied Psychology*, where it was accepted after one round of reviews.

I can go this one better, however. Several colleagues and I submitted a manuscript to an *Academy of Management* – sponsored journal and received an "invitation" to resubmit the manuscript based on a lengthy set of revisions. We dutifully made the revisions and the manuscript was ultimately accepted after two more rounds of referee comments. To our surprise, the manuscript received the journal's annual Best Paper Award. The editor seemed quite pleased that the "developmental review process" had resulted in such a fine paper. In effect, what had happened was that the editor essentially passed judgment on a manuscript that he had ghostwritten and (surprise, surprise) judged to be superior. In short, he liked that which he had created. In essence he had served as author and reviewer of his own work. Should you wonder if I am exaggerating, the initial manuscript we submitted was so different than the manuscript that was accepted we went on to submit it to another Academy journal and it has since been published. Somewhere, at some point, the line between reviewing and ghostwriting had been crossed.

These examples aside, let me be clear in stating that I do not endorse simply repackaging and resubmitting rejected manuscripts without carefully considering referee comments. Whatever the reason for a manuscript's rejection, the benefits of outside feedback for improving a manuscript should not be minimized. In this respect, I agree with Starbuck's (2003) contention that referees' comments should not be viewed as judgments about the value of one's work, but as data about potential readers' reactions to what an author is trying to say. This, however, does not mean that an author should always follow a referee's or editor's bidding before submitting a manuscript elsewhere.

I stress this point because I recall attending a seminar on publishing where an associate editor of a journal, which is published by one of our discipline's primary professional associations, stated that he felt it was "unethical" for an author to resubmit a rejected manuscript without first incorporating the revisions of the rejecting journal's referees. It seems ludicrous to me that anyone would argue that authors are acting unethically if they chose not to revise their work based on the comments of an anonymous referee of unknown pedigree. This is especially true when, by one estimate, 25 percent of editors' and referees' comments "might be wrong, overstated, or off point" (Feldman, 2005, p. 654). Add to this the fact that whereas "peer review" should mean that the merits of a manuscript are assessed by a scientific "peer" working in the same field of research as its author, evidence suggests that this may not be the case when referees are selected on the basis of particularistic criteria rather than their scientific achievements (Bedeian, Van Fleet, & Hyman, 2007).

Faux rigor and playing the game

All this strikes me as an example of what might be termed "*faux* rigor." There seems to be a belief that having three, four, or more referees submit multiple pages of comments is proof that our journals are truly top-tier. What appears to have been overlooked is that "the referees commissioned to read a manuscript may represent, but may not be representative of, an entire discipline" (Bedeian, 2004). Admittedly, we are handicapped as a discipline in that, without a generally accepted criterion for scientific quality, decisions by referees will always be, to some degree, subjective. As a result, in an effort to nevertheless engender faith in publication decisions, we seem to have focused on the extent to which consensus exists across referees as an indication that the review process is a valid indicator of scientific quality. This has always struck me as odd, as we regularly teach in our courses that high reliability (i.e., consensus across referees) is no guarantee of validity. As Daniel (1993) offers, "A high level of agreement between reviewers in itself proves very little, since two reviewers might reach equally erroneous conclusions" (p. 6).

Having said this, however, I do not wish to convey the notion that I have lost faith in the review process, as I do sincerely believe that editors and referees play an invaluable role in saving authors from embarrassing errors. Nonetheless, I also believe that we should be honest in acknowledging that the manuscripts which ultimately appear in our journals are often no less a reflection of the interests of the referees selected to serve as reviewers as the intentions of the authors themselves. It bothers me that publishing, at times, seems to have been turned into a game in which some referees try to find things to object to in a manuscript just to convince an editor that they have done a conscientious job in preparing their review and, in turn, authors admit to having included a specific reference in a manuscript primarily because they hoped that its author would be selected as a referee (Bedeian, 2004).

Further, I continue to wonder if the manuscripts ultimately accepted as a result of the review process make any greater contributions to advancing knowledge than the manuscripts as originally submitted. Additionally, I firmly believe that had these manuscripts been reviewed by sets of different referees (according to their own subjective perspectives) their final content would have been different and, perhaps, even rejected. Whether or not this differing content would have made a greater contribution to knowledge than the content in the original manuscripts remains an open question.

Given my rejected manuscript story, it may come as a surprise to some that I do not encourage arguing with editors and referees and agree with Dov Eden (this volume) only to do so if an issue is of "prime importance" and would otherwise be "intellectually dishonest." I also, however, agree with Dov that authors should not be "obsequious." Like Dov, I have learned from experience not to argue with editors and referees over "little things," such as editors and referees who insist that their own work be cited in a manuscript, regardless of how tangential the connection. I have found, however, that one can disagree with editors and referees without arguing. What I find works in those situations where I am directed to make alternations that I believe to be uninformed is to simply explain my understanding based upon my reading of various sources and then request that the editor or referee advise me about how I may have misunderstood the sources or how the sources are incorrect. If the editor and referee wish to argue with Cohen, Cohen, West, & Aiken (2003) or Pedhazur & Schmelkin (1991) or whomever, let them. Perhaps they do know more than these authorities and, if so, I will have learned something. Nonetheless, I admit to often (not always) agreeing with Nobel Laureate Paul Samuelson, who in addressing referee comments, has confessed that "in my heart of hearts I question that, *net*, they have improved the merits of my papers' contents or expositions" (quoted in Shepherd, 1995, p. 125). Interested readers should know that not everyone is so reticent about arguing with editors and, indeed, have developed quite successful careers doing so, going as far as resubmitting rejected manuscripts to the same journal and ultimately having them accepted (Starbuck, 2006, pp. xi–xv).

What gives me pause, though, are situations in which fledging authors feel pressured to have their work published (to avoid jeopardizing their careers) such that they do compromise on more than the "little things." The extent of the pressure felt in this regard is suggested by a study of 173 lead authors of articles published in the *AMJ* and the *Academy of Management Review* from 1999 to 2001 (Bedeian, 2003). Nearly 25 percent of the authors reported that to placate a referee or editor they had actually made changes in their manuscripts that they (as authors) felt were incorrect. It seems to me that in a Six-Sigma era, we can do better as a profession than having one out of four of the manuscripts published in our discipline's premier journals being flawed (at least in the eyes of their biddable authors).

The best of all worlds

In the best of all worlds, the review process would function in a manner consistent with its ideal image. Editors and referees would enable and amplify rather than sometimes stifle and even replace an author's voice (Beebe, 2006). In such a world, editors would "request" revisions no more than necessary and, all the while, be sensitive to the prerogatives and ethics of legitimate authorship. In this respect, it struck me as odd that a recent editor's forum in the *AMJ* (see Bergh, this volume) seemed to take pride in the fact that the paper selected as the journal's Best Article for 2004 required a full 24 months between initial submission and final acceptance. A third of this time was required for various reviews and 16 months were needed to satisfy referee requests for revision. Allowing, perhaps, for a 12-month lag before publication, one has to wonder about the timeliness of our discipline's research, let alone its prospects for reporting dramatic scientific breakthroughs that will change the world.

In thinking about this situation further, I was reminded of Dick Daft's (1983) comments on the "machine-gun fire of referee criticisms" (p. 544) and also wondered how many within our discipline have simply withdrawn from "the game" as a result of battle fatigue. I have likewise wondered what cost our discipline has incurred in lost knowledge and disenfranchised colleagues who have simply dropped out of the publication process altogether. Is it necessary to spend 24 months to revise a manuscript? Can it be justified in the sense of equating marginal costs with marginal benefits? As Ellison

(2002) has noted, "the review process is the major determinant of how [academics] divide their time between working on new projects, revising old papers, and reviewing the work of others" (p. 949). It thus influences the productivity of our entire discipline, as well as how enjoyable it is to be an academic. Finally, I also wonder to what extent the review process as currently practiced distorts the true record of authors' contributions to our discipline. How are readers to know if they are responding to an author's own words and ideas or those of an unidentified editor or referee, both of whom will escape responsibility for what is attributed to the author?

Beyond these considerations, an additional question looms for our junior colleagues striving to earn tenure. Can 24 months be seen as a viable timeframe for submitting and ultimately having a manuscript (award winning or not) accepted for publication when their tenure clock is ticking down? I've previously argued in favor of re-evaluating our tenure and promotion system so as to reward faculty for doing a few pieces of high-quality research rather than grinding out multiple publications and simply playing a numbers game (Bedeian, 1989). The traditional model, however, with its emphasis on number of publications, still prevails (De Rond & Miller, 2005). As I have stated, it seems to me that we have straightjacketed our junior faculty at the most crucial, formative stage of their careers and that the editorial-review process, with its bias toward established paradigms, not only discourages creative and unorthodox research, but disadvantages those wishing to enter our profession (Bedeian, 1989).

Others have come to share my concern. Acknowledging "the relatively short tenure clock and strong emphasis to publish in 'A' journals in today's business school world," Nifadkar and Tsui (2007) have likewise bemoaned the fact that the contemporary-review process not only discourages the "fainthearted or thin-skinned," but suppresses the "intellectual potential" of our discipline. In this vein, they quote Freeman (2005) to the effect that "overemphasis on reviews, reviewers, revisions, and the socialization of the paper-writing process can lead to a kind of collective group think" (p. 433) that they see as "detrimental to creativity and originality." Echoing sentiments that I have expressed here and elsewhere, Nifadkar and Tsui (2007) similarly conclude that the review process, as currently practiced, has become a barrier to scientific progress in our discipline, stifling intellectual boldness. In this respect, we are at one in the belief that "the community of scholars has a responsibility to ensure that [our discipline's] intellectual environment facilitates rather than inhibits creative scientific activities" (p. 302). Simply put, the future development of our discipline is otherwise at risk.

Conclusion

The scientific marketplace of ideas is unique in the extent to which it is self-managed. In this regard, the manuscript-review process is central to gaining public confidence and, thus, guarding the autonomy and authority we enjoy as academics. It is important that we remain open to examining the "black box of editorship" to ensure that it remains a reliable and valid means for assessing the content of our discipline's published record. To do otherwise would have chilling implications for our scientific progress and be an affront to the prescriptive norms that guide our common pursuit of new knowledge.

In summary, I offer the following conclusions for consideration by authors, editors, referees, and the academy in general:

1 Aspiring authors should not give up on manuscripts easily as most manuscripts are ultimately published.
2 Editors should be especially cognizant of biases favoring established theories and against research reporting creative and unorthodox findings.
3 Although the referees commissioned to read a manuscript may represent, but may not be representative of, an entire discipline, the benefits to authors of outside feedback for improving a manuscript should not be minimized.
4 Authors should not necessarily feel compelled to always follow a referee's or editor's bidding in revising a manuscript or before submitting a rejected manuscript elsewhere.
5 The manuscripts that ultimately appear in our journals are often no less a reflection of the interests of the referees consigned to serve as reviewers as the intentions of the authors themselves.
6 Had a published article been reviewed by different referees (according to their own subjective perspectives) its final content would have been different.
7 Deans and tenure and promotion committees should recognize that articles published in so-called top-tier journals do not necessarily exhibit significantly higher quality than articles published in second-tier and third-tier journals.
8 To preserve the prerogatives and ethics of legitimate authorship, editors and referees should enable and amplify rather than stifle an author's voice, requesting revisions that are no more than necessary.

References

Bedeian, A. G. (1989, October). Totems and taboos: Undercurrents in the management discipline. (Presidential Address.) *Academy of Management Newsletter, 19*, 1–6. Retrieved January 12, 2007, from http://www.bus.lsu.edu/management/faculty/abedeian/articles/Tottems&Taboos-AOM%20News-1999.pdf

Bedeian, A. G. (1996a). Improving the journal review process: The question of ghost-writing. *American Psychologist, 51*, 1189.

Bedeian, A. G. (1996b). Thoughts on making and remaking the management discipline. *Journal of Management Inquiry, 5*, 311–18.

Bedeian, A. G. (1997). Of fiction and fraud. *Academy of Management Review, 22*, 840–2.

Bedeian, A. G. (2003). The manuscript review process: The proper roles of authors, referees, and editors. *Journal of Management Inquiry, 12*, 331–8.

Bedeian, A. G. (2004). Peer review and the social construction of knowledge in the management discipline. *Academy of Management Learning and Education, 3*, 198–216.

Bedeian, A. G., Van Fleet, D. D., & Hyman, H. H., III (2007). Scientific achievement and editorial-board membership. In press, at *Organizational Research Methods*.

Beebe, J. (2006). Editing as a psychological practice. *Journal of Analytical Psychology, 51*, 329–56.

Belcher, W. (2006a). On journal rejection. *Flourish: An electronic journal for scholarly writers, 2* (4). Retrieved January 5, 2007, from http://www.wendybelcher.com/pages/FlourishNewsletter.html

Belcher, W. (2006b). On research on peer review. *Flourish: An electronic journal for scholarly writers, 2* (7). Retrieved January 5, 2007, from http://www.wendybelcher.com/pages/FlourishNewsletter.html

Biagioli, M. (2002). From book censorship to academic peer review. *Emergences, 12*, 11–45.

Cohen, J., Cohen, P., West, S. G., & Aiken, L. S. (2003). *Applied multiple regression/correlation analysis for the behavioral sciences* (3rd ed.). Mahwah, NJ: Erlbaum.

Daft, R. L. (1983). Learning the craft of organizational research. *Academy of Management Review, 8*, 539–46.

Daniel, H. -D. (1993). *Guardians of science: Fairness and reliability of peer review*. (W. E. Russey, Trans.). Weinheim, Germany: VCH Verlagsgesellschaft.

De Rond, M., & Miller, A. N. (2005). Publish or perish: bane or boon of academic life? *Journal of Management Inquiry, 14*, 321–9.

Ellison, G. (2002). The slowdown in the economics publishing process. *Journal of Political Economy, 110*, 947–93.

Feldman, D. C. (2005). Conversing with editors: Strategies for authors and reviewers. *Journal of Management, 31*, 649–58.

Freeman, R. E. (2005). The development of stakeholder theory: An idiosyncratic approach. In K. G. Smith & M. A. Hitt (Eds.), *Great minds in management: The process of theory development* (pp. 417–35). Oxford: Oxford University Press.

Frey, B. S. (2003). Publishing as prostitution? – Choosing between one's own ideas and academic success. *Public Choice, 116*, 205–23.

Miner, J. B. (2003). Commentary on Arthur Bedeian's "the manuscript review process: The proper roles of authors, referees, and editors." *Journal of Management Inquiry, 12*, 339–43.

Nifadkar, S. S., & Tsui, A. (2007). [Review of the book *Great minds in management: The process of theory development*]. *Academy of Management Review, 32*, 298–303.

Pedhazur, E. J., & Schmelkin, L. P. (1991). *Measurement, design, and analysis: An integrated approach*. Hillsdale, NJ: Erlbaum.

Shepherd, G. B. (Ed.). (1995). *Rejected: Leading economists ponder the publication process*. Sun Lakes, AZ: Thomas Horton and Daughters.

Starbuck, W. H. (2003). Turning lemons into lemonade: Where is the value in peer review? *Journal of Management Inquiry, 12*, 344–51.

Starbuck, W. H. (2005). How much better are the most-prestigious journals? The statistics of academic publication. *Organization Science, 16*, 180–200.

Starbuck, W. H. (2006). *Organizational realities: Studies of strategizing and organizing*. Oxford: Oxford University Press.

Weller, A. C. (2001). *Editorial peer review: Its strengths and weaknesses*. Medford, NJ: American Society for Information Science and Technology.

Part III Editing Different Types of Journals

15
Editing a Top Academic Journal
Sheldon Zedeck

As of the writing of this chapter (January 2007), I will have completed five years and about to begin my sixth and final year as editor of the *Journal of Applied Psychology* (*JAP*). The purpose of this chapter is to share some insights and provide advice to authors, and future editors and consulting board members for peer-reviewed journals. I will (1) provide some background regarding *JAP*; (2) share thoughts on how an editor can shape the contents of a journal and contribute to knowledge development of the field, (3) offer advice to authors on how to prepare a well-developed manuscript; and (4) provide insight for prospective editors – a realistic job preview.

Background of the *JAP*

The *JAP* is published by the American Psychological Association (APA). *JAP* is one of approximately 50 journals that APA publishes covering the many diverse fields pertaining to psychology (e.g., social, personality, cognitive, clinical, educational, neuropsychology, etc.). *JAP* is published bimonthly with a current allotment of 1800 pages. The subscription circulation is approximately 4050.

The editorial team is composed of the editor, the associate editors (currently nine), consulting board members (currently 115), and ad hoc reviewers (approximately 400 in the *Journal*'s database). Consulting board members are reviewers who have agreed to review approximately 10–15 manuscripts per year; they are part of the editorial team and as a result, their names are printed in each issue of the *Journal*. Ad hoc reviewers perform the same reviewing function as consulting board members, but on an "as needed basis." These reviewers have agreed to review approximately one manuscript every three months; if they review during a volume year, their names are listed in the last issue of that volume on a special page devoted to ad hoc reviewer acknowledgement.

Each manuscript undergoes blind review by two reviewers and one action editor (editor or associate editor). Beginning January 1, 2002 through

December 31, 2006, *JAP* had received 3440 manuscripts for review, which averages to approximately 700 manuscripts per year (this does not count "revise and resubmits" [R&R]). To the best of my knowledge, *JAP* is the "busiest" journal that deals with organizational and social sciences. The acceptance rate varies from 10 –15 percent per year.

The editors of this volume assigned the title chapter, "Editing a Top Academic Journal"; so allow me to provide some basis and data on why *JAP* is considered a "top academic journal." Journals are informally rated by authors, readers, deans, reviewers, and everyone else who has a stake in the publishing endeavor. The ratings influence the decision of where to submit a manuscript, provide estimates on the likelihood of getting an acceptance of a manuscript, and influence decision-makers with regard to evaluation of a researcher's output when there are hiring, promotion, and merit-increase decisions.

A formal rating system that is adopted by many is the one provided by The Institute for Scientific Information's (ISI) Social Science Index (SSI). The ISI has created databases that provide indicators of journals' and articles' "reputation." They provide quantitative data for evaluating the "impact" and "citedness" of journals, articles, and authors. Citation data can be used to indicate the highest impact journals in different fields and specialties and over varying time frames.

ISI provides a number of indices. "Citations" is based on the assumption that if an author cites a journal, he or she has found it useful. Thus, it follows that the more frequently a journal is cited, the greater its impact in the scientific community. "Impact factor" represents a ratio of citations received to citable items, based on citations made in the current year by all journals in the ISI database to articles published during the previous two years. For example, if a journal published 1000 articles in 2002 and 2003, and there were 250 cites in 2004 to those articles published in 2002 and 2003, its "impact factor" would be 250/1000 or 0.25. "Immediacy factor" reflects the number of cites in a year to articles published in that year. For example, if a journal published 100 articles in 2004 and those articles reference other articles published in that journal 20 times, the immediacy index would be 20/100 or 0.20. Finally, the "half-life" of a journal is the median age of the articles the journal cited in the year in which the index is computed. The half-life calculation finds the number of publication years from the current year in which the index is calculated that account for 50 percent of citations received by the journal.

For the 2005 year (latest year for which data are available as of this writing), I created a listing of journals that ISI had categorized as either "business" or "psychology, applied." This listing yielded 107 journals, though admittedly a good number of these do not compete with *JAP* for manuscripts. Results showed that based on the total cites and impact factor, *JAP* was ranked the number one *empirical* journal compared to others dealing with particular areas of applied psychology (industrial/organizational psychology [I/O psychology], personnel psychology, and organizational behavior). Other analyses support the conclusion that *JAP* is one of, if not, the premier journals in its field (cf., Podsakoff, P., MacKenzie, Bachrach, & Podsakoff, N. P., 2005).

Before concluding this section on the background of *JAP*, I want to note a particular advantage for the editor of *JAP* – which is that the American Psychological Association is the publisher. Having a major organization, which is member-driven and devoted to the fostering of research, as a publisher makes the life of any editor simpler. APA takes care of all of the production, marketing, financial, administrative issues. All the editor has to do is to identify those manuscripts that fit the mission and standards of the journal and produce issues and volumes. Finding yourself in a similar position will facilitate your life as an editor – you should seek such situations if you are inclined to become an editor!

Shaping the content of the journal

The editor can shape the content of a journal in at least three ways: (1) by presenting a mission statement regarding what will be considered for review, and what will *not* be considered; (2) by appointment of the associate editors and consulting board members, and by selection of ad hoc reviewers for the journal; and (3) by publishing "special sections" that highlight particular topics, issues, or concerns of the field. The following will elaborate on each of these strategies with respect to how I attempted to influence the journal, and consequently, the field.

Mission statement

The *Journal*'s mission, as defined by the current editorial team, is:

> *JAP* emphasizes the publication of original investigations that contribute new knowledge and understanding to fields of applied psychology. *JAP* primarily considers empirical and theoretical investigations of interest to psychologists doing research that fosters an understanding of the psychological and behavioral phenomena of individuals, groups, or organizations in settings such as education/training, business, government, or health or service institutions in the private or public sector or for-profit or nonprofit. … We are interested in publishing articles that are empirical, conceptual, or theoretical, or a combination of all three, that enhance our understanding of behavior that has practical implications within particular contexts.
>
> (Zedeck, 2003, p. 3)

The above statement as well as elaboration of the orientation of the journal, the topics it would consider, and its emphases are presented in the editorial statement that appeared in the first issue of the first volume for the editorial team (Zedeck, 2003). In consultation with the associate editors, we tweaked the mission statement of the previous editorial team [see inside cover of *JAP*, 2002, issue number 6]. We specifically noted two topics that we would *not* consider – eyewitness accuracy and consumer behavior. The rationale for this decision was the same that had been mandated by APA and applied by previous editorial teams to manuscripts that dealt with clinical psychology or human factors – there were more appropriate journals for those topics, which would keep them within a journal context devoted to such issues.

On the "increasing the scope side," the associate editors and I also made the decision that we would encourage theoretical and conceptual manuscripts, as well as manuscripts that presented research that could be considered "applied cognition" and were conducted and/or related/generalized to or within a particular context. Finally, we expressed interest in publishing cross-cultural research and encouraged submission from researchers outside the United States. Given the expanding global economy, we hoped to increase the exposure of the journal to those conducting applied research regardless of continent.

The mission also can be conveyed by formal and informal presentations to various groups. During my term as editor, I have been invited to make presentations to doctoral students, new faculty, and research groups, both in the United States and overseas, regarding publishing in *JAP*. These were effective venues to influence the submissions to the journal, in terms of quantity and quality, as well as to identify potential reviewers of manuscripts.

Editorial board

The composition of the editorial board influences the audience that is attracted to submit manuscripts as well as to read the *Journal*'s contents. Readers and authors look to see who is on the board, to assess the reputations of the board members, to note the types of research associated with the board members, and to gain any insight into what might facilitate acceptance of a manuscript.

When I became the editor, APA informed me as to how many associate editors and consulting board members could be appointed. My initial task was to put together the Associate Editor board. One criterion for appointment to the board was acknowledged high reputation of the potential candidates. Familiarity with the field and consultation with colleagues and former editors are the obvious sources for identification of potential members. Once the "excellent reputation" list was formed, I was interested in sending a message to potential authors, and consequently made the appointments of associate editors to reflect that message. My interests were to have a highly distinguished group of associate editors (1) that had an acknowledged excellent track record in empirical and theoretical research; (2) that also had demonstrated excellent skills at reviewing articles, and providing developmental feedback in their reviews; (3) that was diverse with respect to research and methodological orientation; (4) that was diverse in terms of race and gender, (5) that was diverse in constituency represented (academics and the business world), and (6) that was diverse in terms of internationalization of reviewers and substantive content. These considerations were particularly important for me since it was my goal to change, in part, the perceptions of the journal, which had a reputation of a journal focused on "dustbowl empiricism." As indicated in the previous section, I wanted to broaden the mission – to encourage more submissions from overseas scholars, not only reflecting cross-cultural psychology, but also research that was being generated and developed within a non-U.S. context. I also wanted to send a message that scholars working in institutions where "publish or perish" was not the dominant view should and could publish their projects if they furthered the field's knowledge base (e.g., organizations, institutions, or settings where research was being conducted for the purpose of having an impact on operation or policy and the article, *per se*, did not influence the internal evaluation of the researcher).

When choosing reviewers as consulting board members, you need to rely on your knowledge of the field, opinions of colleagues, and, hopefully, data from the previous editor in terms of the quality, timeliness, and developmental feedback that reviewers had demonstrated in the past. The benefits of serving on a consulting board are to have your name and affiliation listed on the masthead, as well as to receive a free subscription to the journal. And, needless to say, a voice in what is subsequently published. These rewards are extrinsically minimal, but they are sought after. During my term as editor, I have received a number of self-volunteer requests to be on the consulting board (and have also had invitations to be an ad hoc reviewer declined because the invitation was not to be on the consulting board). The challenge in putting together a board, and then maintaining it when its size increases (controlled by APA) or there are openings due to resignations or nonreappointment, is to achieve a well-balanced board that again reflects fields of and approaches to research that you want to convey to readers and potential authors. Again, race, gender, and national/international diversity were considerations of mine as I put together and maintained the consulting board team over the years of my editorship.

The formation of a consulting board and ad hoc reviewer database is a difficult one. I mentioned above, my strategy for appointing the consulting board team. The strategy for the ad hoc reviewer team is less restrictive. Associate editors and consulting board members recommended scholars to serve as ad hoc reviewers. Also, we conducted a search to identify authors of articles that appeared in prior issues of the *Journal* and invited them to serve as ad hoc reviewers. The "incentive" for serving as an ad hoc reviewer is the opportunity to provide service to the journal and field, but also to provide "reviewer data" to be used when openings occur on the consulting board (*JAP* evaluates reviewer's reviews). The associate editors and I systematically reviewed the quality and timeliness data of ad hoc reviewers when openings occurred on the consulting board; no one was ever appointed to the board unless there was demonstrated quality in prior reviews.

As mentioned above, *JAP* evaluates the reviews it receives. Reviewers provide numerical evaluations on critical aspects of the manuscript and provide bottom-line accept/not accept recommendations for the manuscript. In addition, the reviewer presents a narrative analysis that should be concrete, clear, precise, and detailed. From my perspective, the most important aspect of the review is that the feedback needs to be developmental. The narrative should identify and discuss why there is a potential problem in the design, logic, or style of the manuscript. There should be suggestions for how to rectify the identified problems. The feedback should be presented in a way to convince the author to accept and implement it. Nothing is gained if the feedback is abrupt, rude, or full of condescending comments. I view the mandate of the editorial role as one of publishing research and contributing to the field's knowledge base. If the view of the review is to show how smart the reviewer is, there is limited value to that review. Reviews should identify issues that can be rectified and the author should have the opportunity to revise and resubmit, when this action is warranted.

What kind of feedback is valued by an editor? The following are some of the characteristics that distinguish a review:

1) Identification of pertinent issues that the action editor did not identify;
2) Identification of creative solutions to address problems;
3) Suggestions for solutions to subtle/complex technical errors;
4) Suggestions for significant new ideas, analyses, and literatures that extend the paper's contribution;
5) Provides the action editor with well-calibrated advice;
6) Provides comments geared to (and identify) specific sections, paragraphs, or lines in manuscript;
7) Offers enough detail for the author to be able to address the concerns without having to guess at the meaning of a reviewer's comment;
8) Offers comments that are constructive and developmental in tone; and
9) Is supportive when possible.

In some ways, the best review is one that borders on being the core of a "companion" paper that warrants consideration for publication!

Reviews that are *not* helpful are ones:

1) that focus only on one or two issues to the exclusion of other significant issues;

2) that are terse and lacking in sufficient detail that would help the author;
3) where the advice to the author lacks proper grounding and usefulness;
4) where the identified points are not on target reflecting that the paper was not carefully read; and
5) where the comments provided are insufficient to justify the reviewer's recommendation.

The bottom-line for such reviews is that they are not useful for helping the action editor make a decision!

Another caveat! Reviewers often assume that the editor will implement the "rejection" recommendation of the reviewer and therefore believe that only a few comments are warranted. If, however, the editor requests an R&R, and the reviewer subsequently identifies an issue that existed in the original manuscript, the tone is set for a negative experience for the editor, reviewer, and author. It is my view that it is inappropriate reviewer etiquette to introduce a problem in a revision that existed in the original manuscript, and was not noted because the reviewer simply was not complete in his/her review.

A final caveat! Most evaluation forms contain two sections, one for "comments for the author" and the other "comments for the editor." Since a particular reviewer is usually one of three who will be providing input, the reviewer should not indicate "acceptance" or "rejection" in the "comments for the authors." The reasons for this advice should be obvious – the editor may not accept the recommendation, which thus causes the editor to devote time and space explaining to the author the counter decision. In summary, reviewers should focus on providing specific, constructive feedback to the authors; ultimate statements regarding acceptance/rejection should not be communicated in the reviewer's "comments for the author."

Before concluding this section on the role of the editorial board in shaping the field, I want to comment on a tangential issue and question: "Why should someone agree to serve on a consulting board or be an ad hoc reviewer?" This issue and question arose more than once when I asked scholars to be on the consulting board or serve as an ad hoc reviewer. When the response was in the negative, I understood and appreciated the declination when it was in terms of "I already serve on too many boards," or "I have other pressing responsibilities such as management or administration that take up much of my time." But there are responses that are as simple as "why should I spend my time reviewing when I could be doing my research?" My reply to such a response is: "you have a professional obligation to review." From my perspective, it is quite simple: Scholars are requested to review manuscripts because they have demonstrated success and effectiveness in conducting research and publishing. The reason they have achieved the status they have in the research world is because someone else took the time to review their work and to work with them to get their research published. Without the peer-review system, we would not have published research that has an impact. It seems to me that as part of professional training and orientation to the research field, we need to train the doctoral students in the "why's and wherefore's" of publishing, which means not only how to conduct research and publish it, but also of the need to be part of the professional community that furthers our scientific base.

Special sections

The editor's message in his/her first issue (e.g., Zedeck, 2003) spells out the goals for the editor. As mentioned above, one of my goals was to increase the theoretical focus of the journal. To achieve this goal, the *JAP* editorial team made use of "special sections." Under the leadership of one of *JAP*'s associate editors, Dr. Katherine Klein, we put out a "call for papers" on "theoretical models and conceptual analysis," requesting potential authors to submit manuscripts that would extend beyond the current literature – that offer more than a review of the existing literature and more than a repackaging of established constructs and models. We emphasized that manuscripts should offer new theoretical insights and propose new explanations of constructs, relationships, and/or phenomena in applied psychology. We hoped to receive innovative manuscripts that would break new theoretical ground while offering testable propositions and applied implications (Klein & Zedeck, 2004). We presented specific instructions regarding the "call" and the papers that could be submitted. The response was that over 90 papers were submitted, and underwent the customary blind, peer review, with the final results being three "special sections" over several issues. The informal response to the manuscripts published in the "special sections" has been quite positive and today there are an increasing number of conceptual and theoretical pieces that are being submitted for review. My assessment is that the message has been received and supported!

Advice to authors

The simplest advice to authors for increasing the probability of an "acceptance" of their manuscript is: Conduct high-quality research on an important and interesting problem, AND write up the project in a manner that communicates what and how the research was conducted, AND "sell" the reader on "why" the research was done, and its contribution to our knowledge base. Somewhat more specifically, likelihood of acceptance increases if the research has multiple studies, multiple measures, and large and representative samples. With this as a preamble, let me provide some more specific suggestions for strategizing the submission of a manuscript.

Know the journal

It is important that you know what the mission is of the journal, the types and content of articles published (e.g., featured or shorter research reports; empirical and/or theoretical; quantitative and/or qualitative; reviews and meta-analyses, etc.), the style in which the manuscript should be written (e.g., APA style), the history of the journal (acceptance rate, lag from submission to publication); and the publication "rules" (e.g., issues pertaining to copyright and confidentiality of materials; conflict of interest regarding "products" that might be mentioned in the manuscript). If the research "fits," submit it. Research has demonstrated that "initial impressions" are important. When an editor or reviewer receives a manuscript that demonstrates that the author has not read the *JAP* prior to submitting the manuscript, that manuscript has a diminished chance of acceptance. It is difficult enough to get "acceptance"; start with a positive impression.

Review the manuscript prior to submission

Ensure that you have presented the project in a logical, orderly, clear, objective, and interesting manner. Ensure that the Abstract contains the information the journal requires and that it does not exceed the journal's limits. Ensure that you have sections covering the Introduction, Method, Results, and Discussion. Ensure that the Reference list is complete and accurate. Before finalizing the manuscript, it is prudent to undertake two more critical actions: (1) ask a "friend" or colleague, with a different perspective, to read the manuscript and give you honest feedback and (2) proof the manuscript for completeness, correct grammar and punctuation, and elimination of spelling mistakes and typos.

Advice to prospective editors

The questions that a prospective editor might ask are: (1) "Why should I be an editor," and (2) "If I accept, what does this mean in terms of my professional and personal life?" Let me try to address these questions now that I have completed five years as editor of *JAP*. (Note that I had been an editor (*Human Performance*) and associate editor (*Human Performance* and *Applied Psychology: An International Review*) of other journals prior to becoming *JAP* editor, so I had some realistic job preview – but the advice that follows is based primarily on my experience as *JAP* editor.)

There are several reasons for agreeing to edit a major journal. First, it is an honor. Appointment as an editor for a top APA journal means that you have survived a diligent selection process whereby nominations, letters of recommendation, and statements from candidates have all been considered by a committee appointed by APA's publication board. This board is not composed solely of scholars within your field, but also includes researchers from other fields. Thus, appointment recognizes your accomplishments in the general field of applied psychology and should be looked upon as an honor – just as one receives a special award.

Second, as stated in prior sections of this chapter, assumption of an editor's position allows you to have some input into the shape of the field. My particular take on this "reason for being an editor" is not to suggest that you will be a gatekeeper or have control over the research that will and should be done. But the editorship provides you with the opportunity to "open" the journal to issues it may not have considered in the past. For example, under my editorship, there has been an increase in manuscripts submitted that are based on qualitative research that stem from researchers outside the United States. In addition, topics such as work and family as well as workplace aggression have received greater attention. These changes may have been on course or more deliberately influenced by the editorial team – but the important point is that there were changes.

Third, as one progresses in his/her career, one becomes narrower and narrower in his/her perspective. When I was in graduate school, I was immersed in the detail of a number of literatures related to I/O psychology. As I have advanced in age, my perspective became narrower and more focused on the particular topics of my research domain. Accordingly, I was not able to keep up with fields that were changing, emerging, or new. But, as editor of a journal such as *JAP*, you have the opportunity to peruse research from all areas of applied psychology. During my term, I have become familiar with approximately 3500 manuscripts, which means that I am now up-to-date with the field of applied psychology (at least as evidenced by what is submitted to *JAP*). Admittedly, approximately 85 percent of what I have perused may not see the light of day, but I am aware of what researchers are doing and thinking about!

How has editorship impacted my professional and personal life? Given the fact that the entire editing process (e.g., uploading submissions, assigning action editors and reviewers, tracking the status of manuscripts, and writing and communicating decisions) is electronic, the role of editor could be with you 24/7. I believe that an editor has an obligation to provide comprehensive and timely feedback – careers involving tenure and promotion are based on the journal's decisions. Accordingly, I have been keen on providing timely feedback, which means that I am frequently monitoring the status of manuscripts. And, I can do this monitoring from any place where I can find a computer (I have personally resisted using a PDA). If so much time is going to be spent on journal activities, then something else has to be sacrificed. The impact for me was to reduce the number of personal research projects with which I would be involved during my term. The good news is that though I have a major grant that coincided with my term as editor, I had excellent colleagues and students to work with which allowed me to be involved in research AND spend time in my editorial role. But do not be misled – as editor of *JAP*, I have invested about 20–30 hours per a seven-day week in the editor's role, hours that therefore were not available for other activities such as research or nonwork.

The above speaks of the editor's role and its impact on research. If you are in academics, you also have commitments to teaching. I strongly urge you to negotiate with your departmental head (chair or dean) and obtain a reduced teaching load. Though the Department of Psychology at Berkeley would not do this, I am willing to write letters for anyone seeking support for a reduced teaching load!

On a personal level, there is no way you can take on the editor's role without an understanding and supportive family. You will seek out and find downtime in family activities to sneak away to a computer to check on the journal. You will use the excuse to "not go to the ballet tonight because I have to catch up on the journal." Electronic submission and processing of manuscripts means that the journal is always with you. Even on vacations! My own experience is that I never had a complete and full vacation, without being concerned about the journal (ask my wife about the times I went to Internet cafes in the Galapagos or in a Tuscany village to check on the journal while she did her tourist thing.) There simply is the obligation to be aware of what is happening with the journal and the status of manuscripts. It may be possible to delegate an associate editor to be responsible for assigning and tracking manuscripts while you are on vacation, but you are the only one who can write the action letter for the manuscript that you assigned to yourself. And that manuscript may be important and critical to the author's tenure case – and there is a deadline by which an answer is needed.

Another role of an editor is to serve as an external evaluator for academic scholars who are being considered for tenure or promotion at universities. Deans and chairs think that an editor should know about every area of research. If the candidate published in the journal you edit, you will be asked to write a letter and do so to meet a deadline. My experience has been that I have been asked to write about 15–20 letters per year, usually in the summer and fall seasons of the calendar year. My position has been to write these letters (I have been a chair of a department and was often the one requesting such letters), especially for those scholars who served on the editorial board or as ad hoc reviewers. They accepted my invitation to serve voluntarily the field, and I believe the editor has an obligation to reciprocate and participate in the academic process.

Finally, I have found that maintaining communication with the associate editors and consulting board to be invaluable in getting a pulse on how the journal is operating. I tried to have annual face-to-face meetings with the associate editors and consulting board members, to review the prior year's accomplishments, identify issues, and obtain suggestions for new directions. Societal or association conferences are the most practical avenues for holding such meetings. But, in addition, annual e-mail "up-dates" to consulting board and ad hoc reviewers regarding the review process are also valuable in maintaining a well-oiled machine.

All of the above relates to the impact the editorship has on your professional and personal life. How can you make the best of the situation? My advice is to negotiate with the publisher for generous financial support.

One, the editor and associate editors should receive compensation for their contributions. Two, the departments or organizations of the editor and associate editors should be compensated for providing space, paper, copying services, and financial accounting. Three, and most important, you need to hire a manuscript coordinator who will manage the entire electronic system, from uploading manuscripts through preparing the content of the issue. The manuscript coordinator is crucial to minimizing the amount of time you need to spend on non-editorial matters, to controlling the requests that you need to respond to or that can be answered by others, and in general, creating the well-oiled machine that I noted above. (I would like to take this opportunity to acknowledge the excellent coordinator for *JAP*, who has served my entire term – Kate Denevan. Her work with editors, reviewers, authors, and the staff at APA has been superb and invaluable.)

Conclusion

The purpose of this chapter was to provide one editor's perspective on the editorial process. Needless to say, other editors will describe different experiences and provide different advice and suggestions. The common goal, however, is that editors are in the business of working with authors to generate research that will contribute to a field's knowledge base. My conclusion as I am about to end my term is that it has been a rewarding experience and hopefully one that has benefited our science. And, in closing, I need to thank all of the people who helped make the journal what it is – the APA staff, the associate editors, the reviewers, the manuscript coordinator, and most surely, the authors. It is truly a team effort.

References

Klein, K. J., & Zedeck, S. (2004). Theory in applied psychology. *Journal of Applied Psychology, 89*, 931–3.

Podsakoff, P. M., MacKenzie, S. B., Bachrach, D. G., & Podsakoff, N. P. (2005). The influence of management journals in the 1980s and 1990s. *Strategic Management Journal, 26*, 473–88.

Zedeck, S. (2003). Editorial. *Journal of Applied Psychology, 88*, 3–5.

16
Editing a Bridge Journal
Theresa M. Welbourne

This chapter started out with a different title. The intention was that I write a chapter about editing a niche journal; however, as I wrote and rewrote, I came to the conclusion that *Human Resource Management* (*HRM*), for which I am editor-in-chief, is not really a niche journal at all. In fact, since taking on the editor's role three years ago, our editorial team has purposely expanded our audience, working to make the Journal less niche-oriented.

Our goal has been to reinstate and reinforce the bridge nature of *HRM*, which requires us to target our work to reach two overlapping, but distinct, audiences. We strive to publish new knowledge that is of interest to both academics and practitioners who work on human resource management topics. We are not focused only on the HR department's work, but on topics related to the management of people at work.

The goal of *Human Resource Management*[1] was defined by my predecessors as being a research-based journal targeting both academics who teach and do research in the field of HRM and senior HRM executives. The idea of being a bridge journal is attractive, but in reality, at least our editorial team has found it quite challenging.

HRM's publishing standards require that articles meet the rigorous standards of scholarly research, and as such, when papers come in, they are reviewed by academics who tend to use the same standards they use for non-bridge journals. Thus, authors are expected to position their papers in the existing literature, apply theory to develop hypotheses, and use rigorous methods (when using either qualitative or quantitative data). At the same time, a successful manuscript has to be interesting to practitioners, and the paper must be written in a way that is accessible and of value to the senior HRM executives, consultants, and MBA students who read HRM.

The problem, we discovered quickly, comes in making this ideal bridge state happen. Academics who are trained to do rigorous, high-quality research rarely have the opportunity to write in a way that is "accessible," and people who write very practitioner-oriented articles have little training in doing rigorous research. Thus, every author is asked to stretch, and this makes the job of recruiting authors and helping authors succeed somewhat more challenging than it would be in a non-bridge journal.

At the same time, the rewards of publishing in a bridge journal and the contributions we make to the field are significant. The research that is published reaches people who can do something with our research. *HRM*, therefore, acts as a conduit providing practitioners with ideas that will help them do their jobs better. There is significant appeal in the potential; the challenge, you will see, is in making the idea a reality.

Leadership forum

After reviewing our competition and looking at the papers being submitted, we decided the most tactical way to bridge research and practice was to create two distinct sections of the Journal. The first section we called the HR Science Forum, which includes the traditional, academic papers. The second section, which we named the HR Leadership Forum, builds on the concept of the Executive Forum that prior editors used with select issues. We published the requirements for each section in our Publishing Cues. We changed the review process for the Leadership Forum section so that high-quality case studies and papers that add value from a practitioner point of view, but ones that may not meet *HRM's* very rigorous standards of a true science paper, could be considered for publication. To date, this process has worked well for us, and we find more authors are submitting Leadership Forum-type papers.

The challenge for our editorial team was and continues to be how to please all of *HRM's* various audiences while maintaining high-quality content. Achieving this has been difficult, but the bridge *HRM* has been building is an important one. We have an incredible opportunity to speak to a much larger audience and have a higher impact on "the real world." From our early research, we found out that *HRM* was being read by academics and practitioners in 58 different countries. We also learned that the global nature of our audience was an important aspect in creating and developing the niche.

Advice to authors from the *HRM* survey

It is a real honor to be the editor-in-chief for *HRM* and to work with so many talented researchers, authors, reviewers, and professionals in the field. I could not help thinking that I should tap into this wealth of experience for this chapter. Therefore, I sent a survey out to all of our board members and reviewers and asked them one simple question. I asked them each to provide their top three tips for authors. I sent the survey out to everyone in our database (1164), and we received a total of 184 responses.

The open-ended comments fall into one of four categories of recommendation. The first, and most frequently mentioned, is the topic of the paper. The second area most frequently mentioned was style of writing. The third most frequently mentioned topic was process, referring to the process by which one moves from idea to published paper. The fourth most frequently mentioned comment category was methods, meaning research methods.

Choose a great topic

Our pool of experts first recommended that authors choose a topic that is of interest and that will have high impact on the field. They also talk about choosing a topic that "bridges" academics and practice. Below are some sample comments:

1. Choose a topic that is unique and interesting and do a good job selling the story.
2. Write on current burning issues / topics in HRM.
3. Insure the topic is relevant to the audience.
4. Write papers with a high-impact factor.
5. Prospective authors should focus on the practicality, timeliness, and importance of the topic.
6. Check the academic / scientific value of the topic.
7. Make sure the article is a topic of importance to both scientists and practitioners.
8. Pick a topic that is current and of importance to the field. Too often, I think, authors write about what interests them and not what interests readers.
9. Ensure the topic would be useful and interesting to a majority of the intended audience.
10. The mindset of the author is critical. Because *HRM* is a bridge journal it is critical that normal scholarly journal norms be met in terms of study design and analysis, but that topics be of interest to the professional community (that is, have some practical application).
11. Make sure your research contributes something of real value to the literature and to practice.
12. Focus on something that is meaningful for the discipline – one that advances knowledge dramatically rather than incrementally.

The rest of the comments follow this basic pattern. The experts recommend that authors pick interesting topics that would be of value to both scientists and practitioners. They also tend to recommend high-impact studies. However, for anyone who is junior in the field, I am certain they would be advised to be careful about how "innovative" they are in their selection of topics because it is often more difficult to get higher risk papers published in "good" journals.

The degree to which your research is "risky" is a personal choice. Search the journals that you like to read, and make your own decision about the kind of work you want to do and seek to publish. My own early career experience was that the papers I really liked to read and that I used as models for my own work were rather cutting-edge (or high-risk) pieces. I wanted to strive to do that type of work, but I also had my second path of "safe" research.

The career decision and how to spend your time is directly related to where you publish and the topics you choose to study. For *HRM*, it is important that the topics be timely because our audience consists of both academics and practitioners. Also, *HRM* is a journal that will go out of its way to encourage a high-risk topic because we want to publish new research. Therefore, one other piece of advice is that if you are going to take on topics that are of interest to you, but that you know are high risk for non-bridge or more traditional academic journals, then *HRM* may be a good choice. Papers that succeed faster are those that are written for *HRM* vs. those that are written for a different type of journal, rejected, and then just sent to *HRM*.

Writing style

The issue of writing style came up as a key recommendation. As a reviewer and editor, I can only support every comment I read in this host of recommendations. Below are a few sample comments:

1. Use a clear, cogent, and non-jargonistic writing style.
2. Write clearly and well. Poor grammar and format will really frustrate reviewers.
3. Use theory to explain, but try to frame your ideas via real-life examples.
4. Be sure to discuss the practical relevance of your study.
5. Be as brief as possible. Cite a few historical sources and refer readers to places to go for more information.
6. Be sure to engage the reader early with a practical problem that your manuscript will address.
7. Minimize technical details in the body of the manuscript. Include any technical material (e.g., formulas, computational details) in an appendix at the end of the main article.Follow the publisher's instructions for submitting the manuscript. Make sure that you have met all the requirements and have addressed all of the questions and comments.
8. You have to come up with concrete suggestions for application. If it cannot make an impact on the organization, then it is not relevant for HRM.
9. Be clear and concise.
10. Contributions should be crystal clear to reviewers and readers. Make sure you explain why the paper is important.
11. Your discussion section should not go beyond the data, overstate, or overgeneralize your findings. Copyedit carefully.

12. The issue of being scientific is especially true for authors who submit qualitative papers and case studies. Lack of numbers shouldn't mean lack of scientific rigor! There are many excellent texts and references discussing the issues of scientific rigor and appropriate standards in qualitative research – there is no reason to not use them. So please make sure you report in your paper what steps you took to ensure the credibility and verifiability of your qualitative research.
13. Tell a story; provide the results of a case study, give demographics, show graphs. Use real examples that are powerful that people can relate to.
14. Be fluent and easy to understand in writing style.
15. The ability to satisfy the needs of the practitioner audience requires taking time to translate the significance of the results into practical advice. This means working through the implications systematically. Often, too little attention is paid to this important part of the manuscript. It is an acid test for relevance that all of our research should go through.
16. Write in the first person.
17. Take time to really get the writing "right." Everything from the flow to the logic to proper grammar to eliminating all typos to always using the correct, most precise word, especially verbs.

In summary, the writing style should be one that is "accessible" to a large audience of readers. The research should be rigorous and compelling, but reading the article should be a pleasure. If you are unclear about your style, we suggest that you hire an editor to review the paper for you; it is helpful to have someone who is not close to the paper to review the manuscript and provide you with detailed feedback.

The thinking to writing to publishing process

Comments about process ranged from preparation in writing to submitting the paper to the revise-and-resubmit stage and lastly to recovery when you get a rejection (which we all receive). When I do presentations on the editorial process, I often am asked about the underlying politics of getting published. Authors want to know if "who you know" matters or if you should be strategic about whom you send the paper to for review. These issues too were addressed, but there were not many comments about pure "politics." This host of comments had three subcategories, which are: (1) relationships with others, (2) tactical advice, and (3) dealing with reviewers. I divided the comments into those three subsections for review.

Comment category #1: Developing relationships, learning from others, and relying on colleagues:

1. Talk to an editor.
2. Know the right people.

3. Talk to someone who has published.
4. Get a friendly review from multiple people before submitting.
5. Before resubmitting our manuscript, we obtained independent reviews from advanced practitioners, whom we instructed to offer feedback on both the readability and conceptual relevance of the paper to a bridge audience. We found this to be very helpful.
6. Build networks / contacts with editors at *HRM*.
7. Participate in the community by reviewing, meeting the people who published and review for *HRM* at conferences.
8. Draw widely on academic and non-academic sources of experience, inspiration and insight. Remember, it's "people" we're talking about here (the human in *HRM*).
9. Believe in yourself and in your contributions.

Comment category #2: Tactical advice

1. Start by presenting your work at well respected academic conferences. From here, refine your work and get it in shape for submission.
2. Meet all the journal guidelines as best as possible.
3. Submit papers that are applicable to the Call for Papers (if a special interest) or in line with what is published in the journal.
4. Read the guidelines for authors and the related details so that you can ensure that your manuscript is suitable for the journal (or not).
5. Very important – have a real interest in HRM and be committed to conducting rigorous research.
6. Become very familiar with the goals and style of *HRM* by reading some of the articles here. Follow the instructions.
7. Keep current on what is happening in the field, both academic and in practice. Read the academic literature, professional literature, media on business; go to conferences.
8. Read conference proceedings from top international conferences such as the *Academy of Management*. Look for emerging trends in management.

Comment category #3: The review process

1. Make convincing attempts to incorporate the reviewers' concerns; don't get into a fighting match with the editor or reviewers.
2. When you get the reviews back, just put them away for a few weeks or months until you are able to think about them rationally. Then read through them again and start thinking about how to address them. Patience is a virtue.
3. Respond to reviewers' and editors' comments; often it seems as if the authors think they can "trick" the reviewers and editors by stating that they made changes and they really did not.

4. The key is persistence. It is easy for a new author to be discouraged by rejection and reviewers' comments that seem harsh. The answer is to respond to reviewer comments, rebut them where you can, or revise your work to answer them. In this way the editor and the reviewers can be valuable teachers if you are open to learning. Regard them as people who want to publish your work.

If you take these comments in total, they provide a very good set of ideas for anyone who is embarking upon a writing career. The networking and tactical work of reading the journal, reading publishing cues, and then knowing how to work with reviewers are all important to success. From the editor's point of view, I continue to be struck by how many people "blame" failure in publishing on not knowing the right people. At least at *HRM* (and I think the same is the same with other journals), we go out of our way to evaluate papers for their merit alone. The names are not attached to papers, and school affiliation is not part of the review process. Papers are judged on their own merit.

However, I do think that it is more common practice at some universities for peers to help each other. Professors read each others' papers; they present their research at seminars, and authors obtain more advice perhaps in some schools than in others. This does not mean that editors favor certain schools; it does, however, mean that there are some institutions that produce more high-quality papers because they have extensive support systems to help authors write and publish. The secrets to success are not secrets at all; they are clear. If only you read these comments, you would see what successful authors are doing. These processes, when broken down into tactical steps, can be replicated wherever you are.

Research methods

The last area where our reviewers and editorial board had significant suggestions is on the subject of research methods. The comments were fairly consistent – use good methods. Use methods that are rigorous and widely accepted. The word "rigor" came up quite frequently, and it was applied to both quantitative and qualitative data. Here are some sample comments:

1. Use the most simple and direct statistical measures to analyze your data rather than first and only use more sophisticated measures when they are not needed.
2. Statistical analysis should match the research question.
3. Rigor – design a study that addresses the research question that you set out to answer. Make sure to search for existing measures of the variables you include. If none are available, validate new measures. Use appropriate statistical methods. If you are using advanced statistical methods, be very clear in your explanation of them and the findings.

4. Focus on measurement. Organizational behaviour/Human resource reviewers tend to be strong on measurement.
5. Take up cross-cultural challenges – the working world has never been as diverse as it is today.
6. Be careful with theory. The Maslows, McGregors, Hertzbergs have been flogged to death. We need new ways of looking at HRM.

Our respondents suggest that authors use the right methods for their research questions, that they execute their study well, and that they explain the methods in terms that are understandable. It was interesting to notice that several reviewers suggested that authors not try to "over-complicate" their methods section. Also, there were good words of advice for authors who use qualitative data. The choice of data type should not dictate rigor; however, we notice that many of the papers we receive using qualitative data do not take the same care to develop research questions, hypotheses, or their methods sections.

Summary of survey data

The reviewers' comments provide an excellent overview for authors. They note that the process of preparing your paper is not really about the paper itself. The tips they provide focus on one's career, overall abilities as a researcher, and ability to tell a story, which is one step beyond pure writing. It may seem that storytelling and scientific rigor are at odds, but they are not. The key to success in writing, whether for *HRM* or any other journal, is to craft your data into a story that others will read. The learning and results are useless unless someone reads them. Good papers will be used in the classroom to spur discussions among MBA students; they will be cited by others because the research causes them to want to extend the work and develop follow-up studies.

For *HRM*, the bridge nature of the journal means that we want good stories for both academics and practitioners. Successful authors must not only be writing on topics of interest to this broad audience but they also must write in a way that is accessible to both academics and practitioners. Whether the paper is conceptual or a research study, whether with qualitative or quantitative data, the paper must represent a rigorous piece of work.

Writing for *HRM* is a challenge for authors who have only written for purely "academic" journals; however, our authors tell us they find the process of preparing and publishing a paper for *HRM* to be very rewarding. You can frame the paper somewhat differently, and the process of writing allows you to think about your work in a different light. Rather than writing for just other academics, you are writing to people who will use your work in their daily jobs. This is a rewarding realization for many people who may have limited audiences for their work.

Editing: the crafter of the story

It has been almost three years since I began working with *HRM*. Editing the journal at this particular time in its history has been an incredible challenge but one that I have valued. In learning from our internal editorial team and from other editors, I would provide the following observations for those of you who are considering being editors or who are starting the editor role.

1. It is a tough job. This is a very time-consuming and difficult job. I must say that I did not know what I was getting into. My motivation for doing the work was my commitment to the HR profession, my personal interest in keeping up to date on research in *HRM*, and my interest in taking on the challenge of the bridge journal (since it fit so well with my personal career). The only way that I could make it work was to put together an active and high-quality management team. I have seen that many editors like to do a lot more of the editorial process themselves. I've talked to editors who say they personally handle 70% of the papers that come through. This has not been the case for me. I do work with papers that are "on topic" with my experience, but I have learned to delegate. I have an active team of associate editors, and they are empowered to do the work needed to keep the journal running. I purposely put myself into a role similar to the one I have at my company (where I am the CEO). This is a decisions everyone must make when coming into the editorial role. How much of the "journal" is you vs. your team?
2. Success in meeting goals creates even more work. When we started with *HRM*, one of our key challenges was getting enough papers. We came into a situation where we did not have enough manuscripts to meet publishing deadlines. Thus, we spent a considerable amount of time working with authors who had revisions outstanding (trying to move papers forward); we recruited people to help with special issues; we started more marketing to reach out to the readers, and more. Today, we have a healthy and growing flow of manuscripts. In our relaunch we expanded the number of pages per issue to accommodate our changing environment. If we continue to get more papers, we may consider moving to six (vs. four) issues per year (but then that's even more work for our team). Our challenge now is to keep the system flowing with a greater workload for all of us.
3. The automated submission process has advantages and disadvantages. I could not do this job without the online submission and manuscript processing system. However, I have heard from other editors that the automation results in authors submitting papers "before their time." This means the editorial team's work goes up considerably. I would agree with this from our experience. We are getting more papers that are really not at all a fit with *HRM*, and it is obvious that authors never read the

publishing cues. The pros, however, of being able to see papers from anywhere, no paper trail, reporting that is much more accurate and efficient, to me at least, all outweigh the cons.
4. Control – is that what it is all about? I have had several people say that it must be great to be an editor because you have so much control over the field, what gets published, etc. The reality is that, like everything that you manage, it is hard work and less control or "power" than you may think. By working with a management team rather than "owning" all the papers myself, I personally have delegated control to others. I think there is less control and more learning. I feel very good about being part of an excellent team that, together, is helping contribute to the field of HRM and overall "people management."

The editorial process is not really such a black box. If you ask people what it is like, they will tell you. This book is a perfect example of the ways editors share information. I was welcomed as an editor; other editors (even from journals that are competitors) all helped me extensively, and I find it a pleasure to work with our authors, associate editors, editorial board, and reviewers. I just wish I had more time to be more involved with the extended team. That is the problem – time. Everyone who works for *HRM* is doing so as voluntary work. We are all busy with other jobs. The most difficult thing, I find, is managing expectations. You can only do so much with the hours in a day given to you. We hope that our hours are spent at *HRM* to create a product that helps both academics and practitioners do their jobs better and learn from each other.

Notes

1. *HRM*, published by John Wiley & Sons, New York, is not the same journal as *Human Resource Management Journal*, which is published by Blackwell Publishing in the UK. People confused the two because the titles are similar.

17
Developing a Global Journal: Embracing Otherness

Haridimos Tsoukas

When David Wilson, then Editor-in-Chief of *Organization Studies* (*OSS*), and Jean-Claude Thoenig, then Chairman of the Advisory Board of *OSS* asked me late in 2002 to consider the possibility of succeeding David as Editor-in-Chief, one of the things I made clear was that one of my aspirations for the journal was to turn it into a *global* one. They agreed and I soon started to work on it (Tsoukas, Garud, & Hardy, 2003).

But what is "a global journal"? *OSS* has always been an international journal anyway, in which scholars from different countries published. Since it is an English-language journal it was to be expected that English-language speakers would dominate submissions. But even so, *OSS* was distinctly European. Set up in 1979 by organizational researchers from several European countries, it has always been a bastion of European organizational research.

Initial conditions are important for the trajectory institutions to follow. The European identity *OSS* was to take was partially imagined on the basis of its differentiation from (or even opposition to, one might argue) the American identity. The positivist scholarly orthodoxy that had long dominated American organizational research was thought too narrow for the Europeans at the time; too lifelessly technical; and too ethnocentric, anyway. Of course, we know that this is only partly true. The American version of organizational scholarship is more variegated than conventional accounts might imply. Karl Weick, James March, Chris Argyris, Ed Schein, and John van Maanen, to mention a few, are some of the most distinguished American organizational scholars but they could hardly be called "positivists." This is not to deny the positivist hegemony one discerns in postwar organizational scholarship in the United States but to merely point out that the adjective "American" is, as adjectives are anyway, too ambiguous for it to be unequivocally given a definitive meaning. This did not stop the institutional entrepreneurs who set up *OSS* at the time to try to construct a homogenous "American" identity to which a "European" journal would be juxtaposed. That is how identities are constructed anyway – through plausible abstraction and symbolic opposition.

What would a European organizational research journal look like? What would its identity be? It is printed on the cover of every single *OSS* issue you get your hands on: "an international multidisciplinary journal devoted to the study of organizations, organizing, and the organized in and between societies." The new journal would explicitly be "international," whereas mainstream American journals at the time were mainly dominated by US authors and American topics of interest. It would not be devoted only to the study of "organizations" but crucially, to "organizing" and "the organized" too. Organizations should not be conceptualized through the commonsensical understandings provided by the "organizers," namely, the managerial elite, but in terms of those who are "organized" as well. Organizations should not be studied only from the "outside-in, namely in terms of properties an independent researcher might try to study in an attempt to find out how they are related and why, but should be studied also from the "inside-out," namely in terms of the *process* through which organizations emerge. Finally, organizational phenomena are not self-contained but deeply social. They are rooted in broader social understandings and embedded in societal and, increasingly, international institutions. Therefore, organizational phenomena should be situated "in" their societies and compared "between" societies. It is not good enough to find out how a particular society's institutions impinge on organizations within a country, but a comparative perspective would help us understand differences across countries. All these nuances were not in evidence in mainstream US journals at the time, and *OSS* explicitly sought to reflect them.

There were other issues as well. The American organizational academic community is the largest single community in the world, with a unified academic labor market and broadly similar doctoral programs and academic standards of assessment. That was (and still is) hardly the case in Europe (Whitley, 2000). With an academic labor market fragmented along national lines; different academic traditions and standards of assessment; and with different doctoral training systems, Europe has not only been different to the United Stated but rather heterogeneous within itself as well. This heterogeneity made it considerably more difficult for a particular research orthodoxy to be established in Europe than in the United States. Like the plethora of nation-states and languages one encounters in Europe, so does one encounter a plethora of perspectives, orientations, and sensitivities. Europe is rooted in pluralism – it has always been. This made *OSS* a deeply pluralistic journal. An underlying open-mindedness, grounded on heterogeneity, as well as a conscious effort to draw on the social sciences at large and, increasingly, on the humanities, made *OSS* a journal open to diverse influences and to different approaches.

But not entirely. After all, the journal did have an identity which, as noted above, was set up in opposition to (or at least in differentiation with) American positivism. That skewed its pluralism in a particular direction, favoring mainly qualitative, interpretive, and critical organizational research with a mainly sociological and, occasionally philosophical slant. It is understandable why this has happened. Pluralism does not imply formlessness, nor is a journal a *tabula rasa* waiting for papers to fill it in. Journals have a historically shaped identity which guides editorial choices and initiatives, and signals to prospective authors the criteria in terms of which their work is to be judged. A journal, in other words, forms over time a discursively produced identity which "'rules in' certain ways of talking about a topic, defining an acceptable and intelligible way to talk, write or conduct one self. [Also it] 'rules out', limits and restricts other ways of talking, of conducting ourselves in relation to the topic or constructing knowledge about it" (Hall, cited in Philips, Lawrence, & Hardy, 2004: 636). Identities carry the marks of their historical beginnings; they focus attention; they enable and constrain.

But identities change too. As the world of organizational scholarship expanded, following on the expansion of business education around the world, so did the different locations within which research was conducted as well as the different approaches for carrying it out. Expansion brought diversity (March, J., 2007). Moreover, thanks mainly to the Internet, collaboration at a distance became far easier than ever before. Although geography has not disappeared, it has lost the significance it once had, at least insofar as the circulation and sharing of intellectual work goes. To be international these days is not enough, for it merely implies that one is not bound by national boundaries. As a European journal, *OSS* has, by design, explicitly been an *international* journal. But as the world of worldwide organizational scholarship becomes ever more integrated, leading journals become increasingly the carriers of a new quasi-global scholarly consciousness which is shaped by multiple communicative interactions (across cultures and disciplines). More than ever before, historically generated intellectual identities are open to new influences. A global journal, for me at least, is one that self-consciously sees itself as the custodian of a culture of intellectual openness. It provides a forum to scholars who may be embedded in distinct academic traditions all over the world to engage in a dialog with(in) the field. Let me explain.

Being historically shaped, the field is an uneven terrain, an institutionalized body of knowledge that inevitably reflects the preoccupations and perspectives of those who have historically been its most significant contributors. At the same time, since researchers are not transhistorical beings but rooted in different countries, which have their own institutionalized systems of scholarship, namely particular intellectual styles and standards of intellectual assessment, their interests and styles are bound to be reflected in papers submitted. The distinguishing feature of a global journal is to understand the inherent diversity of academic scholarship, welcome it, and help the authors shape it into a contribution to the field, thus enriching the field. Structurally, this is manifested with an editorial board and, in the case of *OSS*, with a leading editorial team, consisting of three coeditors and about 20 senior editors, all of whom make editorial decisions, spanning geographically most of the world.

That was not always the case. Historically, *OSS* operated most of the time with a single editor-in-chief, who would be drawn from a major European country; a handful of mostly European associate editors; and an international editorial board. A far more distributed structure has been created since I took over on September 1, 2003. Associate editors have been renamed coeditors and are located in Northern America (Raghu Garud), Australia/New Zealand (Cynthia Hardy) and Europe (David Courpasson), in all of which there are sizeable English-language communities of organizational researchers. The idea was to span several continents. Moreover, senior editors are geographically dispersed all over the world.

These were conscious decisions and signaled the willingness of *OSS* to be, and be seen to be, a journal that wishes to engage with scholars who write in English from all over the world. As we know, structures are set up for problem-handling as well as symbolic purposes. In the case of *OSS*, as well as handling effectively an ever-increasing editorial load (more than 400 papers are submitted every year, twice as much as five years ago), it signals to the worldwide academic community that we care for diversity; we recognize the embeddedness of academic research into different contexts; and we welcome it.

As well as welcoming diversity, however, a global peer-reviewed journal is still a *journal* – it is a disciplinary device that inevitably constrains diversity. To be in dialogue with the field implies that one is in dialogue with those scholars whose voices have been there before his or hers. To join a conversation one needs to accept its currently dominant form and, accordingly, shape one's contributions in a way that will make it recognizable in the conversation. That calls for *discipline* but it also leaves space for difference. To make my contribution recognizable in the conversation, it does not mean that I need to make it identical in form and content to those of others. I can be an interlocutor, with everything this implies for the way I construct my contribution, and yet be a *different* me – someone whose voice is different from those encountered so far. Let me be more specific with an example.

In 2005 a paper was submitted to *OSS* with the intriguing title "Reform without a Theory: Why Does it Work in China?" (Zhu, 2007). It was not a conventional paper: it was not particularly organizationally focused; the study of Chinese reforms and the requisite institution-building involved has not been part of mainstream organization studies, although in the last ten years the study of comparative economic organization has made considerable progress; and, crucially, the argumentation was more discursive and essayistic than would be normal for a journal paper. The paper was offering, however, an intriguing argument to make sense of the Chinese reforms, claiming that the latter were a strategic reform without a theory and, therefore, the gradualism-radicalism debate rested on a false dichotomy. Insofar as the paper blended a cultural understanding of China with an institutional analysis and attention to situationally specific, historical contingencies, it was in line with the explicitly *comparative* lens of *OSS* that emphasized the embeddedness of organizational phenomena within societal institutions.

But, on the whole, the original paper was somewhat awkward. I was not sure whether it was a question of language, mode of arguing, or conceptual construction that led me to that conclusion. Here was a "different" paper, written by someone coming from a distinctly different intellectual tradition. The author, Zhichang Zhu, was affiliated to University of Hull, but he had spent most of his life in China. His background was unusual. In his autobiographical resume it was stated that his normal education had stopped when he was 16, due to China's Cultural Revolution. Without a first degree, he had obtained an M.Sc. in Information Management and a PhD in Management Systems and Sciences, sponsored by British scholarships. He had been, among other things, a communist Red Guard and a farm laborer.

I decided to submit the paper to the review process as an *essai*. The two reviews collected contained constructive and insightful comments, and the senior editor Richard Whitley, a leading expert on comparative economic organization, wrote perceptive comments inviting the author to revise and resubmit. The paper was indeed significantly revised: it came closer to a conventional *OSS* scholarly paper, while retaining its conceptual distinctiveness. Nicole Biggart, University of California-Davis, a distinguished expert on comparative economic organization, was one of the reviewers. Commenting on the second draft, she summarized best what was distinctive about the paper and why it should be published. She wrote to me and to the senior editor:

> I think that "Reform without a Theory" is a successful revision of the earlier manuscript and should be published. It is not an easy-to-read *essai*, but that is not because it is grammatically awkward. The author/editor's revisions have made it much more organized and simple to read, at least on the surface.
>
> The difficulty will be with understanding what is inherently an analysis done in a non-Western manner using non-Western categories, but trying to be sensible to Westerners. It makes me think of what it is like to read a science fiction novel of an alternative reality. China is an alternative reality and has historically developed organizing patterns and conceptualizations that are alien to Westerners. Explaining them is not just a matter of sharing information, but of sharing worldviews and alternative ontologies with the reader, and then asking the reader to adopt them in order to get the analysis.
>
> I actually found much of the discussion of the notes from the author about his/her revisions interesting from this perspective, for example the tension between being "articulate" and "suggestive." This is an excellent

illustration of the different values placed on scholarly discourse and expression between the two traditions.

This is an exemplary attitude to "difference" from an *OSS* reviewer, and I am particularly proud to share it with you. Nicole recognizes that the paper has been brought into a shape that makes it recognizable in the relevant scholarly conversation. At the same time, she also appreciates the contribution of the paper, which comes from its unusual angle. But that contribution is rather unconventional so that, perhaps, it may not make it so easy for the OSS reader to follow the argument. For any reader? Not quite: for the Western reader. Here we are confronted with *otherness*, implies Nicole, and we must make a hermeneutical effort to understand what the paper is all about. It is demanding and occasionally frustrating but, ultimately, rewarding as we get to know the working of another society and a different way of thinking and arguing.

Notice how through the (largely Western, in particular Anglo-American) established conventions of academic scholarship and the hitherto available research on the particular topic of the paper (largely published in English), the field holds its disciplinary power over the author in forcing him to shape the paper in a way that will make it *recognizable* in the scholarly conversation that *OSS* provides a forum for. But, at the same time, the journal, through its reviewers and editors, stretches itself, is open to otherness, and, by consciously expanding its intellectual boundaries, it hopefully enriches the conversation.

Here is, I suggest, what I call *scholarly globalism* (as opposed to parochialism) at its best. Technological and economic developments bring scholars from highly diverse intellectual traditions together and make conversation possible. To join competently the existing scholarly conversation authors need to shape their contributions accordingly *and* strive, at the same time, to retain their otherness. Participants in the conversation stretch themselves intellectually to understand the Other and assess the merits of his/her argument. The act of understanding, if successfully completed, "fuses the horizons" of the interlocutors (Gadamer, 1989). The (typically Western) *OSS* reader's horizon is hopefully extended to make room for the Other and, by so doing, it is changed.

I cannot guarantee that such a fusion of horizons occurs with every "different" paper that is submitted to *OSS*, after all a hermeneutical exercise, being subject-dependent, is always a precarious in its outcome (Taylor, 2002: 286). But the example I have just described is an *example* in Wittgenstein's (1969: 145) sense: it has *exemplary* value and shows in practice how a journal can, indeed, be self-consciously global.

It is not only scholars from non-Western cultures, however, that are likely to write "different" papers. Continental European scholarship provides also an example, different in form from what we conventionally take the

Anglo-Saxon intellectual tradition to be. As a Greek who has spent most of his adult life in English-language universities, I know. In my own country, and in several other Continental European countries, a theoretical scholarly paper is often taken to be a critical summary of, or a commentary on, the literature – it tends to be more of an essay. It is also more likely to be wide-ranging and draws on different disciplines or theoretical frameworks, without necessarily attempting to integrate them, something which would be difficult to do anyway in the limited space of a paper. By and large, in Continental Europe, there is still a certain expectation of the authors to be more wide-ranging and not so discipline-bound than their Anglo-Saxon counterparts. If it is an empirical paper, especially with a quantitative research design, it tends to report data, without necessarily a systematic effort to draw out theoretical implications and how, properly interpreted, those data may contribute to our theoretical understanding of the phenomenon at hand.

In the Anglo-Saxon tradition things tend to be different. Demonstrating a contribution is of paramount importance. Staying focused (even relatively narrow), writing in a straightforward and non-circumlocutory way, building methodically a coherent argument, and "adding value" to what we know, as the current metaphor is, are very important. Moreover, the language of publication – English in this case – is no mere medium; the language is grounded on, and animated within, particular intellectual communities. An English-language journal is likely to draw on the intellectual tradition of Britain and the United States, especially since these two countries have historically been the most significant players in science. To some extent, the language helps shape the argument one puts forward – how it is constructed and what it aims to achieve. To paraphrase Wittgenstein, to ground yourself in a language is to locate yourself in a community.

The difficulty several Continental European scholars have in publishing in international English-language journals is not so much their English as the foreignness of the scholarly *style* that underlies the use of scholarly English. A style is not something merely cosmetic. It "governs how anything can show up *as* anything" (Spinosa, Flores, & Dreyfus, 1997: 20); a style makes certain kinds of purposes and activities matter, and others not. When it comes to publishing in academic journals, demonstrating a contribution is what most matters in the Anglo-Saxon scholarship; voicing one's thoughts in as thorough a manner as possible and/or reporting empirical evidence is what has mattered most in Continental Europe.

Nonetheless, a global journal is aware of the differences of scholarly styles and is not dismissive of them. A global journal is aware of its location within a particular intellectual tradition; it recognizes the latter's contingency and, therefore, is self-consciously open to influences (Rorty, 1989: Ch.1). Just like a journal's identity is a discursively produced object, so is a journal's intellectual tradition. Both identity and tradition guide, but they are susceptible to change. A journal that aspires to be global stretches itself intellectually to extend its horizons. And authors who aspire to contribute to a global journal shape their contributions so that to make them recognizable in the discourse the journal espouses, while seeking to retain their otherness. A global journal is not oblivious to geography, but remains sensitive to otherness – it seeks a "polyocular vision" (Maruyama, 2003: 468–9). A globalized world brings otherness closer to the mainstream and makes the fusion of horizons more possible than ever before.

Conclusions

Parochialism is increasingly difficult to defend today. Scientific research has become a global activity and one is unlikely to be able to do high-quality research unless one is connected to the broader academic community, which transcends borders. The Internet makes global collaboration uniquely possible. However, to work effectively with others from all over the world, one needs to regularly check one's prejudices. A global world is a world that calls for constant other-awareness and tests one's self-awareness.

An editor of a global journal needs to be open to different intellectual styles, while retaining a dynamic identity of his/her journal. No doubt, such a goal generates tension. But it is a tension that can be handled, provided the editor is aware of the historically shaped identity of the journal *and* the ways it is discursively influenced, and therefore changed, in an interconnected world, in which there is ineradicable plurality. A deep appreciation of that plurality makes it possible for an editor to look sympathetically into papers that do not conform to typifications generated by a journal's identity. The following questions an editor needs to address: Does this paper fit in with the objectives of the journal, broadly understood? Irrespectively of the paper's language, argumentation, and structure, is there a kernel of a potentially interesting contribution in it? What do I learn from the paper and how does it compare to what we already know about the phenomenon at hand? Does the paper challenge our cherished ways of thinking? If the claims put forward in the paper were not to see the light, would we be impoverished?

At the same time, a prospective author needs to handle a similar sort of tension: that between otherness and recognizability. Seeking to contribute to an ongoing debate by stressing otherness is welcome, but needs to be balanced with a concern for recognizability by those others who have already been part of the debate. The following questions are important for an author to address: What do I need to do for others in the debate to recognize my contribution as such? Am I addressing an issue of concern to others? How should I link my argument to the scholarly conversation that has been going on? What forms of argument do I need to use in order to draw my interlocutors' attention to what I see as important? How can I convince them of the plausibility of my claims?

Academic publishing is, partly at least, the art of persuasion. An editor needs to be open-minded enough to allow him/herself to be influenced. And an author needs to be determined enough to make his/her voice heard as something both intelligible and original. Like in global politics at large, handling tensions creatively is what publishing in a global journal entails, for both editors and authors.

Acknowledgments

I would like to thank Nicole Biggart, Richard Whitley and Zhichang Zhu for giving me permission to refer to the review process of Zhichang Zhu's paper here and, in the case of Nicole, to include part of her e-mail. Comments from Yehuda Baruch, Cynthia Hardy, Raghu Garud and Nicole Biggart are gratefully acknowledged.

References

Gadamer, H.-G. (1989). *Truth and Method*. Translation revised by J. Weinsheimer and D. G. Marshall. Second, Revised Edition. London: Sheed & Ward.
March, J. (2007). The study of organizations and organizing since 1945. *Organization Studies*, 28, 9–19.
Maruyama, M. (2004). Polyocular vision or subunderstanding? *Organization Studies*, 25/3, 467–80.
Philips, N., Lawrence, T. B., & Hardy, C. (2004). Discourse and institutions. *Academy of Management Review*, 29, 635–52.
Rorty, R. (1989). *Contingency, Irony, and Solidarity*. Cambridge: Cambridge University Press.
Spinosa, C., Flores, F., & Dreyfus, H. L. (1997). *Disclosing New Worlds*. Cambridge, Mass.: The MIT Press.
Taylor, C. (2002). Understanding the other: A Gadamerian view on conceptual schemes. In J. Malpas, U. Arnswald, & J. Kertscher (eds), *Gadamer's Century: Essays in Honor of Hans-Georg Gadamer*, Cambridge, Mass.: MIT Press, 279–298.
Tsoukas, H., Garud, R., & Hardy, C. (2003). Editorial: Continuity and change for *Organization Studies*. *Organization Studies*, 24, 1003–14.
Whitley, R. (2000). *The Intellectual and Social Organization of the Sciences*, Oxford: Oxford University Press, 2nd Edition.
Wittgenstein, L. (1969). *On Certainty*. Oxford: Blackwell.
Zhu, Z. (2007). Reform without a theory: Why does it work in China? *Organization Studies*, 28/10, 1503–22.

18
Sustaining Independent Journals
Timothy Clark and Mike Wright

Introduction

Journals are a key conduit through which knowledge and ideas are certified and disseminated to the broad academy. In the last 20 years or so there have been dramatic changes in the journals market. The merging of publishers has resulted in considerable consolidation and increased levels of concentration. Library expenditure on serials has increased at the expense of books. The Association of Research Libraries (2006) reported that between 1986 and 2005 the unit cost of a journal subscription increased by 5.3 percent a year, whereas that for monographs grew by 3.2 percent. In the same period expenditures on serials increased by 7.6 percent, more than three times that for monographs (2.5 percent). Site licensing and the development of the Internet has had a substantial impact on the way in which academic information is distributed and provided a platform for greater access to journal content and facilitated the establishment of new online journals with open access. There are currently over 2,500 journals listed in the Directory of Open Access Journals (DOAJ) with 33 in management. However, the mortality rate amongst the journals is high. Morris (2006), for example, finds that by end of 2005, 9.7 percent of the 1213 journals in the DOAJ for which information could be traced had not published anything since at least 2003 and appeared to have ceased publication altogether. Given this situation, in this chapter we examine the particular issues editors face when developing and sustaining a distinctive independent journal. We are two of the General Editors of an independent (i.e., nonaffiliated to a professional association) journal – *Journal of Management Studies* (*JMS*) – that has managed to survive and prosper since 1964. Our purpose is to build on our experience of managing this journal and to provide insights for other editors of such journals; although many of the issues we raise have implications for editors of journals more generally.

The first section identifies a number of reasons as to why new independent journals are established. We then turn to discuss a number of factors that may help editors to sustain and build independent journals. Finally, we present some concluding comments and highlight some key lessons for editors and authors.

Why are new journals proliferating?

At a broad level we distinguish three main factors driving the establishment of new independent journals. First, there has been a huge growth in the amount of material being submitted to established journals. Within management many of the leading journals have reported significant increases in submissions over the past five years, some in excess of 100 percent, with a consequent increase in rejection rates (see, for example, Clark, Floyd, and Wright, 2006; Rynes, 2005). With average page budgets and volume sizes in established journals remaining fairly constant, a clear demand has developed for alternative outlets for the material that these journals reject[1].

Second, and this has been a trend within academic publishing since its inception, some areas perceive that established journals are not well predisposed to their work. For whatever reason, broadly based journals that seek to encompass a field often become perceived as narrowing because they are associated with particular theoretical perspectives or methodological approaches (for example, see the recent efforts by the *Academy of Management Journal* to signal its openness to qualitative and international research; Rynes, 2005). Researchers oftentimes want to have the opportunity to address topics or say some thing that may be difficult to convey in mainstream journals associated with a particular theoretical or methodological paradigm or approach. Journals may also require a standardized approach to the presentation of conceptual arguments and empirical analysis. The problem is that there is a high opportunity cost for authors in producing such work if the journal is not recognized as a quality outlet or is perceived as being narrowly based and so closed to certain kinds of work. As publishing consensus-challenging research can be an uncertain process for authors, they may be reluctant to submit what they perceive to be their more novel work to journals that signal that they give primacy to particular approaches. This develops a momentum for the establishment of a journal that is inclusive towards this kind of work.

As an example, in the finance area, the *Journal of Financial Economics* (*JFE*) was established as a result of frustrations by some academics (Michael Jensen and others) that the *Journal of Finance* was not interested in publishing research in their areas (Jensen, 2006). Some time later, the *Review of Financial Studies* was established by those academics who became frustrated at the editorial policy of *JFE* under Jensen's tenure. In addition, an area can develop to such a point that it begins to generate sufficient work at a certain level of quality that is able to sustain a new journal. Human Resource Management is an example of an area which grew exponentially in the 1980s.

Consequently, both the volume and depth of work within this area increased to such a point that two new journals were established in 1990 – *Human Resource Management Journal* and *International Journal of Human Resource Management*. The establishment of specialist journals has also occurred in such diverse areas as entrepreneurship (*Journal of Business Venturing*), careers (*Career Development Quarterly* and *Career Development International*), and business ethics (*Business Ethics – A European Review*).

The third factor driving the launching of new journals is the bundling of journals by publishers. Rather than pay for subscriptions on a journal-by-journal basis, libraries are increasingly purchasing access to large numbers of journals through a single site license. For academics and students this means that they have instant access to the content of a wide range of journals. For the large publishers it means that subscriptions to individual journals are more difficult to cancel and smaller publishers are squeezed out of the market because libraries prefer to purchase the larger bundles. However, to justify the model and the cost journal publishers have to offer a broad range of journals and so set up journals to give the impression to libraries and aggregators that they are getting value for money[2]. There is therefore pressure to constantly strengthen rather than weaken their portfolio (Jeon and Menicucci, 2006). Also, by adding journals to existing bundles, publishers can enter markets and quickly dominate them by leveraging the size of their bundles. Consequently, smaller publishers that do not bundle are vulnerable to large-scale aggregation and to absorption into the larger publishers (Bakos and Brynjolfsson, 2000).

Sustaining independent journals

Whatever the reason for their establishment, if they are to avoid a short lifespan, editors of new independent journals have to overcome the initial excitement and optimism that accompanies the launch of the journal and develop systems and processes that sustain their long-term future as well as aiding the development of an upward quality profile. In what follows we identify a number of critical policies, processes and structures that we believe editors need to establish in order to support journal longevity.

Create the journal community

A key disadvantage for any independent journal is that it does not have a readymade community that comes with being linked to a professional association of some kind. Journals that are part of such associations can clearly feed-off the fact that there is an established membership who will submit articles and act as reviewers. In addition, there may be an annual conference and workshops and seminars throughout the year that help generate a flow of papers. In turn, by reaching out to a broader community the journal can benefit the association through raising its profile and developing membership. In contrast, independent journals have to build their own communities without a readymade infrastructure. Building a community of scholars may be more problematical for independent journals. How might editors do this? The following sections provide some insights into this process.

Journal aims and focus

An important way in which editors of independent journals can build a community is to have a distinctive focus that offers value to authors and readers and which meets a clear gap in the existing research community. However, they need to be watchful that the focus does not become too fuzzy or begin to overlap with existing journals of higher prestige. If this occurs the incremental value falls. To protect themselves against responses from other journals, editors need to revisit the founding focus regularly and adjust in the light of broader developments in the field or subarea.

As we have already said, journals associated with professional organizations and conferences may have the positive benefits of direct access to a community of scholars and a regular flow of papers. However, these factors may also have a downside in terms of encouraging conformity. In contrast, editors of independent journals can be distinctive in promoting and publishing consensus-challenging research. Consensus-challenging papers need to do more than "fill-in the potholes" in an established area. A paper may seek to bring a new theoretical lens to an established area; here it is important to demonstrate the shortcomings of existing approaches and how the new lens causes us to see a topic quite differently. Second, a paper may be opening up an entirely new topic that has not been addressed before. We might expect such work to be published in more prestigious journals only once its validity has been established. Thus, editors can have an active role in establishing new approaches to existing topics as well as legitimizing new areas of research. Such efforts can create a distinctive and long-lasting impact on the field and enhance the reputation of a journal.

There is some debate about what constitutes a distinctive contribution, especially a theoretical one (Sutton and Staw, 1995). Some papers may represent "interim struggles in which people intentionally inch toward stronger theories" (Weick, 1995: 385) and ruling these out may slow inquiry in the early stages of theory development. Yet, as Barley (2006: 19) argues, "there are limits on how far transgressive papers can go." Truly innovative papers cannot "break too many substantive, methodological or theoretical rules" (ibid.) without being considered wacky or offbeam. Thus for Barley even innovative work has to conform to certain "genre constraints" and the review process needs to be of sufficient quality to identify whether these have been transgressed to an unacceptable degree. Editors of fledgling and independent journals thus need to balance the tension between rigor in the review process and maintaining a distinctive ethos and openness to a range of approaches.

Offering a better service to reviewers and authors

Offering a high-quality review process that is perceived to be both quick and fair can quickly establish a journal's reputation. Most authors of journal articles feel that the review process is generally too slow. Partly, this arises because of appointment processes within many universities but also because, as McMullen and Shepherd (2006) point out, time-pressures may make academics reluctant to pursue consensus-challenging research. Regardless of whether these apply, there is also a general impatience linked to any uncertainty. We want to know the outcome as soon as possible. It does not take much of a slip in review-decision times or time to publication for word to spread within the community and for submissions to fall. While broad measures of journal quality, such as citation counts, may not change for some time, academic behavior towards journals does in that word-of-mouth reports, particularly on certain aspects of the reviewing process, can greatly influence submission patterns. Any journal should therefore attach considerable emphasis on the need to provide timely feedback to authors. Editors have a responsibility to their community to publish their turnaround figures so that reviewers and authors are aware of the standards expected.

In these circumstances, editors can ill-afford to be lax. Review systems need to be established that can consistently deliver reasonable review periods. The benchmark within management is between 40 and 60 days (Van Fleet et al., 2006; Kacmar, 2001; Rynes et al., 2005). Our experience suggests that a number of factors can influence the turnaround time of reviews. An electronic review system, either conducted directly with authors via e-mail or indirectly through an online manuscript management system, can dramatically reduce reviewing time. For example, moving from a snail mail-based review system to an electronic system reduced review times by a little more than half, at the *JMS* (see Clark, Floyd, & Wright, 2006), from an average of around 118 days to 65 days.

Linked to the above are two further issues. First, not every article should be sent out to review. Desk rejection rates of 40–50 percent are not uncommon in leading management journals (Clark et al., 2006; Van Fleet et al., 2006), with rates in some journals doubling in recent years (Lee, 2003; Rynes et al., 2005). Filtering articles at this stage means that much-valued reviewers are not overloaded with articles that they themselves would not send out to review. In other words, reviewers are not left feeling (1) the journal's standards are below theirown, and (2) their precious time is being spent on reviewing "no hopers." It also means that those papers which show particular promise receive sufficient development input to ensure that their contribution to the literature is fully realized (Rynes et al., 2005; Clark and Wright, 2007). Second, regardless of when a paper is rejected or a revision is invited, decision-making should be transparent and developmental for authors and reviewers. Increasingly journals are sending copies of the reviews together with an editorial letter to both authors and reviewers. This ensures that the reviewers have an opportunity to read all the information editors receive and enables them to appreciate the context for any subsequent revision and also benefit from seeing how others approach the article and review process more generally.

Journal lists

Whereas the ranking of journals in which people publish has always had implications for personal reputation, peer recognition, career advancement, and pay, increasingly it is impacting much more directly on institutional reputations and rankings and in turn on potential recruitment of staff and students. Individual publication choices and success are therefore assuming greater institutional significance (see Clark and Wright, 2007 for a review). Whether we agree with it or not, editors cannot ignore this trend since various pressures are encouraging institutions around the world to give stronger guidance to faculty in terms of which journals they should submit their manuscripts to. Consequently, publication in such journals has taken a more prominent position in tenure and promotion decisions. Although incentive practices can vary considerably across institutions, the general outcome of this process is that more material is likely to be initially submitted to a narrow group of journals that the community identifies as being of high quality. This again places pressure on editors of distinctive, independent journals to signal their quality and provide a high-quality service to authors and reviewers. But it also means that editors have to be proactive in managing broad community perceptions of their journals and their position within the ranking systems. At the very least, editors need to gain a presence on those lists that are critical to their community if they are to attract a steady stream of submissions.

Choice of editors and editorial board

Ultimately the judgment about a papers' distinctive contribution is the role of the editor(s). A decision will often need to be made about trading off the rough edges of a potentially pathbreaking paper with the need for a paper to meet a threshold of quality and rigor with which the research has been conducted. Editors of independent journals seeking to publish more distinctive research are likely to need to be active editors in terms of working with authors to develop a paper's contribution. Editors have to manage both reviewers and authors. Editors seeking to publish distinctive, consensus-challenging work thus need to exercise great care in selecting reviewers who are unlikely to dismiss a paper out of hand. The well-recognized problem of inter-reviewer disagreement may be particularly acute with more novel contributions (Clark and Wright, 2007; Bedeian, this volume). This can mean that editors need to tread a delicate path between lukewarm or negative reviewers.

It is also important for editors to take great care to select editorial board members who, while able to deal with conceptual and methodological quality issues, are nevertheless sympathetic to more novel approaches.

Regular meetings between the editors and editorial board members can help reinforce a journal's distinctive approach and build a supportive community. Editors can also promulgate a journal's distinctive approach by making presentations in various arenas on how to publish. For example, participation in "meet the editors" panels can enable potential authors to compare approaches of different journals. Awards for best papers and best reviewers also further contribute to building a community as well as signaling the distinctive ethos of the journal.

Interface with the journal

Part of the process of maintaining a close relationship between editors, reviewers, and authors concerns the interface with the journal. While online submission systems can help improve the efficiency of the review process, they nevertheless place a buffer between the author and the journal and between reviewers and the journal. Even though there is typically the option to contact the editors via e-mail, the author or reviewer is rather remote and can form the impression that direct contact, if not actively discouraged, is not encouraged. Furthermore, such systems are vulnerable to technical glitches with the consequence that articles and reviews may not be logged even when apparently submitted.

We would argue that for a distinctive, independent journal, direct access to the administrators and editors is an essential part of building and sustaining a community. Consequently, manuscripts should be sent directly to the administrators and by the administrators to reviewers. The administrators then liaise with reviewers to ascertain that they are able and willing to conduct the review within the time specified and, by establishing a personal link, are able to follow-through the review process in a timely manner. Having established such relationships it also helps in persuading colleagues to referee papers quickly in the occasional cases where journals are let down by a reviewer. This process also encourages active dialog between editors, authors, and reviewers, ranging from clarification of points in reviewers' or editors' comments to discussion over decisions.

Debates and special issues

A further mechanism to encourage distinctive contributions is to establish a debate section within one or two issues a year. Such sections might involve shorter papers that take different perspectives on an emerging or currently contentious topic. These shorter papers may be invited by the editors and typically are not subject to the normal anonymous review process but are reviewed by the editors and relevant editorial board members. These sections typically offer short lead times and so can contain much more up-to-date content. Because of this they may be a way to attract contributions from more established academics who may otherwise be unwilling to pursue consensus-challenging work because of the uncertainty as to whether or not it will be accepted (McMullen and Shepherd, 2006).

An example of a debates section is the Point-Counterpoint sections in *JMS* and *Journal of Organizational Behavior*. These sections seek to provoke lively debates by inviting short contributions from two or possibly three different perspectives on topical and important aspects of management. In *JMS*, each contribution is approximately half the length of a regular paper. These have become some of the most downloaded and highly cited recent publications in the Journal. Debates have been varied and included papers such as the Future of the Business School, Executive Remuneration: Theory and Context; Edith Penrose and the Resource-based View of Strategic Management; and, the Peer Review Process.

Where there may be divisions of opinions among reviewers relating to a paper that nevertheless has significant merit in challenging existing views in a particular area, a second possibility is to publish the dissenting reviewers' comments alongside the paper. Again such pairings are found to generate considerable interest within the academic community because they contain the various angles of a particular debate.

Special issues provide a further means to publish distinctive, consensus-challenging work and at the same time to signal the intellectual scope of the journal to a broader community. However, care is needed in a number of areas. Guest editors who are aware of the general ethos of the journal and who will also ensure that quality thresholds are met need to be selected. While the aim of special issues is to delegate decision-making to guest editors, the general editors may need to take an oversight role in order to ensure quality. There is also a need to ensure that a topic for a special issue is substantial enough to attract sufficient quality contributions yet novel enough to be the stimulus for a new research stream.

Once an independent journal becomes established, there may be less need for special issues to popularize the journal. However, to sustain the journal, the nature of special issues can be changed to bring to bear different cognate disciplines that may help to extend both the research domain and the community of scholars. For example, the *Journal of Business Venturing*, which is now in its 22nd year and which has established itself in the ISI rankings, it has adopted a policy where special issues are now used as a way to engage researchers who may otherwise not have thought to link their work to entrepreneurship. This change has also been accompanied by adjustments to the editorial team to include associate editors with a broader discipline base.

A further possibility for editors of independent journals to offer a distinctive contribution is to invite review articles from established scholars. Rather than merely being summary overviews of a particular domain, such articles can be used to develop novel insights. For example, Zahra, Sapienza, and Davidsson (2006) review the literature on dynamic capabilities and their role in value creation.

Governance mechanism

While editors of independent journals may value potentially greater freedom in decision-making, there are potential downsides to this that can be detrimental to the longevity and standing of the journal. A sure way of destroying the early momentum and excitement that a new journal may establish is to atrophy under the leadership of a coterie of scholars whose decisions are unchallenged. Alternatively, as a journal becomes established it can become mainstream and subject to a perceived loss of distinctiveness. As we showed earlier, new journals may be developed to compete with it. If a journal is to maintain its distinctiveness in such circumstances, editors may need to be prepared to change the aims and focus of the journal. It may also be necessary to change the editors and editorial board.

To mitigate the potentially harmful effects that may arise from too great a control resting in a small group for too long, we would suggest that all journals should establish a management board to which the editors are accountable for the way in which they manage the journal. This board should be composed of independent-minded members of the journal's community. This board would be responsible for advertising all editorial positions in the journal and selecting the editors. It would also set the length in which an editor can be in post. The board should not become involved in the day-to-day aspects of the journal but members should be free to quiz the editors on any aspect of how the journal is run. Editors can benefit from the advice and tremendous support provided by such boards, especially where they encounter difficulties with authors or elements of the community, as can happen from time to time in even well-run journals.

Editors of independent journals should in any case establish mechanisms to monitor their performance. Regularly reviewing the performance of the editorial team in relation to a number of key measures provides a check on whether they are maintaining the ethos of the journal as well as whether they are swift or slow, fair, biased, clear, opaque, and so forth. For example, our Editorial Office at *JMS* collects all feedback from authors, reviewers, and editorial board members on the nature of our general procedures, as well as how they have been applied and experienced in particular circumstances. Separately authors and reviewers submit to the Office comments based on their individual experiences of our procedures.

Concluding comments

In this chapter we set out to examine the particular issues associated with developing and sustaining a distinctive independent journal from our perspective as two of the General Editors of an independent journal. We identified a number of issues that editors of independent journals need to address: creating the journal community; journal aims and focus; offering a better service to reviewers and authors; dealing with the growing pressure from journal rankings; choosing editors and editorial boards; interface with the journal; the use of debate sections and special issues; and journal governance. The significant mortality of journals emphasizes the need for independent journals to adapt, in order to maintain their distinctiveness and their communities. In the context of a proliferation of new journals and efforts by existing journals aligned with particular academies to enhance their scope and service, this is a formidable challenge.

Implications for prospective editors

This chapter suggests that editors of independent journals need to address the following issues:

- establish a vibrant and committed journal community in order to encourage submission of papers and willing reviewers;
- be clear about the journal aims and focus, but revisit these in light of developments within the field and subject area more generally;
- offer a high-quality service to both authors and reviewers so that each feels that it is mutually beneficial and results in a positive learning experience;
- be transparent about turnaround times;
- manage broad community perceptions of the quality of the journal in part by ensuring the journal enters important rankings but also by publishing distinctive and consensus-challenging work;
- do not think of the journal simply as containing refereed articles. Strategically use dialog sections and special issues in order to capture contributions to current debates and forge an identity to existing communities and new and emerging areas of research;
- establish an appropriate governance mechanism so that editors have a group of advisers to whom they can turn for support but who also ensure consistency in management beyond the tenure of any one editor or editorial team.

Implications for authors

The chapter also has the following implications for authors:

- if you believe your work is consensus-challenging or is likely opening up a new area, give serious consideration to submitting your work to independent journals rather than mainstream affiliated journals;
- approach editors of independent journals where you identify a topical and controversial area that may be suitable for debate between different perspectives;

- volunteer as a reviewer in order to obtain inside knowledge about the standards of your favorite journals and to become an active member of that community;
- engage in dialog with the editor of an independent journal both in terms of exploring whether a particular paper may, in principle, be of interest and with respect to developing and shaping your work;
- ask about turnaround times if you are looking for a decision within a particular time-frame.

Acknowledgments

We are grateful to Geoff Easton for his valuable comments on an earlier draft.

Notes

1. In addition, users have developed a voracious appetite for new material. Electronic downloading of papers has grown exponentially in recent years. For example, between 2005 and 2006 the average increase in downloads per journal in Blackwell's business and management list was 30 percent. In 2006, 345,911 articles were downloaded from *Journal of Management Studies* alone, a 22 percent increase on the 2005 figure.
2. We are grateful to Geoff Easton for bringing this point to our attention.

References

Association of Research Libraries (2006). *Monograph and Serial Expenditures in ARL Libraries, 1986–2005.* http://www.arl.org/stats/arlstat/index.html.

Bakos, Y., & Brynjolfsson, E. (2000). 'Bundling and competition on the internet'. *Marketing Science*, 19 (1), 63–82.

Barley, S. R. (2006). 'When I write my masterpiece: thoughts on what makes a paper interesting'. *Academy of Management Journal*, 49 (1), 16–20.

Clark, T, Floyd, S., & Wright, M. (2006). 'On the review process and policies of *Journal of Management Studies*'. *Journal of Management Studies*, 43 (5), 655–64.

Clark, T., & Wright, M. (2007). 'Reviewing journal rankings and revisiting peer reviews: editorial perspectives'. *Journal of Management Studies*, 44 (4), 612–21.

Jensen, M. (2006). Seminar on publishing in finance. Nottingham University Business School, November 13th.

Jeon, D. S., & Menicucci, D. (2006). 'Bundling electronic journals and competition among publishers'. *Journal of European Economic Association*, 4 (5), 1038–83.

Kacmar, M. (2001). 'From the editor'. *Journal of Management*, 26 (1), 1–4.

Lee, T. (2003). 'From the editors: reflections on the first 18 months'. *Academy of Management Journal*, 46 (1), 7–9.

McMullen, J., & Shepherd, D. (2006). 'Encouraging consensus-challenging research in universities'. *Journal of Management Studies*, 43 (8), 1643–70.

Morris, S. (2006). 'When is a journal not a journal? A closer look at the DOAJ'. *Learned Publishing*, 19 (1), 73–6.

Rynes, S. (2005). 'Taking stock and looking ahead'. *Academy of Management Journal*, 48 (1), 9–15.
Rynes, S., Hillman, A., Ireland, D., Kirkman, B., Law, K., Miller, C., Rajagopalan, N., & Shapiro, D. (2005). 'Everything you always wanted to know about *AMJ* (but may have been afraid to ask)'. *Academy of Management Journal*, 48 (5), 732–7.
Sutton, R., & Staw, B. (1995). 'What theory is not'. *Administrative Science Quarterly*. 40, 371–84.
Van Fleet, D. Ray, D., Bedeian, A., Downey, H. K., Hunt, J. G., Griffin, R., Dalton, D., Vecchio, R., Kacmar, K. M., & Feldman, D. (2006). 'The Journal of Management's first 30 years'. *Journal of Management*, 8 (32), 477–506.
Weick, K. (1995). 'What theory is not, theorizing is'. *Administrative Science Quarterly*, 40, 385–90.
Zahra, S., Sapienza, H., & Davidsson, P. (2006). 'Entrepreneurship and dynamic capabilities: a review, model and research agenda'. *Journal of Management Studies*, 43 (4), 917–55.

19
Reflections on Creating a New Scholarly Journal: Perspectives from a Founding Editor

Larry J. Williams

Most faculty and students in organizational studies can probably remember some of their earliest experiences with receiving or accessing journals from their chosen academic field. For many, becoming a reader or subscriber of such journals represents a key first step in their professional development, and provides their first exposure to the end products of scientific endeavors. As developing scholars learn more of the research and publication process, they quickly learn of the important role that journal editors play in the publication process. During doctoral training, both in seminars and in other discussions with fellow students and faculty, young researchers are given advice on how to increase their chances of success in getting their articles published. Further, the experiences of those who have served as reviewers and editors are also shared with aspiring scholars. Through all of these types of events, young scientists learn about the publication process.

Throughout this developmental process, however, little if any attention is given to the issue of how and why different journals get started, and the issues involved in creating or founding a scientific journal. In most instances this may be because the journals that are most talked about are those with the greatest prestige, which are also likely to be those that have likely been around the longest. As a result, there may not be access to those involved in starting these journals, and as a result there may be no capability for describing or reflecting on the process. Also, it appears there is little if any published guidance for or accounts of the journal start-up process.

I am extremely fortunate to have been involved in creating a scholarly journal in the organizational studies area, *Organizational Research Methods* (*ORM*), and I am happy to be given the opportunity to share my experiences. I do so hoping to document how things evolved during the start-up process, and perhaps identifying things to do and not do in the process of launching a new journal. Of course, such "documentation" is greatly influenced by my selective perceptual processes and memory, and undoubtedly there will be things I will not recall due to effective, if not necessary, defense mechanisms. Nevertheless, I will describe my experiences as best I can, with the hope of providing something of value to those who find themselves starting a new journal, and those who may consider submitting their research to a new journal.

What is the need?

Given the historical origins of the various management-related disciplines, which can be traced back many years, it should not be surprising that there is an abundance of publishing outlets for research on organizational topics. Indeed, in the category of Management, Thomson Scientific in its annual Journal Citation Reports provides rankings for 78 journals. In addition, there are other categories that also include journals that publish content directly relevant to Management and related fields. For example, the Applied Psychology category includes 54 journals. Within this environment, the first obvious question that arises for those considering a journal start-up is why another journal is needed. There are numerous journals that have a very broad focus, for which submissions from many disciplines of management would be appropriate, and there are also many specialized journals supporting what may seem as narrow areas of management. As one considers these journals of both types, the key issue is determining what value will be provided by the establishment of a new outlet.

In my particular situation, the answer was clear and provided by experienced members of the research methods community, as this was the area of my career focus. I can remember participating in many conversations at professional meetings where I heard senior scholars from my area describe the challenges of getting their research methods articles accepted at traditional management outlets. I knew of the considerable success of these scholars in getting their substantive work published, so I could rule out the explanation that the discussions I was hearing were simply the "sour grapes" that might be expected from those whose work was not up to the standards of these traditional management outlets. These frustrated authors shared their experiences of having reviewers who might be substantive experts but who were lacking in their methods training, and of having editors who wanted their work to pass a dual standard of making both substantive and methodological contributions.

As I reflected on these discussions, I came to recognize that there was no outlet devoted to research methods scholarship conducted by organizational based scholars. Indeed, it became apparent that members of the research methods community within the Academy of Management (AOM) were the only group of management scholars whose work did not fit within the general scope of existing Academy publications. For example, while over the years the *Academy of Management Review* (*AMR*) had published reviews of existing data analysis techniques, empirical research on various research methods problems was not within the domain of *AMR*. Similarly, while the

Academy of Management Journal (*AMJ*) occasionally published articles that might be seen as having a research methods emphasis, to be accepted articles for *AMJ* were required to make a substantive contribution to management, as well as a contribution to the research methods literature. Finally, while journals devoted to research methods did exist in other disciplines (e.g., *Sociological Methods and Research*), career advancement considerations made these less than an optimal outlet for organizational researchers working within the disciplines of management.

As I considered this state of affairs, I came to believe that there was a need for an outlet that would be considered by management and organizational researchers focusing on research methods as a natural home for their scholarship. Such an outlet would also need to be seen by those making personnel decisions (e.g., promotion and tenure committees, department chairs and Deans) as management-based, which would lead potential authors to believe that they would get fair rewards for their efforts. In short, I believed that I had identified a void in the market of scholarly outlets for an important segment of the population of organizational scholars, those interested in research methods, and I was ultimately able to convince the AOM and Sage Publications, Inc., of this claim.

Thus, a first lesson is that anyone considering starting a new journal must be sure that there is some gap in existing outlets that will be met by a new journal. They can increase their certainty by understanding the beliefs and perceptions of those who might serve as potential contributors of their work, and by having a good understanding of the missions and strengths/weaknesses of existing outlets with a similar focus. These considerations can result in the belief that a new outlet will ultimately generate the flow of submissions required for long-term success.

What will the mission be?

The above discussion suggests that at some point a person considering starting a scholarly journal identifies a general need that is not being met or an audience that is being underserved by the current configuration of outlets, in my case those associated with the organizational research methods community. At this stage in the overall development the conceptualization is very general, and the next key step involves becoming more specific in articulating the mission of the new journal. There are many ways in which the needs of a neglected community of scholars can be addressed, and important strategic decisions are faced. Some of these decisions need to be based on substantive considerations, and others are more practical, but neither type can be neglected.

The specific action that can be most helpful at this stage is the development of the policy statement, which describes the types of articles appropriate for the new journal. In some instances guidance can be obtained from the policy statements of journals with similar missions. In my case, I carefully considered such statements from *Sociological Methods and Research* and *Psychological Methods*, outlets which I saw as having a similar mission but that targeted a different audience. I was able to use these to help shape the vision of the new journal I was pursuing, but I also needed to be aware of specific nuances associated with working within the management and organizational context.

Similarly, I had to decide if the audience of *ORM* was to be only those who conduct methodological work, or whether it should also include substantive researchers looking for guidance as to how to best conduct their research. I was concerned that these two potential constituents might have conflicting needs that would create problems. For example, a well-executed simulation study of a specific statistic might be seen as an important contribution by those doing similar work on the statistic, but seen as less important to someone needing to analyze their data. Alternatively, while a general review paper might be seen as very valuable to a substantive researcher, a methodologist might view it less favorably and conclude that there is nothing new that cannot be found in original sources. Ultimately, I decided that there was equal intellectual value to work aimed at both audiences and that both types of scholarship could ultimately improve the quality of substantive management research.

Thus, a second lesson is that the process of starting a new journal is likely to involve decisions where arguments can be made in favor of either side (for example, as noted about focusing on methodologists and substantive researchers). In making these decisions, anyone considering starting a journal should be guided by a long-term vision of what is necessary for success, which ultimately gets translated into the Policy Statement that will guide authors, reviewers, and the editor. Finally, in developing this Statement, it is very important to obtain feedback from experienced scholars in the area who will be deciding whether to submit their work to the new outlet.

The importance of a sponsor for the new journal

In addition to determining the need for a potential new journal and the development of the Policy Statement, another key consideration in the start-up process involves the organizational context. Simply, there are several advantages for those who can link their new journal to an existing organization via an affiliation or sponsorship. Such an arrangement benefits the publisher and may be critical in persuading the publisher that there will be a base of support needed for the new journal. The economics of starting a new journal are challenging (it can take several years for a new journal to be profitable), and a tie to a sponsoring organization can help the publisher decide that there will be a subscription base needed for long-term financial success. The partnership with a sponsoring organization can also provide a relatively easy way to promote the new journal, using means such as the organization's newsletter or website.

Affiliation with a sponsoring organization also can benefit the editor and potential contributors. Linking with a sponsor can send an important signal about the quality of the new outlet. As is often said, you only get one chance to make a first impression, and being able to send out the initial Call for Papers with such a link can play an important role in solidifying the journal's image before the first submission is received and before the first page is published. Assuming that the sponsoring organization holds some type of annual meeting, this partnership creates the opportunity for increasing awareness of the new outlet via a special reception or party recognizing and celebrating the establishment of the new journal. The start-up process can benefit greatly by the existence of favorable "chatter" created by such a social context, which can increase awareness of the new outlet among potential contributors. Further, if the sponsoring organization allows the presentation of research papers appropriate for the mission of the new journal, the presenters can be approached about submitting their research to the journal.

Of course, there must be reasons for the sponsoring organization to commit to such a partnership, and I think several advantages are possible. In many instances members of the organization receive a discount on the journal they are associated with. The existence of a dedicated outlet can also increase the perceived scientific legitimacy of the area of the journal by those from other scholarly areas. And, the availability of an outlet can have a positive influence on scholars deciding whether to do work in the area, in that they are more likely to do such research if they are sure there is a home for the final product.

In my case, there was an organization eager to establish a partnership, the research methods division (RMD) of the AOM. Indeed, the senior scholars whose conversations I witnessed (mentioned earlier) included several past leaders of the RMD, and they were very instrumental in generating the support within the membership of the RMD. The RMD also had a history of increasing participation in the Program of the annual Academy meeting, creating a potential pool of papers that could be submitted to *ORM*. Further, the RMD co-sponsored a social event in the first year of *ORM*, helping increase awareness. Finally, and I am sure most importantly, the link of *ORM* with the AOM and its RMD was critical in how *ORM* was perceived in its first few years. Simply, authors considering submitting their work to *ORM* were able to know that *ORM* would be discussed by their evaluators (promotion committees, department chairs, deans) as a journal affiliated with a division of the AOM. While ultimately the value of *ORM* would be determined by information related to the quality of the articles published, submission and rejection rates, and impact factors, it can take years for data on these criteria to be available. During this time the link with the RMD sent a signal about quality, and in fact through contributing to high-quality submissions helped contribute to the favorable data on citations and impact that ultimately has emerged.

Before proceeding, it should be noted that difficult issues can emerge in the process of establishing a link between a new journal and a sponsoring organization. Topics to be addressed include who has control over the selection of the editor and the degree to which the sponsoring organization has input. Allocation of responsibilities during the review and publication process must also be resolved, as do any liabilities for the sponsoring unit. Ultimately, questions related to ownership and revenue control have to be addressed. In my case, with the start up of *ORM* all of these issues came up during the process through which the Board of Governors of the AOM approved the request from the Executive Committee of the RMD to sponsor *ORM* (up to this time, divisions of the Academy were not allowed to be affiliated with non-Academy journals). Fortunately, as a result of diligent efforts by all the parties involved, this sponsorship was approved, and from the first public notice about *ORM* the link with the RMD was emphasized. A key lesson is that anyone attempting to establish such a partnership must remember that the sponsor (and the publisher) is putting its reputation on the line by being associated with the new outlet, and all the pieces must be in place to support the viability and quality of the new journal.

Having the right team

So far my discussion has focused on the editor, authors, and a potential sponsoring organization. There is another group of players whose contribution is equally important, the editorial and review team. Once the Policy Statement has been developed and sponsorship issues have been resolved, the editor must put in place a group of partners that can insure success. I do feel that there are some aspects of this process that may be different for a start-up journal.

In the absence of a tradition and reputation, the qualifications of the editorial team are very important. From the first distribution of promotional materials, the early decision letters on the journal's letterhead, and the publication of the first issue with the listing of the editorial Board, the reputation and status of the team sends a critical signal as to the quality of the new outlet. The operating perception is that if good people lend their names to the emerging effort, it will be a good product. I do believe it can be more difficult to select a team in this context, because without a history of submissions it can be difficult to predict the range of topics of the papers, making it more difficult to know the types of expertise needed to obtain good reviews. In the beginning it may also be more difficult to recruit members to the new team, as the prestige and reputation of the new journal has yet to be established. Someone starting a new journal will also not inherit an extensive list of ad-hoc reviewers, as would an editor of an existing journal.

Finally, it is very important to have the commitment of all members of the team, who must be willing to do more than just lend their names to the new venture. These members must provide timely and constructive reviews that will help shape the positive image of the journal during its early years. They also can serve as a valuable source of information about the new journal as they discuss their work activities with their students and colleagues, which can potentially result in submissions that would otherwise not occur. And, since the team members are chosen in part because of their reputations in the journal's area, and these are based on their research achievements, these members can serve as an important source of high-quality submissions during the emergence of the journal.

Thus, the lesson is to remember that ultimately the publication of a journal is a team effort. An editor must have submissions and they must have feedback on submitted papers that is technically correct. The editorial team can contribute to both causes, and difficult issues can develop. The editor of a new journal might have to exert considerable effort to obtain tardy reviews, they will likely have to reject an article recommended by an editorial reviewer or accept an article reviewed unfavorably by such a reviewer, and they may have to reject a submission by an editorial board member. Clear and effective communications, and a well-designed and executed review process, can minimize the problems associated with these situations and help with the long-term success of the endeavor.

Is this the right job for me?

Before turning to lessons for potential contributors to new journals, let me address an issue that is obvious but that must be considered, namely, is the job of being the founding editor of a new journal the right job to take? Anyone with such an opportunity will recognize immediately the positive benefits of being in such a position. The impact on one's status, reputation, and career should be obvious. Also obvious is the workload, which, for every editor I have talked with and from the information included in other chapters in this volume, has been greater than what was expected. To help inform those who might be considering such an endeavor, I would like to share some thoughts based on my experiences, and I will try to keep the focus on those aspects of the process unique to starting a journal, as compared to stepping into an editorial role with an established journal.

A first thing that comes to mind is the wide range of activities and tasks that confront someone starting a new journal. While we tend to think of an editor as mainly assigning reviewers, evaluating their feedback, and making one of three decisions (reject, revise, accept), much more is required during the start of a new journal. First, it is likely that this person will conceive and develop the Policy Statement, which, as discussed earlier, plays perhaps a more important role in shaping the identity of a new journal before members of the community can look to many published issues to determine the domain of the journal. There is considerable pressure associated with this process, given the importance of this Statement, and it is not faced by anyone who steps into an existing journal. Second, there are several types of activities that the editor of a new journal may want to pursue that are less important with an established outlet. For example, a person in this position may want to take more advantage of opportunities to be visible at conferences and in giving invited talks, so as to create more awareness of the new journal. Of course, one must be careful to not allow these activities to slow down the review process, as review times are increasingly being used competitively by competing journals.

Further, in this situation the editor may have to be relatively more aggressive in generating submissions than someone working with an established journal. Several things can be done in this regard, including sending invitations to those presenting papers at relevant professional meetings (who may be looking for the best place to submit their paper). Such invitations can also be sent to those who have recently published articles within the domain of the new journal in existing outlets. These researchers have a track record of success (by virtue of their publications), and may also be looking for an expanded list of potential outlets for their work.

A final characteristic of being involved in a journal start-up is the time pressure that can be involved. Any editor faces the task of processing papers as quickly as possible. However, a new editor of an existing journal is likely to have a backlog of papers in the publication cue, as well as a substantial set of papers that will be processed by the outgoing editor, both of which lessens the pressure of filling the first issue that will list them as editor. The editor of a new journal has neither of these resources. Complicating the matter is that when the new outlet is first formally announced, a commitment is made to the publication date of the first issue. And, the publisher typically has reasons to want to make that date as soon as possible, as the actual publication of the first issue can play an important role in generating subscriptions and revenues. So, when taking into account the time required to process those initial submissions, time for authors to develop revisions, and the time required to review the revisions, there may not be a lot of slack in the system to accommodate delays. And, the editor knows that while there must be papers to put in the first issue, the quality of those early papers will go along way to establishing the early reputation. This aspect of the situation is the main reason it is so important for the editor of a new journal to aggressively recruit submissions, so as to insure an adequate set of high-quality articles in the first few issues, which will have several important effects on subsequent activities.

Implications for potential contributors to a new journal

In terms of any lessons based on my experiences in starting a new journal that might be relevant to potential contributors, a few considerations come to mind. First, give special attention to the task of insuring that the journal is an appropriate outlet for your work. For this, you may have to examine the Policy Statement to make this judgment more than you normally would, as there will not be years of Tables of Contents to examine to see if the journal has published work on this topic before. You may also want to contact the editor with a brief description of your topic before actually submitting your paper. Second, if a potential contributor is a junior faculty member, they may want to seek the input of those who will be evaluating their publication record to obtain reactions as to how a publication from the new journal would be received (i.e., how would it be judged).

Third, while it does take time for citation and impact rating information to be available, information of acceptance rates can usually be obtained from the editor, and if the contributor feels this information would be helpful they should not hesitate to contact the editor. This information can help the potential contributor judge their relative chances of success, and it can also be provided to those who will evaluate their performance to legitimate any claim as to the quality of the outlet. Finally, someone with an ongoing research stream in the domain of the new journal might consider volunteering to serve as an ad-hoc reviewer. Identifying qualified ad-hoc reviewers can be a challenge for an editor involved in all the other aspects of starting a new journal, and they might appreciate such an offer. And, one can learn about the new journal as an ad hoc reviewer by tracking the comments provided by other reviewers and by examining the decision letters of the editors.

Final thoughts

In closing, let me first say that in my comments I have tried to provide guidance that will be helpful to those seeking to better understand the journal start-up process. In my efforts at being complete, I hope that I have not discouraged anyone for considering such an endeavor. It can be a stressful and demanding role to play, and must be considered in the context of one's stage of career, their ability to cope with uncertainty, and their interest in the broad range of activities associated with being the editor of a new journal. One's comfort level with technology should also be considered, as most journals are using an electronic submission and review process. However, two things come to mind as I reflect on my own start-up experience. First, intellectually I have not found anything that creates the same sense of excitement as sitting down with a submission and a set of reviews and trying to help an author develop the best paper they can within the data or objectives that they have. Second, it is very rewarding and fulfilling when doing this in the context of a new journal, knowing the impact of these activities on the emergence of the journal, the growth of the discipline, and the opportunities that a successful new journal will provide to the scholars from the area.

20
Running an Electronic Journal: Considerations and Possibilities

Bernard Forgues and Jeanie M. Forray

A revolution is taking place in scholarly publication. Fueled by rapid technological advances and an exponential diffusion of the Internet, the way scientists exchange knowledge is experiencing its most dramatic change since Gutenberg invented type printing 550 years ago. Yet, social scientists lag far behind their colleagues in physics or biology in reacting to these changes. In this chapter, we present developments in electronic publishing and some of the opportunities and challenges that face prospective editors and authors in this new academic reality.

Many elements involved in running a peer-reviewed electronic or online[1] journal mirror those of any scholarly publication: working with authors, developing an editorial review board and overseeing their work, attracting high-quality submissions, etc. As such, we refer readers to other chapters for some of the more standard considerations of editorship that affect all academic journals regardless of their mode of delivery.

Our focus is on some of the more unique aspects of editing an internet-based journal, offering potential editors and authors some useful insights into the world of online publications. We begin with a brief history of three online management journals to highlight some of the considerations we believe most salient for an online publication. Next, we discuss these key issues in greater detail, providing insight into the important decisions that editors of online journals must make. Finally, we discuss two fundamental concerns for online journals: access and legitimacy. In so doing, we describe some of the changes taking place that we believe will affect the future of electronic publishing and offer suggestions for prospective editors and authors wanting to take advantage of these opportunities.

History lessons

Scholars first began to explore the potential for computer-based academic journals as early as the 1970s (cf., Bamford, 1972; Senders, 1976). At that time, the Internet was seen as a potential solution to the apparent limits of a print-based system where rising costs restricted the number of articles that could be published while the number of articles produced by researchers was on the rise. It was theorized that unless something changed, the result of these publication pressures would be threefold: potentially valuable papers would not be published or would be severely delayed, individuals and libraries would not be able to subscribe to journals to which they wanted access, and readers would pay for journals in which many of the articles were of little interest (Turnoff & Hiltz, 1982). It was hoped that the prospective solution to these issues would come from the use of electronic technology.

Each of these outcomes has come to pass in the last 40 years and, as access to the Internet has grown, electronic technology has provided some solutions. Indeed, most print journal publishers have moved toward greater electronic presence with prepublication articles posted on the Internet (e.g., *Academy of Management Journal*), and electronic distribution via proprietary websites (e.g., Sage, Emerald) or commercial database (e.g., Academic Source Premiere, Infotrac). While these changes enhance the timeliness of scholarly articles, they do not – in and of themselves – speak to the increasing institutional pressures for publication among management scholars and, as a result, the growing numbers of management articles being written that are in need of a legitimate outlet.

In conjunction with the growth of electronic communication and increased publishing pressures, entrepreneurial individuals and scholarly organizations in the management domain began to inaugurate peer-reviewed online journals. While these journals followed the same editorial processes as print journals, they represented a completely electronic presence, did not require a traditional publisher, and were not restricted by page limitations and print costs. As such, inaugurating and running an online journal can be a faster and less costly means of publishing a journal. Three examples are described below.

With its inauguration in 1995, the *Electronic Journal of Radical Organization Theory (EJROT)* became the first online journal for management scholarship. Conceptualized and edited by Clive Gilson at the University of Waikato, *EJROT* drew on the interest and commitment of a community of critical organizational scholars. In addition to publishing articles using a traditional peer-review system and editorial board, the journal also publishes the Proceedings of the Critical Management Studies conferences. *EJROT* began as an open access (free) peer-reviewed journal, with interested individuals registering to become members of the *EJROT* community. Although the journal recently affiliated with Informit e-Library for institutional access, *EJROT* remains a niche publication with one issue per year. Increasingly, *EJROT* publishes as special issues, with content and editorial work overseen by the special issue editors.

A different approach was taken by *M@n@gement*, a peer-reviewed online publication whose inaugural issue appeared in 1998. *M@n@gement* was launched when a small group of individuals based in Europe reasoned that one of the barriers they faced when trying to publish in established American journals was their poor command of English. Local journals, on the other hand, often lacked the rigor found in peer-reviewed journals and had a very limited circulation. Thus, they decided to launch a journal that would publish articles in their original language. In addition, while maintaining a low acceptance rate the journal would be highly demanding but developmental so as to train people to later try their luck at top-tier journals. Articles for the journal are published as soon as they are accepted and, like its predecessor, *M@n@gement* is an open access journal with interested individuals signing-up to receive notification of new article publication. Since 2005, it has been the official journal of AIMS, the French strategic management association.

Unlike the previous two examples, *Organization Management Journal* (*OMJ*) began in 2004 as a sponsored publication of the Eastern Academy of Management (EAM). *OMJ* was designed to enhance the reputation of the organization, to reflect the various interests of its membership, and to contribute to the advancement of management theory, research, education, and practice. As such, it was designed with different sections, each with a unique focus and editorial board. The editor-in-chief, who supervises the entire publication, is appointed by the EAM's Board of Governors and serves a three-year term. In addition, each section is overseen by two editors: one from North America and the other located in an area outside North America. Also, unlike its predecessors, *OMJ* is affiliated with a publisher and requires individuals to become subscribers in order to gain access to journal articles (all EAM members are subscribers automatically). The journal is published on a set schedule four times a year.

Each of the three publications discussed above highlights some of the editorial issues facing scholarly online journals and the individuals who edit and/or submit to them. In the next section, we discuss some of these issues in detail.

Pragmatic issues

Who should hold copyright on the article once published?

In general, authors of articles in print journals must assign copyright to the publisher of the journal. But this is not the case for all online journals. *OMJ* acquires copyright authority from authors prior to publication while *M@n@gement* shares copyright with the author(s) upon publication. In addition, many online journals apply the Creative Commons Attribution License (see creativecommons.org) under which authors retain ownership of the copyright for their article while allowing anyone to download, reuse, reprint, modify, distribute, and/or copy it, as long as the original authors and source are credited. Whether or not to hold copyright is a decision generally based on financial as well as control considerations. If the journal is intended to generate revenues, even at some future time, then the journal is best served by maintaining copyright authority for its articles. A journal may require a subscription fee or fee-for-download of articles that would require payment of royalties for any article whose copyright is not controlled by the journal. In the case of *OMJ*, the journal requires authors to assign copyright prior to publication and is then able to control the use of articles after publication. For *M@n@gement*, individuals desirous of using articles for any commercial purposes must obtain permission of both the journal and the author(s).

How is the website developed and maintained?

Any online journal requires a website and ongoing technical support. This can be a relatively simple matter using free or low-cost resources available on the Internet,[2] or it can be a more costly endeavor involving individuals with sophisticated technical capabilities. For example, because the EAM is a non-profit organization and does not charge a fee for the journal, *OMJ* received technical design for the website and continues to receive ongoing support from an educational institution. If this kind of support is not available, other arrangements must be made. Some websites are maintained by the individuals who edit the journal, while others are supported by interested individuals not involved with the editorial content or process.

Should issues be published on a set schedule or as they are ready?

As noted above, *EJROT* publishes articles as they are ready and includes them all as part of one issue per year. While *M@n@gement* also publishes on an "as ready" basis, it does so quarterly so that there are four issues per year. Alternatively, *OMJ* establishes a short pipeline of accepted articles for future issues by publishing on a set schedule of three issues per year. The first two examples use the speed of the electronic format to provide timeliness for authors, and this method is simpler to coordinate than a set schedule process. The latter example uses a more traditional approach that mirrors print publications in order to enhance its legitimacy and to manage its section format, and allows the journal to regularly publicize each new issue to the management community.

Should the journal publish in English only or in other languages?

By and large, all scholarly journals aspire to be international in terms of readership and impact but few publish articles in their original language if it is not English. This may result from the dominance of English-language print publishers in management scholarship, with the obvious problems of copyediting in languages other than English, or it may result from the difficulty editors face in identifying reviewers for scholarly work not in their own (the editor's) language. However, insofar as they are able to attract a truly international readership and editorial board, electronic journals often have a "wider net" with respect to these resources. And there are benefits to providing material in the original language that may enhance the reputation of an electronic journal. Authors are always best able to express themselves in their "first" language, thus enhancing the quality of the article by maintaining the richness and subtlety of the author's thought. This, in turn, allows readers (many of whom are able to read more than one language) to benefit from this clarity. With this approach (as with English-only, of course) citation is limited to those who read and understand the language in which the article is written.

How should the journal be funded?

An online journal requires financial resources. While the costs are certainly lower than those of a print publication, who have obvious printing and mailing costs, online journals also incur costs related to their publication. These may include copyedit and formatting costs, promotion costs, and editor-travel costs, etc. How much is needed and how it is to be generated are critical issues for online editors and publishers.

There are four basic ways to cover the costs of an online journal. The first is by charging an individual and/or institutional subscriber fee. This practice mirrors that of print journals but (1) is inconsistent with an open access philosophy and (2) is difficult to employ when so many online journals are available for free. The second option is to charge authors upon submission or publication (the fee often being paid by the author's employer or funding agency). Contrary to what many believe, a recent survey by the Kauffman-Wills Group (2005) notes that fewer than half of the available open access journals charge authors. Indeed, subscription-based journals actually charge authors more often than open access ones. A third possibility for covering costs is to rely on grants or subsidies from sponsors. This is often the case for journals published by scholarly associations, with the associations making money from conferences or membership and earmarking some of it for journal support. The fourth way to generate income is through related services such as on-site advertising, on-demand print publication, or other value-added fee-based services. These various possibilities are in no way mutually exclusive, but can be combined. In any case, publishers need to have a clear understanding of the costs of publication and the ways in which revenues will be generated to cover them, editors need to be aware of the resources available to them, and authors need to be cognizant of the ways in which viable publications generate revenues that may impact them.

While each of the foregoing pragmatic issues is salient for online editors and authors, in the next section we turn to two broader issues underlying the nature of all electronic journals.

Access and legitimacy

All journals, whether published on paper or on the web, face issues of access and legitimacy. It is often assumed that there is a direct relationship between circulation rate (number of subscribers) and legitimacy, but this is not always the case. Indeed, one study found that rank correlations between impact factor and circulation in 21 disciplines were between 0.25 and 0.50 (Peritz, 1995). E-journals achieve much larger circulation at a quicker rate than print journals, but they face more resistance as to their legitimacy. However, because of technological advances and greater numbers of peer-reviewed online publications, this situation may be changing.

"Open access" refers to free access to scholarly literature over the Internet. Most electronic scholarly journals are open access, providing free and unrestricted access to published research results to anyone. Among the reasons behind the open access movement, the main one is that while authors and reviewers work for free, subscription prices have increased far above inflation rates (e.g., McCabe, 2000; Bergstrom & Bergstrom, 2006). Thus, the increases in price for print journals are not a reflection of increases in academic costs but of print publication industry changes. Supporters of open access, view free and unrestricted access as an answer to the commercialization of academic research.

Indeed, proponents of open access claim it accelerates research, enriches education, and levels the economic playing field for researchers outside well-funded universities (Chan et al., 2002; Jaschik, 2006). Benefits for authors include larger potential audience, increased impact, and shorter delays between research and publication (SPARC, 2004).

Access to journals is a crucial issue for editors because it involves both economic viability and scientific influence. Those two issues need careful examination. As noted above, an open access policy affords journals higher circulation at a more rapid rate than their print counterparts. This exposure enhances the potential impact of journal articles, which in turn enhances the legitimacy of the journal. On the economic side, however, open access means that no revenue can be obtained through subscription. While printing and distribution are (almost) accomplished for free over the Internet, some production costs remain.

Access is related to scientific influence, although the relationship is not as straightforward as one might expect at first glance. Because journal circulation is highly responsive to price differences (Bergstrom & Bergstrom, 2006), an open access journal can be expected to have higher circulation. Further, as DuBois and Reeb (2000) argue, "the probability of citation of a journal as well as impressions of journal quality is positively influenced by journal availability" (p. 702). Given their broader circulation possibilities, open access journals should have broader influence, but this doesn't currently show in ISI impact factors. Open access journals may fare poorly in rankings for a number of reasons. First, they are of newer origin and have had less time to get established and cited. Second, in the absence of an institutionalized standard to cite electronic journals, authors do a poor job at referencing them and, as a consequence, citation counts frequently miss them and thus underestimate their impact. As a result, online management journals are rarely included in journal-ranking schemes because those who develop such rankings have little evidence to support an assessment of an online journal's impact.

The situation may be improving as open access journals start to achieve their promise. In a carefully designed study, Eysenbach (2006) compared citations received by open access articles and non-open access articles published in the same journal. To do so, he took advantage of the *Proceedings of the National Academy of Sciences* (*PNAS*) switch to an open access option, where authors of accepted articles are offered the possibility of paying a fee to have their paper available for free on the publisher's website. Such a natural experiment allowed the author to control many confounds, including the number of days since publication, number of authors, and previous citation records of authors. He also sent a questionnaire to authors to check that they did not opt for open access only for their more important articles. Eysenbach's (2006) results clearly showed that open access articles received more citations than those behind a paid subscription barrier. Open access articles were twice as likely to be cited four to ten months after publication, and three times as likely between 10 and 16 months. The benefit to authors and to the advancement of knowledge is thus important, especially as *PNAS* is a journal widely available in libraries.

Journals also need legitimacy to attract submissions. In scholarly publishing, legitimacy comes primarily from the journal's reputation or the editorial process it uses. More precisely, a journal is credible if it has already established a strong reputation or if it belongs to some legitimate learned society. As for processes, the one perceived as most legitimate is the double-blind, peer-reviewed process used by the overwhelming majority of journals in our field, including open access ones.

Additionally, journals can gain legitimacy by staffing their boards with prestigious scholars, seeking institutional endorsements, and publishing papers by prominent authors; these practices are available (and used by) online journals. Electronic journals can also mimic print journals by "looking alike" (e.g., using page numbers, establishing an institutional "header," publishing issues on a quarterly basis, etc.).

Legitimacy usually translates into the journal's impact factor, which is sometimes used as a measure of excellence and certainly of prestige, but new technologies might shake the status quo. Indeed, one problem is that prestigious journals do not always publish the best articles. Using a statistical analysis of differences in citation rates between the top 20 percent, the middle 40 percent, and the bottom 40 percent of a sample of journals in economics, psychology, sociology, and management, Starbuck (2005) observed that "highly prestigious journals publish quite a few low-value articles, low-prestige journals publish some excellent articles, and excellent manuscripts may receive successive rejections from several journals" (p. 196). In other words, legitimacy does not automatically equate to quality. As a result, although being a convenient shortcut for promotion committees making tenure decisions or for busy scholars selecting which journals to browse, no one criterion alone can designate the quality, relevance, or contribution of a journal or the articles it publishes.

Concluding thoughts

All in all, the future for editors of online journals and the authors who submit to them looks promising. As the number of such journals increases, and the scholarly community responds to their quality and familiarity, their acceptance as a format for scholarly publication grows. Online journals hold a clear advantage as to ease of access and use, two paramount features for scholars. Thanks to their format, readers are only one click away from relevant works cited in electronic journals if these are also available on the Internet. Readers also save the time they used to spend going to their local library or requesting reprints from distant libraries. For authors, Internet journals provide an enhanced distribution for their work because it is available to the widest possible readership. Clearly, as more and more research is made available electronically, patterns of use change[3].

Launching a journal on the Internet, or switching from print to electronic distribution, offers many opportunities. Such a move requires careful preparation, for which useful guides are available. Both technical and economic advice abound on the Internet: prospective editors might want to start with a look at those offered by the Budapest Open Access Initiative (http://www.soros.org/openaccess/resources.shtml), which was instrumental in initiating the open access movement.

Notes

1. Our use of this term signifies journals that have no form of distribution beyond the Internet, i.e., online-only. We distinguish these publications from journals that now commonly offer both a print version and electronic access to articles. In addition, our comments in this chapter are made with respect to peer-reviewed publications and are not intended to address issues with respect to "blogs" or other non-refereed publications.
2. A popular end-to-end journal management system available for free is OJS (http://pkp.sfu.ca/?q=ojs).
3. Incidentally, JSTOR (www.jstor.org) succeeded in reviving old articles by making them instantly available in full text.

References

Bamford, H. (1972). A Concept for Applying Computer Technology to the Publication of Scientific Journals. *Journal of the Washington Academy of Science*, 62, 306–14.

Bergstrom, C. T., & Bergstrom T. C. (2006). The Economics of Ecology Journals, *Frontiers in Ecology and the Environment*, 4 (9), 488–95.

Chan, L., Cuplinskas, D., Eisen, M., Friend, F., Genova, Y., Guédon, J.-C., Hagemann, M., Harnad, S., Johnson, R., Kupryte, R., La Manna, M., Rév, I., Segbert, M., de Souza, S., Suber, P., & Velterop, J. (2002). *Budapest Open Access Initiative*. Retrieved 12 January 2007 from http://www.soros.org/openaccess/read.shtml

DuBois, F. L., & Reeb D. (2000). Ranking the International Business Journals, *Journal of International Business Studies*, 31 (4), 689–704.

Eysenbach, G. (2006). Citation Advantage of Open Access Articles, *PLOS Biology*, 4 (5): e157. Retrieved 12 January 2007 from http://biology.plosjournals.org/perlserv/?request=get-document&doi=10.1371/journal.pbio.0040157

Jaschik, S. (2006). Rallying Behind Open Access, *Inside Higher Ed*, July 28, Retrieved 12 January 2007 from http://www.insidehighered.com/news/2006/07/28/provosts

Kauffman-Wills Group (2005). *The Facts about Open Access: A Study of the Financial and Non-Financial Effects of Alternative Business Models on Scholarly Journals*, ALPSP Research Report, Worthing, UK: Association of Learned and Professional Society Publishers. Retrieved 12 January 2007 from http://www.alpsp.org/ngen_public/article.asp?id=200&did=47&aid=270&st=&oaid=-1

McCabe, M. J. (2000). Academic Journal Pricing and Market Power: A Portfolio Approach, Paper presented at the American Economic Association conference, Boston, MA. Retrieved 12 January 2007 from http://www.prism.gatech.edu/~mm284/JournPub.PDF

Peritz, B. C. (1995). On the Association Between Journal Circulation and Impact Factor. *Journal of Information Science*, 21 (1), 63–7.

Senders, J. (1976). The Scientific Journal of the Future. *The American Sociologist*, 11, 160–4.

SPARC (2004). *Open Access*, Brochure no. OA2004, Washington, DC: Scholarly Publishing and Academic Resources Coalition. Retrieved 12 January 2007 from http://www.arl.org/sparc/oa/docs/OpenAccess.pdf

Starbuck, W. H. (2005). How Much Better Are the Most-Prestigious Journals? The Statistics of Academic Publication, *Organization Science*, 16 (2), 180–200.

Turnoff, M. & Hiltz, S. R. (1982). The Electronic Journal: A Progress Report. *Journal of the American Society of Information Science*, 33, 195–202.

Part IV Editorship and Academic Career

21
Opening the Black Box of Editorship: Editors' Voice

Yehuda Baruch

In this chapter I examine the experience of academic-journal editors, building on data collected from over 50 editors of such journals. I explored their positive and negative experiences, what helped them and what hindered their progress, asking them what it takes to make a successful editor, what advice they would give to a novice editor, and about their route to editorship.

Becoming an editor is a clear indication and manifestation of academic career success. Editors are a minor, but significant, group of individuals who have the most power over what is going to be published versus what is not going to make it. Being in this critical junction of power, where a culture of "publish or perish" prevails, represents both significant honor and major responsibility. To succeed they need certain qualities, which I will discuss in this chapter, focusing on the "why, what, how, and when" of editorship.

The chapter is based on qualitative and quantitative data collected from editors of journals in the management and social sciences. It is arranged in the following sections: (a) Method, (b) The identified qualities of successful editors, (c) "Things I wish I had known before becoming an editor," based on the "advice for a novice editor" provided by the respondents, (d) The psychological contract of editorship – what editors give and what they get, and (e) Implications: for both serving editors and academics aspiring to serve as editors in the future.

Method

Procedure

The target population was of current editors of academic refereed journals in management and behavioral sciences in the English language. A list comprising editors from the following organizations and publishing houses was made: The Academy of Management, American Psychological Association, Oxford University Press, Blackwell, Elsevier, Wiley, Sage, and Palgrave Macmillan. E-mails were sent to those editors who had their e-mail addresses presented, overall some 250 editors. The 53 responses received account to just over 20 percent response rate, below the norm for surveys conducted at the individual level, but within the norm when referring to representatives of organizations (see Baruch, 1999), though this does not eliminate the prospects of response bias. One reason for this low rate, which emerged from the responses, is the significant overload and time pressure editors have to cope with. The data produced, though, is rich and revealing, as will be demonstrated below.

Research instrument

I collected data via semiopen questionnaires attached to the e-mails. Some questions comprised standard measures for variables such as career and job satisfaction, others were specific to the subject of the study. In addition, a number of open-ended questions were presented, to learn about issues such as: What would you argue was (a) your best achievement or best experience while leading this journal? And (b) your worst experience while leading this journal? What do you think are the most important qualities that make a successful editor? Reasons for present research output compared with pre-editorship period; and, what advice do you have for a novice editor?

This volume of data enabled me to employ a content analysis, conducted manually, according to the principles identified by Kirppendorff (1989) and Carley (1993). In addition, quantitative analysis was performed on the numerical section of the questionnaires.

Sample

The sample reflects both the people – editors, and the journals they edit. In terms of people, the sample was very biased toward the traditional archetype, which seems to represent the specific population of academic editors – the vast majority were white, and gender wise 37 were males, 8 were females (the 8 did not refer to the gender question). Average age was 52.9 (sd. 8.56), which is a typical stage for academics to reach seniority position, though far from retiring age. Surprisingly, they came from a variety of universities, not necessarily top ranked, but, nevertheless, from established, research-led institutions.

All the journals were academic blind refereed. The average rejection rate was 78.09 (sd 13.60), and the average ISI (Institute for Scientific Information) was 1.59 (sd 1.0). About half did not have ISI rating (though six were in the process of gaining it). T-test comparison between the responses of ISI journal editors and others revealed no significant differences in their attitudes, though the rejection rate was higher in the ISI journals (83%) compared with the non-ISI (75%). ISI editors also felt a slightly higher level of the impact of editorship on their career, but the impact felt on professionalism was similar (and high – 5.6 on a Likert scale; from 1, meaning 'not at all', to 7, meaning 'very much'). ISI editors had less support from their publishers, but similar support from other sources. Overall it seems that while more visible journals (with ISI ranking) may receive more submissions and have a larger number of reviewers, the editor must manage that, essentially, those issues and inputs provided by them are qualitatively similar to those faced by journals not included in the ISI.

Results

I will discuss both qualitative and quantitative findings which emerged from the data. In doing so, I will reflect on the "why, what, how, and when" issues.

Qualities that make a successful editor

One of the most significant questions the respondents were asked to reflect upon in an open question was, "What are the most important qualities that make a successful editor?" This was also complemented by another open question – "what would you advice a novice editor?" My implicit assumptions were that the participants are good editors, well informed, and have high self-awareness, as well as the integrity to reflect on their experience in the form of worthy advice. Starting with the first question, the answers varied significantly, but several elements became clear (and were supported by some of the quantitative items in the questionnaire). The content analysis of the qualitative data conducted for these open questions revealed a variety of categories and dimensions: four clear dimensions have emerged, which I categorized under: Thinking and vision, Feeling, Willing, and Acting (the latter including managerial and organizational issues).

Thinking and vision

Under the "Thinking and vision" banner, the most prominent aspects were, as one may anticipate, mental ability, knowledge (general as well as field-specific), and the ability to make decisions.

Representing the mental ability were indications for the need of "analytical intelligence"; "curiosity for learning"; "attention to detail"; and "open-mindedness." These were complemented by the need for the ability "to synthesize," "to read fast," and to "be clear, crisp and concise." Two editors mentioned the need for "creativity to spot interesting/novel areas" and ability to generate ideas.

The need for academic knowledge of the field was the most cited element, with typical quotes such as "Needed in-depth knowledge of subject … Very broad knowledge of the field … Good grounding in the subject covered by journal … Mix of depth and breadth of knowledge … Understand the broad area, be able to think beyond the confines of one's own narrow discipline … Mastery of the journal's literature, intimate knowledge of what's been published historically and mastery of the journal's niche topic."

However, the need for knowledge was not enough, and as a number of editors argue, knowledge was essential, but should be coupled with visionary direction: "vision for the field; vision for the future of the journal ... A sense of what's 'hot' ... vision for how the literature relates to and serves the field ... Clear vision shared with colleagues." At the more practical level of vision, the following two observations are revealing: "A sense of what it takes for a paper to be downloaded and cited ... Understanding of place of the journal in the field." Knowledge and reputation as a leading scholar are important for other editorship-sensitive requirements (e.g., for being able to reject the submissions of big names).

The required ability of decision-making competence was manifested by quotes indicating the need for "good judgment," "competent decision making," "unbiased decisions," and "good and quick judgment." One editor emphasized the need to have "independence of judgment" (i.e., not being just a mailbox between authors and reviewers).

Last but not least, emerged the requirement for editors to be distinguished scholars in their own right: "Editor should be at the top of his academic field (so as to know well the issues ... be able to reject senior scholars' work that is below par)." This was manifested by the need to have strong research and publishing experience ... academic credibility ... be respected in the discipline, have "a good reputation," and "engagement with research." Interestingly, one of those mentioning "hard work" added, "willingness to work hard (and to forget about your own publishing record)."

Feeling

The most surprising outcome for me was the Feeling issues. The second most frequently used word (following "knowledge") was "patience"! If we add "compassion" and "being sensitive," this "touchy-feeling" element, then, becomes the quality mostly mentioned as relevant to the editorial role overall. As another editor reflected, to be a good editor, one should "be prepared to 'go the extra mile' to help." Other feeling-related qualities mentioned were "appreciation/empathy," "being understanding," "being supportive," and "being conscientious."

Nevertheless, qualities such as extroversion, firmness, and persistence were mentioned too, reflecting on the need to sometimes be tough and hard when difficult decisions have to be made (though it still needs to be delivered in a fair manner). The last quote I am happy to seal this "feeling" element with is the need for "love of the subject field."

Willing

Here the element of "passion for the job and for knowledge creation" and "passion for learning" was coupled with a need for commitment: "commitment to the journal and its mission"; "commitment to research," dedication, and tenacity, plus "intellectual curiosity." Similarly, persistence and determination appeared in different wordings. To quote one editor: "a desire and willingness to serve the wider academic community" (what was termed "servant leadership" – See Chapter 3 in this volume).

In line with the other dimensions of thinking and feeling, I counted here the elements of decisiveness as well as the need to be uncompromising in terms of standards, though also a desire to help researchers improve.

Acting

Under "acting" the striking word that reappeared, though not surprising, was "hard work." It seems that workaholism might be a required quality for editorship (this is also reflected in the analysis of working hours that will be presented later). Stamina is an essential ingredient for this required "capacity for a high volume of work, work habits." One editor nicely put what he felt were the two most crucial qualities – "Hard work and intelligence (in that order)."

Second, but not least important, is the developmental quality, that is, this action should be directed with "developmental orientation," though at the same time a good editor should be "comfortable saying 'no' with grace and sensitivity." Here "being decisive" does not mean opposite to having "tact and diplomacy," another quote was "diplomacy in managing both authors and reviewers." Another developmental action quality necessary was implied when an editor argued that "A good editor is a good writing teacher."

Further "acting" issues deem required are managerial competencies. Good organizational skills and being an excellent communicator were frequently mentioned. Some elaborated on the nature of the required communication skills, such as "Ability to make constructive suggestions for improving articles."

The most frequently mentioned issue was networking. Knowing many scholars in the field and their work is crucial for editors, naturally, for example, "to build a thoroughly professional team" and "ability to pick good associate editors and good reviewers."

Other organization-related skills were time management and the ability to "be the journal's ambassador; selling the journal to potential authors, reviewers and Board Members." Administrative skills, editing/writing skills (e.g., clarity of writing), attention to detail, having collegial style, being a team worker, and mentoring were also suggested. As explained, editors need "effective organizational skills given large volume of MS and entrepreneurial skills to renew journal on a regular basis." These are really needed because editors must have the "Ability to persuade a host of academics to do a massive amount of voluntary work on time and to constantly push the reviewers to be more thorough in their reviews."

Things I wish I had known before becoming an editor

The advice offered to novice editors fairly reflected the above-discussed qualities deemed necessary for being a good editor. There were several general advices, which I will start with, and a number of advices that can be categorized under the why (of being an editor), the what/how of running the process, and the when – timing issue.

Why

"Do it for love of the contribution to knowledge creation ... [Editors] have to love the job and consider it as a great service to the development of researchers ... Do not take this role on with a view to self-aggrandizement; it's about serving ones colleagues in the hope that the field continues to grow and develop above and beyond that which can be achieved through one's own contribution to research and scholarship ... I would advise colleagues to pursue actively opportunities to join editorial boards and engage with the peer review process which relies on the service of the whole academy." And finally, "Have a clear vision of what you want to do with the journal."

These responses reflect viewing this role as a service to the community (see Chapter 3 in this volume, on servant-leadership), as well as the unwritten requirement to have academic leadership, a vision for the field of study.

What to do, how to do it

Some of the comments about how to perform the role were of a holistic nature, other comprised more practical advice. A general advice was the need to have a strong and wide editorial board and reviewers; for example, "Get a good team behind you" or "Surround yourself with quality reviewers who get their stuff in on time." "Build an editorial team! It's not a one-man show" and following from the last comment, "Don't allow your Ego to get in the way" "It is a balancing job. Have confidence in your judgment, but not excessively so. Take reviewers' assessments and comments seriously, but recognize that some serious flaws can be fixed, salvaging articles that reviewers might reject ... Keep reader's perspective in mind, but respect authors." And finally, "Reach out to other editors. I found other editors to be very helpful."

These are very useful comments, though some are easier said than done (e.g., having high-quality, quick-responding reviewers). Others correspond to the needed ability for a learned decision-making competence.

More practical advice

Some advised to be sensitive and full of empathy, others suggested to be tough: "You cannot 'save' every paper nor can you 'develop' every author – sometimes it is not a good idea to invest too much time and energy into letters to those that are so far off the mark – however, you should invest time and energy into those that do miss the cut but where you see that promise and potential." In line with this comment came "Don't spend too much time on articles that won't make the grade – but do spend time on raising standards."

Some reassurance about the supportive nature of collegial work among editors of competing journals could be gathered from, "Don't be afraid to ask for help, know you won't get everything right (and no one else has either)."

The managerial issue of goal setting was seen as instrumental: "Set clear expectations – for your Associate Editors; for reviewers; and for authors. Also from the institution (e.g., make sure that appropriate administrative support is in place.) ... Setup/develop a peer-review system and keep reviewers on board with regular updates (I update 2x per year) – have some targets to attract peer reviewers from across the range of topics." A different editor added the caveat, "Expect referees to be slow."

"Hire the very best Managing Editor you can" – this advice is limited, of course, to the cases where the editor has the power to do that; sometimes it is for the publisher to appoint the managing editor. "Automate the tasks associated with processing manuscripts" (see later comments under "best achievements, best experience"). And, yes, a couple of editors who were aware of this book simply recommended, "Read the book!"

At the more personal level, one comment (reflecting the "feeling" dimension mentioned above) was, "Realize that there is someone reading your letter; try to provide them with advice about how to proceed; do not view your decision letter as your task to finish, but a communication to an author who has hopes about their work. Focus not only on the rationale for the decision but also serve to give them direction about how to further improve their work." Another personal comment reflected on the need for sensitivity and being supportive: "The more polite, supportive and civil you can be to all persons with whom you come into contact as editor, the better your work will go. Emphasizing civil and constructive feedback to authors and mentoring young authors through their initial publishing attempts will pay off well in the long run. There is no excuse for overly harsh or brutal communication." While these are sound, the counter-voice was reflected in "Be tough – there are many poor or incompetent authors who argue that their work is deserving."

There were also certain warnings, such as: "It's a lot of work; forget your research for the duration of your editorship but it is very enjoyable seeing certain papers evolve and develop through rigorous peer-reviewing" and "Think carefully whether you really want to do it." "Be prepared to work hard, be able to work consistently." And lastly, institutional support from both the university and the publisher might be critical: "Don't do it without explicit financial and moral support of your Dean." "Find out if being an editor counts at your university BEFORE accepting the position; get as much help from the publisher as possible; don't work for free (publishers make money on the journal, so should you)."

Timing

When to take up editorship is an important consideration, as it may come in at different career stages. The advice here was clear – "Don't do it until you are tenured." And "Make sure you have tenure first; don't let the editorship get in the way of your academic career."

For how long – "Make sure it is a three-year stint." Others commented similarly for not doing it "forever," or changing journal, though no clear-cut time limit can be determined.

Final advice

"It's a great career opportunity [which] provides 'esteem factor' ... Generally a great opportunity ... Take an active role as, in most cases, Editorship has to be its own reward! ... Just do it, and have a good time ... Enjoy it, it is a privilege." Also: "Enjoy and never fret because no matter how hard you try someone will be upset by your decisions," and lastly, "Go for it, do your best to do a good job, be sincere, positive and constructive in your approach."

The psychological contract of editorship – what editors give and what they get

How editors gain the role

There are various ways to be appointed or selected to the role. In a number of journals, especially those run by established academic organizations (e.g., Academy of Management, American Psychological Association), there is a selection process, usually a call for nomination followed by a committee search recommendation (see Black, Newing & McLean, 1998; Cascio, 2007, this volume). Sometimes the publisher is much involved with the search. Yet in a significant number of cases, it was the direct recommendation of the former editor to the publisher that paved the way for the appointment. This recommendation was typically based on good experience of reviewing competence and personal knowledge. The typical progress towards editorship started with reviewing for journals, which in itself is an indication of the readiness to invest effort and commitment to the process of knowledge development (Baruch, Sullivan, & Schepmyer, 2006). To sum up, *hard work and networking* are the essential inputs needed to gain the role, and once an editor, these two factors seem to gain in significance.

Support

What are the sources of support the editor may expect and how strongly did they fair in this survey? Based on initial discussions, the questionnaire

Table 21.1 Support from various sources

Source of support	Average	sd	Valid N
Your publisher	5.8	1.32	50
Your university/institution	4.9	2.01	50
Your associate editor(s)	6.03	1.16	39
Your editorial board	5.69	1.18	52
The former editor	4.89	2.16	36

included the item "How would you rate the support you have from …" (on a Likert scale of 1 [poor] to 7 [great]). Five sources were tested, as presented in Table 21.1. The most supportive source was the associate editor(s). It should be noted that the high variance in the perceived support from the institution and from former editors emerged due to uneven distribution (i.e., some very low scores and many very high scores, rather than a normal distribution around the 5 score).

Impact on academic performance

The editors were asked what their present level of publication is compared with the level at a time when they were not serving as editors. Based on a comparative self-perception, the overall average impact is deemed negative (though for some, the impact was not related to the editorship). For 21 of the 53 (some 40%) there was no change, but over 43 percent felt they publish less (18) or much less (5), compared with only 17 percent that felt they publish more (4) or much more (5) than before. While 17 percent is a minority, it is still a significant minority, and it may be more revealing to examine the reasons attributed to the change (or stability). Reasoning for lower publication output, the overwhelming factor was time and time pressure. Typical quotes ranged from the simple "The Journal absorbs every spare minute," to the more elaborate ones such as "I had so much to read as an editor that was unrelated to my own work that I had no time left for my own research." Other reasons were mentioned too, such as "Less necessary … less interest" "I now do not have to publish just to satisfy a misguided employer" as well as "age" and "career stage."

Very few felt there was no impact. One such untypical comment was "Being editor has not been enough of a burden to get in the way of my research."

Reasons cited to explain a higher level of publishing outcome are more exciting, though referring to a smaller share of the population. Some were academically oriented: "More experienced, more opportunities, more collaborators" "Gained insight about how reviewers and editors think," and "have a better sense of what I want to be writing and how it serves a broader population." Others were at the practical level (e.g., "I have more release time from teaching that I am using for research").

Interestingly, one editor said, "While I was an editor I published *much* less, but since leaving the editorship I have published much more and it takes less time (less revisions) to get them in …" – this may point out that the editorship experience bears fruits, which may ripen at a later stage.

Best achievement, best experience

"What would you argue was your best achievement or best experience while leading this journal?" – this question produced intriguing responses. Some were concerned with the journal, starting with general improvement, but particularly moving to web-based management process (mentioned as a significant achievement by a number of the editors). Others included:

- Improving quality, number of submissions, reviewers, and range and size of readership
- Enhancing the field's perception of the journal's openness and fairness
- Getting ISI rating
- Establishing a truly interdisciplinary and international journal; keeping balance among multidiscipline focus
- Repositioning the journal to appeal to a global management audience and to attract more management readers
- Being in a special position which enables "Reading not only the best manuscript in the field but ALL of them"
- Helping authors improve their work and helping reviewers improve theirs too
- For a couple of editors who started their own journal, this "start-up" experience was their best
- "Being thanked by authors of rejected papers" and "getting positive feedback from authors about their experience with us"

Worst experience(s) while leading this journal?

A correspondent question was "What would you argue was your worst experience while leading this journal?" The issues were mostly about administration, academic (in particular decision making), and ethical issues (see also in Chapter 9, in this volume).
Administrative issues:

- Persuading reviewers to review
- Having them review it in the expected time-frame
- Problems of managing the process (e.g. with the publisher or the institution)

Academic – decision-making issues:

- Rejecting a paper that was later published elsewhere and became a big hit citation wise
- Inheriting a pipeline of manuscripts of questionable scholarship that one has had to clean up

- Dealing with unprofessional authors
- Rejecting submissions after they have been revised in response to reviews
- Relating to the administration issue were cases of need to remove people, including friends, from the editorial boards or from being associate editors
- Lastly, and perhaps surprising to some authors – a significant problem to editors is *"the lack of quality manuscripts"* – yes, editors yearn for quality manuscripts. They want to publish, not to reject.

Ethical and political issues:

- Having to deal with senior scholars who felt their papers should be published primarily because they were the author
- Established scholars who have forgotten the maxim – there are no bad readers, only bad writers
- Having to reject papers from colleagues – I have always maintained that the journal standard comes first but it has created conflict (See also Chapter 24 in this volume)

A worrying sign that might mark things to come is the arrival of the litigious society to the academe: *Being sued by an author whose paper had originally been accepted and I withdrew the acceptance when I discovered that 90% of the paper had been previously published in another journal. My publisher stood behind me 100% and covered all costs. (I prevailed.)*

Overall, the negative experiences seem to be of a lower tone than the positive ones. Several specifically added – "No bad experience" and "Nothing of note." I see this as an encouraging message to the community.

Satisfaction from editorship and from career

The level of satisfaction was very high in serving as an editor and with regards to the more general career satisfaction. The distributions were not normal, but much skewed toward the upper end. The very few untypical cases of intention to quit editorship (four cases) seem to reflect circumstantial factors (e.g., getting close to ending the role). The average satisfaction from serving as editor was 5.96 (sd 1.16) on a 1–7 Likert scale; Satisfaction from career in general was even higher – 6.29 (sd .72).

Did they have a clear career target of becoming an editor? Editing a journal can be a significant aim in an academic career. As one editor commented, "My motivations are very intrinsic. Actually, I am one of those who have things I want to do before I retire. Editing a journal was one of them."

The majority (38, 72%) indeed wished to become editors; a further 10 (19%) were not sure, while only 5 (less than 10%) claimed that they did not want to be an editor.

On an average, the editors spent 25 years (sd 9.42) in their academic careers, and it took them 15.62 years (sd 8.06) to reach their present hierarchy level. Almost all of them started as assistant professor or the equivalent European level, and the majority reached the level of full professor by now. Bearing in mind the flat hierarchy system of the academic ladder, it is difficult to project from this data on the pace of progress as a career success indicator, in particular because much of meaning of "progress" depends on the institution where a scholar gained a full professorship. Yet, it implies from the data that, typically, people first became full professors, then were appointed to the editorial role.

In what way did editorship help or hinder the career of the editors?

Based on their self-evaluation, being editors helps their career positively (4.16, sd 2.02 on a scale of 1–7), and even more, their professional development (5.58, sd 1.58 on a scale of 1–7). Further, they were asked specifically about how their expectations (both positive and negative) were fulfilled by their editorship. The statistics is presented in Table 21.2a and Table 21.2b.

The following two tables present the level of fulfillment of expectations from the role.

This came at a certain cost – the average weekly working hours for the sample was 55 (sd 9.15), of which 14.80 (sd 10.90) were dedicated to editorship. It seems that being a workaholic is an inherent requirement for this job.

Table 21.2a Positive outcomes

	N	Mean	Std. Deviation
Generating a strong network	40	5.70	1.29
Improving self academic competence	39	5.54	1.12
Improving academic discipline knowledge	47	5.55	1.12
Gaining respect from colleagues	40	5.23	1.33
Improving income	28	4.25	1.86
Developing my self-esteem	28	5.07	1.44
Improve my influential power	26	4.77	1.50
Improving chances of academic promotion	21	3.86	2.10
Other	8	5.75	1.91

Table 21.2b Negative outcomes

	N	Mean	Std. Dev
Generating work-related stress	45	4.82	1.63
Generating a non-work-related stress	24	3.58	2.21
Harming relationship with colleagues	23	3.17	1.80
Creating frustration	28	4.39	1.62
Hindering research development/progress	37	4.24	2.01
Other	3	5.67	.577

Implications for aspiring editors

Serving as an editor is a great privilege, accompanied by high level of work investment, obligations, and stress, but nevertheless gratifying, developmental, and enriching, both personally and professionally. As was demonstrated in this chapter, "you will not be alone." Editors share similar joys, suffer similar challenges and struggle. We can do that more together, as a community, and when "joining the club" a new editor is adviced to look for ways to collaborate. Editors compete for submissions, but can collaborate on other issues, and certainly form a caring community to help each other. This can be done at the professional realm (e.g., recommend authors to try a different journal that may be a better fit for their manuscript) and at the personal realm (e.g., ask for advice about how to deal with a problematic author or with an ethical issue).

How long should editorship last

Even if successful, editors should not "stick to the chair" forever, though some did have a long tenure. Echoing the "timing" section above, one said that "I have considered giving up the editorship as I have been doing it for 6 years and I am concerned that the Journal will not progress with the same person staying for too long." This was echoed by, "I have an open-ended appointment. However, I believe in helping other careers. It is important to let others get this experience so they are more likely to get awards, promotions, and recognition. So, max 4 years is all I will do."

What next?

The editors were asked about their anticipated career move next. The most opted for option was, "Continuing my academic career without editorship" (24, 45 percent). Nevertheless, 12 suggested that "I do not see myself ending this editorship before I retire," and further 6 planned or expected to run another editorship. Six plan to move to managerial-academic career, and the rest (8) had other plans (e.g., to pursue different, more applied roles). These findings, in line with other inputs from this group of scholars, manifest their professional integrity and willingness not to exploit the power bestowed on them by the academic community.

Implications for authors

We are all in the same boat. Editors are scholars just like authors. While being editors for their journal, they are also authors trying to publish elsewhere, and they certainly go through the hassles and hurdles of being rejected, and ultimately have their work published before becoming editors – thus they sympathize with authors more than one might believe. Overall, we share the same purpose – to promote academic knowledge for the wider scholarly community, or sometimes for the smaller niche community. They are on your side, but have strong obligations to the general academe. Moreover, they want your submission, and aim to improve it if possible, so eventually they will publish high-quality papers. Work *with* them, not *against* them.

References

Baruch, Y. (1999). Response Rate in Academic Studies – A comparative analysis. *Human Relations*, 52, 421–38.

Baruch, Y. Sullivan, S. E. & Schepmyer, H. N. (Eds.) (2006). *Winning Reviews: A Guide for Evaluating Scholarly Writing*. Basingstoke: Palgrave Macmillan.

Black, D. Newing, R. A. & McLean, I. (1998). *The Theory of Committees and Elections*. Springer.

Carley, K. (1993). Coding Choices for Textual Analysis: A Comparison of Content Analysis and Map Analysis, *Sociological Methodology*, 23, 75–126.

Cascio, W. F. (2008). How Editors are Selected. In Y. Baruch, A. M. Konrad, H. Aguinis, & W. H. Starbuck (Eds.), *Opening the Black Box of Editorship* (pp. 231–8). London, UK: Palgrave Macmillan.

Eden, D. (2008). What Authors Need to Know to Navigate the Review Process Successfully: Understanding and Managing the Editor's Dilemma. In Y. Baruch, A. M. Konrad, H. Aguinis, & W. H. Starbuck (Eds.), *Opening the Black Box of Editorship* (pp. 239–49). London, UK: Palgrave Macmillan.

Kirppendorff, K. (1989). *Content Analysis: An introduction to its methodology*. Beverley Hills: Sage.

Ryan, A. M. (2008). How May I Help You? Editing as Service. In Y. Baruch, A. M. Konrad, H. Aguinis, & W. H. Starbuck (Eds.), *Opening the Black Box of Editorship* (pp. 27–38). London, UK: Palgrave Macmillan.

Shapiro, D. L., & Bartunek, J. (2008). Being an Ethical Editorial Board Member and Editor: The Integral Role of Earned Trust. In Y. Baruch, A. M. Konrad, H. Aguinis, & W. H. Starbuck (Eds.), *Opening the Black Box of Editorship* (pp. 88–96). London, UK: Palgrave Macmillan.

22
The Motivating Potential of an Associate Editor's Role

Carol T. Kulik

I served as associate editor for the *Journal of Management* (*JOM*) from 2002–05. This role was the single best service responsibility I have had during my academic career. I enjoyed it more, and found it more fulfilling, than any leadership role I held in any professional association or any committee I served on at any academic institution. In fact, I'll share a deep, dark secret: I enjoyed my editorial work so much that I regularly moved it to the top of my to-do list – ahead of other responsibilities (including, sometimes, my own research agenda) that might have had more direct instrumental benefit to my career. I don't mean to sugarcoat the experience. It was a lot of work on a relentless schedule, and there were times when I felt a bit like a hamster on one of those exercise wheels, struggling to keep the flow of manuscripts moving forward at a steady pace. But on the whole, I loved it. I relished it. I thrived in it. My personal experience indicates that the role of associate editor can be a good, positive, and developmental one – but I suspect that it's not for everyone. In this chapter, I analyze my experience as an associate editor, and I offer some diagnostic tips to the academic considering an associate editorship.

The motivating potential of the associate editor role

In reflecting on the quality of the associate editor role, I turned to a tried-and-true framework: Hackman and Oldham's (1980) Job Characteristics Theory (JCT). The theory's basic premise is both straightforward and intuitive. A job that has high levels of five key job characteristics (Task Significance, Task Identity, Skill Variety, Autonomy, and Feedback) has a high "Motivating Potential Score" (MPS). High MPS jobs create a self-sustaining motivational cycle in which a jobholder is continually rewarded for performing well on a challenging job. High MPS jobs usually (but not always!) result in positive outcomes for both the jobholder and the larger organization. All five of JCT's characteristics were maximized in my role as associate editor, making it a very high MPS job indeed.

The role had high Task Significance, Task Identity, and Skill Variety–contributing to my Experienced Meaningfulness. I knew that my work had an impact on other people's lives (Task Significance), because publishing an article in *JOM* would affect an author's career – maybe only in an incremental way as one more publication on the author's vita, but possibly more significantly, in making the difference in a close tenure case. I personally shepherded a manuscript from its initial submission to its final decision, and through all the review rounds in between (Task Identity). And no two submitted manuscripts had more than a passing resemblance to one another. Every manuscript exposed me to different areas of the management field, used different methodological techniques and strategies, and challenged me to bring a variety of skills to help the manuscript to develop (Skill Variety).

The role had huge amounts of Autonomy – contributing to my Experienced Responsibility. The only constraints I faced were acting consistently within *JOM* policy and procedures. But the specific steps I took in responding to each submission were at my full discretion. And at the end of the day, it was my decision, and my decision alone, whether to "green light" a submission to the next stage.

And finally, the role had built-in Feedback channels – giving me direct knowledge of results. One feedback channel came from the iterative review process associated with manuscripts that cleared the initial hurdle. Another feedback channel came from observing my convergence (and sometimes, learning from my divergence) with the reviewer panel. And a third feedback channel came directly from the authors themselves.

But what are the outcomes?

Hackman and Oldham (1980) emphasize the "intrinsic" outcomes (e.g., high jobholder satisfaction and motivation) that result from working on a well-designed job – not the "extrinsic" ones. A person performing a high MPS job wants to do the job right – even if doing the job poorly might mean completing more products in the same period of time and earning more pay. That's one of the hallmarks of a high MPS job, that a person reaps psychological benefits from the work.

A person considering an associate editor position might anticipate career benefits that result from being associated with a journal's editorial team, particularly a journal with a positive reputation. But I am hard-pressed to identify any specific instrumental outcomes that resulted directly from my affiliation with *JOM*. I can't name any jobs I was offered because of the editorship; I am unaware of any pay raises I received due to the editorship. Consistent with the predictions of JCT, when I reflect on my experience as an associate editor at *JOM*, it's the psychological rewards that are most salient. I can vividly recall some emotion-laden events without having to jog my memory by looking through the electronic files: The times I had a "Eureka!"

moment that helped an author solve a sticky methodological problem and satisfy a reviewer's concerns. The time a rejected author wrote the *JOM* reviewers and me a grateful thank you note for our developmental feedback. The times *JOM* reviewers celebrated the dramatic improvement delivered by a second-round submission. The times we shepherded "diamonds in the rough" through the review process. The first time one of "my" authors' papers appeared in hard copy print. Each event provided exactly the kind of positive emotional "oomph" that reminded me why I signed on for the job in the first place.

While I cannot identify direct instrumental benefits resulting from my *JOM* experience, I am distinctly aware that there have been some *indirect* career benefits. As a result of my editorial experience, I have a broader appreciation of the field than I have had since my graduate school prelim exams. That's because I was exposed to areas (social network theory and stakeholder theory spring to mind) outside my immediate expertise. My methodological toolkit is more fully stocked. That's because I had to get up to speed quickly on the rules-of-thumb for data collection strategies and statistical techniques (cluster analysis and hierarchical linear modeling among them) I wasn't using in my own research. Now that I've made the investment to learn about those techniques, I can see their applicability to my own research agenda. I am a better writer. That's because I had to explicitly learn the grammar rules that lay beneath my gut instinct that written material didn't "sound right" in order to justify the changes to authors. Knowing the rules, I can now apply them to my own writing without having to think consciously about them. And I am definitely a better supervisor to my students. My editorial experience taught me that it's not enough to show someone the "right" way to present an idea. I had to be able to explain why I was recommending an alternative to the author's personal preference, and as I developed that explanation, I usually discovered a way that was even "better" than my first-considered alternative.

So, in combination, my editorial experiences should make me a better researcher, a better scholar, a better academic. And I believe that they have. But here's the diagnostic opportunity for the academic contemplating a stint as an associate editor: How well do you cope with delayed gratification? During the three years (or a little more) that you serve as associate editor, your own research agenda will inevitably slow. It's almost impossible to devote yourself to developing other people's research in the editorial process and simultaneously keep your own research program going full steam. I am very aware that during my three-year term at *JOM*, my publication record owes a lot to my co-authors who took the lead on ongoing projects and maintained our momentum on them.

Therefore, before accepting the responsibility of an associate editor position, it's worth doing an assessment of your research portfolio and considering whether your projects can be sustained during the editorial term. Can you afford to make other people's research a higher priority than your own for a few years, knowing that the experience will ultimately enrich your research program? And do you *want* to make other people's research a personal priority? Career models (e.g., Super, 1957; Super, Savickas & Super, 1996) describe a classic "turning point" in many people's careers, when they transition from a "me-centered" orientation (with a focus on personal development) to an outward-focused orientation (with an emphasis on developing others). Are you at that turning point? I was exactly at that point when the *JOM* opportunity came up. I was being very productive in my research career, but I worried that I might be becoming "stale." *JOM* was an opportunity to step back, take a broad view, and re-energize.

MPS enhancers or constraints

Hackman and Oldham (1980) caution that lurking between the five job characteristics and positive jobholder outcomes are a variety of individual and contextual factors that can either enhance the motivating potential of a well-designed job or turn that same job into a frustrating experience. High MPS jobs have high motivating *potential* – but there's no guarantee that every person will experience positive outcomes in every context. Looking back, I can see that in my case, individual and contextual factors converged into a favorable situation for a fledgling associate editor. And these factors can be used as diagnostics that I urge anyone considering an associate editor position to reflect upon before accepting the job.

What is your skill set?

Inevitably, associate editors are asked to manage manuscripts outside of their particular area of expertise. That's particularly true at journals like *JOM*, who claim the entire broad domain of "management" and receive manuscripts across the micro-macro continuum. A researcher with narrow interests and limited research experience could easily feel over-stretched in the associate editor role. Broad research interests and experience with a variety of research methods are big plusses. However, associate editors don't need to be top-shelf experts in every area as long as the journal maintains a high-quality roster of reviewers who embody that expertise. What's most important, I believe, is a skill for seeing the "big picture" potential of a manuscript. A reviewer with experience in social identity theory will identify the flaws in the theoretical logic of a submission. A reviewer with experience in survey data collection will point out the potential biases resulting from the survey administration. A reviewer with experience in structural equation modeling will pick up the data analysis problems. The challenge for the associate editor is putting these puzzle pieces together to see if a manuscript with that particular configuration of theoretical flaws, methodological biases, and analytical problems nonetheless has the potential to make a contribution to the field.

Before accepting an associate editor role, I encourage you to think back on other opportunities you had to integrate feedback from multiple sources. For example, when you chair dissertation committees, are you able to integrate committee members' feedback to give the student a clear and unified sense of direction? How about when you look at reviews of your own research? Can you take three reviews written in different styles and emphasizing different issues, and identify the top three or four issues (*across* reviewers) that need to be addressed in the revision? These situations draw on the same integration skills that you'll need as an associate editor – better to know whether that skill is sufficiently developed before you jump into the deep end of the pool.

What is your confidence level?

At some journals, editors are not very proactive. They might simply pass the reviews forward to the author and leave it to the author to decide on the best way to tackle the revision. But at *JOM*, we had a conscious policy to make a "go/no go" decision after the first revision, so we didn't have time for much trial-and-error. The first revision had to be the author's absolute best shot at a publishable product. *JOM*'s policy meshed well with my personal philosophy about effective editing: I strongly believe that effective editors are directive. That doesn't mean that editors should be autocratic dictators or place "one best way" demands on authors. But I see an effective editor as one who helps the author to work through the accumulating (and sometimes conflicting) reviewer advice. That requires providing the author a road map – identifying which issues are most important, and suggesting which avenues have the highest probability of success.

I couldn't have done that early in my career. Confidence comes with experience. By the time I stepped into the associate editor role, I had accumulated experience as an author and as a reviewer. I knew that there was no "one best way" but I also knew that some ways were better than others, and I had confidence in my ability to identify the better ones. Associate editors have to stick their necks out – to point the author in a particular direction, and then hope for the best. So here's another opportunity for self-assessment: Do you have a healthy amount of confidence in your ability to sort the wheat from the chaff? Are you willing to disagree with your reviewers if you see a solution that they didn't? Are you ready to go with a minority viewpoint if you disagree with the majority stand?

Who are you working with?

Journals, I've learned, vary tremendously in their organizational structure. At some journals, each associate editor handles his or her own administration – assigning reviewers, chasing down late reviews, distributing reviewer feedback. That wasn't the case at *JOM*. The central *JOM* office maintained reviewer files, sent out reminders, and generally managed all the paperwork.

This freed the associate editors to concentrate on the really satisfying part of the job – reading and reviewing the submissions. As a result, even during a stretch with a particularly heavy workload, I could look back on my *JOM* time and count a very large percentage as quality work and not administrivia. Before you commit to an associate editor role, find out as much as you can about the journal's overall organization and structure. You might find that the high-MPS job I described in opening this chapter has a hefty low-MPS administrative component. If the administrative part of the job takes up a considerable amount of time, it might begin to overshadow the more satisfying parts of the job. And talk with the senior editor about his or her editing philosophy and make sure that you have a shared view of the role, especially of the amount of autonomy you will have in the decision-making.

What else are you doing?

My opportunity to join the *JOM* editorial team came just as I was moving to a new job and a new country. My plate was very full for several years, but in fact the *JOM* opportunity blended well with my other academic responsibilities. My new academic job had a lighter teaching load than my previous one – which meant that I had a looser schedule within which to fit the editorial responsibilities. And I found that *JOM* enabled me to meet some of the expectations associated with my academic job. In my academic job, I was encouraged to mentor junior colleagues and involve them in professional activities. Several of my junior colleagues served as ad hoc reviewers for *JOM*, and a couple of them even "graduated" to the editorial board. Before accepting an associate editor role, look around at your other responsibilities and ask yourself whether your journal experiences will complement, enhance, or interfere with them.

Do you have a mission?

Personally, I've always had two axes to grind about the management field: First, I believe that we do not make sufficient use of experimental research designs in management. We have begun to emphasize field contexts and survey methodologies to the point that we are losing experimental rigor and the ability to draw causal inferences (see Scandura & Williams, 2000 for an analysis reaching a similar conclusion). Second, as a US-trained but Australia-based management researcher, I worry about the barriers faced by international researchers that limit their access to US journals as forums for their research. In my role as associate editor at *JOM*, I was able to supplement my editorial responsibilities with an additional educational focus. As an associate editor, I was regularly invited to participate in publishing workshops or editorial panels where I could educate authors about ways to frame and position their research to increase the possibility of publication. And during the review process, I could sometimes educate reviewers about artificial barriers that might disadvantage experimental or international researchers.

And then an interesting thing happened. Somewhere down the line, I shifted my concept of the "editor" job to a concept that was more of an "editor-and-educator" job – not just for experimental research or research by international authors, but for all manuscripts and all authors. Thinking of myself as an "editor-and-educator" helped me to bring a longer-term perspective to the job. Rejecting manuscripts isn't fun, and an associate editor at a high-quality journal rejects a *lot* of manuscripts. Inevitably, an associate editor has a bad stretch and has to write a series of rejection letters one after another – and that's downright depressing. Thinking about the "educator" component of my role helped me to appreciate the benefits that accrue from a high-quality rejection and motivated me to invest energy in papers that were clearly not publishable now (but might be publishable down the track). I might need to reject this particular manuscript, but ideally the experience of going through the *JOM* review process would help that author to clear the hurdle at another good journal. Journals regularly generate statistics about percentages of manuscripts accepted or manuscript turnaround time. Focusing exclusively on those objective indicators can sometimes obscure the real value of the work editors do.

Do you have a personal mission that can sustain you during a "down" period when you reject manuscript after manuscript, always with an eye toward meeting deadlines? Can that mission keep the associate editor role "fresh" for you, without turning it into a manuscript-processing assembly line?

Dead end or springboard role?

I think my own answer to this question is clear. My experience as an associate editor was an enriching one, one that I would have hated to miss. But the associate editor role is by no means a clear path to tangible career success. It's best to think of it as an opportunity to have an immediate positive impact on a small set of individuals – and a non-duplicable opportunity to have a *long-term* positive impact on your own research agenda. The emphasis in the previous sentence on "long-term" is deliberate – while an associate editor will experience immediate psychic rewards, the real career benefits are subtle and may not be visible until after the associate editor term is complete. There's nothing wrong with making the "selfish" choice to advance your own research agenda and turning down an associate editor opportunity. In fact, that's certainly the right choice early in a research career. But at the right time and place, the associate editor role can be a mechanism for pushing your career motivation to a new level.

Acknowledgment

The author thanks Daniel Feldman, Allen Amason, the *JOM* editorial board, and the entire cast of *JOM* ad hoc reviewers for making the 2002–05 *JOM* experience such a rewarding one.

References

Hackman, J. R., & Oldham, G. R. (1980). *Work design*. Reading, Mass: Addison-Wesley.

Scandura, T. A., & Williams, E. A. (2000). Research methodology in management: Current practices, trends, and implications for future research. *Academy of Management Journal*, 43, 1248–64.

Super, D. E. (1957). The psychology of careers. New York: HarperCollins.

Super, D. E., Savickas, M. L., & Super, C. M. (1996). The life-span, life-space approach to careers. In D. Brown, L. Brooks, and Associates (Eds.), *Career choice and development* (pp. 121–78). San Francisco: Jossey-Bass.

23
How Editors are Selected
Wayne F. Cascio

Selection of a new editor for a journal is (or at least it should be) a significant undertaking in time and effort, for it will have long-lasting effects. Editors are gatekeepers of knowledge. As such they affect the development of a field, as reflected in the articles their journals publish, and they also affect the development of individual professional careers. The tone of the letters the editor writes to authors may instill feelings of hope, anger, self-confidence, despair, or a variety of other reactions. In all cases, the editor is the face that represents the journal to the outside world. Hence, the decision to select a new editor should not be taken lightly.

This chapter is not an exhaustive review of editor-selection processes across the full range of journals in the broad field of management and other social sciences. Rather, its focus is considerably narrower, for it describes the process used by the Academy of Management (AOM) to select editors for its four journals. By way of introduction, therefore, it is important to provide some background information about the AOM.

The AOM is one of the largest associations of (predominately) business school professors in the world. As of 2007, it includes more than 10,500 members from the United States, and almost 6000 members from 79 countries outside the United States (aomonline.org, 2007). The Academy is committed to what might be called its knowledge-centric publications mission (Journals Committee, 2004). That is, it seeks to contribute to the theoretical development of management knowledge, to the empirical testing of that knowledge, and to the use of that knowledge in both educational and organizational settings. The Academy's four journals are the forums through which these contributions take place.

Each of the Academy's four journals emphasizes a different scholarly aspect of its mission. The *Academy of Management Review* (*AMR*) provides a forum to explicate theoretical insights and developments. Articles published in the *Academy of Management Journal* (*AMJ*) examine theory-based knowledge empirically. The *Academy of Management Learning and Education* (*AMLE*) provides a forum to examine learning processes and management education.

Articles published in the *Academy of Management Perspectives* (*AMP*, formerly the *Academy of Management Executive*) use research-based knowledge to inform and improve management practice.

The AOM is widely recognized for the quality of research published in its journals. Serving the scholarly needs and interests of its membership as well as those of scholars in related disciplines is an important outcome of the Academy's efforts. As the Journals Committee of the Academy's Board of Governors (2004) noted:

> In addition to the stature of the research published in its journals, the Academy is known for its high-quality review processes. In general, our journals are known for providing authors with timely, thorough, and constructive reviews. This type of feedback is possible because of the collective efforts of the journals' editors, associate editors, and editorial review board members. The nature of the feedback our journals provide and the processes used to generate the feedback appear to combine to form a "source of competitive advantage." In this context, it perhaps can be argued that when considering a set of high-quality journals as possible outlets for their work, scholars/authors will select the journal known to offer thorough, constructive, and timely feedback, assuming equivalency across other dimensions (e.g., journal prestige).
>
> (p. 1)

This information is extremely important to the editor-selection process, because it provides clues about standards of performance, along with a profile of the types of personal characteristics and the types of support that new editors of the Academy's journals must have. During my three years as a member of the AOM's Board of Governors (2003–06), I was privileged to be involved, either as a member or as Chair of the Board's Journals Committee, in the selection of all four new editors of the Academy's journals. The information that follows is drawn largely from the March, 2005 article that I wrote in the *Newsletter of the Academy of Management,* in which I provided a broad overview of the process and its outcome in the interests of providing as much transparency as possible to the membership (Cascio, 2005).

The Journals Committee of the Academy's Board of Governors is a subcommittee of the Board. It comprises four members of the Board, one of whom serves as Chair, along with the four current editors of the Academy's journals (*AMR*, *AMJ*, *AMP*, and *AMLE*).

The search process begins with an effort to provide widespread notification to the members of the AOM of an upcoming editor vacancy in one of its journals, in order to solicit interest from as many individuals as possible. To do that the Academy uses multiple channels to advertise the upcoming vacancy. Specifically, the process begins at the annual conference of the AOM one year in advance of the vacancy, when the Academy solicits candidates for the editorial position through announcements included in the package of materials that each individual receives when he or she attends the conference. The availability of the editor's position, together with requests for nominations (including self-nominations), are also posted on the Academy's website for all members to see. This is very important, since not all members are able to attend the annual conference, particularly international members, yet it is important that they have the same opportunity to apply for vacant editor positions as do those members who do attend the annual conference. Other channels, as described below, also reflect this objective.

Printed announcements appear in each of the four Academy journals in the issues published immediately after the annual conference, as well as on each journal's respective website. A full-time AOM staff member works closely with the Chair of the Journals Committee to ensure that each of these steps is followed each time an editorial vacancy arises.

These methods appear to be quite effective, in that highly qualified individuals either are nominated by others or self-nominate as candidates for these editorial positions. The Academy is quite fortunate to have a large number of talented scholars willing to serve as an editor for one of its journals. Potential candidates are asked to contact the Chair of the Journals Committee if they have specific questions about the position. Many avail themselves of that opportunity, and that is one channel through which candidates can receive a realistic preview of the editor's job. Candidates can also contact former editors or associate editors on their own for such a realistic preview. There is a genuine effort to shield the current editor from these types of calls, so as not to distract him or her from editorial duties. Of course that is not possible in every case, but for the most part the current editor tends to incur only peripheral involvement at this stage of the selection process.

In terms of the editor's job at one of the Academy's journals, the appointment is for a three-year period, with a six-month transition period from the current editor. The Academy provides funds for secretarial support, supplies, limited travel (through a discretionary fund disbursed as an annual check that is deposited in the editor's name in an account held at the host university), and some administrative work. It does not provide funds to pay for release time for the editor, office space, or benefits for part-time employees (although it would if it were a requirement of a school's compensation and benefits package). The editor's host institution is expected to provide release time for editorial duties (usually one-half release time), computers, office space, and access to fax, copy machines, and Internet service.

In terms of the volume of manuscripts (new submissions) to be expected, *AMJ* receives more than 700 per year, *AMR* roughly 600, and *AMP* and *AMLE* more than 100 per year, on average. Discretionary funds to the editors reflect these divergent workloads. Editors are all volunteers, as are associate editors and editorial board members. As such, the Academy strives to provide as much support to them as possible, for example, by authorizing additional associate editors to cope with increasing numbers of submissions, or by purchasing editing software (e.g., Scholar One) that makes the submission and management of manuscripts a completely electronic process (for more information on this topic, see Chapter 10 by Martin Kilduff).

It is important to ensure that candidates for editorial positions receive as realistic a preview of the job as possible, because at least some individuals are motivated to apply because of the "glamour" and visibility of the position, without a clear understanding of its time-consuming (some editors would say all-consuming) demands. For example, if an editor takes a one-week vacation (and stays away from the Internet), or if he or she is ill and cannot get to manuscripts as they arrive, then a backlog develops, and is there to greet the editor when he or she can get to them. That is a realistic feature of the job and candidates need to be aware of that constraint.

In terms of the actual application process, each candidate is asked to submit various items to the Journals Committee. Included among these items is a statement of her/his vision for the journal, a letter from his/her dean indicating that the host institution will provide resources to support the candidate's editorial service, and a recent copy of her/his curriculum vitae (CV). Outside letters of recommendation may also be submitted on a candidate's behalf. Failure to include these items is grounds for exclusion from consideration by the committee.

The Chair of the Journals Committee, working closely with a designated staff member from the Academy's headquarters office, tracks the submission of each candidate's materials, assembles them into a binder, and distributes the combined set of information to the other committee members for their review.

In a face-to-face meeting, the committee carefully considers each of the items submitted by each candidate. Several criteria, including the following ones, guide, but do not singly determine, the committee's deliberations and selection:

(1) as required by policy, a candidate must be a member of the Academy of Management;
(2) the breadth and depth of the candidate's vision statement for the journal;
(3) the nature of recommendation letters that were submitted to the committee;
(4) sufficient, clear, and written support from the candidate's dean; and
(5) an appreciation for the range of the research areas in which the journal publishes articles.

Each of these criteria is important. Lack of Academy membership is a disqualification factor, while the breadth and depth of the candidate's vision statement for the journal often reflect his or her familiarity with it, either as a reviewer or as a contributor. The task of the committee is to retain the basic mission of each journal, while remaining open to new directions or initiatives. The persuasiveness of the candidate's statement carries considerable weight in the overall selection process, and there is often spirited discussion of the practicality and merits of each candidate's vision statement.

Sufficient, clear, and written support from the candidate's dean is another potential qualification factor. Some deans are positively enthusiastic about providing generous support in order to house one of the Academy's journals at his or her university. Others are more guarded in their statements. Reticence and vague generalities on the part of a dean do not help a candidate, and they can actually detract from the overall appeal of a candidate to the committee.

CVs as well as outside letters of recommendation are extremely helpful to the committee in assessing the extent to which candidates have an appreciation for the range of the research areas in which the journal publishes articles. For example, if the journal's orientation is more "macro," yet a candidate's research focuses almost exclusively on "micro" issues in organizations, that fact signals a poor match between the focus of the journal and the candidate's interests. If a journal publishes articles whose focus is on the development of theory, yet almost all of a candidate's work is empirical in nature (or vice versa), again this is a sign of a poor match. Finally, if a journal publishes research conducted both at the macro and micro levels, such as *AMJ*, it takes a truly broad breadth of scholarly interests and publications by an individual in order to appreciate the full range of the research areas in which the journal publishes articles. In all cases, a candidate's CV and external letters can help the committee to understand more fully his or her qualifications to serve as editor.

At the meeting in which a final choice is made, all of the current editors join with the members of the Journals Committee in thorough, candid, in-depth discussions about the candidates. The Committee proceeds in a systematic manner, using flip charts to display a matrix that depicts each candidate's standing on each criterion. Through its discussions, the Committee arrives at a consensus rating for each candidate on each criterion. Candidates with the lowest ratings are eliminated first, and then additional deliberations on the remaining candidates ensue. When discussion is finished, and the members of the Journals Committee are ready to vote, the current editor whose replacement is under discussion is asked to leave the room. To avoid potential conflicts of interest or undue influence, the current editor is not present when the final vote is taken to choose his or her successor.

Once the vote is taken, the candidate receiving the highest number of votes is selected. The Chair then calls that candidate to inform him or her of the selection, and to verify that he or she indeed is willing and able to assume the position of incoming editor.

The committee then recommends to the full Board of Governors one candidate as incoming editor of the journal in question. The Board discusses the choice and the process used to arrive at the choice, and votes to accept or not to accept the committee's recommendation. In almost all cases, the recommendation of the Journals Committee is accepted by the full Board of Governors.

I make no claim that this process of editor selection is universal in the field of management and other social sciences. Rather, it represents the evolution of what successive Journals Committees of the AOM have regarded as good professional practice. Surely it can be improved further, and now that the process is transparent, there is every reason to expect that it will be.

Implications for authors

One purpose of this chapter is to help authors understand that the editor-selection process is thorough, detailed, and exhaustive from several perspectives. It is important for prospective authors to realize that editors are selected in a very professional and objective manner. At the same time, not all authors will be pleased with the final selections, and there are sometimes legitimate differences of opinion, even among selection-committee members, about the merits of particular candidates.

Authors should know, however, that the individuals selected, to the greatest extent possible, do their very best to remain impartial and objective throughout the process of manuscript reviews, and to provide feedback to authors that is constructive in tone. Ethically, editors are expected to recuse themselves from reviewing manuscripts where they might have, or even be perceived as having, a conflict of interest. This could occur, for example, if the editor was an author, or a co-author, of a manuscript submitted to his or her journal. If such a manuscript is published eventually, the editor typically includes a footnote that explains the process by which the manuscript was reviewed and accepted for publication.

In other cases, authors may feel that they did not receive a fair review, or that other information, material to the accept-or-reject decision, was not considered. Unless the decision is outright rejection, editors generally ask authors to respond point-by-point to the issues raised in reviews. That is the opportunity for authors to make the editor aware of new information, logical predictions or arguments based on theory, or perhaps the use of biased language, in a review. Even in the case of outright rejection, editors of Academy journals try to write letters to the authors that are constructive in tone and that might help them craft better manuscripts in the future. It is true that editors are gatekeepers of knowledge, but there is at least the opportunity for authors to pry those gates open a bit in order to receive fair, balanced treatment in the review process.

Authors should understand that editors are incredibly dedicated to the journals they represent, and that each issue that is published becomes a historical record that reflects directly on the judgment and competence of the editor and his or her editorial team. It is the task of the selection committee to assess each candidate's breadth of expertise in the relevant domain, his or her openness to new ideas, willingness to be constructive and objective in the manuscript-review process, and commitment to the demands of the editor's job. Authors can be confident that the persons they deal with throughout the review process reflect these characteristics.

Implications for prospective editors

After reading material in this chapter, prospective editors might well be asking themselves what they can do to prepare well for the selection process. What kinds of knowledge, skills, abilities, and other characteristics (KSAOs) should they try to acquire in preparation for competing for the position of editor with other well-qualified individuals? What evidence should they marshal in support of these KSAOs? Are there any specific experiences and personal characteristics considered to be "deal breakers" by the selection committee? Is the selection process relative (i.e., candidates competing against each other in any given year and the best one wins), are there absolute standards, or both? What type of support (specifically) should be sought from one's dean?

These are all reasonable questions, and in this final section I will try to provide brief answers to each of them. The first, and in my opinion most important, piece of advice is to follow your passion. Focus on research and writing that is important to *you*. Worry less about positioning yourself strategically to be able to qualify for an editor's job. If you are interested in someday being considered, however, do volunteer to serve as an ad hoc reviewer for several journals. Work hard to provide constructive, thorough, and timely reviews. Current editors notice that, and they are always on the lookout for prospective editorial board members whose reviews reflect those characteristics. Take the opportunity to serve on several editorial boards, and to work with a variety of editors and associate editors. In your efforts to please editors and authors through the quality of your reviews, however, do not be afraid to tell an editor that a manuscript is not within your domain of expertise. Be honest about your intellectual strengths and weaknesses, as well as your personal proclivities (e.g., to procrastinate or to not allow things to pile up on your desk). Ask yourself if you have the deep commitment, the drive, and the intellectual fortitude to assume the job of editor. Above all, be realistic about the demands of an editor's job. Talk with current or past editors about the workloads and time commitments required to do the job effectively. If, after weighing all of this evidence carefully, you still want to pursue the job of editor, then by all means make yourself available as a candidate in the selection process.

From the perspective of a selection committee, there are certain "deal breakers" that committees generally adhere to. Aside from possible association membership requirements (e.g., AOM or American Psychological Association), a key consideration is domain expertise, as reflected in published articles, monographs, and books. A second is personal experience with a candidate. Selection committees are extremely reluctant to select an individual as editor whom nobody knows, except through his or her published work. As should be clear by now, after domain expertise, personal characteristics are critically important considerations. Play an active role in your professional association, network extensively, and allow others to develop first-hand knowledge of you as a person.

Assuming that the candidate pool includes individuals who meet basic qualifications, as described above, selection is relative. In cases where no candidate is acceptable to the committee, a rare occurrence in my experience, the current editor might be asked to stay on for an additional period of time until a suitable replacement can be found. Alternatively, if an editor becomes ill, dies, or quits, typically an associate editor will assume the editor's duties for the remainder of his or her term, and then a new selection process takes place.

Finally, it is important to recognize that one's dean plays a very important role in the editor-selection process. The letter that the dean writes in support of a candidate will be read very carefully by members of the committee. Otherwise deserving candidates may be excluded if the Committee perceives that a dean is willing to provide only lukewarm support. As a candidate, it is important that you identify for the dean the types of support that you need. I described those kinds of support earlier (e.g., release time, office and secretarial support). It also is important for the dean to state unequivocally that he or she sincerely *wants* to house the journal at his or her school, and that he or she is willing to provide resources to make that happen. In short, a strong letter from your dean can add considerable "heft" to your candidacy for an editorship.

The editor-selection process is neither unknowable nor inscrutable. As an author, you can rest assured that individuals selected as editors have been vetted with the utmost care and thoroughness. As a prospective candidate for an editor's position, you can take steps now to develop a portfolio of important KSAOs that will make you an attractive candidate when the time comes to compete.

References

Aomonline.org (2007). Membership statistics downloaded from the Academy of Management Web site, aomonline.org, on January 5, 2007.

Cascio, W. F. (2005, March). Selection of new editor for the *Academy of Management Review*. *Newsletter of the Academy of Management*, p. 2.

Journals Committee, Academy of Management Board of Governors. (2004, April). Editorial support: A white paper. Unpublished manuscript. (Available in redacted form from Academy of Management Headquarters by writing to SZaid@pace.edu).

24
What Authors Need to Know to Navigate the Review Process Successfully: Understanding and Managing the Editor's Dilemma

Dov Eden

Who am I to be writing this?

After 30 years of experience publishing articles in scientific journals and service on editorial boards of leading journals, I accepted appointment to a three-year term as associate editor of *Academy of Management Journal* (*AMJ*). Because of the trailing pipeline, the job actually extended beyond four years, during which I served as action-editor on over 300 submitted manuscripts, over 60 of which went through revision. As I became immersed in the role, I was surprised myself at some basic things I had not known about the refereeing process despite having published dozens of articles. This essay is intended to help young colleagues learn these things earlier than I did. I'm assuming the reader has read some of the basic books (e.g., Huff, 1999) and edited volumes (e.g., Cummings & Frost, 1995; Baruch, Sullivan, & Schepmyer, 2006) regarding the publication process, and especially specific chapters focused on the relationship between editor and author from both points of view (e.g., Daft, 1985; Zahra & Neubaum, 2006). Indeed, the availability of so much useful material gives me the feeling of, "Here we go again, one more time: How does one navigate the review process successfully?"

Reviewers advise, but editors decide

Quite often it may seem as though the editor decides to accept a manuscript once authors answer the reviewers' concerns. However, this is not always the case. A surprisingly large proportion of authors do not realize that reviewers make recommendations to the editor but they make no decisions. It is the editor that makes the decisions. Often the editor's decision is informed by the reviews, but editors are not *always* swayed by the reviews. Though infrequent, there are instances in which an editor may decide contrary to the unanimous recommendation of the reviewers. This can happen in both directions: the editor may think that the reviewers were overly harsh or missed or undervalued some important contribution in the submission, or that they were remiss and failed to detect major shortcomings that disqualify the manuscript for publication. What this means for authors is that the name of the game is not "Satisfy the reviewers"; rather, it is "Convince the editor."

While we were serving together as *AMJ* associate editors, my colleague Marshall Schminke (2004) wrote an editorial in which he divulged what he called the editors' "secret" to potential authors at *AMJ*. The secret is, *"We want to publish your study."* This implies that it is your job to provide what it takes to fulfill that desire. I know that what Marshall wrote is true of *AMJ* editors. I believe generalization to most editors at most journals is warranted because all editors want to publish high-quality research in their journals. Nevertheless, the author's imperative is the same: you must persuade the editor, who wants to publish the best research in the field, that the right decision is to accept your submission. This essay is based on the assumption that the better you understand the editor's dilemma, the better you can navigate the rocky road to publication.

In this essay, I'm assuming that the editor takes his or her role seriously as one who makes the accept/reject decision. Some editors may seem to give all the weight to the reviewers, taking the role of "vote" counters. Authors understandably feel unfairly treated when an editor seems to lay responsibility for the decision onto the reviewers. Were that the editor's job, a competent secretary could tally the reviewers' votes and inform the author of the decision. As an author, I expect the editor to express his or her responsibility for the rejection decision in the letter and to detail the justification for the decision using such terms as, "I have decided ..." and "My decision is ..." Making such decisions is the crux of the job, and I'm assuming that we are discussing the role of an adjudicating editor, not a vote counter. Of course, being the former is what makes the job so difficult.

There is an inherent contradiction in the dual nature of the editor's decision-making. Similar to managers using a performance appraisal system, the editor must be simultaneously judgmental and developmental. This means I must tell you what I do and do not like about your research and suggest (instruct?) how to improve it. To the extent that authors do not like being judged (who does?), judgment must be rendered in a way that is neither denigrating, condescending, nor paternalistic, but is constructive, supportive, and acceptable to the author. In this sense, the editor's relationship to the author shares a challenge with managers, officers, teachers, and parents vis-à-vis their subordinates, soldiers, pupils, and children: the task of giving authentic feedback that produces growth. We should be good at this: many of us have been trained in psychology and we are presumably experts in giving and receiving feedback. The well-known guidelines for giving effective feedback are highly appropriate to the editor's role, and the well-known guidelines for receiving effective feedback are highly appropriate to the author's role. However, we do not always practice what we preach, producing role dilemmas: how should I react as an editor when the author is not accepting feedback appropriately, and how should I react as an author when the editor is not giving feedback appropriately? Each will profit by understanding the other's difficulty and by responding rationally to the other even when the other's reaction seems inappropriate.

Editors as decision makers

The core of the editor's role is decision making. Some of these decisions are easy, others are hard, and still others are like passing the proverbial camel through the eye of a needle. The easiest are the so-called "desk rejections." These are submissions that are obviously outside the journal's purview and do not get reviewed. In most cases, these are simply not in the journal's content areas or are inappropriate for its publication policy. *AMJ* gets submissions with no empirical research and *AMR* gets submissions reporting empirical research. Similarly, a human resources management journal may get a submission dealing more with economics or marketing. These manuscripts are simply returned to authors with a short letter informing them of the lack of fit and suggesting where they might submit their manuscript. Some submissions are on target regarding content but too far out of line with the journal's guidelines for authors. This can include exceeding the journal's length limitation, ignoring format instructions regarding how to list references or font size, and the like.

Such inappropriate submissions can be prevented by simply *reading the journal's web site* before you submit. This is simple and time-saving. It is astonishing how many authors submit manuscripts that do not conform to the journal's mission, style, or technical specifications. This is unwise. It wastes everybody's time. It makes a negative impression on the editor. Meeting any journal's format and style requirements involves mere clerical tasks. Not doing it can be interpreted as slovenly work, disrespect for the journal, or even a lackadaisical attitude. It's like showing up in class or at a meeting unprepared, not having done your homework. Given all the things going against you in a top journal, don't give reviewers and editors another reason to develop a negative attitude toward your work, especially one that's so easy to avoid.

Some desk rejections result from the editor's on-the-spot decision that the submission does not meet the journal's quality standards. Again, by not sending it out for review the editor is husbanding scarce reviewing resources judiciously. If the editor knows without review what his or her decision will be, desk rejection is the most efficient action. Editors differ in where the threshold for desk rejection is. Some editors will send a submission out for review despite knowing it has meager chances. They may do this because they think the author can learn a lot from the reviews.

A desk rejection means that the editor sees little chance that the revision process will eventuate in a publishable manuscript. For authors, the lesson in receiving desk rejections is that you have that much more to improve to get your work up to the journal's minimal standards, or you must seek journals that publish research at the quality level at which you are working.

Easy decisions

Of the submissions sent out for review, two types make the editor's decision easy. These are the ones that obviously fall short of the journal's standards and cannot be accepted and those that are obviously excellent and appear likely to be acceptable after revision. Unfortunately, the former far outnumber the latter, but both kinds are easy decisions. Journals dedicated to providing mentoring service to the research community to help develop excellent scholarship provide even authors of obviously substandard work with copious constructive feedback from reviewers and the action editor. This is a "free" service to those authors. At *AMJ* such service is touted as a mission eagerly taken on under the name of "developmental reviewing." It is a give-away form of tutoring, mentoring, advising, and counseling to developing scholars seeking to increase their research prowess. To my knowledge and direct, personal experience, *AMJ* is exceptionally generous with its reviewer resources in providing rich, developmental feedback as a service to the academic community. Countless young (and not so young) scholars have benefited from this service over the years.

The submissions that are obviously worthy of publication are put through the reviewing process in the attempt to make them better still. Often reviewers raise points that lead to improvements in revision even of work that was already excellent when first submitted. Managing this process involves work for the editor, but not agonizing decision-making.

Hard decisions

It is the bulk of submissions that are not obviously outstanding or substandard that confront the editor with a succession of dichotomous decisions. First, after the first round of reviews he or she must decide whether the manuscript warrants a revise-and-resubmit (R&R) decision or whether it should be rejected. This decision is inherently difficult because it is always a judgment call whether a submission has the potential to be improved sufficiently to meet the journal's standards. This decision is harder still when the editor sees potential but also harbors doubt. It can be exasperated by mixed reviews or by reviews expressing the same ambivalence as the editor is experiencing about the manuscript. When doubt overshadows hope, the decision must be rejection; when hope outweighs doubt, the decision is to invite a revision. The *AMJ* editorial culture values seeking the "diamond in the rough" (see Chapter 12 in this volume by Donald Bergh, my colleague on that *AMJ* editorial team). It is the editor's responsibility to seek and discern these obscure gems and not to rush to reject a potential contribution. Different editors will have different preferences for Type I and Type II errors. Some will be reluctant to "waste" reviewer resources – and his or her own very scarce resource, time – on a revision that has little likelihood of passing muster, whereas others will "invest" those scarce resources in the attempt to salvage even a very dubious manuscript that has some nonzero chance of making it. This decision is never easy. Socialization into *AMJ*'s developmental culture made me far more wary of rejecting a potential gem than concern over consuming reviewer resources.

Sometimes a decision to accept a submission has been made and the editor issues the R&R invitation simply seeking one more effort to improve an already strong, publishable manuscript. In other instances, the editor is highly doubtful but gives the author an opportunity to revise and resubmit believing chances of success are slim and signaling this to the author by dubbing it a "high-risk" revision. The distinction between the two is often encoded in the editor's written statement regarding how risky the revision may be. In either case, it is necessary to invest maximal effort in the revision.

Sometimes top scholars submit manuscripts that fall short of the journal's standards. This is also something that makes editors very uneasy. When the author, or one of them, has a great reputation and you recognize that he or she has a finer record than you yourself have, it is with great trepidation that you write that rejection letter. I did this several times, expecting the sky to come crashing down on me; it didn't.

Agonizing decisions

Almost the hardest decision is rejecting a revision. It's worse if it's a second revision. I've been on the receiving end of this enough times to know this one is especially painful for authors. Having been on the other end makes the editor empathize with the author's sense of loss, letdown, frustration, unfairness, and often sheer rage. Beyond that, for the editor it is disappointing because hopes of salvaging a publishable manuscript have not panned out. By this time, much effort has been invested on the part of all concerned – the author, the reviewers, and the editor – and the only payoff will be to the authors who got abundant constructive feedback but are probably so vexed – or enraged – at this point that they are unlikely to appreciate that. Often when this happens the dilemma is so acute that the accept/reject decision gets deferred as the editor decides to give the author one more chance to bring it up to expectations. This may involve still another round of reviews, or the editor may make the decision at the next stage without seeking additional input from the reviewers. Sometimes I would mull over such decisions for several days, unable to choose because both options were unsavory. Onerous is too mild an adjective to express the feeling.

Worse than agonizing

Sometimes you know the author is untenured and your decision may be crucial. In such cases, your decision may mean the difference between promotion or separation, tenure or protracted limbo, employment or an embarrassing job search, moving a family, and all that it can mean. Awareness of these stakes makes the emotional burden heavier and harder to bear. Only mildly less burdensome is the thought that a tenured author's promotion will be delayed.

Untenured authors might wonder whether they should inform the editor of their status and of the potential cost to them of a rejection. My advice is to refrain from this. It is superfluous. You can assume that the editor knows what the potential costs to you are because they are always in the back of his or her mind. If this particular editor is one that does not care about such concerns, your raising it won't help. Worse, it may backfire, especially if the editor interprets this as an attempt to influence his or her decision in an unethical way. Your best course of action is to do your best work prior to submission and let the editorial review process play out with no further attempt to influence it after submission. Your time for action is before submission and after getting an R&R; between those two events, work on your next submission. If after getting an acceptance you need an earlier publication date (though you shouldn't – an acceptance letter from an editor should be sufficient for the article to "count" toward tenure or promotion), I think that request could be made without penalty of any kind, though the editor might be unable or unwilling to accommodate your request.

Finally, it gets worse still when an editor must reject a manuscript submitted by a friend. Yes, we are all professionals and we exert objective judgment, but we also have colleagues who are friends. When for some reason you cannot recuse yourself from being action-editor on a friend's submission, and the submission does not warrant acceptance, the dilemma may not be so severe. But writing that rejection letter is torture. You know you are doing the right thing, but you have a bad feeling, bordering on betrayal. Could you or should you have done more to help your friend? Conversely, were you overly strict to avoid any suspicion of leniency on behalf of your friend?

Editors hate having to make and notify about these decisions. This is what the editor is going through while you are waiting on pins and needles to hear his or her decision.

Put yourself in the reviewers' and editor's shoes

One savvy National Football League (NFL) player wanted to understand better how the referees judged things. He did something few players have ever done: he enrolled in the official NFL referee course. Now, that is one smart football player. Knowing how the referee was trained, he knows what the referee will be looking for and how he will be making his penalty decisions. This knowledge helps this player to choose the right moves and avoid the wrong ones on the playing field. The parallel is that one way to get closer to understanding editors' and reviewers' thinking is to review for the journals to which you intend to submit your manuscripts. You can learn a lot from how editors weave your comments and the other reviewers' comments into their decision letters. To do this, you need not wait to be invited to be a reviewer. Many journals accept volunteers. For most journals, all you have to do is to inform the editor of your interest in reviewing. If you prove to be a good reviewer, you will be asked to review more. If you do a poor job of it, you will not be asked to review again. Some journals rate the quality of each review and maintain a data set that is used as a basis for judging how good a reviewer you are.

Whether or not you actually do review, a proxy, albeit an anemic one, for attaining some understanding of what reviewers look for would be to read the journals' instructions to reviewers. These are commonly accessible to the public on journal web sites. Reading these instructions will inform you what the editor expects to get from the reviewers and this makes pretty clear what the reviewers will be looking for in your manuscripts. Obviously, this will also give you further insight into what the editor will be looking for when he or she reads your manuscript and the reviews.

How to revise

The first thing to realize is that an invitation to revise and resubmit means that the editor liked your submission, wants to accept it, and thinks it can be successfully revised. A common mistake is to think the editor expects you to meet the deadline set in the R&R letter. This is usually not the case. The editor wants to be able to decide to publish your revision and will be willing to wait for it much longer. A simple email promptly accepting the R&R challenge and asking for more time will usually get you the time you need.

Another common mistake is to think the editor expects you to accept and act on all the reviewers' comments. This simply is not true. Naturally, the editor wants to see a substantially improved revision that is responsive to reviewer feedback and that makes a meaningful contribution. Some authors are overwhelmed by the sheer volume of feedback and daunted by the sometimes contradictory suggestions made by different reviewers. This should be viewed as an opportunity, not a disaster. The editor, normally, will be aware of the contradictions and may suggest how to deal with them. If the editor makes no such suggestions, he or she is leaving it to you to decide how to handle them. In such cases, make your choices and explain them in your cover letter. If your explanations are reasonable, they will be accepted as such even though you were more responsive to one reviewer's suggestion than to another's. This is the basic definition of conflict: the more you respond to one demand the less the likelihood that you will be able to respond to another demand. The editor understands this and wants you to make a convincing choice. We all know you can't work miracles.

In his or her decision letter, the editor will repeat, mention, point out, or expand certain points in the reviews. Other points will not be mentioned. Those that go unmentioned are not the major issues that the editor thinks need revision. Describing in your cover letter what changes you have made based on such points or explaining why you have preferred not to revise according to such points will usually be acceptable to the editor.

Editors and reviewers speak of "responsiveness" to the feedback in the reviews. This means weighing them and either adopting them or explaining why you did not; it does not mean subjugating your own best judgment to someone else's and slavishly accommodating any and every suggestion made to you (see also Bedeian, this volume). Two bases for judging your responsiveness are your letter accompanying the revision and, of course, the revision itself. Successful writing of that letter may entail some measure of impression management. Be responsive and make yourself "sound" responsive. But do not be obsequious. No one respects that. It is poor impression management.

When the editor disagrees with a certain point in a review, he or she makes no mention of it. Except in the most extraordinary circumstances, editors do not edit reviews; what the reviewers said is what you get. Furthermore, editors do not give reviewers feedback on their reviews. When they disagree with a point in a review, they most often ignore it. Sometimes, to relieve the author of uncertainty an editor may say something like, "With regard to Reviewer C's Point 7, you might handle this by ..." or, "it may be less of a problem once you take Reviewer A's advice in his or her Point 3 into account" or, "If you emphasize in the Method and Discussion sections that your experimental design justifies causal conclusions, it should answer Reviewer C's Point 7 adequately." These are all ways of signaling to you that the editor does not agree with the reviewer on this point without stating it bluntly and putting the reviewer on the spot. Just take the hint and do as the editor suggests.

Having said that, two things are worth keeping in mind. First, you should detail in your accompanying letter what changes you have made, what you have left unchanged despite the advice of the reviewers and editor, and explain why. Second, whatever you may have concluded from reading Art Bedeian's chapter on "Balancing Authorial Voice and Editorial Omniscience" in this volume, my advice is: don't fight back. It consumes enormous energy and it arouses reviewer animosity. Furthermore, it makes you look argumentative and, worse in the minds of reviewers and editors, unresponsive. Unless the issue is of prime importance and it would be intellectually dishonest to go along with the reviewers' suggestions, make those revisions and get your work published. Accepting or rejecting advice from editors and reviewers should not be viewed as a matter of saving face or of that omnipresent obsession of ours, academic freedom. If by compromising on little things you can get your main message out to your colleagues in the academic community, my advice is to compromise. Not to do so due to your stubbornness in relation to minor, inconsequential things would be needlessly shooting yourself in the foot.

In any case, don't play sophomoric games. If the editor invited a revision limited to a certain number of pages, don't reduce margins, font size, or font style to get more text into less space. It will almost always be detected, in particular in the computer age when the 'word-count' function and a font-size check will easily expose such monkey business (we have all been there and we know all the tricks) and you might pay a very dear price for appearing to be dishonest. The best way to play this game is to play by the rules.

So what?

Editors of leading journals are looking for major contributions that will advance the field, especially theoretical contributions (Bergh, 2003). They want your submission to tell something important, significant, meaningful, insightful, innovative, or pioneering; something that colleagues will make note of and tell their friends about. Too often the work submitted is very well done, with the data competently collected and analyzed, and the manuscript well written, but with no real contribution. Nothing new. No new concepts. No fresh take on an existing stream of research. No new ground has been broken. In discussing this "So what?" problem, Sara Rynes (2002), my former editorial teammate and subsequent editor of *AMJ*, detailed the most common deficiencies that lead to contrary reviews and rejection decisions as too little incremental contribution or too narrow a contribution, a trivial contribution that would surprise no one, and a contribution that was simply not made clear. It is not enough to be competent and to get the stats right. For a top journal, you must generate something that sparks the reader's imagination. Although it need not be totally new, you must be creative. It can be an interesting extension of a construct that's already out there, or a constructive replication of previous research. It might be a neat addition to your own or someone else's existing oeuvre. But it must make an added-value contribution that will make readers sense that your article was worth reading. If it lacks that special zing, the editor will think, "so what?" and will expect readers to think the same. That is not the kind of article that top journals want to publish. The cliché, "If it's not worth doing, it's not worth doing well" applies here. Excellent method is wasted on trivial ideas, and it will impress only the undeveloped mind of someone with a methods fetish.

The practical imperative may go beyond what this chapter is supposed to deal with. My advice is to do less but better. Put quality before quantity.

Good ideas don't come to most of us easily or frequently, and they take time to germinate. When they do come, they may be harder and take longer to bring to fruition, both theoretically and empirically, than just doing an unimaginative study in existing molds. To increase your chances of publishing in top journals, be choosey. Don't let yourself get sucked into doing an uninspiring and unimaginative study just because the opportunity to do some research has arisen, even if you have received a complimentary invitation from a colleague or client to do so. Wait for opportunity to do something really *worthwhile*.

Better yet, be proactive in seeking out or creating opportunities for innovative research. One such gold mine is, of course, graduate students. Another is executive education. Successful teaching in executive courses sometimes ignites the imagination of participants with clout in their organizations and they invite you to "come and do something in their company." Another opportunity is what you may encounter while consulting. If you can't turn your teaching and consulting into opportunities to do innovative research, you may be in the wrong profession.

Once you have your research or theory in hand and are ready to write for publication, the single most important thing you can do is to read and constantly refer to the *APA Publication Manual* even if you are not submitting to an APA journal. It is the standard to which your writing is expected to conform. Some degree of compulsivity in adhering to it is the single best thing you can do to succeed at impression management, and it can significantly improve your chances of getting your work accepted. Concentrate on the nontechnical sections of the Manual, which put forth a philosophy of scientific writing. The adaptation to non-APA journals is a minor clerical task.

To conclude, I repeat the basics for emphasis. Study and apply the *APA Publication Manual*. Read the instructions to authors and the instructions to reviewers of any journal before you write for it. Be responsive to feedback and make yourself "look" responsive. Be sincere and you will look sincere. Be honest and you will look honest. Above all, make it easier for the editor to accept your submission by doing imaginative research that will displace "So what?" with "Wow!"

Summary of implications for authors:

- Be choosey about what kind of research you invest your time and effort in; try to "wow" them.
- Read some basic writings about the publication process. Make sure to include the *APA Publication Manual*.
- Volunteer to review for the journals to which you intend to submit.
- Read the instructions for authors on the journal's web site before submitting to a journal.
- Read also the journal's *instructions for reviewers* on its website.

- Ask the editor for more time if it is needed to revise the article.
- Be maximally responsive to reviewers' and the editor's comments and suggestions.
- Read the editor's letter carefully for cues revealing what's really important.
- Answer every point raised in the reviews and explain your decisions in your accompanying letter, but don't exaggerate the length of this letter.
- Don't waste time and effort trying to persuade the reviewers; try to convince the editor.
- Regard the reviewers as advisors and the editor as a mentor giving developmental feedback, even if they do not execute these roles with finesse.
- Resist the tendency to reject the reviewers' comments, even if they are not stated constructively. Treat them as valuable feedback and make the best of it.
- Don't fight with the reviewers and don't play infantile games.

Summary of implications for prospective editors:

- Read this chapter again before you decide to accept the job!

References

Baruch, Y., Sullivan, S. E., & Schepmyer, H. N. (Eds.). (2006). *Winning reviews: A guide for evaluating scholarly writing*. Basingstoke: Palgrave Macmillan.

Bergh, D. (2003). Thinking strategically about contribution. *Academy of Management Journal, 46*, 135–6.

Cummings, L. L., & Frost, P. J. (Eds.). (1995). *Publishing in the organizational sciences* (2nd ed.) Thousand Oaks: Sage.

Daft, R. L. (1985). Why I recommended that your manuscript be rejected and what you can do about it. In L. L. Cummings & P. J. Frost (Eds.), *Publishing in the organizational sciences* (2nd ed., pp. 164–182). Thousand Oaks: Sage.

Huff, A. S. (1999). *Writing for scholarly publication*. Thousand Oaks: Sage.

Rynes, S. (2002). Some reflections on contribution. *Academy of Management Journal, 45*, 311–13.

Schminke, M. (2004). Raising the bamboo curtain. *Academy of Management Journal, 47*, 310–14.

Zahra, S. & Neubaum D. (2006). How to answer reviews to get an article published. In Y. Baruch, S. E. Sullivan, & H. N. Schepmyer, (Eds.), *Winning reviews: A guide for evaluating scholarly writing*. Basingstoke: Palgrave Macmillan.

25
Epilogue: Trade-Offs among Editorial Goals in Complex Publishing Environments

William H. Starbuck, Herman Aguinis, Alison M. Konrad, and Yehuda Baruch

Trade-offs among editorial goals in complex publishing environments

The extrinsic rewards from editorial work can be erratic and disappointing. Even those who edit highly prestigious journals may find it difficult to persuade their deans to allocate resources to this activity, and their deans or department heads may advise them to publish more articles themselves instead of publishing articles by other authors. Those who receive payments from commercial publishers are likely to find that these payments translate into ludicrously low hourly wages. Those who edit journals published by their universities may hear their colleagues asking why resources are going to that specific field or topic rather than to other topics or fields.

Editors may also find it difficult to assess the impacts they are having at the time they are having them. Most editors receive respect and deference, and these rewards are likely to decline when they leave their editorial jobs. Editors, who spend many hours trying to help authors express their ideas, may hear later that some authors greatly appreciated their suggestions whereas others saw the editors' efforts as intrusive. Editors have opportunities to influence the development of knowledge and agendas for teaching and research. However, they may see these effects wane when their successors pursue different agendas and adopt different policies. Any effort to exert influence or to exercise judgment has the potential to upset someone, so all editors make some authors angry or upset and some editors discover that their editorial activities won them enemies.

Thus, editors need to think about their intrinsic rewards, and hence about their motives and goals. Why do you want to serve as an editor? What satisfactions do you hope to receive from the experience? Recognition? Visibility? Methodological change? Establishment of a nascent research domain? Incremental improvement in an established domain? Promote the development of a subdiscipline? This chapter offers an explicit analysis of some central choices that editors can make about their roles. Reflecting on these choices can help editors to use their time and efforts more effectively and to see the advantages and disadvantages of their activities. This chapter also has implications for authors: by understanding the choices that specific editors make in their roles, authors can gain a better understanding of what to expect from the review process.

This book presents very diverse viewpoints that collectively show that there are many ways for an editor to achieve success ... and just as many ways for an editor to perform poorly. Because every editor has limited time, a limited supply of manuscripts, and personal strengths and weaknesses, no editor can attain excellence on every dimension of performance. An editor has to choose some foci. However, there is also no need for an editor to attain excellence on every possible dimension of performance. Journals have different reputations, occupy different market positions, possess different opportunities, espouse different missions, and need different developmental impulses. Thus, editors have latitude to adapt their talents and experience to the needs and opportunities of the journals they are editing.

At the same time, it is apparent that some editors achieve greater success than do others. Circulations, subscription revenues, downloads, and citations offer quantitative evidence. The historical statistics include instances in which citations to a specific journal have risen dramatically, or plummeted, during one editor's term and then stabilized when that editor left the job. Figure 25.1 illustrates some of the possibilities by graphing real data regarding the impact factors during the terms of four successive editors of a management journal. The dashed horizontal lines show the averages during the editors' terms, and the axes are unlabeled to mask the identities of the editors. Although documentation about reputations is nonexistent, every

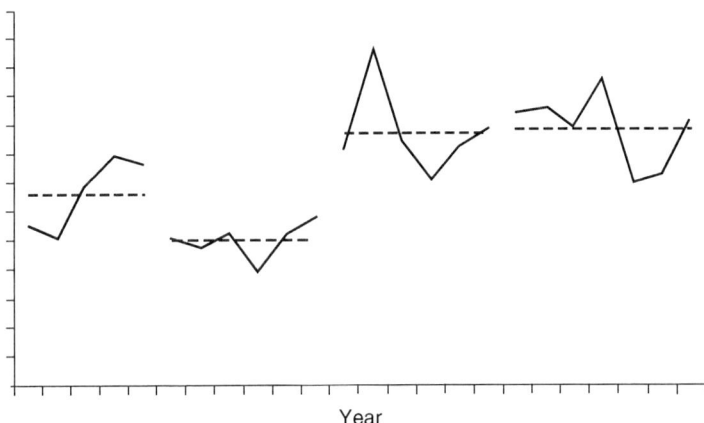

Figure 25.1 Impact factors with four editors

academic author has participated in conversations about the apparent editorial policies of various journals. Some journals, it is said, are open to new ideas; others, it is said, will consider only X or Y. Yet another indicator of editorial success may be the votes cast in the elections of professional societies. Because people vote for names they recognize and editorships create visibility, those who have recently been editors tend to attract votes. However, there are instances in which candidates who recently left editorships have attracted either remarkably many votes or shockingly few of them.

Journal editors face too many strategic and tactical options to enumerate here. However, four pairs of options receive frequent mention throughout this book. To make the pros and cons very clear, we present these options as sharply distinct alternatives. However, most editors mix these options in practice. Instead of consistently choosing option A in preference to not-A, editors choose A for some manuscripts and not-A for others. For example, an editor may have much more confidence in some reviewers than in other reviewers, or an editor may believe that she has much more expertise about some topics than about other topics.

Because many contingencies affect editorial actions and their consequences, and because some editors deviate from generalizations that describe many editors, all of the arguments to follow have exceptions and their validity depends upon the specifics of individual situations. For example, some journals try to select editors through systematic processes. They identify reviewers who offer especially useful and constructive advice, and invite these people to become associate editors. Then, they select editors from among the associate editors (Cascio, 2008, this volume). Although such processes tend to select editors who do not perform poorly, the selected editors do not all perform equally well, and different editors emphasize different aspects of their roles. The processes that winnow candidates may take account of issues such as areas of specialization or geographic location that do not correlate with editorial performance. Furthermore, careful selection is not the only way to find exceptional editors. The editors who have performed exceptionally well include people who became editors because they proposed the creation of new journals or because they worked in specific departments at specific universities.

Option 1A: An editor should personally make evaluations of manuscripts and these evaluations should dominate those of other reviewers.

versus

Option 1B: An editor should not evaluate manuscripts but instead should manage the reviewing process to implement the evaluations and suggestions of reviewers.

In Chapter 13, "The Case for an Activist Editorial Model," Jacobs (2008, this volume) argues that the decision following a first review should be a crucial one. He advises editors to read carefully every manuscript and the reviewers' comments about them, and also to make sure that the reviews are "informative" and that they discuss all of the important issues. Editors' central goal, he says, should be to avoid encouraging revisions to manuscripts that have little chance of acceptance because authors find rejections more "painful" after they have made revisions. Jacobs also argues that early rejections save reviewers' time and authors may be able to publish their work sooner by resubmitting to an alternative journal.

Such an activist approach assumes that a specific editor has better judgment than do the reviewers of a specific manuscript. It assumes that the editor can and will make better decisions or more definitive decisions than the reviewers do concerning the issues that most need attention and the likelihood that a manuscript will eventually warrant publication. Such assumptions may not be valid when applied to many manuscripts on diverse topics, but they may be reasonable assumptions where an editor has especially relevant expertise or experience, or where reviewers lack relevant expertise or experience. Ironically, whereas the editor of a highly specialized journal might have relevant expertise more frequently, reviewers for a highly specialized journal might also have relevant expertise more frequently. Certainly, editors have stronger motivation than reviewers do to invest time and effort in making correct judgments. Anonymous reviewers do not have to take personal responsibility for the quality of published articles and reviewers may see the reading and evaluation of manuscripts as intrusions into their busy lives. Editors have their names publicly associated with the published products and they are performing editorial work because they feel personally committed to the specific journal.

Because journals, editors, reviewers, authors, and manuscripts are diverse, many contingencies affect the usefulness of an activist approach. One important contingency is a specific editor's ability to enlist appropriate and effective reviewers for a specific manuscript. An editor who has difficulty finding appropriate and effective reviewers must try to compensate by doing more reviewing personally. In the contemporary academic environment where professors around the world are experiencing pressure to publish in academic journals, the numbers of manuscripts to review are increasing substantially. As a result, editors must recruit more reviewers, and often must rely on the judgments of people they do not know personally. Indeed, in recognition of the growing diversity of authors and research topics, many editors feel a responsibility to draw upon reviewers from around the world. Thus, editors sometimes find themselves calling upon reviewers about whom they know little, with one possible result being reviews of poor quality. In fact, some editors even recruit editorial board members with less than stellar research records, which may suggest that these reviewers may not have the qualifications and experience needed to evaluate research produced by others (Bedeian, Van Fleet, & Hyman, 2007).

As well, reviewers sometimes do not complete their work promptly so that an editor may decide that further delay would be unreasonable, and one possible response is a review by the editor personally.

Another contingency is the size of the audience to which editors and authors seek to communicate. Some journals have identities that attract manuscripts on narrow ranges of topics, which implies that editors, reviewers, and authors come from specialized subpopulations. Editors in such situations can enlist reviewers from these subpopulations. However, much research indicates that people have different perceptions and different propensities for activism in familiar domains than in unfamiliar domains, and a few studies suggest that some editors treat manuscripts in their own specialties differently from other manuscripts (Ellison, 2002; Martinko, Campbell & Douglas, 2000; Miller & Perrucci, 2001). Such biases likely occur in reviewers' treatment of manuscripts in their own specialties. In addition, a study by Mahoney (1977, 1979) suggests that reviewers are more likely to approve of manuscripts that support the reviewers' own published studies and that they are more likely to disapprove of manuscripts that contradict the reviewers' own published studies. Thus, editors of specialized journals confront frequent challenges to their objectivity and fairness that arise from the homogeneity and small sizes of their audiences. The editors of general journals face inverse challenges that arise from the diversity and breadth of their audiences. When these editors find themselves looking at reviews by unknown people concerning manuscripts on unfamiliar topics, they have to regard submitted reviews as providing evidence about reviewers and manuscripts simultaneously (Konrad, 2008, this volume). This shifts the evaluation toward indirect evidence about the reviewers' evaluations: Does a reviewer appear to have read the manuscript carefully? Does a reviewer seem to have familiarity with relevant literature? As well, the communicative properties of manuscripts have more importance: Is the manuscript understandable by a diverse audience? Is the manuscript's topic of widespread interest? Overall, editors of general journals participate in editorial processes somewhat differently than do editors of specialized journals. Editors' willingness to ask questions about manuscripts outside their own specialties can help authors to communicate the value of their contribution to a wider audience. Indeed, forcing authors to explain the value of their research clearly to nonspecialists greatly improves the quality of writing and clarifies manuscripts' contribution even to specialist readers.

Strong editorial interventions are two-edged swords that can produce either better outcomes or worse ones. This attendant uncertainty arises from the many ways to perceive a manuscript and the many criteria that readers can apply to a manuscript. For example, Starbuck (2006a) reported how abnormal editorial actions affected several of his most-cited articles. Indeed, his most cited article received "rejects" by both of two reviewers but that journal published the article because the editor accepted it against the reviewers' advice. In another instance, an editor did not even consult reviewers before accepting an article that later drew many citations. Of course, such interventions may work to an author's disadvantage as well. Starbuck has had a manuscript rejected by an editor despite receiving two "accepts" and a "revise" from three reviewers. Konrad (2008, this volume) points out that editors may offer recourse to authors when reviewers have missed a point, made incorrect assumptions, or held authors to excessive standards of excellence.

There are also various reasons why an editor might have a policy of abstaining from direct involvement in the evaluation of manuscripts. One of these reasons is to increase the involvement and commitment of members of editorial boards. For instance, when Starbuck became the editor of *Administrative Science Quarterly* (*ASQ*) in 1967, there was no field called "organization theory," and scholars regarded that journal as a representative of Cornell University's School of Business and Public Administration. Indeed, James D. Thompson and Edward Litchfield had created *ASQ* to promote the school's central theme that successful administration in business requires the same abilities as successful administration in public agencies or hospitals or military organizations. Although *ASQ* had published several articles by well-known authors, it had a diffuse identity that resulted from its efforts to encompass a wide range of administrative activities and settings. Starbuck saw *ASQ* as an opportunity to pursue a different agenda – the crystallization of organization theory. Although Simon had spoken of organization theory since the 1950s, March and Simon had published the book titled *Organizations*, and March had edited the *Handbook of Organizations*, in the mid-1960s, this potential field lacked a focal point. As Simon and March had visualized it, organization theory should draw participants and topics from all of the social sciences, but this heterogeneity meant that relevant research appeared in many specialized journals. Starbuck sought to give *ASQ* an identity as the focal journal for organizational research by anthropologists, economists, management theorists, political scientists, psychologists, and sociologists. He recruited a large editorial board of very well known researchers, who were almost the only people who reviewed manuscripts, and he made every effort to convince them that they had responsibility for the editorial decisions and recommendations to authors. His goal was to persuade the members of editorial board to identify with *ASQ*, expecting that this identification would induce them to submit their own manuscripts to the journal and to recommend the journal to their colleagues and students. Keeping himself in the background and demonstrating respect for the reviewers' opinions were important aspects of this persuasion process. Of course, this policy also meant that the journal sometimes published articles that Starbuck himself would not have chosen and it sometimes rejected manuscripts in which he saw promise. At the same time, members of the editorial board devoted many, many hours to reviewing and they often had insights and made discoveries that surprised Starbuck.

Other editors may defer to reviewers because the editors perceive themselves as having abnormal values or unusual biases that would make their own evaluations unrepresentative of their journals' audiences. For example, when authors asked one editor to intercede in the review process, this editor systematically replied by saying that he would render a judgment if the authors insisted but he nearly always wanted to reject manuscripts. Few editors have time to read carefully and comment on many manuscripts, which implies that the editors of journals that publish many articles need to restrict their personal involvements to tiny fractions of the manuscripts.

Like directors of research laboratories who do not conduct research themselves and instead rely on the expertise of the research scientists, editors who refrain from making evaluations have to focus on process management. Are manuscripts being reviewed promptly and generally fairly? Are the comments to authors polite and constructive? However, process management works better if the editor concentrates on preventing problems rather than on correcting problems. Probably the most important management activity is deciding who should be on the editorial board and which people should review each manuscript (cf. Bedeian, Van Fleet, & Hyman, 2007). By prescreening reviewers to identify people who show good judgment and write helpful reviews, editors can avoid situations in which authors feel they are receiving unjust treatment. Highly regarded journals are not only publishers of frequently cited research. They gain their strong reputations in part because they provide post-doctoral education in research methods and research presentation, and the members of their editorial boards and ad hoc reviewers function as faculty for this education process. Thus, selecting board members and reviewers deserves cautious care.

Laband (1990) studied referees' comments and authors' reactions to these comments on 89 papers that appeared in top journals over five years. His statistical analyses led him to infer that editors' comments had had no discernible influence on later citations of the published papers but that reviewers' comments had significantly increased citations. Thus, he concluded that editors add value to manuscripts mainly by choosing reviewers well. Of course, just as some reviewers make more useful comments than others do, some individual editors doubtless make useful comments. Nevertheless, Laband's study says that editors add very little on average.

Option 2A: An editor's primary goal should be to help authors express their ideas and findings as effectively as possible.

versus

Option 2B: An editor should not attempt to advise authors about presentation style, but instead should allow authors to exercise their own judgment.

Konrad (2008, this volume) argues that authors greatly appreciate guidance from editors, who will have responsibility for making the final publication decisions on their manuscripts. Knowledge development entails difficulties, especially ones arising from abstract and complex ideas. Editors can help authors by adjudicating the reviews, helping authors to sort out reviewers' demands that contradict one another, shedding light on a line of action that might address a particular reviewer's concerns, and sharing their own thoughts. Providing that sort of guidance, she says, gives authors better chances of focusing their efforts on areas likely to result in acceptance.

Just as editors have opinions about the research that manuscripts describe, they also have opinions about the ways in which authors describe their research and opinions about the advice offered by reviewers regarding presentation. Most of the contingencies that make it more or less reasonable for an editor to intervene between authors and reviewers apply to presentation style as well to research substance and methodology. Does the journal target a specialized audience or a general one, and hence, does the presentation speak better to a specialist audience or a general audience? Does the author have much experience and many publications, or is the author inexperienced and possibly looking for guidance? Are some of the comments of reviewers unclear or misguided?

The pros and cons of such editorial activities are visible in the story of an editor who made strong efforts to assist authors. A few years ago, an editor of a very prominent journal gained a reputation for very detailed commentary. This editor had once worked as a journalist and he expressed himself very well. He also sought to behave in a nurturing way. Thus, the editor routinely sent very long commentaries to authors; every author received at least two single-spaced pages and many received four or five pages. These commentaries restated the comments of the reviewers, emphasizing some of their points more than others, and they gave rather detailed suggestions about how to revise manuscripts. He even wrote long commentaries that were filled with suggestions for revision when he rejected manuscripts, and he phrased his comments so tactfully that some authors of rejected manuscripts thought he was asking them to revise-and-resubmit. Authors reacted variously but predictably to this behavior. For one thing, authors interpreted the editor's comments as contracts: they expected that if they did as the editor proposed, the editor would accept their manuscripts for publication. As a result, authors were shocked when they resubmitted manuscripts that they believed fulfilled the editor's requirements and then they subsequently received yet another revise-and-resubmit that was accompanied by another long, detailed commentary by the editor. For another thing, most authors objected to a few of the editor's suggestions, so they viewed these as unreasonable demands with which they had to comply if they wanted to publish in that journal. Authors who were very eager to achieve a publication in a very prestigious journal found themselves deeply conflicted: Their goal appeared to be within reach but to reach that goal, they would have to say things they did not believe or do things that made no sense to them. Some authors felt that this editor was demanding co-authorship of their work, anonymously of course, but enforced by the implicit threat to reject noncompliance (Bedeian, 1996).

That editor could have caused less anger had he handled his relationships with authors in a more forthright way. However, his example highlights the incompatibility among four editorial roles: resource allocators, evaluators, mediators, and coaches. Editors ultimately have to allocate space in their journals. Which of the available manuscripts is going to occupy that space? With typical editorial practices and allowing for multiple revisions, the reviewers make definitive decisions concerning 55–65 percent of the manuscripts. Therefore, editors make the final decisions concerning 35–45 percent of the manuscripts (Starbuck, 2005). Editors must evaluate manuscripts carefully enough to choose among the candidates that reviewers leave unclear, and most editors prefer to involve themselves much earlier in the review process. Editors must also mediate between authors and reviewers. Authors may believe that they must do everything that every reviewer says in order to receive an acceptance, and they may find it difficult to distinguish between an inflexible demand and a casual suggestion. Authors want a court of appeal when they believe that reviewers are making incorrect or unreasonable demands, and they would like to think that editors provide fair mediation. Finally, editors have opportunities to act as coaches. Some authors genuinely want advice, and even those who do not want it may find it useful if phrased appropriately. When should authors be strongly encouraged to undertake revisions? Which of the various suggestions by reviewers are likely to prove most useful? Editors often fail to make clear which of these roles they are performing. Aguinis (2007) has pointed out that similar challenges and issues occur with other supervisory roles.

Editors sometimes forget that authors regard editors and reviewers with fear. Bedeian (2003) surveyed authors who had published in two highly regarded journals. One-third said that they had made revisions that expressed an editor's or reviewer's personal preferences, and one-fourth said that they had had to make statements that they believed to be incorrect. These findings show the importance of flexibility in editorial processes. A reviewer or an editor may believe that a particular change would substantially improve a manuscript. However, the author should have latitude to argue an alternative view, and the reviewer or editor should be open to changing their judgments. Indeed, such debates can strengthen the manuscript if authors include their arguments in the manuscript. If a reviewer or editor has questioned a particular conceptual or methodological point, other readers are likely to have the same question, and persuading those readers should be one of the author's goals (Starbuck, 2003). Bedeian (2004) has argued that the issue is less one of flexibility than of equality between authors, editors, and reviewers. Giving authors more equal standing, he argued, would enhance knowledge development.

Option 3A: An editor should seek to publish manuscripts that are consistent with values and paradigms that currently dominate the thinking of readers of the editor's journal. That is, the editor should promote evolutionary change rather than revolutionary.

versus

Option 3B: An editor should seek to publish manuscripts that challenge the values and paradigms that currently dominate the thinking of readers of the editor's journal. That is, the editor should promote revolutionary change rather than evolutionary.

Option 3A's focus on evolutionary development may require adamant and persistent demands. Almost all of the editors who have attempted revolutionary change have had small impacts that might better be described as incremental evolution, and the changes produced by one editor have often been undone by the succeeding editor. To effect revolutionary changes, editors need help from textbooks, professional societies, and many other editors.

Consider the consequences of efforts to eliminate null hypothesis significance tests (Starbuck, 2006b). These tests are supposed to assess the adequacy of sample sizes, but researchers who are willing to continue gathering data until their samples are large enough can eventually show that any "finding" is statistically significant. Indeed, published correlations indicate that researchers do gather more data when their studies are yielding effects that do not reach conventional levels of statistical significance, and the average correlations computed from small samples are much larger than the average correlations computed from large samples (Webster & Starbuck, 1988). Some argue that because statistical significance is very easy to achieve, journals often publish statistically significant findings that have little or no substantive meaning. Another problem is that the public, journalists, MBA graduates, and researchers misunderstand the actual meaning of the tests, and so misinterpretations of test results are very prevalent. People often discuss statistical significance as if it indicates substantive importance. Other prevalent misinterpretations are that rejection of a null hypothesis indicates support for the alternative hypothesis that inspired data gathering, or that failure to reject a null hypothesis indicates that a variable has no effect. As well, people sometimes speak as if the 0.05 probability tail is the probability that a null hypothesis is true, whereas most null hypotheses could not be true on logical grounds, no matter what data research produces (Armstrong, 2007; Cascio & Aguinis, 2005).

The elimination of statistical significance tests from social-science articles has to be regarded as a revolutionary proposal because such tests are deeply imbedded in social-science traditions and many social scientists do not understand why these tests might be detrimental. The liabilities of significance tests have roused criticism since they were first proposed, but their critics have found it very difficult to persuade social scientists to use other ways of assessing their research (Falk & Greenbaum, 1995). For example, in the mid-1990s, several respected psychometricians urged the American Psychological Association (APA) to ban significance tests from its journals (Starbuck, 2006b, p. 137). Subsequently, leading psychologists participated in symposia at the annual meetings of both APA and the Association for Psychological Science (then called American Psychological Society), and APA appointed a task force to assess the pros and cons of banning such tests. However, the APA task force met briefly and then announced that it "does not support any action that could be interpreted as banning the use of null hypothesis significance testing or p values." The task force did recommend that researchers should augment significance tests by also reporting confidence intervals for effect sizes.

Partly because of the APA task force, two dozen journals in psychology and education are now asking authors to estimate effect sizes (Thompson, 2007). Other journals ask authors to estimate confidence intervals rather than or in addition to point estimates. However, the evidence so far has been that merely asking authors to do this is insufficient to produce much compliance (Cumming et al., 2007). Authors have conformed symbolically, but not substantively. For example, authors may state effect sizes in tables but ignore effect sizes when they discuss their findings, or they may state confidence intervals in tables but say nothing about these in their discussions. For example, in 1996, 36 percent of the articles published in the *Journal of Consulting and Clinical Psychology* (*JCCP*) discussed the clinical significance of their findings (Fidler et al., 2005). That year, the APA task force made its recommendations, both American psychological societies held symposia on statistical evidence during their annual meetings, and *American Psychologist* published a debate about significance tests. In 1997, an editorial in *JCCP* asked authors to report effect sizes and indicators of clinical significance. In 1999, *JCCP* sought to promote the use of indicators of clinical significance by publishing a special forum about such indicators. Yet in 2001, 40 percent of the articles in *JCCP* discussed clinical significance, just 4 percent more than in 1996. Also in 2001, only 17 percent of the articles reported confidence intervals, and only 11 percent of the articles mentioned the confidence intervals in their discussions of results. As well, Leahey (2005) inferred that authors – especially, well-known researchers from prestigious departments – have had more influence than journal editors on the ways sociologists use significance tests.

Editors have rarely refused to publish manuscripts that did not conform to specific guidelines. However, such strong editorial interventions appear to have stimulated major changes in statistical reporting in medical journals. One extreme example occurred when Ken Rothman became an editor of the *American Journal of Public Health*. His revise-and-resubmit letters told authors: "All references to statistical hypothesis testing and statistical significance should be removed from the papers. I ask that you delete *p* values as well as comments about statistical significance. If you do not agree with my standards (concerning the inappropriateness of significance tests) you should feel free to argue the point, or simply ignore what you may consider to be my misguided view, by publishing elsewhere." Later, Rothman became the editor of another journal, where he announced: "When writing for *Epidemiology*, you can enhance your prospects if you omit tests of statistical significance ... In *Epidemiology*, we do not publish them at all. Not only do we eschew publishing claims of the presence or absence of statistical significance, we discourage the use of this type of thinking in the data analysis, such as in the use of stepwise regression." Not surprisingly, these policies altered the frequencies of significance tests in these two journals dramatically. Somewhat surprisingly, Rothman's policies set behavioral patterns that persisted after he left those journals.

However, Rothman did not produce a revolution in medical reporting all by himself. Various medical researchers, journals, and societies had been campaigning against significance tests for many years. Although Rothman's actions drew attention and they influenced many people, a unity of efforts by many people appears to have been what brought about widespread and persistent change in medical research. After studying efforts to change statistical practices in ecology, medicine, and psychology, Fidler et al. (2004: 615) concluded: "The nature of the editorial policies and the degree of collaboration amongst editors are important factors in explaining the varying levels of reforms in these disciplines. But without efforts to also re-write textbooks, improve software and research understanding of alternative methods, it seems unlikely that editorial initiatives will achieve substantial statistical reform."

There are much larger fluctuations in the impact factors of small-circulation journals that change editors than in the impact factors of large-circulation journals that change editors. Presumably, these fluctuations reflect the stronger effects of editorial policies in small-circulation journals. Journals with small circulations also have greater incentive to develop policies that give them distinctive identities. However, there is a risk that idiosyncratic policies and values may alienate some potential authors and readers. On the other hand, the editors of journals with large circulations are very likely to feel that they have a responsibility to uphold norms that have wide acceptance, and those who choose editors for such journals are very likely to choose editors who subscribe to widely accepted norms. As well, large-circulation journals draw reviewers from diverse populations so these reviewers are unlikely to endorse manuscripts that espouse revolutionary ideas. Thus, the editors who have the greatest opportunities to attempt revolutionary change are ones who have limited influence on researchers in general, whereas those who have the greatest opportunities to exert influence face stronger moral and practical constraints.

It is possible that editors' abilities to bring about change fluctuate over time. Tushman and Romanelli (1994) observed that the strategic development of business firms shifts between brief periods of dramatic change and long periods of incremental convergence. Similarly, Kuhn (1970) argued that scientific knowledge fluctuates between brief periods of revolutionary change and long periods of widespread agreement and incremental development. Revolutions become increasingly likely as more and more people become dissatisfied with the shared beliefs that pervade incremental development. Widespread consensus might mean either that the current values and paradigms are well founded or that the field has grown stale and complacent. Thus, an editor who attempts revolutionary change may be a lone dissident who attracts few supporters or one of a rather large group of dissidents who support the change.

Option 4A: An editor should focus on publishing outstanding articles.

versus

Option 4B: An editor should focus on not publishing bad articles.

The pros and cons of these options have been evolving as the publishing industry has experienced dramatic changes over the last three decades. Publishing companies have merged and consolidated their operations. Printing technology has revolutionized, making it possible to publish books in small quantities. The journal-publishing segment has become much more commercial, focused on profit making. Many journals are now being delivered via the Internet, and journals on paper may soon become rare.

During the 1980s and 1990s, publishers introduced many, many new journals (Starbuck, 2005). Although each of these new journals gained a small market segment, collectively they took a significant share from the established journals. Because academic libraries had to acknowledge these new entrants, they shifted funds from books to journals. To make these shifts on defensible grounds, librarians focused on journals' impact factors. In reaction, journal publishers also began to pay much more attention to impact factors, which not only indicate salability to libraries but also the potential value of future reprints. The Institute for Scientific Information (ISI) stopped trying to compile citations in books and limited citation counts to citations in journals, which made the citation data more reliable but also increased the influence of journals over books. Thus, the success of journals and their editors has become a matter of citation counts. Articles that receive many citations encourage librarians to subscribe to journals and publishers to continue publishing them; articles that draw no citations may enhance their authors' résumés but they do not improve journals' visibility or economic viability.

The strongest correlate of journals' impact factors is their circulations. The larger the number of people who receive journals, the larger the number

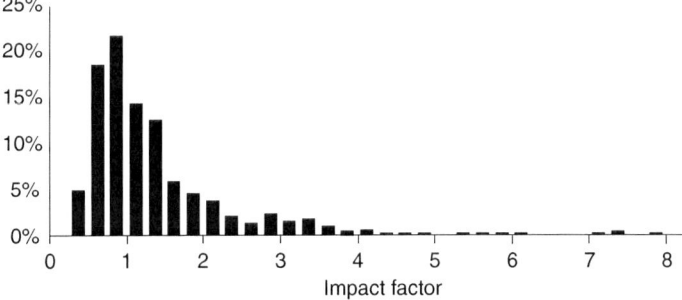

Figure 25.2 Percentages of business journals with different impact factors in 2004

of people who cite articles in those journals. However, journals published by professional associations have lower impact factors than their circulations would otherwise imply, presumably because some of their subscribers do not read them. Editors can use at least two tactics to increase the circulations of their journals: They can try to publish articles that attract a more diverse readership, and they can publish special issues that attract readers who are interested in specific topics. Other factors that correlate positively with impact factors are journals' reputations for high quality, the average lengths of articles, the prevalence of frequently cited authors, and emphasis on theoretical-review articles versus empirical articles (Laband & Piette, 1994; Medoff, 2003). Figure 25.2 presents the 2004 impact factors for 508 journals that business journals cited frequently during 2001 and 2002. These are all of the journals that received at least 12 citations over two years by the 150 journals that the ISI classified as business, business finance, industrial relations, or management. The distribution has a long tail to the right, and the impact factor for the most cited journal is over 34 times the average impact factor, which is only 0.85. That is, an average article in an average journal receives less than one citation during the first two years after its publication. A lack of submitted manuscripts may influence the editorial processes at little-cited journals.

The average impact factors that publishers and journals advertise and librarians study can be misleading. Impact factors give a misleading impression of the total citations to articles in that they focus on just the first two years following publication and they assume that some notes or letters might receive citations. Most published articles receive very few citations, and small fractions of the published articles attract most of the citations. Figure 25.3 shows total citations to full-fledged articles over many years – based on 1,000 articles published during the last eight months of the year

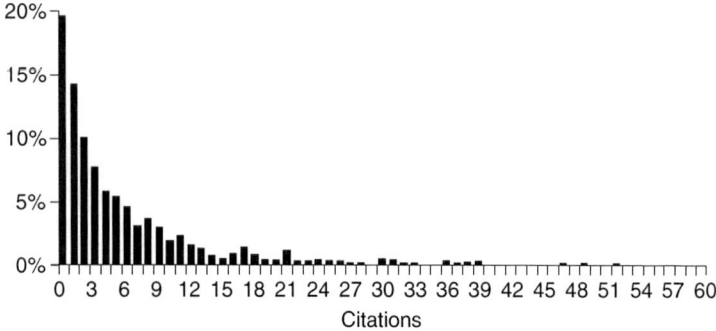

Figure 25.3 Percentages of articles that received different numbers of citations over 17 years

2,000 and having the words "compensation," "management," or "strategy" in their titles. Because these data encompass many journals that have diverse circulations and reputations, the articles published in any single journal would not have so much diversity. According to these data, an average article in an average journal received 7.3 citations during the first 17 years after its publication. However, 71 percent of the articles had below-average numbers of citations and 20 percent of the articles received no citations at all. The 29 percent of the articles that received more than seven citations accounted for 78 percent of all citations. Furthermore, the data in Figure 25.3 understate the effects of the most highly cited articles because this specific sample includes no articles that received more than 118 citations, whereas there do exist rare articles that draw hundreds and thousands of citations.

Readers seem to have very poor abilities to judge the impacts of below-median articles, but better abilities to judge the impacts of above-median articles. Gottfredson (1978) related citations to evaluations made by knowledgeable readers. The logarithms of citations correlated 0.21 with readers' judgments of articles' quality and 0.27 with readers' judgments of articles' impact on their fields. Because readers made their judgments retrospectively, both correlations might overstate reviewers' abilities to make predictive judgments. As well, the practical correlation is nil for many articles. When Gottfredson separated the more-cited and less-cited articles, he found that reviewers' judgments of impact correlated 0.03 with citations for articles that had fewer citations than the median, and correlated 0.36 with citations for articles that had more citations than the median. These differences suggest that readers may be better able to judge and to agree with each other about the small fraction of manuscripts that attract unusually many citations. If so, an implication would be that journals' visibility and economic viability depend strongly on the very few manuscripts that receive "accept" ratings from all reviewers. However, reviewers' evaluations have low reliability (Starbuck, 2005), and journals have rejected some articles that later proved to be very influential because some of the most cited articles have confounded reviewers and editors by deviating from widely accepted norms about methodology or presentation style (Gans & Shepherd, 1994). Such events are consistent with the evidence that people tend to be better able to identify conventional excellence than innovative excellence, and they are better able to appreciate findings that support prevalent beliefs than findings that contradict prevalent beliefs.

Two studies suggest that editors' most important contributions to their journals come from interpersonal networking. A survey by Sherrell, Hair, and Griffin (1989) found that professors considered the two least ethical editorial practices to be (1) favoritism toward friends and colleagues and (2) biasing reviews toward acceptance or rejection by selecting reviewers with strong biases about a manuscript's content or methodology. Laband & Piette (1994) investigated the effects of favoritism. They found that articles by authors who had personal connections with editors were more likely to be lead articles and these articles received significantly more citations after publication. Therefore, Laband and Piette (1994) inferred that "although journal editors occasionally publish subpar papers authored by colleagues and former graduate students, on balance their use of professional connections enables them to identify and 'capture' high-impact papers for publication" (p. 194). Medoff (2003) also studied the effects of favoritism and drew a similar conclusion. Medoff concluded "that articles authored by those with editorial connections, particularly serving on the publishing journal's editorial board, are both statistically and numerically of higher quality. ... The empirical results support the proposition that journal editors, in order to reduce the search costs involved in identifying high-quality manuscripts, use personal ties and institutional connections to persuade high-quality authors to submit their papers to them. Journal editors/coeditors attract these submissions by inducing high-quality authors to serve on their editorial boards as well as by offering constructive comments and suggestions on a high-quality author's paper, reducing the author's transaction cost of publishing" (p. 434).

Yet, editors and reviewers devote nearly all of their attention to trying to improve normal manuscripts. A focus on identifying defects and suggesting corrections means that reviewers and editors spend their time on the manuscripts that have many defects and need many corrections. Although improving a not-quite-good-enough manuscript until it is publishable may contribute to the general development of academic research, but it does not raise a journal's standing to a significant degree. Editors also devote time to rejecting some manuscripts without sending them to reviewers – manuscripts that aim at another audience, that focus on topics outside the journal's range, or that seem to be of low quality. Unfortunately, empirical studies say that readers' judgments (including the judgments of editors and reviewers) about manuscripts' quality have very low correlations with citations to published articles, and these unreliable judgments mean that journals likely reject about half of the best manuscripts that they receive (Gottfredson, 1978; Starbuck, 2005). Of course, this unreliability also means that about half of the best articles appear in second-tier or third-tier journals.

The foregoing studies imply that in an era of "impact factor" dominance, editors' most significant contributions may be to use interpersonal networking to search for and to attract unusually high-quality manuscripts or manuscripts that promise to create breakthroughs. Both strategies entail risk. The former strategy violates cherished professional ethics. The latter strategy relies on editors' having better judgment and better insight than most people.

Striking realistic balances

This chapter has critically reviewed four dimensions on which editors can make strategic choices. Although the alternatives are phrased as polar opposites, it is very unlikely that any editor would choose one of these extremes. More likely, an editor would blend the alternative strategies even within the handling of one specific manuscript.

For example, Options 1a versus 1b contrast a strategy in which an editor participates in evaluation so dominantly that reviewers have little say, with a strategy in which an editor merely manages the reviewing process and defers completely to reviewers on substantive issues. These two strategies might be policies that an editor applies consistently to every manuscript. However, an editor might use one extreme policy for some manuscripts and the other extreme policy for others, and might deal with most manuscripts by asserting the editor's own opinions on some points while yielding to reviewers on other points. An appropriate mixture of strategies depends upon the editor's abilities and goals, the editor's confidence in each reviewer, each reviewer's expertise, the topic and methodology of the manuscript, the author's reputation and expertise, and properties of the journal such as its age, circulation, or ownership.

Likewise, an editor might perceive that one manuscript could become much more informative and persuasive if the author would change some presentational elements, but that another manuscript is already exceedingly well written. Or, one editor might perceive that conditions are right to attempt a revolutionary change – support from like-minded editors and textbook writers, possibly an influential professional society that is advocating change – whereas another editor might believe that no matter how desirable a change might be, the timing is not right or support is lacking. Or, even an editor who devotes much time to soliciting manuscripts likely also devotes some time to weeding out unsolicited manuscripts that deviate from that journal's topics.

Because editors have so many ways to use their time and effort, it is hard for them to behave poorly, but it is also hard for them to behave optimally. Optimization requires awareness of the many strategic options and the contingencies that make strategies more or less effective. Because each manuscript entails somewhat different contingencies, an editor that seeks to optimize both macroscopically and microscopically would need to reassess endlessly. Shades of Herbert Simon! This changing complexity raises the issue of what heuristics editors adopt and what biases editors exhibit.

Editors need to beware of the so-called "fundamental attribution bias," a propensity for people to overestimate their own influence on events and to underestimate external or situational influences. For instance, Meindl and Ehrlich (1987) and Meindl, Ehrlich, and Dukerich (1985) argued that both researchers and the general populace attribute too much control and influence to leaders; they inferred that these attributions become more frequent after successful performances. A related and prevalent phenomenon is the "self-serving bias," a propensity for people to overestimate their own influence on successes and to overestimate external or situational influences on failures (Heider, 1958). People also tend to exhibit the opposite biases when interpreting other people's successes and failures. For instance, Wagner and Gooding (1997) found that managers who face equivocal information about their own businesses tend to attribute positive outcomes to strengths in their own organizations, while they blame negative outcomes on environmental circumstances. However, when managers are asked to interpret information about businesses managed by others, they attribute positive outcomes to opportunities in the environment and negative outcomes to organizational weakness.

Biases in reviewing processes also confront editors with challenging ethical and political issues. Prominent among these is the treatment of authors' social statuses. Some of the studies mentioned above imply that editors can increase their journals' visibility and influence by making special efforts to attract manuscripts by prestigious authors. One of the most cited journals, the *Journal of Economic Literature*, has an acceptance rate close to 100 percent because nearly all of its articles are invited ones written by very well-known authors. Similarly, the *Annual Review of Psychology*, which includes invited articles only, has the second highest impact factor (i.e., 11.71) among 99 journals included in the "psychology-multidisciplinary" category (ISI rankings, 2007). However, some professional norms assert that all manuscripts should receive evaluations that are independent of their authorship. Thus, Peters and Ceci (1982) roused strong responses when they resubmitted 12 articles to the journals that had published them just 18 to 32 months earlier. All 12 of these journals were prestigious ones, and the articles had originally been authored by researchers from highly rated psychology departments. However, Peters and Ceci gave the resubmissions fictitious authors and return addresses at obscure institutions. The submissions went to 38 editors and reviewers. Three editors and reviewers detected that the manuscripts had already appeared in print, which reduced the study to nine manuscripts that had 18 reviewers. Sixteen reviewers recommended rejection, and editors rejected eight manuscripts, leaving only one acceptance. Of course, the original editorial processes may have erred by accepting undeserving manuscripts that had been written in prestigious departments, or the experimental editorial processes may have erred by rejecting deserving manuscripts that had been written in obscure departments, or the quality of manuscripts may be so ambiguous that reviewers and editors eagerly grasp for external evidence to guide them such as the imputed reputations of authors. During Peters and Ceci's experiment, the most prevalent reasons for rejection were "serious methodological flaws," including inappropriate statistical analyses and faulty study design. As Mahoney (1977) found, methodology seems to serve as an all-purpose façade for other considerations.

Thus, editors' most valuable assets may be awareness of their own limitations and the limitations of their coeditors and reviewers. Editing is above all an imperfect activity that incorporates human weaknesses and errors and has no optimal solutions. However, editors can do more and feel better about their effects if they make realistic assessments of their personal capabilities and situations.

Acknowledgment

We thank Arthur Bedeian for help in locating some relevant research. This research was conducted in part while Herman Aguinis was on sabbatical leave from the University of Colorado at Denver and Health Sciences Center and holding a visiting appointment at the University of Salamanca (Spain).

References

Aguinis, H. (2007). *Performance Management*. Upper Saddle River, NJ: Pearson Prentice Hall.

Armstrong, J. S. (2007). Significance tests harm progress in forecasting. *International Journal of Forecasting*, 23, 321–7.

Bedeian, A. G. (1996). Improving the journal review process: The question of ghostwriting. *American Psychologist*, 51, 1189.

Bedeian, A. G. (2003). The manuscript review process: The proper roles of authors, referees, and editors. *Journal of Management Inquiry*, 12, 331–8.

Bedeian, A. G. (2004). Peer review and the social construction of knowledge in the management discipline. *Academy of Management Learning and Education*, 3, 198–216.

Bedeian, A. G., Van Fleet, D. D., & Hyman, H. H. (2007). Scientific achievement and editorial-board membership. *Organizational Research Methods*.

Cascio, W. F. (2008). How editors are selected. In Y. Baruch, A. M. Konrad, H. Aguinis, and W. H. Starbuck (Eds.), *Opening the black box of editorship*. Basingstoke, London: Palgrave Macmillan.

Cascio, W. F., & Aguinis, H. (2005). Test development and use: New twists on old questions. *Human Resource Management*, 44, 219–35.

Cumming, G., Fidler, F., Leonard, M., Kalinowski, P., Christiansen, A., Kleinig, A., Lo, J., McMenamin, N. & Wilson, S. (2007). Statistical reform in psychology: Is anything changing? *Psychological Science*, 18, 230–2.

Ellison, G. (2002). The slowdown of the economics publishing process. *Journal of Political Economy*, 110, 947–93.

Falk, R. & Greenbaum, C. W. (1995). Significance tests die hard: The amazing persistence of a probabilistic misconception. *Theory & Psychology*, 5, 75–98.

Fidler, F., Cumming, G., Burgman, M., & Thomason, N. (2004). Statistical reform in medicine, psychology and ecology. *Journal of Socio-Economics*, 33, 615–30.

Fidler, F., Cumming, G., Thomason, N., Pannuzzo, D., Smith, J., Fyffe, P., Edmonds, H., Harrington, C., & Schmitt, R. (2005). Evaluating the effectiveness of editorial policy to improve statistical practice: The case of the Journal of Consulting and Clinical Psychology. *Journal of Consulting and Clinical Psychology*, 73, 136–43.

Gans, J. S. & Shepherd, G.B. (1994). How are the mighty fallen: Rejected classic articles by leading economists. *Journal of Economic Perspectives*, 8, 165–79.

Gottfredson, S. D. (1978). Evaluating psychological research reports: Dimensions, reliability, and correlates of quality judgments. *American Psychologist*, 33 (10), 920–34.

Heider, F. (1958). *The psychology of interpersonal relations*. New York: Wiley.

ISI rankings (2007). Reports on Impact Factor for the year 2006. Retrieved from http://www.annualreviews.org/catalog/isi-rankings.aspx on September 26, 2007.

Jacobs, J. A. (2008). The case for an activist editorial model. In Y. Baruch, A. M. Konrad, H. Aguinis, & W. H. Starbuck (Eds.), *Opening the black box of editorship*. Basingstoke, London: Palgrave Macmillan.

Konrad, A. M. (2008). Knowledge creation and the journal editor's role. In Y. Baruch, A. M. Konrad, H. Aguinis, & W. H. Starbuck (Eds.), *Opening the black box of editorship*. Basingstoke, London: Palgrave Macmillan.

Kuhn, T. S. (1970). *The structure of scientific revolutions*. Chicago: University of Chicago Press.

Laband, D. N. (1990). Is there value-added from the review process in Economics? Preliminary evidence from authors. *The Quarterly Journal of Economics*, 105, 341–52.

Laband, D. N. & Piette, M. J. (1994). Favoritism versus search for good papers: Empirical evidence regarding the behavior of journal editors. *The Journal of Political Economy*, 102, 194–203.

Leahey, E. (2005). Alphas and asterisks: The development of statistical significance testing standards in sociology. *Social Forces*, 84, 1–24.

Mahoney, M. J. (1977). Publication prejudices: An experimental study of confirmatory bias in the peer review system. *Cognitive Therapy and Research*, 1, 161–75.

Mahoney, M. J. (1979). Psychology of the scientist: An evaluative review. *Social Studies of Science*, 9(3), 349–75.

Martinko, M. J., Campbell, C. R. & Douglas, S. C. (2000). Bias in the social science publication process: Are there exceptions? *Journal of Social Behavior and Personality*, 15, 1–18.

Medoff, M. H. (2003). Editorial favoritism in Economics? *Southern Economic Journal*, 70, 425–34.

Meindl, J. R. & Ehrlich, S. B. (1987). The romance of leadership and the evaluation of organizational performance. *Academy of Management Journal*, 30, 91–109.

Meindl, J. R., Ehrlich, S. B., & Dukerich, J. M. (1985). The romance of leadership. *Administrative Science Quarterly*, 30, 78–102.

Miller, J. & Perrucci, R. (2001). Back stage at "Social Problems": An analysis of the editorial decision process, 1993–1996. *Social Problems*, 48, 93–110.

Peters, D. P. & Ceci, S. J. (1982). Peer-review practices of psychological journals: The fate of published articles, submitted again. *Behavioral and Brain Sciences*, 5, 187–255 (page range includes 50 pages of comments by others and a response by Peters & Ceci).

Sherrell, D. L.; Hair, J. F., Jr.; & Griffin, M. (1989). Marketing academicians' perceptions of ethical research and publishing behavior. *Journal of the Academy of Marketing Science*, 17, 315–24.

Starbuck, W. H. (2003). Turning lemons into lemonade: Where is the value in peer reviews? *Journal of Management Inquiry*, 12, 344–51.

Starbuck, W. H. (2005). How much better are the most-prestigious journals? The statistics of academic publication. *Organization Science*, 16, 180–200.

Starbuck, W. H. (2006a). Preface: Realistic perspectives on organizing and strategizing. In *Organizational realities: Studies of strategizing and organizing*. Oxford: Oxford University Press.

Starbuck, W. H. (2006b). *The production of knowledge: The challenge of social science research*. New York: Oxford University Press.

Thompson, B. (2007). Various editorial policies regarding statistical significance tests and effect sizes. Retrieved from http://www.coe.tamu.edu/~bthompson/journals.htm on September 26, 2007.

Tushman, M. & Romanelli, E. (1994). Organization transformation as punctuated equilibrium: An empirical test. *Academy of Management Journal*, 34, 1141–66.

Wagner, J. A. III & Gooding, R. Z. (1997). Equivocal information and attribution: An investigation of patterns of managerial sensemaking. *Strategic Management Journal*, 18, 275–86.

Webster, E. J., & Starbuck, W. H. (1988). Theory building in industrial and organizational psychology. In C. L. Cooper and I. Robertson (Eds.), *International Review of Industrial and Organizational Psychology*, 93–138. London: Wiley.

Author Index

Agarwal, R.   61, 67, 119, 123
Aguinis, H.   xii, xxvi, 3, 14, 250, 258, 259, 268, 269
Aiken, L. S.   118, 123, 138, 142
Allscheid, S. P.   34, 38
Altman, G.   xxv
Anderson, N.   11, 113
Argyris, C.   4, 15, 167
Armstrong, J. S.   259, 268
Arnswald, U.   175
Ashforth, B. E.   28, 37

Bacharach, S.   23, 26
Bachrach, D. G.   38, 147, 156
Bakos, Y.   178, 186
Bamford, H.   197, 204
Barbuto, J. E.   35, 37
Barley, S. R.   xiii, xxiii, 39, 99, 103, 119, 123, 179, 186
Barnes-Farrell, J. L.   33, 38
Barron, F.   26
Bartunek, J.   xiii, xxiii, 3, 11, 59, 88, 89, 119, 123, 222
Baruch, Y.   xii, xxii, xxiv, xxv, 15, 37, 38, 56, 88, 96, 101, 103, 175, 209, 210, 216, 222, 239, 249, 250, 269
Bazerman, M.   87
Bedeian, A. G.   xiv, xxi, xxiii, xxv, 29, 37, 80, 87, 134–142, 181, 187, 246, 253, 256, 258, 268
Beebe, J.   139, 142
Belcher, W.   135, 136, 142
Bem, D. J.   101, 103
Bergh, D. D.   xiv, xxiii, 13, 114, 115, 119, 122, 123, 139, 243, 247, 249
Bergstrom, C. T.   202, 205
Bergstrom, T. C.   202, 205
Beyer, J.   94
Bhappu, A. D.   34, 37
Biagioli, M.   134, 135, 142
Bies, R.   77, 87
Biggart, N.   171, 175
Bitner, M. J.   33, 37

Black, D.   216, 222
Bolino, M. C.   31, 37
Booms, B. H.   33, 37
Borchgrevink, C. P.   34, 38
Bowen, D. E.   32, 37, 38
Brett, J. M.   91, 96
Brockner, J.   77, 87
Brody, T.   113
Brooks, L.   230
Brown, D.   230
Brynjolfsson, E.   178, 186,
Buchler, J.   16, 26,
Burgman, M.   269

Calhoun, M. A.   4, 12, 15
Callero, P. L.   38
Campbell, C. R.   254, 269
Campbell, D. T.   23, 26
Caplow, T.   88, 96
Cardinal, L. B.   xxii, xxv
Carley, K.   210, 222
Carr, L.   113
Cascio, W. F.   xii, xiv, xxiv, 89, 93, 216, 222, 231, 238, 252, 259, 269
Ceci, S. J.   267, 268, 270
Chan, L.   202, 205
Chang, C.   33, 37
Cherry, B.   34, 37
Christiansen, A.   269
Clark, T.   xiv, xxiv, 176, 177, 180, 181, 186
Clary, E. G.   28, 37
Cohen, J.   20, 138, 142
Cohen, P.   138, 142
Colquitt, J.   77, 87, 96
Conlon, D.   87
Cook, T. D.   23, 26
Cooper, C. L.   270
Courpasson, D.   170
Cranage, D.   33, 38
Creamer, V.   33, 38
Cumming, G.   260, 269
Cummings, L. L.   xxi, xxv, 67, 239, 249

271

Daft, R. L. xxi, xxv, 63, 64, 67, 139, 142, 239, 249
Dalton, D. 187
Daniel, H.-D. 138, 142
Daniels, D. 31, 37
Davidsson, P. 184, 187
Davis, M. 19
Davis, J. H. 89, 96
Davis, M. S. 119, 120, 123
De Cock, C. 8, 15
De Rond, M. 140, 142
Denevan, K. 156
DeNisi, A. S. xv, xxiii, 64, 67, 75
Deutsch, Y. 31, 38
Donnelly, J. H. 32, 37
Douglas, S. C. 105, 113, 254, 269
Downey, H. K. 187
Dreyfus, H. L. 173, 175
DuBois, F. L. 202, 205
Duell, B. 31, 37
Dukerich, J. M. 119, 123, 267, 269
Dutton, J. 119, 123

Easterby-Smith, M. 15
Echambadi, R. 61, 67, 119, 123
Eden, D. xv, xxiv, 138, 222, 239
Edmonds, H. 269
Ehrlich, S. B. 267, 269
Eisenberg, N. 12
Ellison, G. 139, 142, 254, 269
Eysenbach, G. 203, 205

Falk, R. 260, 269
Feldman, D. C. xv, xxiii, 12, 13, 15, 30, 37, 68, 137, 142, 187, 229
Ferris, G. R. 38
Fidler, F. 260, 261, 269
Flores, F. 173, 175
Floyd, S. 177, 186
Ford, J. K. 113
Forgues, B. xvi, xxiv, 197
Forray, J. M. xvi, xxiv, 197
Foss, N. J. 10, 11, 15
Franco, A. M. 67, 123
Freeman, R. E. 140, 142
Frey, B. S. 10, 15, 65, 67, 135, 142
Frost, P. J. xxi, xxii, xxv, 67, 239, 249
Fyffe, P. 269

Gadamer, H.-G. 172, 175
Gans, J. S. 265, 269

Garud, R. 170, 175
Geary, J. 113
Gephart, R. P. 59, 67
Gilson, C. 198
Glick, W. H. xxii, xxv
Gooding, R. Z. 267, 270
Gottfredson, S. D. 264, 266, 269
Greenbaum, C. W. 260, 269
Greenberg, J. 96
Greenleaf, R. K. 35, 37
Griffin, M. 265, 270
Griffin, R. 187
Grube, J. 28, 37, 38
Guralnik, D. B. 16, 26
Gutek, B. A. 34, 37

Hackman, J. R. 223, 224, 226, 230
Hair, J. F., Jr. 265, 270
Hall, D. T. xxi, xxii, xxiv, 88, 96, 169
Hanke, R. 122, 123
Hardy, C. 170, 175
Harnad, S. 113
Harrington, C. 269
Harrison, D. 98
Harvey, P. 105, 113
Heider, F. 267, 269
Henle, C. A. 3, 14
Herriot, P. 111, 113
Hertzberg, F. 164
Hillman, A. xxv, 56, 187
Hiltz, S. R. 198, 205
Hitt, M. A. 75, 142
Hodgkinson, G. P. xvi, xxiii, 104, 107–109, 111, 113
Hollenbeck, J. R. xvii, xxii, 13, 16
Huff, A. S. xxi, xxv, 239, 249
Hunt, J. G. 187
Hyman, H. H., III 137, 142, 253, 268

Ireland, R. D. xxv, 56, 123, 187

Jacobs, J. A. xvii, xxiii, 65, 67, 124, 252, 253, 269
Jaschik, S. 202, 205
Jeanes, E. L. 8, 15
Jensen, M. 177, 186
Jeon, D. S. 178, 186
Joireman, J. 31, 37

Kacmar, K. M.   xvii, xxiii, 34, 38, 49, 180, 186, 187
Kalinowski, P.   269
Kamdar, D.   37
Kauffman-Wills Group   201, 205
Kelley, S. W.   32, 37
Kertscher, J.   175
Kilduff, M.   xvii, xxiii, 97, 101, 103, 107, 119, 123, 234
Kirkman, B.   xxv, 187
Kirppendorff, K.   210, 222
Klein, K. J.   152, 156
Kleinig, A.   269
Kluger, A. N.   64, 67
Koch, W. A.   xxv
Konrad, A. M.   xii, xxii, xxiv, xxvi, 3, 250, 254–256, 269
Kuhn, T. S.   16, 19, 26, 262, 269
Kulik, C. T.   xvii, xxiv, 223

Laband, D. N.   256, 263, 265, 269
Latham, G. P.   57, 67
Law, K.   xxv, 56, 187
Lawrence, T. B.   169, 175
Leahey, E.   260, 269
Lee, T.   180, 186
Legnick-Hall, C. A.   32, 37
Leonard, M.   269
Lewicki, B.   88
Lewin, A. Y.   63, 67
Liao-Troth, M. A.   34, 37
Lilienfeld, S. O.   30, 37
Litchfield, E.   255
Lo, J.   269
Locke, E. A.   57, 67
Luhmann, N.   xxi, xxv
Lundberg, G. D.   30, 37
Lyles, M. A.   15

MacKenzie, S. B.   30, 38, 147, 156
Mael, F.   28, 37
Mahoney, M. J.   254, 268, 269
Malpas, J.   175
March, J.   167, 169, 175, 255
Marriott, L.   113
Marshall, D. G.   175, 240
Martinko, M. J.   105, 113, 254, 269
Maruyama, M.   174, 175
Maslow, A.   164
Mattila, A. S.   33, 38
Mayer, R. C.   64, 89, 90, 92, 96

McCabe, M. J.   202, 205
McCarty, R.   30, 38
McGee, R. J.   88, 96
McGregor, D.   164
McLean, I.   216, 222
McMenamin, N.   269
McMullen, J.   180, 182, 186
Medoff, M. H.   263, 265, 269
Meindl, J. R.   267, 269
Menicucci, D.   178, 186
Meyer, A. D.   56, 57, 63, 64, 65, 67
Miller, A. N.   140, 142
Miller, C. C.   xxii, xxv, 56, 187
Miller, J.   254, 270
Miner, J. B.   135, 136, 142
Moag, J.   77, 87
Mohr, L. A.   33, 37
Morris, S.   176, 187

Neubaum, D.   239
Newcombe, N. S.   30, 38
Newing, R. A.   216, 222
Ng, K. Y.   77, 87
Nifadkar, S. S.   140, 142
Nonaka, I.   5–8, 10, 13, 15

Oldham, G. R.   223, 224, 226, 230
Organ, D. W.   30, 38
Otley, D.   105

Paine, J. B.   30, 38
Pannuzzo, D.   269
Patterson, K.   35, 38
Pedhazur, E. J.   138, 142
Peirce, C.   16, 26
Penner, L. A.   27, 28, 29, 38
Peritz, B. C.   202, 205
Perneger, T. V.   113
Perrucci, R.   254, 270
Perry, J.   122, 123
Peters, D. P.   267, 270
Petkova, A. P.   90, 96
Pfeffer, J.   8, 9, 15
Philips, N.   169, 175
Piette, M. J.   263, 265, 269
Piliavin, J. A.   28, 37
Piliavin, P.   28, 38
Platt, J. R.   17, 19, 26
Podaskoff, P. M.   30, 38, 147, 156
Podsakoff, N. P.   147, 156
Pondy, L. R.   64, 67

Porter, C. 77, 87
Priem, R. L. 27, 38

Rajagopalan, N. xxv, 56, 187
Rasheed, A. A. 27, 38
Ray, D. 180, 187
Reeb, D. 202, 205
Reinke, S. J. 35, 38
Ridge, R. D. 28, 37
Rindova, V. P. 90, 96
Robertson, I. 270
Rogelberg, S. G. 14, 33, 38
Romanelli, E. 61–64, 67, 262, 270
Rorty, R. 173, 175
Rothman, K. 260, 261
Rowland, K. M. 38
Rowlinson, M. 113
Russell, R. F. 35, 38
Russey (Trans.), W. E. 142
Ryan, A. M. xviii, xxii, 27, 222
Rynes, S. L. xviii, xxi, xxiii, xxv, 56, 94–96, 119, 123, 177, 180, 187, 247, 249

Salamon, S. D. 31, 38
Sapienza, H. 184, 187
Sarkar, M. B. 60, 67, 119, 123
Savickas, M. L. 226, 230
Scandura, T. A. 228, 230
Schein, E. 167
Schepmyer, H. N. xxv, 15, 37, 96, 216, 222, 239, 249
Schmelkin, L. P. 138, 142
Schminke, M. 240, 249
Schmit, M. J. 34, 38
Schmitt, R. 269
Schneider, B. 32, 37, 38
Schon, D. 4, 15
Schoorman, F. D. 89, 96
Senders, J. 197, 205
Sever, J. M. 90, 96
Shapiro, D. L. xviii, xix, xxiii, xxv, 3, 11, 56, 88, 89, 91, 96, 187, 222
Shepherd, D. 180, 182, 186
Shepherd, G. B. 135, 139, 142, 265, 269
Sheppard, B. 87
Sherrell, D. L. 265, 270
Simon, H. 255, 267
Sitkin, S. B. 88, 91, 96
Skinner, S. J. 32, 37

Smith, J. 269
Smith, K. G. 142
Snyder, M. 28, 37
Spinosa, C. 173, 175
Starbuck, W. H. xiii, xxiv, 3, 4, 12, 15, 136, 137, 139, 142, 203, 205, 250, 254, 255, 258–260, 262, 265, 266, 269, 270
Staw, B. 179, 187
Sternberg, R. J. 17, 26
Stichweh, R. xxi, xxv
Stone, A. G. 35, 38
Suddaby, R. 59, 67
Sullivan, S. E. xxv, 15, 37, 38, 96, 216, 222, 239, 249
Super, C. M. 226, 230
Super, D. E. 226, 230
Susskind, A. M. 34, 38
Sutton, R. 180, 187

Taylor, C. 172, 175
Taylor, C. W. 26
Taylor, M. S. xxii, xxv
Thoenig, J.-C. 167
Thomas, W. I. 40
Thomason, N. 269
Thompson, B. 260, 270
Thompson, J. D. 255
Tsang, E. W. K. 10, 15
Tsoukas, H. xix, xxiv, 167, 175
Tsui, A. 140, 142
Turnley, W. H. 31, 37
Turnoff, M. 198, 205
Tushman, M. 262, 270
Tywoniak, S. A. xi, xxv, 4, 5, 6, 12, 13, 15

Vakil, T. F. 67
Van de Ven, A. H. 8, 9, 15
Van Fleet, D. D. 137, 142, 180, 187, 253, 268
Van Maanen, J. 8, 9, 15, 167
Vecchio, R. 187
Vermeulen, F. 7, 15
Voelpel, S. 5, 15
Von Krogh, G. 5, 15

Wagner, J. A., III 267, 270
Webster, E. J. 259, 270
Weick, K. E. 24, 26, 167, 179, 187

Weinsheimer, J. 175
Welbourne, T. M. xix, xxiii, 157
Weller, A. C. 135, 142
Wesson, M. 77, 87
West, S. G. 118, 123, 138, 142
Wheeler, D. W. 35, 37
Whetten, D. 119, 123
Whitley, R. 168, 171, 175
Wilderom, C. 108
Williams, E. A. 228, 230
Williams, L. J. xix, xxiv, 188,
Williamson, I. O. 90, 96

Wilson, D. 167
Wilson, S. 269
Wisenfeld, B. 77, 87
Wittgenstein, L. 172, 173, 175
Wright, M. xx, xxiv, 176, 177, 181, 186

Zahra, S. 184, 187, 239, 249
Zedeck, S. xx, xxiii, 145, 147, 148, 152, 156
Zevon, W. 16, 17
Zhu, Z. 170, 171, 175

Subject Index

academic freedom, 247
Academic Source Premier, 198
Academy of Management (AOM), xii, 62, 66, 83, 89, 107, 189, 209, 216, 231, 234
Academy of Management Ethics Committee, 95
Academy of Management Executive, 232
Academy of Management Journal (AMJ), xiii, xiv, xv, xvii, xviii, xix, xx, xxiii, xxiv, 56–62, 65–67, 75, 77, 78, 89, 92, 94, 96, 118, 119, 136, 139, 177, 190, 198, 231–233, 235, 239–243, 247
Academy of Management Learning and Education (AMLE), 231–233
Academy of Management Perspectives, 232
Academy of Management Review (AMR), xiii, xix, xxiii, 59, 92, 97–102, 108, 139, 189, 231–233, 238, 241
acceptance
  conditional, 64, 80, 124, 126, 129, 130, 133
  final, 126, 139
  likelihood of, 29, 146, 152, 153, 180, 253
  rates, 196
Administrative Science Quarterly (ASQ), xiii, xvii, xix, xxiii, 10, 39, 43, 59, 97, 98, 108, 255
Advanced Institute of Management (AIM), 113
advance(s),
  revolutionary, 7
agency
  funding, 201
ambassador
  journal's, 39, 40, 42, 107, 213
American Journal of Public Health, 260
American Psychological Association (APA), xiii, 83, 84, 145, 147, 148, 149, 153, 156, 209, 216, 237, 248, 260
American Psychologist, 260
American Sociological Association, xxii

American Sociological Review (ASR), xvii, xxiii, 124, 129, 130
animosity
  reviewer, 246
Annual Review of Psychology, xvi, 267
Aomonline.org, 231, 238
APA Publication Manual, 248
applied organizational sciences, 18, 19, 26
applied psychology, 147, 154
Applied Psychology: An International Review, xx, 153
article(s)
  award winning, 120
  high quality, 12, 195
  important, 203
  influential, 29
  invited, 267
  most cited, 254, 265
  practitioner-oriented, 157
  research methods, 189
assessment(s), xviii, 105, 118, 127, 152, 168, 169, 203, 214, 225, 227, 268
associate editors
  qualifications, 68, 193, 235
Association for Psychological Science (APS), (formerly American Psychological Society), xiii, 260
Association of Research Libraries, 176, 186
Australia, xii, xvii, 71, 170, 223, 228
authors and reviewers
  consensus between, 114, 257
authorship, 139, 141, 257, 267
  ethics of, 139, 141
  legitimate, 139, 141
  prerogatives of, 139, 141
autonomy, 3, 135, 141, 223, 224, 228
award(s), xiii, 67, 69, 92, 182, 221
  best reviewer, 67, 69, 92
  journal, 69
  special, 153

backlog, 98, 195, 234
balance, 75, 85, 87, 100, 109, 114, 149, 174, 179, 218, 236, 265, 266

behavioral science, xiv, xxiii, 92, 95, 96, 209
Best Article Award, xv, 119
Best Paper of the Year Award, 136
Best Reviewer Award, 67, 69, 92
biases, 10, 41, 81, 82, 141, 226, 254, 256, 265, 267
  methodological, 226
  opposite, 267
  potential, 226
Board of Governors (of the Academy of Management), xix, 193, 232
boardroom, 84
book review editor, 39
branding opportunities, 73
breakthroughs, 139
Britain, iv, 173
British Academy of Management (BAM) Annual Conference Issue, 108
British Association of Sociology, 106
British Journal of Management (BJM), xvi, xxiii, 104–113
British Psychological Society, 106
Budapest Open Access Initiative
budgets
  page, 36, 177
burden
  emotional, 244
  professional service, 28
burnout
  editorial, 45
Business Ethics - A European Review, 178
byline, 135

calculation
  half-life, 146
call for papers, 152, 162, 192
capability(ies), 31, 100, 105, 107, 110, 184, 188, 200, 268
  organizational, 105, 110
  personal, 268
  resource, 107
  sophisticated, 200
  technical, 200
  to manage costs, 31
capacity(ies), 5, 6, 36, 40, 106, 113, 213
  operational, 112
  strategic, 106
career, 24, 28, 31, 64, 111, 224

Career Development International, xii, xxiv, 178
Career Development Quarterly, 178
case studies, 158
censorship
  reverse, 135
certifications, 134
chairs, 155, 190, 192
change(s)
  editorial policy, 35
  evolutionary, 259, 261, 262, 266
  journal focus, 35
  methodological, 250
  revolutionary, 259, 261–262, 266
  technological, 97
Chief Executive Officer (CEO), xix, 165
China, xii, 170, 171
choices
  publication, 181
  strategic, 266
circulation(s), 145, 169, 199, 202, 251, 261–264, 266
citation counts, 18, 92, 180, 202, 262, 264
citation frequency, 90
citation rates
  differences in, 203
citation(s)
  few, 263
  increased, 256
  many, 255, 262, 264
  number of, 136
  ratio of, 146
  subsequent, 11
  total, 263
citedness, 146
citizenship, 27, 30, 31, 36
civic virtue, 30
civility
  norms of, 99
co-author(ship), 225, 236, 257
code of ethics, 14
coeditors, xii, xxiv, 45, 169, 170, 265, 268
collegiality, 11, 61
  lack of, 11
commentary(ies), 61, 101, 173, 257
  detailed, 257
commercialization, 202

commitment, 21, 72–74, 87, 98, 110, 128, 154, 165, 194, 195, 198, 212, 216, 237, 255
  time, 237
committee(s)
  advisory, xvi, xviii, 89
  promotion, 141, 192, 204
  selection, 236, 237
  tenure, 190
  see also Journals Committee
communication(s), xix, 4, 5, 7, 11, 12, 13, 42, 57, 87, 91, 109, 123, 155, 194, 198, 213, 215
community
  academic, 106, 168, 170, 174, 179, 183, 185, 198, 213, 214, 221, 242, 247
  American, 168
  caring, 221
  ethical, 95
  journal, 178, 185
  niche, 222
  of scholars, 140, 179, 183, 190
  practitioner, xxiv
  professional, 89, 91, 95, 152, 159
competence(y), 44, 89, 90, 92–94, 96, 212–214, 216, 220, 236
  decision making, 214
  reviewing, 216
competition, 76, 108, 158, 186
complaints
  common, 132
compliance
  organizational, 30
compulsivity, 248
conferences, 32, 41, 109, 155, 162, 179, 195, 198, 201
confidentiality, 153
conflict of interest, 30, 153, 236
conformity, 179
conscientiousness, 62
consciousness
  quasi-global, 169
  scholarly, 169
consensus, 17
  lack of, 16, 17, 20, 24
consensus creation, 16, 17, 20, 24, 26
consensus shifting, 16, 17, 19, 20–26
consensus-challenging work, 182, 185
consequence(s), xix, 19, 40, 43, 63, 98, 109, 135, 182, 202, 252, 259

consistency, 69, 89, 92, 185
  level of, 69
consulting editor, xv, xix, xx, 69, 75
content analysis, 210, 211
contingency(ies), 4, 24, 171, 173, 252–254, 257, 268
  behavioral, 4
  different, 267
  historical, 171
  situationally-specific, 171
continuum
  micro-macro, 226
contract, 110, 209, 216, 257
  psychological, 209, 216
coordinator
  manuscript, 156
coproduction, 32, 33, 36
copyediting, 130, 131, 200
copying services, 156
copyright, iv, 153, 199, 200
  ownership of, 199
Cornell University, xiii, xvii, xviii, xix, 255
correspondence
  inappropriate, 33
  personal, 72
cost containment, 83
cost(s)
  marginal, 139
  of printing, 97
  opportunity, 177
  production, 202
Council of the British Academy of Management (BAM), 105
counseling, 242
counter-voice, 215
court of appeal, 258
Creative Commons Attribution License, 199
creativity, 26, 86, 119, 122, 140, 211
credibility, 71, 134, 161, 212
criteria, 26, 30, 58, 87, 91, 92, 94, 137, 169, 192, 234, 254
  particularistic, 137
  publication, 58
criticism(s), 82, 85, 91, 94, 139, 259
  constructive, 94
  developmental, 91
  referee, 139
critique, 7, 42, 44, 71, 91
  journal, 71

Cultural Revolution, 171
culture(s), xix, 71, 169, 172, 209, 243
  developmental, 243
  editorial, 243
  non-Western, 172
curiosity, 211, 213
  intellectual, 213
current thinking, 7
Curriculum Vitae (CV), 234 (*see also* resumé)
customer service, 27, 31–34
customized interactions, 33
cycle
  decision, 97

deal breakers, 237
deans, 106, 141, 146, 155, 190, 192, 235, 250
  business school, xix, 106
  enthusiastic, 235
decision making, xiii, xvii, xxiii, 12, 17, 75, 93, 96, 99, 100, 180, 183, 184, 212, 214, 218, 240–242
  agonizing, 242
  editorial, xxiii
Decision Sciences, xvii, xxii
dedication, 66, 69, 109, 110, 212
deference, 250
delay(s), 36, 43, 49, 53, 126, 127, 195, 198, 202, 225, 244, 254
delegation, 100, 129, 132
Department of Psychology at Berkeley, 155
desk reject(ion), 52, 53, 56, 58, 59, 66, 180, 241, 242
developmental feedback, 78, 149, 225, 242, 249
diamond in the rough, 95, 243
dignity, 91, 92
diplomacy, 80, 83, 213
Directory of Open Access Journals (DOAJ), 176, 201–203
disagreement
  inter-reviewer, 181
disrespect, 241
diversity, xii, xvii, xviii, xxiii, 8, 71, 149, 169, 170, 253, 254, 264
  epistemological, 44
  gender, xii
  inherent, 169
  international, 149
  national, 149
  public and private universities, 71
  race/racial, 71
dustbowl empiricism, 149

Eastern Academy of Management (EAM), 199
eclectic field, 104
ecology, 261
education
  business, 169
  executive, xix, 248
  management, xvi, xviii, 231
  post-doctoral, 256
educators
  graduate, 29
effectiveness, 99, 100, 102, 151
efficiency, 51, 72, 97, 99, 100, 102, 182
  control of, 100
ego, 28, 214
  editor's, 131
e-journals, 202
elections, 236, 252
electronic form/version, 50, 130, 200
Electronic Journal of Radical Organization Theory (EJROT), 198
electronic journal(s), xvi, xxiv, 197, 198, 200–204
electronic publishing, 98, 197
electronic review(s), 50, 180
electronic submission(s), 50, 52, 71, 101, 155, 196
electronic system, 92
empathy, 29, 212, 214
empowerment
  editorial, 93
endorsements
  institutional, 203
entrepreneurs
  institutional, 167
entrepreneurship, xx, 178, 183
Epidemiology, 261
epistemology(ies), xix, 8, 9
error(s)
  human, 268
  technical, 150
  Type I, 10, 243
  Type II, 10, 243
esteem, 28, 216, 220
  ego-growth, 28
  self, 220

ethical dilemmas, 109
ethical violations, 11
ethics, xiv, xvii, 84, 95, 139, 141, 178, 266
etiquette
  inappropriate reviewer, 151
excellence, xxiii, 89, 104, 203, 251, 255, 265
expenditure
  library, 176
  on serials, 176
experiment(s)
  laboratory, 84
  natural, 203
explicit knowledge, 5–7
extrinsic outcomes, 224
extroversion, 212

factor(s)
  circumstantial, 219
  contextual, 226
  immediacy, 146
  impact, 106, 108, 113, 146, 159, 192, 202, 203, 251, 261, 263, 267
faculty, xiii, xv, xvii, xviii, xix, 68, 69–74, 140, 148, 181, 188, 196, 239, 256
  junior, 71, 73, 140, 196
  new, 148
  senior, 71, 73
fairness, xviii, 78, 218, 243, 254
  perceived, 78
  procedural, xviii
faith, 137, 138
faux rigor, 137
favoritism, 40, 265
fear, 258
feeling, 9, 31, 33, 45, 56, 65, 105, 115, 180, 211–213, 215, 231, 239, 244
figure(s)
  public, 39
  supplemental, 130
  turnaround, 180
finance, xx, 107, 177, 263
financial accounting, 156
Financial Times, xix, 90
finding(s), 14, 20, 111, 115–117, 120–121, 125, 141, 160, 163, 211, 221, 256, 258–260, 266
first impression, 102, 120, 192

fit(s), 4, 7, 8, 30, 43, 53, 57, 59, 60, 78, 87, 118, 119, 147, 153, 165, 174, 189, 221, 228, 241
  lack of, 60, 241
flaws, 9, 14, 42, 90, 119, 214, 226, 268
  methodological, 268
  serious, 214
  theoretical, 226
flexibility, 55, 258
foreignness, 173
form letter, 9, 77–79
format(ting), 52, 94, 160, 200, 201, 204, 241
  electronic, 200
  give-away, 242
  journal's, 241
  poor, 160
  section, 200
Forum
  Executive, 158
  HR Leadership, 158
  HR Science, 158
forum(s), 32, 119, 139, 158, 169, 172, 228, 231, 260
  editor's, 139
  special, 260
framework(s), 9, 28, 58, 115, 116, 118, 119, 173, 223
  extended, 116
  generalized, 119
  simplistic, 115
  theoretical, 58, 173
  tried-and-true, 223
framing, 19, 21, 26, 64, 102, 128
  conceptual, 8, 128
  theoretical, 102
framing manuscripts, 21
fraud, 8
freedom
  academic, 247
frustration, 10, 32, 177, 220, 243
fulfillment
  level of, 220
functions of volunteering
  protective, 29
  understanding, 29
funds, 233, 262
  discretionary, 233
fusion
  possible, 174

games
 evolutionary, 183
 infantile, 249
 sophomoric, 247
gatekeeper/gatekeeping, 7, 8, 88–92, 95, 96, 154, 231, 236
 editorial, 7, 8
gathering
 data, 259
gender, xii, xvi, 71, 137, 149, 210
generalization, 240, 252
ghostwriters/ghostwriting, xxii, 63, 134, 135, 137
gifts, 44, 73, 74
 token, 74
glamour, 234
good reviewers, 42, 74, 76, 81–83, 213
goodwill, 119
governance mechanisms, 184, 185
grace
 sensitivity, 213
grade, 215
graduates
 MBA, 259
grammar
 poor, 160
grant(s), 20, 31, 154, 201
graphs, 161
gratification
 delayed, 225
Greek, 173
grievance, 124
ground(s), 44, 234, 259, 262
 defensible, 262
 logical, 259
 new, 247
 theoretical, 152
group
 distinguished, 148
 large, 262
 minor, 209
 only, 189
 significant, 209
 small, 184, 199
Group & Organization Management, xii, xvi, xxii, xxiv
group think, 140
guidance, xxvi, 3, 9, 11, 13, 33, 58, 59, 83, 115, 121, 124, 126, 128, 133, 181, 188, 190, 191, 196, 256, 258, 260
 published, 188

guidelines, 32, 36, 53, 58, 61, 78, 84, 119, 162, 241, 260
 ethical, 84
 journal, 32, 162
 reviewer, 53
 style, 58
 submission, 36, 53

half-life, 146
Handbook of Organization, 255
hermeneutical exercise, 172
hierarchical linear modeling, 33, 225
higher education, 106
high quality, xxi, 3, 12, 13, 35, 40, 82, 89, 94, 107, 112, 140, 152, 157, 158, 163, 165, 174, 180, 181, 185, 192, 194, 195, 197, 214, 222, 226, 229, 232, 240, 263, 265, 266
high-risk revision, 243
history of science, 16
hit
 citation wise, 218
home institution, 69
homogeneity, 254
hospitals, 255
HR Leadership Forum, 158
HR Science Forum, 158
HRM , 157, 166
HRM Survey, 158
http://www.soros.org/openaccess/resources.shtml
 Budapest Open Access Initiative, 204
Human Performance, xx, 153
Human Relations, xii, xv, xvii, 92
Human Resource Management (HRM), xii, xiv, xv, xvii, xviii, xix, xxiii, xxvii, 157–160, 162–166, 177
Human Resource Management Journal, xvii, 166, 178
humanities, 168
hypothesis(es), 24, 86, 116, 117, 157, 164, 259
 alternative, 259
 knowledge-driven, 24
 new, 116
 null, 259, 260
 problem-driven, 24
 statement of, 86
 true, 259

idealism, 122
idea(s)
  marketplace of, 115, 135, 140
  revolutionary, 261
  value-added, 90
identification, 28, 30, 121, 148, 150, 255
  professional, 38, 30, 35
identity(ies), xxiv, 28, 35, 107, 111, 167–169, 173, 174, 185, 194, 223, 224, 226, 251, 254, 255, 261
  American, 167
  diffuse, 255
  discursively influenced, 174
  discursively produced, 169, 173
  distinctive, 111, 261
  dynamic, 174
  European, 167
  historically generated/shaped, 169, 174
  homogenous, 167
  intellectual, 169
  journal's, 173, 174
  professional, 35
  task, 223, 224
  volunteer role, 28
image
  ideal, 135, 139
  journal's, 110, 192
imagination, 247, 248
  reader's, 247
immaturity
  disciplinary, 17
immediacy factor, 146
impact factor(s)
  different, 263
  instability of, 4
impact(s), 26, 158, 176, 179, 202, 203, 217, 229, 259, 263, 264
implications, xxiv, 3, 7, 9, 23–26, 36, 37, 53, 54, 63, 84, 86, 104, 110, 111, 120, 121, 125, 141, 147, 152, 161, 173, 176, 181, 185, 195, 209, 221, 236, 237, 248, 251
  applied, 152
  communal, 104
  personal, 181
  practical, 147
  theoretical, 173
  for practice, 23

implied mediator, 23
impulses
  developmental, 251
  different, 251
inappropriateness, 261
inauguration, 198
incentive, 82, 149, 181, 261
inception, 177
inclusion, 8, 106
income, 39, 201, 220
incompatibility, 258
incorporation, 126
incremental contribution, 13, 247
independence, 119, 212
independent journals, xxiv, 176–186
  non-affiliated to a professional association, 176
index (indices),
  immediacy, 146
indicator(s), 90, 112, 146, 229, 260
  career success, 220
industry
  publishing, 262
Informit e-Library, 198
Infotrac, 198
infrastructure
  administrative, 112
  electronic, 109
  journal, 49
  ready-made, 179
initiative(s), xii, 30, 89, 120, 169, 204, 234, 261
  editorial, 261
insider, 40
insights, xxii, 49, 53, 90, 116, 117, 118, 129, 145, 152, 176, 179, 184, 197, 231, 255
  theoretical, 118, 152, 231
  useful, 197
instability, 4
instinct
  gut, 225
institution(s), 69, 100, 200, 210, 215, 217, 218, 220, 223, 233, 234,
  host, 233, 234
  international, 168
  obscure, 268
  research-led, 210
  societal, 171
  sponsoring, 111
  trajectory, 167

instructions, 50, 62, 63, 152, 160, 162, 241, 245, 248,
  format, 241
  journal's, 248
  publisher's, 160
  specific, 152
  submission, 50
insurance, 126
integrity, 30, 65, 89, 91–96, 134, 211, 221
intellectual property, 80
intelligence, 211, 213
  analytical, 211
intention(s), 23, 106, 138, 141, 157, 219
interest(s)
  collective, 31
  conflict of, 30, 153, 236
  conflicting, 75
  readers', 130
  self-, 31, 34
  vested, 77
interface, 103, 182, 185
interlocutor, 170, 172, 174
international conference circuit, 105
International Journal of Human Resource Management, 178
internationalization, 100, 101, 108, 109, 149
internet, 11, 101, 155, 169, 174, 176, 186, 197, 198, 200, 202, 204, 233, 234, 262
  access to the, 198
intervals
  confidence, 260
intervention(s)
  editorial, 128, 254, 260
  strong, 254
investigations
  original, 147
  theoretical, 147
ISBN number, 84
ISI (Institute of Scientific Information) Journal Citation Reports
  rating or ranking, 3, 90, 106, 146, 183, 189, 202, 210, 211, 218, 262, 263, 267
issue(s)
  special, xii, xx, 69, 93, 108, 135, 165, 182, 183, 185, 198, 263,

iteration(s), 115, 122, 129
  final, 129
  several, 115, 129
iterative effects, 224

Job Characteristics Theory (JCT), 223, 224
  predictions of, 224
Journal Citation Reports
  see ISI (Institute of Scientific Information) Journal Citation Reports
journal lists, 181
Journal of Applied Behavioral Science, xiv, xxiii
Journal of Applied Psychology (JAP), xiii, 60, 136, 145
Journal of Business Venturing, xx, 178, 183
Journal of Consulting and Clinical Psychology (JCCP), 260
Journal of Economic Literature, 267
Journal of Finance, 177
Journal of Financial Economics (JFE), 177
Journal of Management (JOM), xii, xiv, xv, xvi, xvii, xviii, xix, xx, xxiii, xxiv, 30, 49, 50–53, 55, 68, 104, 176, 186, 223–229
Journal of Management Studies (JMS), xv, xix, xx, xxiv, 176, 180, 183, 184, 186
Journal of Organizational Behavior, xv, xvi, 59, 92, 183
Journal of Personality and Social Psychology (JPSP), xvii, 80
journal web sites, 58, 245
Journals Committee, xxiv, 231–236, 238
  successive, 236
judgment(s), xxi, 3–5, 7–10, 12, 13, 65, 134, 136, 137, 181, 196, 212, 214, 236, 240, 242, 244, 246, 250, 253, 256, 258, 264, 266
  editorial, 4, 10
  independence of, 212
  objective, 244
  readers', 264, 266
  reviewer(s), 65, 264
justice, xix, 77, 91

key job characteristic
  Autonomy, 223
  Task Identity, 223
  Task Significance, 223

keywords, 102
knowledge
  academic, 211, 221
  accumulation, 11
  advancement of, 203
  advances(ing), 35, 138, 159
  appropriation, 11
  common body of, xxii, 3, 7, 8, 12
  communicating, rules for, 5
  creation, xxi, xxii, 3, 7, 8, 10, 88, 212, 214
  current, 18, 90
  deficiencies in, 116
  definition of, 4, 13, 17
  development, 4, 16, 17, 26, 145, 216, 256, 258
  discipline, 220
  dissemination, xxi, xxii, 88, 114
  existing, 13, 19, 24, 25
  explicit, 5, 6, 7
  inside, 186
  inter-subjective, xxii, 3, 6, 9, 11
  research-based, 232
  scientific, 262
  sharing, 11
  social construction of, 134
  tacit, 5–7, 13
  theory-based, 231
  transmission, 5
  validating, rules for, 5
knowledge base, 8, 18, 21, 24–26, 37, 147, 149, 150, 152, 156, 203
knowledge conversion, xxii, 3, 6–10, 12
knowledge generation, 6, 21, 23–25
knowledge management, 3
knowledge sharing, 5, 11
KSAOs
  knowledge, skills, abilities, other characteristics, 237, 238

laboratories
  directors of, 256
  research, 256
leaders, 84, 110, 192, 267
leadership
  academic, 214
  servant, xxii, 27, 35, 213, 214
learning, xiii, xvi, xviii, 4, 29, 43, 82, 98, 114, 161, 163–166, 185, 211, 212, 224, 231
  single-loop, 4

legacy of service, 37
legitimacy, 70, 71, 192, 197, 201–204
  institutional, 71
  perceived, 192, 203
length(s), 34, 43, 58, 60, 70, 129, 130, 136, 183, 184, 241, 249, 263
  article or manuscript, 58
  average, 263
  maximum, 130
leniency, 69, 244
letter(s)
  acceptance, 244
  accompanying, 246, 249
  action, 155
  conditional accept, 129
  cover, 12, 53, 77, 246
  decision, 27, 29, 31, 32, 34, 35, 43, 45, 49, 50, 53, 57, 59, 60, 63–65, 69, 78, 83, 85, 98–100, 102, 126, 193, 196, 215, 245, 246
  editorial, 93, 128, 180
  personalized, 79
  R&R/revise-and-resubmit, 60, 245, 260
  recommendation, 234
  rejection, 57, 59, 66, 79, 229, 243, 244
liabilities, 117, 193, 259
librarians, 262, 263
library(ies), 107, 110, 204, 262
license(ing), 176, 178
  Creative Commons Attribution License, 199
list serves, 11
listing
  business, 106
  management, 106
lists
  evaluation, 3
  journal, 181
literature review, 32
literature search, 14
load
  editorial, 170
  increasing, 170
  reduced teaching, 155
  teaching, 155, 228
lobbying, 106
location(s), xvi, 50, 98, 100, 129, 169, 173, 193, 252
logistical issues, 51
longevity, 178, 184
  journal, 178

luck of the reviewer draw, 136
Luddite, 97

M@n@gement, xvi, xxiv, 198–200
mailing process, 49
   international reviewers, 49
mailing time
   international, 49
mainstream, 168, 170, 174, 177, 184, 185
managing editor, 97–101, 215
Manuscript Central, 92
manuscript tracking database, 52
market(s), 112, 122, 134, 168, 176, 178, 190, 251, 262
   journals, 176
   labor, 168
   unified, 168
marketing, xxvi, 69, 73, 107, 110, 112, 147, 165, 241
   campaigns, 110, 112
marketplace, xxiii, 68, 104, 106, 111, 115, 135, 140
   economic, 135
   global, xxiii, 104,
   scientific, 135, 140
masthead, 65, 81, 149
   journal, 81
material(s),
   offensive, 135
   permanent, 130
   promotional, 193
   supplemental, 130
   technical, 160
mechanism(s)
   defense, 188
   governance, 184, 185
   internal support, 107
   market, 112
   quality-control, 134
   support, 112
meddling,
   editorial, 131
mediator(s), 22–24, 120, 258
   editorial roles, 258
   implied, 23
medicine, 261
member(s)
   editorial board, 61, 68, 71, 72–74, 83, 88–94, 96, 110, 129, 181, 182, 184, 194, 233, 237, 253
   editorial review board, 89, 232

international, 233
junior faculty, 71, 196
prospective, 237
membership, 71, 89, 178, 179, 192, 199, 201, 232, 234, 237,
memory, 4, 70, 71, 100, 101, 188, 224
   institutional, 70, 71, 101
   selective perceptual, 168
mentor(s), 39, 41, 42, 89, 228, 249
   role of, 42
mentoring, xxii, 42, 62, 66, 213, 215, 242
meritocracy, 71
meta-analysis, 20
method(s)
   qualitative, 14
   quantitative, 58
   research, xix, 9, 63, 107, 159, 163, 189, 190, 192, 226, 256
   rigorous, 157
   statistical, 163
   vote-counting, 9
methodology(ies)/ methodologist(s), xiv, 8, 9, 12, 14, 68, 71, 76, 93, 115, 117, 118, 121, 191, 228, 257, 265, 266, 268
   survey, 228
mindset, 86, 159
minority
   significant, 217
misconceptions, 36
misinformation, consequences, xxi
mission statement, 58, 147, 148
mission(s)
   editorial, 107
   journal, 52, 58, 60, 119, 122, 147, 241, 242
moderator(s), xii, 22, 24, 120
monographs, 176, 237
Motivating Potential Score (MPS), 223, 224, 226, 228

National Football League (NFL), 244
network(s), xvii, 5, 56, 68, 162, 220, 225, 238
networking, 70, 163, 213, 216, 265, 266
   interpersonal, 265, 266
neuroscience, 183
New Orleans, 98
New Zealand, xiii, 170
Newsletter of the Academy of Management, 232

nomination, 28, 70, 102, 153, 216, 233
  call for, 216
noncompliance, 258
norm(s), 71, 77, 99, 125, 141, 159, 210, 261, 265
  journal, 159
  professional, 265
North America, 105, 108, 110, 199
notification, 58, 199
  widespread, 232
novelty, 116
nuances, 118, 168, 191

obligation, 42–43, 73, 154–155, 221, 222
  professional, 151
obsession
  omnipresent, 247
OCB
  organizational citizenship behavior, xxvii, 30–31
office
  central, 98–99
  editorial, 102, 109, 112, 184
  headquarters, 234
  journal, 49–50, 54, 101
  virtual, 50
officers, 240
online journal/publication, xxiv, 176, 197–205
ontologies
  alternative, 171
oomph
  positive emotional, 225
open access, xxii, 176, 198–199, 201–204
open ended appointment, 221
Open Journal Systems (OJS)
  http://pkp.sfu.ca/?q=ojs, 204
open-mindedness, 94–95
  underlying, 168
openness, 8, 177, 179, 236
  intellectual, 169
  journal's, 218
optimization, 267
oracle, 40–41
Organization Management Journal (OMJ), xvi, xxvii, 199–200
Organization Science, xiv, xvi–xvii, xix, 92
organization studies, xiii, xix, 7–8, 99, 104, 106, 170
Organization Studies (OSS), xii, xvii, xxiv, xxvii, 167–172

organization theory, xvi, 60, 255
organizational behavior, 147
Organizational Behavior and Human Decision Processes (OBHDP), xxvii, 60, 98
organizational citizenship behavior (OCB), xxvii, 30–31
organizational compliance, 30
organizational loyalty, 30
organizational positions, 6
Organizational Research Methods (ORM), xiii–xiv, xvi, xix, xxix, 60, 188, 190–199
Organizations, 255
outcome(s), 3, 6, 18, 24, 25, 29, 36, 43, 67, 75–76, 79, 90, 114, 180, 254
  acceptance, 79–80
  desired, xxi, 4, 31
  intrinsic, 224
  negative, xi, 220, 267
  positive, xi, 80, 220, 223, 226, 267
  precarious, 173
  rejection, 36, 79
outlet(s), xvi, xix, 19, 43, 60, 74, 78, 84, 86, 106, 107, 118, 123, 177, 189–193, 195, 196, 198, 232
  alternative, 60, 78, 177
  international, 107
  legitimate, 198
  possible, 232
  potential, 195
outline(s), 81, 129
over-editing, 63
overload, 8, 31, 61, 180, 210
  information, 8, 61
  significant, 210
oversights, 42, 83, 183
Oxford English Dictionary (OED), xxvii, 41–42

p values, 260, 261
pages
  allotment of, 145
  number of, 131, 165, 247
  per volume, 108
panel(s)
  editorial, 228
  meet the editor, 182
  reviewer, 224
paperwork, 227

paradigm(s), 8, 9, 20, 44, 95, 125, 140, 177, 259, 262
  Statistical Hypothesis Inference Testing, 20
parochialism, 172, 174
passion, 212, 237
patience, 162, 180, 212
payment(s), 200, 250
peer(s), 163, 181
peer evaluations, 113
peer judgment(s), 134
peer review, 27, 30, 33, 53, 124, 133–135, 137, 151, 152, 183, 198, 214, 215
penalty, 244, 245
Penn State, 99, 100, 102
perceived justice, 77
perception(s)
  operating, 193
  public, 70
performance, xxiii, 57, 64, 66, 70, 96, 104–107, 184, 196, 217, 232, 240, 251, 252, 267,
  editorial, 252
  improving journal's, xxiii, 104
performance-quality
  constructiveness, 92
permission, 175, 200
personal touch, 78
personal work values, 28
personality, 29, 145
Personnel Psychology, xiii, xvi, xvii, xviii, xxii, 19, 147
persuasion, 13, 175, 255
  art of, 175
persuasiveness, 234
philosophy
  editing, 228
  open access, 201
  personal, 227
philosophy of science, 16
pipeline, 40, 83, 200, 218, 239
plagiarism, 8, 11, 95
plagiarizing, 94
pluralism, 168, 169
plurality
  ineradicable, 174
policy makers, 106
Policy Statement, 190, 191, 193, 194, 196

policy(ies), xxi, 14, 32, 35, 41, 43, 45, 58, 60, 62, 66, 80, 84, 93, 106, 107, 110, 131, 149, 177, 178, 183, 190, 191, 202, 224, 227, 234, 241, 250, 252, 255, 261, 266
  editor submission to own journal, 84
  editorial, xxi, 35, 41, 66, 107, 177, 252, 261
  extreme, 266
  idiosyncratic, 261
  open access, 202
  Revise and Resubmit Once, 45
politics
  underlying, 161
polls, 122
pool
  candidate, 238
  potential, 192
positivism
  American, 168
positivists, 167
power, xxi, 12, 39, 65, 75, 76, 85, 87, 102, 166, 172, 209, 215, 220, 221
  disciplinary, 172
  influential, 220
power, editorial, 39
practice(s)
  contribution to, 111, 159
  implications for, 23
practitioner(s), xviii, xxiv, 12, 25, 43, 157–162, 164, 166
praise, 81, 91
  false, 91
pre-conditions
  submitting, 58
prejudices, 174
pressure to publish, 43, 125, 253
pressure(s),
  institutional, 198
  social, 28, 29
  time, 126, 180, 195, 210, 217
prestige, xxi, 18, 76, 84, 179, 188, 193, 203, 232
  journal, 232
  measure of, 203
probability
  publication, 13, 14
problem-solving, 24, 25
Proceedings, 84, 162, 193, 198, 203

Proceedings of the Critical Management Studies conferences, 198
Proceedings of the National Academy of Sciences (PNAS), 203
production(s), xxvi, 32, 34, 35, 39, 43, 103, 110, 112, 142, 147, 202,
productivity, 31, 55, 140
  research, 31, 55
professional association, xxi, 40, 70, 84, 98, 137, 176, 178, 223, 238, 263
professional citizenship, 30, 36
professional community, 89, 91, 95, 152, 159
professional identification, 28, 30, 35
professional values, 28
profit making, 262
program(s)
  doctoral, xiii, 168
promotion, 140, 141, 146, 154, 155, 181, 190, 192, 201, 204, 220, 221, 244
  academic, 220
proofreader, 33
Psychological Bulletin, 12, 19, 77
psychological contract, 209, 216
Psychological Methods, 191
psychology, xiv, xv, xviii, 84, 105, 145–149, 152–154, 189, 203, 241, 260, 261, 267
  applied, xii, xiii, xx, 60, 136, 145, 147, 152–154, 189
  clinical, 148, 260
  cognitive, 145
  cross-cultural, 149
  educational, 145
  neuropsychology, 145
  personality, 145
  social, xvii, 80, 105
psychometricians, 260
public good, 70
publication(s)
  downloaded, 183
  non-refereed, 204
  number of, 140, 146
  number of days since, 203
  time to, 180
publish or perish, xxi, xxii, 88, 149, 209
publisher(s)
  academic, 112
  commercial, 250
  English-language, 200
  online, 201
  private, 83
  professional, 112
publishing
  academic, 3, 175, 177
publishing company(ies)
  Blackwell Publishing (Blackwell), 83, 106, 108, 110, 166, 186, 209
  Elsevier, 209
  Emerald, 198
  John Wiley & Sons (Wiley), 83, 166, 209
  Oxford University Press, 209
  Palgrave, 209
  Sage Publications, Inc. (Sage), 190, 210
publishing work by Associate Editors, 11
publishing work by members of Editorial Board, 70

qualifications, 68, 193, 235, 238, 253
  associate editors, 68
  editorial board/team, 193, 253
  reviewers, 253
queries, 98, 128
quotes, 211, 212, 217

R&R 9, 10, 43, 45, 60, 62, 79, 80, 124–129, 131–133, 146, 150, 151, 161, 171, 242, 243–245, 257, 260 *see also* revise-and-resubmit,
ranking(s), 113
  institutional, 181
  journal, xxiv, 3, 104, 106, 181, 185, 202–203
rate(s)
  acceptance, 129, 136, 146, 153, 196, 199, 267
  circulation, 202
  citation, 203
  desk-rejection, 66, 180
  rejection, *see also* desk-rejection rates, 108, 112, 177, 192, 210
  response, 210
  submission, 69, 74
readership, 9, 30, 84, 204, 218
  diverse, 263
  international, 200

reception(s), 109–110, 192
recognition, 19, 28, 30, 103, 111, 114, 221, 250, 253
  name, 28
  peer, 181
recommendation(s), 25, 64, 78, 85, 235–236, 260
  accept/not accept, 150
  author, 102, 120, 130, 159–160
  bottom-line, 150
  direct, 216
  for reviewers, 100
  letters of, 153, 234–235
  opposing, 121
  potentially conflicting, 109
  reviewer/referee, 78, 81–83, 85, 121–122, 135, 151, 216, 239–240, 255
  unanimous, 240
record(s), 25, 89, 92, 96, 140, 243
  citation, 94, 203
  historical, 236
  performance, 107
  publication, 66, 70, 195–196, 225
  publishing, 212
  scholarly, 93
referee(s)
  ad hoc, 110
  delinquent, chasing of, 110
  interests of, 138
  see also reviewers, 134–141, 215, 244, 256
regression
  stepwise, 261
rejection(s), 9, 27, 36, 43, 53, 57, 59–61, 64, 66, 77, 79, 94–95, 108, 112, 129, 135–137, 151, 161, 163, 177, 192, 210, 229, 240, 243–244, 247, 254, 259, 265, 268
  desk, 52, 58, 59, 66, 180, 241–242
  early, 253
  high-quality, 229
  of revised papers, 80, 132
  outright, 236
  painful, 80, 126, 243, 253
  reason for, 57, 137
  successive, 203
relevance, xxii, 28, 94, 161, 204
  conceptual, 162
  practical, 160
reliability, 97, 138, 265

reminder(s), 51–54, 95, 100, 227
  built-in, 54, 100
  email, 51, 53
  message, 52
replication
  constructive, 247
reprints, 204, 262
reputation(s), 68, 84, 86, 105, 148, 193–195, 199, 212, 224, 243, 256
  articles', 146
  author('s, s'), 243, 266, 268
  department scholarly, xxi
  imputed, 268
  individual scholarly, xxi
  institutional, 111, 181
  integrity, 30
  journal('s, s'), 29–30, 42, 49, 77–78, 83, 105, 146, 149, 179–188, 193, 195, 201, 203, 224, 251, 256–257, 263–264
  professional, 70
  scholarly, xxi, 212
research
  applied, 148
  approaches, 8
  compelling,
  consensus confirming, 22
  consensus-challenging, 177, 179–8
  creative, 140
  critical, 160
  cross-cultural, 148
  development of, 7
  directions for future, 32
  empirical, 58, 189, 241
  European, 168
  frequently cited, 256
  high quality, 13, 107, 140, 152, 157, 174, 240
  imaginative, 248
  implications for, 7
  innovative, 248
  international, 59, 177, 228
  interpretive, 169
  micro, 235
  non-U.S. context, 149
  provocative, 87
  qualitative, 154, 161
  quality of, 232
  quantitative, 173
  rigorous, 158, 162
  theoretical, 149

research (Cont).
  theory-testing, 58
  types of, 148
  unorthodox, 135, 140
research methodology(ies), 71, 115
research methods, 9, 63, 107, 159, 163, 189–190, 226, 256
Research Methods Division (RMD), xxvii, 192–193
research productivity, 31, 55
research question(s), 7–9, 13, 24, 112, 115–116, 118–119, 121, 163–164
researcher(s)
  independent, 168
  international, 228
  medical, 261
  US-trained, 228
respect, 77–79, 91, 93, 215, 220, 250, 255
respondents, 164, 209, 211
response(s), 28, 33, 52, 61, 86, 94, 151–152, 158, 179, 210, 219
  informal, 152
  intriguing, 218
  negative, 151
  possible, 254
  strong, 267
responsibility(ies), xxi, 12, 62, 88, 94, 140, 180, 209, 193, 224, 228, 253, 255–256, 261
  academic, 228
  administration, 151
  editor, 21, 34, 45, 65, 69, 88–89, 91–92, 96, 100, 104, 109, 111, 122, 225, 228, 240, 243
  major, 209
  management, 151
  personal, 253
  sense of, 105
  single best service, 223
  ultimate, 85
responsiveness, 246
resubmission(s), 61, 79–80, 268
resumé (see also Curriculum Vitae) 171, 262
revenues, 195, 200–201
  subscription, 251
reverse censorship, 135
review cycle, 50, 52, 56
Review of Financial Studies, 177
review process, vii, ix, xxiii, xxiv, 9–12, 18, 27, 30, 33, 36, 43, 49–67

automated, 50
developmental, 136
disadvantages, 49–50, 80, 165
electronic, 50, 180
integrity of, 65, 134
phases, 43, 44
ritualized, 57
review(s)
  constructive, 53, 150, 194, 232, 237
  contradictory, 12
  cycle, 50, 52, 56
  delayed, 49
  developmental, 77, 94, 136, 242
  exhaustive, 231
  expedient, 49
  fair, 77, 236
  first set of, 127
  helpful, 44, 83, 256
  inappropriate tone, 34
  independent, 162,
  informative, 77
  informed, 53
  late, 227
  lost, 49
  mixed, 242
  request, 44, 52–53
  round of, 12, 76, 124, 136, 242–243
  second round of, 45, 126–127, 129
  time to complete, 44, 50
  timeliness, 73, 93–94, 149–150
  timely, 77, 81, 83, 91, 94, 112, 182, 194, 232, 237
  weak, 34
reviewer feedback, 78, 83, 149–151, 184, 224, 227, 236, 242, 245–246
reviewer role
  prosecutor, 65
reviewer(s)
  ad hoc, vii, xxiii, 51–53, 68, 71–74, 92, 94, 110, 112, 145, 147, 149–151, 155, 193, 196, 228–229, 237, 256
  allocation, 100
  appropriate, 151
  assigning, 99, 102
  behavior of, 32
  best, 44, 67, 69, 92
  choice of, 99
  consensus among, 17
  delinquent, 110

reviewer(s) (*Contd*).
  discontent, 101
  insulting a, 86
  international, 49
  late, 77
  lukewarm, 181
  negative, 181
  non-responsive/ unresponsive, 34, 52
  original, 52, 126
  overdue, 98, 100
  overemphasis on, 140
  poor, 82,
  practice-oriented, 24
  qualified, 51, 85, 253
  quality, 11, 52, 70
  reluctant, xxiii
  responsive, 44
  timeliness of, 52, 92
  unconstructive, 52
  valued, 83, 180
  see also referee(s)
revise and resubmit (R&R), xxvii, 9–10, 43, 45, 60, 62, 67, 79, 80, 124–133, 146, 150–151, 161, 171, 242–245, 257, 260
revision(s), xxiii, 9, 10, 12, 29, 33, 35, 56, 61–63, 65, 78–80, 82, 85, 95, 116, 121–122, 124–129, 132, 136–137, 151, 171, 180, 195, 227, 239, 242–243, 245–247, 253, 257–258
  acceptable, 129
  first, 227
  high risk, 64, 67, 243
  likelihood of a successful, 79, 81
  multiple, 80, 126, 258
  responsive, 10, 245–246
  rounds of, 131
  second, 21, 243
  subsequent, 181
  successful, 79, 81, 127, 171
reward(s), 30, 31, 36, 44, 123, 149, 158, 250
  fair, 190
  immediate, 229
  intrinsic, 250
  psychological, 224
  salient, 224
rigor/rigour, 163–164, 179, 181, 199, 228
  faux, 137
  theoretical, 109

Royal Economics Society, 106
royalties
  payment of, 200

sales, 32, 110
  overseas, 110
satisfaction
  career, 210, 219
  customer, 34
  editor, 34, 45, 219, 250
  job, 59, 67, 210
scholar(s), xxi, xxii, xxiv, 8, 10, 28, 41, 68, 70, 72, 74, 81, 87–96, 107, 126, 132, 149, 151, 153, 155, 167, 169–173, 183–184, 189–192, 196–198, 204, 213, 220–221, 225, 232, 255
  academic, xxii, 155
  aspiring, 188
  community of, 140, 179, 183, 199
  distinguished, 212
  leading, 84, 212
  prominent, 129
  senior, 66, 71, 189, 192, 212, 219
  young, 97, 242
scholarly community, 59, 91–92, 105, 204, 222
scholarship, 8, 45, 89–90, 96, 106, 214
  academic, 170, 172
  American, 167
  Anglo-Saxon, 173
  British, 171
  continental, 172
  European, 172
  organizational, 167, 169, 190
  personal, 111
  worldwide, 169
science(s), xxi, 16, 24, 158, 171, 173
  applied organizational, 18, 26
  basic, 99
  behavioral, xxii, 92, 95–96, 209
  management, 92, 209, 231, 236
  organizational, xxii, 18
  philosophy of, 16, 26
  social, xxii, 6, 106, 121, 125, 146, 156, 168, 209, 231, 236, 255, 259
sector
  for-profit, 147
  nonprofit, 147
  private, 147
  public, 107, 147

selection process/ procedures, 71, 89, 94, 153, 216, 231–238
sentiments, 62, 140
separation, 244
servant leadership, 27–37, 213–214
service, 18, 27, 28, 32–37, 41, 50, 109, 112, 150, 185, 201, 223, 234
  better, 29, 180, 185
  conscientious, 74
  editing as, 27–37, 234
  free, 242
  invisible, 27
  legacy of, 37
  mentoring, 242
  professional, xxii, 27–28, 35
  recovery, 32–34
  reviewing, 34, 66, 68, 214, 242
  terms of, 72
  years of, 70, 239
service behavior
  discretionary, 30
service orientation, 27
service provider, 27, 32–34
service recovery activities, 34
significance
  institutional, 181
  statistical, 259–261
single-loop
  learning, 4
Six-Sigma era, 139
sizes
  effect, 260
  sample, 259
skill(s), xxvii, 30, 42, 83, 90–91, 109, 226, 237
  communication, 213
  editing, 213
  entrepreneurial, 213
  requisite, 109
  variety of, 224
  writing, 213
social interaction, 5
social construction of knowledge, 134
social dilemma, 31
social sciences, 6, 106, 121, 125, 146, 168, 209, 231, 236, 255, 259
Social Sciences Citation Index (SSCI), xxviii, 104, 106, 108, 113
socialization, xvi, xxi, 140, 243

Society for Industrial and Organizational Psychology, xiii, xxvii
Sociological Methods and Research, 190–191
sociologists, 255, 260
sociology, 203
sophomoric games, 247
source of competitive advantage, 232
special issues, xiii, xx, 69, 108, 165, 182–183, 185, 198, 263
special sections, 147, 152
sponsor(ship), 191–193, 201
sportsmanship, 30
staff, 42, 97–99, 156, 181, 233–234
  administrative support, 101, 109
  clerical, 109
  day-to-day support, 112
  strong, 133
stage
  career, 140, 196, 210, 216–218, 224
  conditional accept, 124, 129–130, 133
  copy editing, 130
  revise and resubmit, 126–127, 129, 131–133, 161
stakeholders, 91
  advisory board, 104
  authors, 94, 104–105
  editorial team, 94, 104
  journal, 90
  key, 105
  professional field, 90
  reviewers, 94, 104–105
  submitter, 90
  subscribers, 104
stamina, 213
standard(s), 3, 30, 36–37, 40, 76, 89, 91, 93, 147, 157, 161, 168–169, 180, 213, 215, 232, 242, 255, 261
  absolute, 237
  journal, 36, 41, 58, 180, 186, 189, 242–243
  quality, 29, 34–35, 91, 241
  rigorous, 157–158
standing, xxiii, 21
  candidate's, 235
  equal, 258
  increase in, 109
  international, 110
  journal, 104–113, 184, 265

statement(s), 7, 13, 17, 84, 86, 125, 148, 151, 153, 235,
  candidate's, 234
  editor, 148, 243
  incorrect, 258
  policy, 190–6
  vision, 234–235
statistics, 32, 77, 84, 220, 229, 251
status(es)
  author's, 244
  social, 267
stereotyping, 10
stewardship, 35, 36, 111
story telling, 164
strain, 31
strategic management, 69, 183
Strategic Management Association, xvi, xxii, 199
Strategic Management Journal, xiv, xvi, xix, 60
strategy(ies), xiii, 69, 86, 112, 147, 149, 264, 266–267
  competitive positioning, 112
  corporate, 107
  editorial, 70
  internationalization, 108–109
  niche, 76
strengths, 9, 116–118, 120, 131, 267
  personal, 251
strengths and weaknesses, 14, 87, 114, 190, 237, 251
stress, 31, 35, 82, 220, 221
structural equation modeling, 226
style, 32, 150, 153, 160–162, 170, 173, 241, 247, 256–257, 265
  collegial, 213
  guidelines, 32, 58
  intellectual, 169, 174
  matters of, 133
  non-jargonistic, 160
  scholarly, 173
  writing, 58, 64, 159–261
style guide, 58
subjectivity, 3–4, 7, 10
submitter, 90–91
subscriber fee
  individual, 201
  institutional, 201
subscriber(s), 104, 188, 199, 202, 263

subscription, 43, 73, 145, 191, 195, 200, 202, 203, 251
  free, 149, 199
  journal, 71, 176, 178, 201
subsidies, 201
success(es)
  career, xxi, 209, 220, 229
  chances of, 59, 188, 196, 243
  editor, 68, 74, 252, 262
  financial, 191
  highest probability of, 227
  journal, 105, 262
  likelihood of, 25
  long-term, 18, 190, 194
  prospects for, 60
  publication, 87
succession, 69, 242
successor, 41, 235, 250
summary, 95, 111, 122, 141, 151, 161, 164, 248, 249
  critical, 173
sunk costs, 10
support, 112, 266
  administrative, 109, 215
  clerical, 109
  course release, 69, 155
  financial, 155
  institutional, 215
  journal, 201
  ongoing, 200
  perceived, 217
  secretarial, 69, 233, 238
  technical, 200
  type of, 232, 237
support function
  back office, 109
support system, 105, 163
supporters, 202, 262
system(s), xxi, 4–5, 10, 12, 30, 34, 56, 70–71, 97–103, 125, 165, 178, 182, 185, 220
  administration, 109
  electronic, 72, 92, 110, 156, 180–181
  evaluation, 114
  flat hierarchy, 220
  institutionalized, 170
  knowledge as, 39543
  manuscript management, 49–50, 180
  manuscript processing, 49–55, 165
  manuscript tracking, 50, 133

system(s) (*Contd*).
    online, 166, 180, 182,
    parallel, 98
    peer review, 151, 198, 215
    promotion, 140
    ranking, 181
    rating, 146
    review, 54, 180
    support, 105, 163
    web-based, 98–102

Tables of Contents, 196
tabula rasa, 169
tacit knowledge, 5–7, 13
technical glitches, 182
technology(ies), 97, 99, 101, 102, 103, 196, 203
    change, 97–98, 198
    distributed, 101
    electronic, 198
    graphical interface, 103
    paperless, 97
    printing, 262
    voice recognition, 103
template(s), 59, 96
    desk rejection letter, 59
tenacity, 213
tenure, 33, 79, 134, 140, 154–155, 181, 190, 204, 216, 224, 244
    editor's, 34, 45, 77, 108, 130, 179, 186, 221
tenure case
    important and critical to, 155
tenure clock, 43, 140,
tenure system, 140
term(s), 16–35, 65, 70, 79–80, 92, 97, 98–99, 102, 106, 111, 114–115, 121, 148–153, 159, 164, 168–169, 178–181, 186, 190–195, 200, 204, 210, 213, 229, 233–234, 240
    complete, 153, 229
    editor's, editorial, 52, 59, 64, 68, 71, 74, 80, 98, 108–113, 127, 148, 153–156, 199, 225–229, 238–239, 251
terms of service, 72
testing
    hypothesis, 259
    statistical, 259
    theory, 58, 116–121
tests
    detrimental, 259

null hypothesis significance, 259
    significance, 259–261
textbook protocols, 25
textbook(s), 259, 261, 266
theory building, 24, 58
theory development
    contribution to, 111
theory(ies), 8–9, 19, 23–24, 39, 41, 51, 58, 64, 84, 86, 95, 102, 105, 111, 115–118, 121, 141, 157, 160, 164, 180, 183, 199, 236, 248
    complex systems, 183
    cutting edge, 84
    development of, 111, 157, 179, 235
    existing, 116–118
    importation of, 117
    knowledge driven, 24
    organization, xvi, xix, 60, 255
    overlap of, 117
    problem driven, 24
    social identity, 226
    social network, 225
    stakeholder, 225
thin-skinned, 140
Thomson Scientific, 189
threshold(s), 181, 242
time frames
    expected, 218
    varying, 146
    viable, 140
time(s)
    review, 98, 180, 195
    turnaround, 43, 52, 180, 185–186, 229
timeline, 58
timeliness, 52, 69, 73, 92–93, 139, 149–150, 159, 198, 200, 266
title(s), 16, 130, 134, 146, 157, 270
    awkward, 130
    clear, 130
    intriguing, 130, 170
    inviting, 130
    long, 130
    similar, 166
    succinct, 130
    uninviting, 130
tracking
    manuscript, 50, 109, 133, 154–155
    number, 52
tradeoffs
    methodological, 9, 14
tradition(s), 8, 26, 172, 193

academic, 168–169
Anglo-Saxon, 173
discursively produced, 173
distinct, 171
diverse, 168
European, 111
intellectual, 171–173
scholarly, 8
social-science, 259
USA, 111
training, xviii, 62, 129
  doctoral, 152, 168, 188
  economics, 60
  management, 60
  methods, 189
  operations research, 60
  professional, 152
transparency, 121, 232
trust, 89, 92–95
trustworthiness, 88, 93, 94, 96
turnaround
  prompt, 43
turnover, 73
tutorial, 33
tutoring, 242

unethical acts, 95
unfairness
  sense of, 243
United States (USA), xiii, 107–108, 111, 120, 167–168, 173
  outside the, 148, 154, 231
University of Hull, 171
University of Texas, xii, 100, 102
University of Waikato, 198

vacancy, 232
  editor, 232–233
  upcoming, 232
vacation(s), 51, 52, 54, 155
  one-week, 234
validity threat, 37
value(s), 3, 9, 12, 14, 20, 28, 29, 30, 49, 51, 63, 68, 69, 99, 114, 121, 127, 134, 140, 142, 150, 157, 159, 172, 178, 179, 184, 189, 192, 203, 243, 254, 256, 259, 260, 261, 298
  altruistic, 28
  current, 262
  idiosyncratic, 261
  incremental, 179

intellectual, 191
limited, 135, 150
overall, 121
personal work, 28
potential, xxii, 262
professional, 28
proposed, 115
real, 21, 159, 229
well founded, 262
work, 69
value added, xxii, 17, 18, 20, 90, 91, 120, 158, 173, 201, 247, 256, 297
variability, 128
variable, 23, 117, 120, 122, 132, 163, 210, 259
  dependent, 15, 22
  different, 117
  independent, 22
view(s)
  alternative, 258
  discrepant, 42
  existing, 183
viewpoint(s)
  diverse, 251
  evolutionary psychology, 31
  minority, 227
virtue, 31, 110, 132, 133, 162, 195
vision, 68, 72, 74, 93, 126, 129, 211–212, 234
  clear, 68, 111, 127, 212, 214
  journal, 93, 122, 123, 191, 212, 234
  long-term, 191
  polyocular, 174
  strategic, 107, 112
vision statement, 234, 235
  breadth of, 234
  depth of, 234
voice(s), 8, 42, 109, 149, 170, 215
  authorial, 134–141, 246
  diversity of, 8
  editor, editorial, 131, 209–222
  intelligible, 175
  stifle, 109, 139, 141
volumes, 147, 239
  edited, xvi, 239
volunteering/volunteerism, 28–29, 36, 71, 196
  sustained, 27
volunteers, 36, 44, 234, 245
votes, 235, 252
  reviewers', 65, 240

wages
   ludicrously low hourly, 250
winner
   best paper, 58
wisdom
   collective, 125
word-scrubbing, 122

work sample, 94
workaholic, 220
workaholism, 213
workshop(s), 178
   professional development, 62
   publishing, 228
writers, textbook, 266